"PAT.
KILLED WITH AN AX.

"Oh God, Candy, how horrible."

Her husband shook his head and grimaced, then went back to mowing the lawn. Candy went back into the house, where the phone was ringing again.

"I've been listening on the radio, and they say there were bloody footprints all over the house. How could this happen to someone like Betty?"

Another call, another explanation. The phone was ringing constantly.

Candy couldn't stand the phone any longer.

The police will be calling. A bloody footprint.

Candy sat in a chair by the kitchen table, a pair of garden shears in her hand. She began to work the shears back and forth, pressing with all her might as the metal blades cut through the soles of a pair of rubber sandals. She continued her work for several minutes, long enough to render the shoes into messy little heaps of rubber. Then she gathered up the scraps she had made and carried them to an outside garbage can . . .

EVIDENCE OF LOVE

EVIDENCE OF LOVE

John Bloom and Jim Atkinson

BANTAM BOOKS
TORONTO · NEW YORK · LONDON · SYDNEY · AUCKLAND

This low-priced Bantam Book
has been completely reset in a type face
designed for easy reading, and was printed
from new plates. It contains the complete
text of the original hard-cover edition.
NOT ONE WORD HAS BEEN OMITTED.

EVIDENCE OF LOVE

A Bantam Book / published by arrangement with
Texas Monthly Press

PRINTING HISTORY
Texas Monthly edition published March 1984
A Preferred Choice Bookplan Selection, July 1984
Appeared as a two-part serialization entitled "Love and
Death in Silicon Prairie" in Texas Monthly magazine,
January/February 1984. Serialized in Cosmopolitan, May
1984.
Bantam edition / June 1985

ISBN 0-553-24873-1

Published simultaneously in the United States and Canada

PRINTED IN THE UNITED STATES OF AMERICA
H   0 9 8 7 6 5 4 3 2 1

Dear Allan,

Sometimes I have doubts about my worth as a person, and wonder if I'm really accomplishing anything and am doing what God would want me to do. But if you express your pride in me, then I feel reassured that I am really important. . . . I need to be reassured and told this often, just as I need to see and feel tangible evidence of your love. . . .

I Love You!

Love,
Betty

—from a letter by Betty Gore, to her husband, October 28, 1979

1 · GOD'S PLAN

"Once upon a time there were three trees."

The children stopped fidgeting in the church pews, and all you could hear was the whir of the ceiling fan and the occasional rattle of paper as the younger ones played with their song sheets. All fifty pairs of eyes focused front and center, where Candy Montgomery stood before the altar, waiting for absolute quiet. She always got it, too. Children have little patience for most activities that go on within a church sanctuary, but Candy's daily parables were an exception.

"Once upon a time there were three trees high up on a hill," she began again. "And for centuries and centuries they grew and grew. Sometimes they would talk to each other. The biggest tree used to say to the others" (here her voice became deep and masculine) "'When I grow up, I want to be made into a big boat, the finest ocean liner in the world.'

"And the second, medium-sized tree would say, 'When I grow up, I want to be made into a baby cradle, which is the most marvelous thing of all.'

"But the third tree, the littlest one, said, 'I don't ever want to be cut down; I want to stand here forever, pointing to God.'"

As Candy said this, she pointed toward the ceiling, just the way she had practiced it with her husband Pat the night before. The kids were enthralled. When Candy told these stories, there was something about her manner that was itself childlike; she glowed with simple, genuine delight. She even looked a little like a child, or at least like one of the teenagers, with her worn blue jeans and rubber thongs and loose-hanging gauzy blouse. Her blonde hair was close-cropped and tightly curled, almost kinky, in the style of the early seventies. Pat

1

didn't like it that way; he said it made her look loose. But everyone else seemed to like it, and besides, it made her feel free. Candy was the kind of mother you could call by her first name, a part of the child's eternal conspiracy against order. It was almost as though she didn't know how the story ended and was making it up as she went along.

"But one day a group of woodcutters came to the hill of the three trees," said Candy, puckering her brow, "and one of them looked at the biggest tree and said, 'This tree looks like it would make a fine fishing boat.' The big tree cried and cried. But the woodcutters cut it down anyway."

She paused for effect.

"And it became the very boat that Peter used as his altar to spread the Good News."

Candy had a sudden and unexpected smile that could transform the face of a brooding introvert into that of a mischievous party girl. She flashed it now, as though to say, "Isn't this wonderful fun we're having?"

"Then a little while later the woodcutters came back," she said, "and one of them took a look at the second tree and said, 'This one looks like it would make a great barnstall.' And the medium-sized tree cried and cried, but the man cut it down anyway. . . . And it turned out to be the stable the baby Jesus was born in, the best baby cradle of all."

Candy let the expectation build.

"And then," she said, more softly, "a little while after that, the woodcutters came for the third tree. And one of them said, 'This tree will make a fine cross.' And the little tree cried most of all. . . . But it ended up as the cross that Jesus hung on, and it's still standing today, pointing to God."

"We should always remember," Candy concluded solemnly, "that what we are is not what we plan for ourselves, but what God plans for us."

It was the thirteenth of June, 1980, the beginning of a punishing, oppressive Texas summer, and Candy Montgomery had arrived at the United Methodist Church of Lucas, Texas, a little before nine that morning. As soon as she pulled onto the gravel lot, two doors of the old white family station wagon flopped open and the children piled out and ran inside. Ian, her "baby," went his own way, but Jenny and her best friend Alisa Gore stuck together, inseparable as only six- and seven-year-old girls can be. It was the last day of Vacation Bible

School, a mixed blessing for the dozen or so mothers who reported for duty that morning. On the one hand it would be a celebration for those who had taught and shepherded the children all week: their reward was to be a noon luncheon in the old sanctuary. On the other, they would be more than happy when it was over. Even though the school ran only five days a year, and only in the mornings at that, it was such an inflexible schedule, requiring car pooling, refreshment preparation, babysitters, and lesson planning, that it was all the women could do to get through the week. The final day brought additional burdens, what with the cooking to do and a special puppet show for the visiting parents. More than one of them had joked about the "graduation" falling on Friday the thirteenth.

Candy Montgomery had a hundred other things to do besides. At breakfast the kids had all badgered and begged until she gave up and said that, yes, perhaps Alisa Gore could spend the night again that evening, even though they usually didn't allow the girls to sleep over two nights in a row. And, yes, she would ask Alisa's mother whether Alisa could go to *The Empire Strikes Back* that night with the Montgomery family. But the changed plans meant that Candy's driving strategy for the day would have to be rearranged. (In the "distant suburbs" of Dallas, as Collin County was known, the success of an entire day could revolve around a housewife's efficient use of the car.) The extra night would mean accepting the responsibility for Alisa's afternoon swimming lesson in Wylie in addition to the other errands in various outlying towns: the station wagon needed gas (in Allen), she wanted to help with the luncheon (in Lucas), she needed to get to the store to buy Father's Day cards (in Plano), and she had promised to lend a card table to her best friend, Sherry, who had relatives coming for the weekend (in Fairview). Five errands now, in five different towns—the price of living in the country. No telling when she would have time to take care of it all. Now Alisa had told her that her swimsuit was still at home, which meant driving all the way to Wylie to get it from Betty Gore.

First came Bible School. As soon as she arrived that morning, Candy grabbed her purse and headed over to the parsonage. Reverend Adams would want to know that she had finished the phone lists for her committee. She didn't call him "Reverend," of course. She had never been able to call him anything except "Ron," perhaps because he was only twenty-five years old, perhaps because the Methodists of Lucas had never stood on any kind of ceremony. She knew Ron wouldn't be at the Bible School program that day; she suspected Ron didn't even *like* the Bible School. It was frivolous, something the women did. Poor Ron. Somewhere behind that head full of building plans and budgetary procedures and the arrogance of a young man in his first pastoral appointment, there might be a nice guy. Ron would never show it, though. Candy told Ron about the lists, and he grunted his approval. Then she bustled into the sanctuary just as the children were bowing their heads for Betty Huffhines' first prayer.

Candy had saved "The Three Trees" for the last day of school. It was a special story for Candy, a modern parable she had picked up at the Methodist Annual Conference in Dallas that year. Candy had been the church's lay delegate for the past two years, a job she accepted for reasons that had little to do with Methodism but a great deal to do with the feelings of warmth and security and belonging that this little church by the roadside gave her. It was a place where people could have religion without "*being* religious," a distinction in her mind that separated Lucas from the narrow-minded orthodox Presbyterians of her childhood. She had never spoken about these feelings to anyone except Jackie, the woman who had pastored the church before Ron, but it all came down to one word: love. All Jackie had ever preached about was love. That's why Candy liked "The Three Trees" so much; it was so *loving*. It was Christian but it didn't have all the biblical references that got in the way of a child's understanding; it was a little like the story she had told on Tuesday, about the little gingerbread man and the little gingerbread woman. The kids wouldn't have liked it nearly as much if they had known it was the story of Adam and Eve. But when Candy had performed "The Three Trees" for Pat the night before, he had pronounced it the best story of the week. "Fantastic!" he said. "The kids will love it." Pat loved Lucas Church almost as much as Candy did. In a way, the church represented everything the Montgomerys had moved to the country to find. Here, for the first time in their lives, they felt like they had a home.

After the day's parable, Candy had the children bow their heads for a final prayer, and then they all scurried off to their 9:30 classes. Betty Huffhines was in charge of the school that year, so she and Candy were the only women who had no classes to teach. Instead they stayed behind to straighten up the sanctuary and collect the song sheets. Afterwards Candy walked over to the old sanctuary, a deteriorating white clapboard building with concrete steps and a skinny metal cross perched on its peaked roof. She had an affection for the old building; it was drafty and crudely constructed and too small, but she found it charming nonetheless. The new sanctuary was fine, too; it had pile carpet and stained glass and cushioned pews for up to 120 people. But there was something warm and nostalgic about the old place that had made her love it the very first time they had visited, three years before.

Candy mounted the steps and walked through the foyer to the old worship room, where the pews had been replaced by cafeteria tables and the altar had given way to a lopsided pool table. She could hear the scuffling of children's feet on the hardwood floors as a class met in a corner. She continued into the kitchen, where she knew she would find Barbara Green preparing Kool-Aid and cookies for the 10:30 recess.

"Here, let me help you with that," she said brightly. "I'll do the ice." Candy had a way of making everything she did sound fresh and insouciant.

Barbara assented and showed her where the glasses were. Candy enjoyed chatting with Barbara. The Greens lived two houses down, and Barbara's husband Phil worked with Pat at Texas Instruments. Candy felt she could confide in Barbara about almost anything. The only exceptions were the secrets Candy shared only with Sherry Cleckler, her closest friend of all. Candy admired Barbara, but she was also a little intimidated by her. Barbara was one of the few people in the world, Candy imagined, who may never have had an impure thought, or almost never. Barbara was embarrassed by even mildly vulgar language, but she had the grace and good sense to ignore it when she heard it. Barbara was devoted to her family and had a simple, genuine faith. Sometimes Candy envied her.

Candy did most of the talking, about everything and nothing.

"Well, all the kids want to see the new Star Wars movie, and so Jenny and Alisa were after me this morning to let Alisa stay over another night so the girls could go with us. Ian just loves Star Wars, you know. He has all the Star Wars characters; he always wants to be Luke when Pat plays with him. Pat promised Ian he would take him tonight, so we're all going. I think I'm going to run down to Betty's and ask her about it and get Alisa's swimsuit while I'm there. If I leave now, I might have time to do that and go over to Target and get some Father's Day cards for Pat."

"Don't forget the puppet show today," said Barbara.

"I'll be back for that. It shouldn't take me more than an hour. I'm sure Betty will be glad to have us keep Alisa another night, since she's got her hands full trying to take care of the baby and plan their vacation at the same time."

After rushing through a few more simple kitchen chores to satisfy her conscience, Candy hurried out of the church building, pausing only long enough to speak to her favorite babysitter, Connie Holmes. Connie was teaching the six-year-olds that day. No one else saw Candy get into her station wagon and pull out onto the highway.

They called it simply "the country," this place where the women had come with their men and their children to settle. Specifically, it was eight to ten amorphous little towns in eastern Collin County, Texas, but it really had no name. The church where the Montgomerys worshipped was located in a tiny farming community called Lucas, but most of the farming had ceased and few of the church members lived there anyway. The church buildings sat on a slight rise surrounded by fallow blackland wheat fields on three sides and a farm-to-market road on the fourth. When the sky was clear and the wind strong, as it usually was, the landscape had the feel of a rough and untamed outpost, solitary and a little forbidding, not beautiful but stunning in its brown and gray emptiness. In the nineteenth century, this had been the place where the westering families from Kentucky and Tennessee had stopped and turned back, unable to cope with the violence of the weather or the naked vulnerability of the land. Only a few had stayed, and you could still hear in the voices of their descendants the clipped cadence of a people who had found no great joy in their triumph. The people of Lucas Church, by and large, knew little of this, for now the land was giving way to a second wave of immigrants.

Most had come to escape something: cities, density, routine, fear of crime, overpriced housing, the urban problems their parents never knew. They came in the seventies, just about the time the Dallas developers started buying out the farmers one by one, and they settled on pasture-sized lots in homes designed exclusively for them by architects happy to get rich by satisfying their personal whims. They sent their children to a little red schoolhouse, joined a civic club or ran for the town council, and started going to church again when they found the quaint little chapel by the roadside in Lucas. Twenty miles to the southwest were the teeming freeways of Dallas, the huge electronics corporations where many of them worked as engineers and physicists and computer analysts, the endless chain of suburban housing developments and shopping malls and office centers running due north out of the city. But here there was quiet and solitude and a kind of control over their lives. Some of them spoke of it proudly. "This is the way things were back home," they would say, or "This is how things used to be," or "Thank God we had enough money to move to the country so the kids could get a good education." The country was pure, untroubled, safe, innocent, a vision of regenerate America.

Slicing through the heart of the country was Farm-to-Market Road 1378, a tortuous two-lane blacktop connecting McKinney, the county seat, with Wylie, an old railroad town now given over to tract homes and light industry. Both towns were older and more authentically western than anything in the twenty miles or so between them. For 1378 had become the main artery for the new subdivisions full of fantasy architecture: houses shaped like Alpine villas, houses dolled up like medieval castles, houses as forbidding as national park pavilions or as secluded as missile bases, hidden in thickets along the shores of Lake Lavon. Juxtaposed with these personal statements were the more familiar examples of prairie architecture: trailer homes, bait shops, windowless lodge halls, an outdoor revival shelter, barns, ghost-town cemeteries. The only connection between past and present was the ubiquitous white horse fences which proliferated along the highway, and around many of the brand-new houses, in inverse proportion to the number of horses needing corrals.

Candy Montgomery pulled onto 1378 and quickly gunned the station wagon up to fifty. She was in no particular hurry, but she tended to get impatient when things weren't done. She was a morning person, at her best when she was up early and finished with most of her work by noon, giving her plenty of time to mess around with Sherry Cleckler. Today she'd had to call Sherry and tell her there just wasn't time, even for coffee, because of the need to take care of Alisa's swimming lesson. She didn't call Alisa's mother, though. Instead she just jumped in the car and headed south; she could tell Betty Gore when she got there, and she'd have to go anyway to pick up the swimsuit. If the truth were known, she often avoided talking to Betty at all. She found Betty cold and distant, and one reason she wanted Alisa to go with them to the movie is that, otherwise, Alisa might not get to see it at all.

Wylie was hardly Candy's favorite place to visit. The Gores lived in the best part of town, a new subdivision on the southeast side, near the school where Betty taught. But it was still a far cry from the estates and custom homes of the country to the north. A few miles south of Lucas, Candy made an abrupt left turn, and the scenery began to change from waving prairie grass and pillared entryways to tiny farmhouses with aluminum siding, weedy front lawns surrounded by chain link fences, abandoned cars, barbed wire animal pens, and neon signs. She continued on into the town itself, down the main street, past the discount drug, the funeral home, the feed and seed, and a squat cinder-block building that announced simply "POLICE." She crossed the railroad tracks and the main highway to Dallas, cruised through a shantytown, and turned left again toward a sea of tract homes, huddled closely together on the town's outskirts. The air was not yet hot but it was heavy, which usually promised a suffocating Texas afternoon. There were a few children playing on the lawns, since their mothers would want them in the house during the scorching midday hours, but otherwise all was quiet. Candy turned onto Dogwood Street and crept along until she recognized the brick and white trim of the Gore home. She angled across to the left side of the street and parked against the curb. She picked up her purse off the front seat, walked down the sidewalk to the front door, and rang the bell.

At Bible School, Marie Childs was taking care of the four- and five-year-olds that morning. After Candy's parable, she had herded them into the old building and led a song to establish some semblance of order. She gave the lesson for the day: "Do unto others as you would have them do unto you." Then, as she was finishing, she noticed Candy walking toward the parking lot and called to her. She wanted her to know that she had finished using Candy's cassette recorder and would give it back later that day. Candy waved and said, "Fine, I'll be back in a little bit. I'm just running down to Betty Gore's and to

Target." Marie turned back to her daily story—the miracle of the fishes and loaves—and then got the kids started on the crafts period. Today the little ones were making bread and fish out of clay and construction paper. Then they started preparing their puppet show for the 11 A.M. assembly; all their mothers were invited to see their rendition of "Noah's Ark," complete with stick puppets of the animals marching two by two.

Ninety minutes later, the day's second assembly went off as scheduled, with several mothers in attendance and the kids all boisterously involved in playing with their handmade puppets. Because the meal was being prepared at the same time, people were constantly bustling in and out of the sanctuary, increasing the general level of chaos, but no one really seemed to mind. When it came time for Ian Montgomery, Candy's quiet little five-year-old, to do his part in the Noah story, Marie Childs scanned the audience and noticed that his mother wasn't there. Candy Montgomery had been gone for at least an hour and a half.

The toe on Candy's left foot was bleeding profusely. She stared at it and fished in her purse for the keys to the station wagon.

Now you're in the car. You're normal. The car is still here. Everything looks the same.

Her mind went blank, and in the few lost moments, she was vaguely aware of the car beginning to move.

Father's Day cards. Puppet show. One step at a time, just do one thing at a time and it will be all right. Don't think about the house . . . Father's Day cards.

She stared down the main street of Wylie and imagined her car was not moving at all. Then the main street was gone. She stared at a stop sign. It scared her; she needed movement. She needed something to do.

You can't lose control now. Nothing is changed.

The car turned left, onto a lonely farm road that leads due west, toward the Dallas suburb of Plano. The road jogged across a railroad track and opened into an expanse of empty farmland. Weeds grew right up to the shoulder.

Think of something.

She glanced down at her lap and felt a sudden chill in her legs. Her blue jeans were soaked through with water. Her nostrils flooded with the antiseptic smell of fabric softener, and for a moment she thought she would be sick.

Why am I wet? That smell. Can't panic. Normal. Left, right . . . Father's Day, left, Target . . . Why won't the car go faster?

Candy's toe began to throb.

Oh God it hurts . . . Cut it on the storm door, that's what happened . . . How can I be wet?

The car coasted past an abandoned railroad coach and a row of trailer homes and slowed to a crawl for a flashing yellow light. Then it turned abruptly right, onto a little-used blacktop that cuts through the community of Murphy, and then northwest, away from Plano, away from Lucas Church, away from Wylie, into the emptiness of the open prairie.

You're so dirty . . . Where is the church? . . . You love the church . . . oh God it hurts . . . No one will know . . . You couldn't do it . . . No one will know.

Two miles north of Murphy, on the right side of the asphalt road, was a long winding drive leading to a white pillared mansion. The mansion was set in the midst of an immaculate pasture encircled by horse fence. Situated along the driveway and parked at odd angles beside the main road were a dozen cars and buses. Most of their occupants were milling around with cameras, shooting pictures of a high arched gate that read "Southfork Ranch." They had come, that day as every day, to see the exterior set where a television series is filmed, a show populated with a family of exaggerated Texas stereotypes for whom the ranch has become a symbol of failed dreams. None of the tourists noticed the old white station wagon that sped by that day. Its driver had her eyes fixed firmly on the white line of the road.

Tina was only five, but she liked to play with the bigger girls down the street whenever they would let her. Especially Alisa Gore, who was seven and lived in the brick house with the white trim and had a little baby sister. Grandma was at Tina's house today. She let Tina go outside for a while but told her not to go very far. Tina decided to go to Alisa's. She knew Alisa was home because of that woman. She saw her. She had blonde curly hair and blue jeans and Tina saw her come out of Alisa's and get in her station wagon. She was in a hurry, because she drove right by Tina and she never even looked.

She just drove down to the end of the block and turned and went away.

That's what made Tina think of Alisa. She looked both ways before crossing the street, and then she went up to the front door and rang the bell on Alisa's door. She could hear Alisa's little baby sister crying in the house. It was real loud crying. So Tina waited a while for Alisa to come. But the baby kept crying, real loud, and nobody came to the door and Tina rang the bell again and again.

After a while Tina quit ringing the bell, and then she knocked on the door, and then she went around to the back where Alisa's mother and father parked the cars and saw that they were still there, and then Tina went home to tell her grandmother that Alisa's little sister was crying but Alisa wasn't home.

Tina never noticed the red droplets on Alisa Gore's front porch.

No one must know.

The white station wagon wound through the Collin County back country. It pulled up to an intersection one-half mile from Lucas Church. To the right was the church. The car continued forward.

Dry and clean, you need to be dry and clean . . . calm now . . . no one must know.

The car angled up an empty, little-used road midway between the county's two main highways. After a while it pulled back onto Farm-to-Market 1378, but far north of Lucas Church. It continued north past an old church and a red schoolhouse, across a narrow stone bridge, and up a hill. At the crest, it turned right onto a pitted gravel road that disappeared into a forest of oaks and hackberries.

On the left, across a ravine, was a large two-story Tudor home; that would be Mayor Haas'. He had a gas lamp with a wooden rabbit on it. Now the landscape was familiar again. Down a slight incline, left onto the gravel, and up the steeply inclined driveway. Only now could the house be seen from the car, sitting on a little knoll, shrouded by two or three red oaks, a contemporary cathedral-like structure in wood and glass, with the kind of stylishly unfinished look common in Colorado ski lodges. Around the expansive yard was a corral of white horse fence. The station wagon nosed into the double garage and stopped.

Nothing is changed. Out of these clothes and calm. Dry and clean. Normal.

God, the toe.

She unlocked the door leading from the garage into the house and quickly ran upstairs, stripping off her blouse and blue jeans as she entered the master bedroom. She fumbled through shelves in the bathroom but couldn't find what she was looking for. So she went back downstairs and into the hall bathroom and grabbed a box of Band-Aids. She put her left foot up on the commode and lowered her head down close to the third toe. She wiped the blood away and wrapped the Band-Aid as tightly as she could. She flinched as she felt how deep it was.

I did it on the storm door. We never have fixed the storm door.

She retrieved her blouse and took it into the kitchen and placed it in the sink. She poured the detergent and turned on the water.

Oh no, the smell again.

She started to retch but regained her composure quickly.

She left the blouse soaking in the sink and went upstairs to find a pair of blue jeans; she matched the shade against the ones she had just taken off and carried them into the bathroom. She took a quick shower and washed her hair. As she did, she noticed an open cut at the hairline on the right side of her forehead. She dried her hair with a towel and then went to get another Band-Aid. But the bandage wouldn't stick. No matter how she positioned it, the springy hair around the wound kept it from adhering to the skin. Finally she gave up, wrung out her blouse, put on the new blue jeans, threw the old ones in the washer, and waited while the dryer dried her blouse.

Thank goodness it was burgundy-colored.

The last thing she did was find a pair of blue tennis shoes in the upstairs closet. She traded those for the rubber sandals and laced them up tightly to keep pressure on the toe bandage. She picked up her purse. She was ready to go to church.

Betty Huffhines stood at the back of the sanctuary, watching as the last of the four puppet shows came to a close.

Mothers began gathering up their purses and their children to leave. As they did, little seven-year-old Jenny Montgomery walked up to Betty with a perplexed expression.

"Do you know where my mom is?" she asked.

"No," said Betty, "but you should go ask Mrs. Green." Barbara Green didn't know either.

Betty started moving toward the door with the rest of the mothers, anxious to check on the lasagna she was preparing for the luncheon. As she did she happened to see Candy Montgomery's station wagon as it pulled onto the parking lot. Candy jumped out of the car and met Barbara Green as Barbara was passing from the new sanctuary to the old.

"Oh, Barbara," said Candy breathlessly, "I went down to Betty's and we just got to talking and then I looked at my watch and thought I had time to go to Target to get Father's Day cards and I drove all the way to Plano. But then when I got to the parking lot, I realized my watch had stopped and I was late so I didn't even go in. I'm so upset, because I wanted to see the program."

"Jenny was just now asking about you," said Barbara.

"Oh no, well, I'll just have to make it up to them."

Candy and Barbara continued on into the old building and headed straight for the kitchen. As they entered, Betty Huffhines looked up and said, "So where have *you* been?"

"Oh, I'm so upset," said Candy, "I went down to Betty's and we just got to talking and then I thought I had time to go to buy Father's Day cards at Target but I realized my watch had stopped when I got there and so I was late."

As she was talking, Candy filled the glasses with ice and started pouring tea from a pitcher. Most of the women were only half listening to her rather complicated story.

"I had to get Alisa's swimsuit from Betty or I wouldn't have been late. My watch stopped."

Someone handed Candy a plate and all the women filed into the open room of the old sanctuary. The women sat at one table, their children at another. Candy took a place between Rhonda Hensley and Connie Holmes and ladled a helping of lasagna onto her plate. Craig Huffhines and Jimmy Wright, the two teenagers, were doing their best to keep the kids entertained, but the room was noisy with children's squeals and conversational chatter. Connie and Rhonda started talking about new movies.

"We're taking Alisa with us tonight to see *The Empire*

Strikes Back," Candy said. "That reminds me, I'd better go check on the kids."

Candy took her napkin as she got up and headed for one of the classrooms. Once there, she found a mirror and dabbed at the cut near her right hairline. She returned to the table but sat very still.

"Why are *you* so quiet today?" said Rhonda.

Candy cleared her throat. The back of her mouth was dry. Her toe throbbed painfully. She smiled. "Because I'm eating and it's not nice to talk with your mouth full."

Rhonda smiled. The conversation turned back to movies. Candy got up from the table again. The thought crossed her mind that she might be limping. She made a special effort to walk straight. She found another mirror and dabbed the blood again. Even when it was staunched, she could feel it running down her forehead, exposing her.

No one must know. Day like any other.

When Candy returned, the women had started clearing off the table. She stayed for a few minutes, helping to wash dishes and put things away, until Jenny came into the kitchen and tugged at her blouse.

"Mom, you have to take us to buy Father's Day cards, remember?"

"Oh, I almost forgot. Okay, dear, almost ready."

As Candy left the kitchen to find Ian and Alisa, Betty Huffhines happened to notice something odd. Candy Montgomery, who always wore rubber sandals in the summer, was wearing a pair of blue tennis shoes.

The afternoon passed in a fog. Candy bundled the three kids into the station wagon and headed for Allen, a town some five miles away, just large enough to have supermarkets and department stores. The four of them trooped into the Wal-Mart on Highway 5, but Candy couldn't get them all to the card counter before they started getting sidetracked. Jenny started it when she noticed a candy rack; she knew what she wanted and the others encouraged her. "Nestle's Crunches, Nestle's Crunches, Mom, can we?"

Candy had a strict rule against buying any Nestle product. She was participating in a mother's boycott against Nestle's because of that company's sale of a controversial baby formula in the Third World. Perhaps because the kids knew a Nestle's

Crunch was forbidden, they wanted one all the more. Today Candy didn't feel like fighting, so she gave in.

"We'll get one each when we leave," she said.

At the card counter, the kids wanted to look at them all. Ian chose his first, a card with a funny man with a moustache and a straw hat on the front. When you opened it, his straw hat popped up out of the middle. The greeting read "HATS OFF for a wonderful Father's Day." Jenny wanted one with a poem. She settled on this one:

> To wish you a
> Happy Father's Day
> And then to tell you, too
> There's always lots of love and pride
> In every thought of you.

Candy chose a joke card, as usual; she and Pat had exchanged them for as long as they had known each other. This one featured a cartoon drawing of a curly-haired wife with rouged cheeks. "Happy FATHER'S DAY Honey," it read, "it really means a lot to have a husband like you!" The second page showed the same figure and said:

> a lot of time
> a lot of frustration
> a lot of headaches
> a lot of worry . . .

And then the third page:

> . . . BUT A LOT OF FUN!

Pat would love it.

The kids were an odd kind of comfort; they kept her occupied, kept the dragons at bay.

When they got home, Candy gave Alisa her swimsuit and told her to get ready for her afternoon lesson. Then she checked the washer, wrung the water out of a pair of worn blue jeans, and transferred them to the dryer. Ian wandered out into the back yard while the girls were upstairs. Candy picked up the kitchen phone and dialed her husband at work.

"Pat, we just got home from Bible School and wanted to be sure you get enough money at the bank, because Alisa is going to the movie with us. The kids nagged about it after you left this morning, and so I promised them I'd ask Betty if Alisa could stay another night. But then I had to go to Betty's to pick up Alisa's swimsuit and we got to talking and I lost track of time, and then when I went to Target I noticed my watch had stopped and I missed the whole Bible School program."

"Uh-huh," said Pat. He had just returned from a Texas Instruments office picnic, and was anxious to get over to the North Building to make some computer runs. "So Betty's letting Alisa go to the movie with us?"

"She never did say anything about the movie really," said Candy, "but she said Alisa could spend the night again."

"Listen, honey, that's fine with me, I'm about to go to the bank now."

"Pat, would you happen to know where Allan is working today?"

"Allan Gore? No. Why?"

"It's not important. Okay, we'll meet you in the parking lot about fifteen of five."

"Okay, fine."

Pat hung up and thought, "What was that all about?"

At 410 Dogwood Street, the home of Allan and Betty Gore, their two children, and their two cocker spaniels, no one came or went on the afternoon of June 13, 1980. The phone rang intermittently but wasn't answered. Around noon, a delivery man for a parcel service rang the doorbell but got no response. Around four, Allan Gore himself placed a call from the Dallas–Fort Worth Airport, where he was about to board a plane. After ten or eleven rings, he hung up. The only sign that the house was occupied at all was the muffled sound from within of a small baby, crying at the top of its lungs.

Behind the house, the two dogs skittered nervously around the yard, howling and whimpering by turns, as if they were confused, or perhaps simply frightened.

2 · CANDY AND PAT

All her life she would remember the tidy little village on the west coast of France, the one where the peddler's carts rattled down the cobblestone streets, firewood stacked precariously high. The Wheelers lived in a big stone house on the outskirts of town, where gently undulating farmland stretched for miles beyond the back door, gateway to the world's richest wine-growing regions. There were other American families there, too, all waiting for the new Army base to be finished. Their young children roamed the shady lanes and the countryside, teasing the goats and scaring the chickens, climbing in forbidden trees, treating the strange, wondrous place as a perpetual amusement park created for their benefit. Candy Wheeler was tiny, blonde, cute as a button, and already showing signs of being the more high-strung of the Wheeler girls, but she was still too young to go far on her own. She rode the school bus each day to a room where a pale black woman would teach them how to count and say simple French phrases, but Candy seemed more interested in her classmates, especially the ones always referred to as "the two little Communist boys," deposited in La Rochelle by some sad circumstance of the war.

Candy gravitated to the older kids right away, perhaps because she had no trace of shyness and always liked boys' games, even when her mother would scold her for getting her clothes dirty. In kindergarten, she was already flirtatious, trying to attract the attentions of a classmate named Steven who brought Graham crackers to school every day. Candy would watch his temples move as he ate them; it made him look nice, she thought. Once, when a nine-year-old named Johnny was spending the night, she challenged him to a race:

whoever got to the water pump first got to pump the handle until a big glass jar was filled. Johnny, bigger and faster than Candy, was off right away and won easily, but as soon as Candy caught up she grabbed the jar from him and smashed it against the pump in rage. One piece of glass hit the top of Candy's nose, right between the eyes, and blood started to pour. By the time they got her to the local hospital, she was kicking and screaming so much that she had to be held down by nurses. Her mother seemed put out with her, placing her forefinger to her lip and saying, "What will the people in the waiting room think?" But Candy kept screaming until all the stitches were in. She would bear the scar the rest of her life, but she would try to forget the race. It was something ugly in such a pretty place. She preferred to remember France as her happiest time.

Candy was an Army brat, the daughter of a radar technician who spent the twenty years after World War II bouncing from base to base, putting in two- or three-year stretches, trying to keep some thread of continuity in the lives of his two daughters, destined to attend six or seven schools in as many places before high school graduation. First there was Fort Gordon, then Fort Sam Houston in San Antonio, followed by the three years in France, then Virginia, El Paso, West Germany, Washington, D.C., Fort Meade in Maryland—after a while the places all ran together and seemed like a very small town that happens to be scattered over half the globe. Candy seemed born to the wandering life, though, blessed with an easy rapport with strangers and the sort of coquettish exuberance that taught her at a very early age what power women could exert over men. In the fifth grade she was showered with bracelets by an impetuous admirer; in the sixth she felt her greatest embarrassment when a friend wrote "Donnie Loves Candy" all over the blackboard during recess. Her first kiss came from a guy with the improbable name of Jack Spratt; it happened one night outside the base Teen Center somewhere in rural Germany after an eighth-grade Coke dance. But Jack, like most boys she knew, soon had to leave, and she would have started going steady with Jack's best friend had it not been for her mother's stern admonition that she was too young for any such thing.

Candy learned most of what she knew of sex from Joy, her older sister, who traded secret knowledge in giggling, whispered confidences and showed Candy how to use exotic paraphernalia like lipstick and nylons. Candy wanted to know everything, and learned it soon enough. By the time both girls were teenagers, and the Wheeler household started filling up with a constant stream of homesick GI's, Mrs. Wheeler decided it was time for preventive education and gave Candy a book on sex to read. The information was superfluous by that time, but Candy was troubled by the terminology. "Any questions?" asked her mother when she had finished.

"No," she said honestly, "but what's a penis?"

After a transfer back to a base in Maryland, conversations between mother and daughter became more strained. When Candy turned thirteen, she told her mother she wanted to wear a girdle. You don't need one, her mother told her. I don't care, said Candy, everybody is wearing them. That's silly, said her mother. I need one to hold up my stockings, she said. You don't need those either, came the reply. But Candy wouldn't give up, arguing and protesting in ways that only made her mother more adamant. Finally Joy intervened on Candy's behalf and talked their mother into a girdle. By the time she got it, though, Candy didn't feel too grateful, knowing that there would be more and tougher fights.

At the age of fourteen she ran away from home. She had no particular reason, but her best friend Chloe had had a fight with her father, so the two of them met at the base Teen Club one night after a roller-skating party and decided to see the world together. They set off on foot, only to be found the following day at a nearby shopping center. Candy was hungry, but otherwise she had no regrets.

She despised school, because it was boring and because no particular subject ever seemed to get her attention. At sixteen she became a full-time loiterer, spending most weekends sitting at fast-food joints, cruising, playing pool, drinking beer (though without ever developing a taste for it), telling what she believed to be dirty jokes, and especially hanging out at the base rifle range late at night, where boys' hands were sometimes known to wander underneath girls' dresses. Candy was curious and aggressive, anxious to try anything, but sometimes that was difficult. Since she had started school a year early, Candy was the baby of the rifle range crowd—the last of the girls to start having her period and, worse yet, the last to be allowed to "car-date." She continued to quarrel frequently with her mother—over dating, makeup (she wasn't allowed to wear it to school), the telephone (Candy remained glued to it for hours on end), and especially smoking. Both parents smoked but didn't want her to start. Finally, after several mother-daughter spats, her father—always the push-over when it came to his "baby girls"—said it wasn't *that* important, not if they were going to be fighting all the time, and gave her permission to do it. She immediately stopped smoking.

Still, until she was a high school junior, the most daring thing Candy had done was go skinnydipping late at night, with and without males, whenever the girls in her group could sneak out their windows without getting caught. That kind of suggestive but innocent fun all changed when her best friend got pregnant and had to leave school. Upset more by her girlfriend's keeping it a secret than by the pregnancy itself, Candy set her sights on her first steady boyfriend. The magic "car-dating" age of sixteen had arrived, and Candy was tired of spending all her time with the girls.

His name was Chris, and he was one of the senior-class "darlings" that all the junior girls drooled over. He was the first thing in Candy's life that seemed to matter. As Candy would later say, "I fell madly in love with him." She couldn't wait to lose her virginity.

"We had dated for a couple of months before I went to bed with him," she would recall. "Actually, went to car with him would be more appropriate, since it was the back seat of his Ford. I was very disappointed. From all the trashy novels I'd read, I expected fireworks and explosions and to be all aquiver with lust. I had certainly wanted him before he actually entered me, but afterwards was a big letdown. Oh, it felt good, and it didn't hurt like I had expected it to, but it didn't feel as good as I thought it should. I wondered afterwards if my eyes were all glassy and my cheeks rosy like in the novels. It got better, though, as time went on, and we became more experienced and experimental with each other. I don't think Chris ever felt guilty for having done it, and I knew I didn't. We were in love and it seemed a natural course. And yet it was something that we kept very private. Some of our friends copulated more openly and that Chris was so quiet about it pleased me. It put our relationship above that of our friends. The Christmas after my senior year Chris wanted to give me an engagement ring and my mother wouldn't allow him to. Daddy at this time had been sent to an isolated base in Alaska, Mama and I were both working, and she felt I was too young.

She always 'felt I was too young' for everything, it seemed. I guess she was right, though. When Daddy came home, he was sent to Illinois. I was in California at the time with my sister—she had been having a difficult pregnancy and miscarried while I was there. But rather than going back to Maryland to marry Chris, I went to Illinois. I guess I thought I was too young, too. Soon, Chris and I didn't even write anymore."

Pat Montgomery met her one summer in El Paso, a summer so crowded with images of love and death that in later years he would have trouble piecing them all together. For much of that summer he sat in the lab at Texas Instruments, staring at his pallid scientific theorems without the least interest, his mind eight hundred miles away. Pat Montgomery was one of the brightest young electrical engineers in one of the fastest-moving American electronics companies, and for several years he had told himself that was all he wanted in life. For a while he just about gave up on women, and the only times he went out now were when somebody fixed him up. He lived in a Dallas singles apartment—his buddies at the lab talked him into it—where everyone was supposed to have such a great sex life. But all Pat ever seemed to do was go to movies he didn't want to see with nice young schoolteachers he didn't like; they were all polite but intimidating women whom he would leave at the doorstep after a nervous pause and an awkward kiss. Afterward he would go home and feel foolish. They were all like the women his mother tried to set him up with—nice but not his type. It was all fake, Pat decided. Who needs it? Then Pat took a week off to go fishing with his father in Arizona, and when they got back to El Paso his mother had done it again. "She's a very nice girl I met at work," was all she said. Great, thought Pat. One of the women at the furniture factory. Then he thought, what the hell? And that's how Pat met Candy Wheeler.

She was petite and blonde and a little impish, with a thin pointed nose and a contagious high-pitched laugh. But Pat didn't notice those things until later. When she opened the door to her apartment, he thought two things: overweight and a double chin. Typical mother's choice. Not his type. Fake date.

He took her across the river to Adrian's, one of the nicest restaurants in Juarez, and tried to make conversation, but Pat honestly didn't know how to "make conversation." Later

Candy would describe it, with characteristic candor, as the dullest date in her life. Mostly she listened to Pat talk about his childhood, especially his memories of the trips he made with his uncle out to the sand dunes southeast of El Paso. Candy had enough interest in "paperback archeology" to keep up with his description of some old Indian ruins, but mostly she just wanted it to be over. On the way to a shopping mall to see *Airport* afterwards, Candy tried to fill the awkward silences.

"Your mother told me you wanted to be a doctor."

Pat nodded.

"Well, you must really like to work with your hands."

Pat explained that he wanted a Ph.D., not an M.D., and then he tried to explain what electromagnetics is.

Candy was in a holding pattern when she met Pat Montgomery. After Chris, she had altered her ambitions a bit, especially after a brief stint doing secretarial work for the National Security Agency. It was even more boring than high school. What she needed, Candy decided, was a husband. Candy had always assumed she would be a mother but rarely thought of being a wife. In her favorite childhood fantasy, she lived on a great country farm full of animals and children ("at *least* eight children," she said in later years), and yet there was no man in her dream vision. "I don't know how I intended to *have* those children," she said, "since I never thought about husbands." Nevertheless, she scouted around from time to time, beginning in January 1970 when, at the age of twenty, she moved out of her parents' house for the first time, rented a duplex, got a secretarial job at the *El Paso Times*, and dated successively a man named Fred (ruled out due to poor income level), a guy named Dave (ruled out for lack of education), and one whose name she could never remember. (She did seriously consider marrying the one whose name she couldn't remember, but only because his best friend had married Candy's best friend, Cathy. "It seemed the natural thing to do at the time," she said later.) Then Cathy moved away, and Candy took up with a Mexican-American girl named Frances, whose fondness for tennis, movies, shopping, wasting time at the Fort Bliss Service Club, and bar-hopping in Juarez perfectly agreed with Candy's own. The two of them were especially taken with a Juarez emporium called Pete's, where Pete himself would mix exotic but relatively harmless Purple Passions just for them. Candy's mother constantly warned her not to have anything to do with Frances's Mexican boyfriends, a warning that went unheeded after Candy got her duplex, not because Candy had any great fondness for Mexican men but because she considered her mother's opinion hypocritical. Mrs. Wheeler's dating code didn't proscribe Frances from dating *Anglo* men.

Nevertheless, the last place Candy would have expected to find herself was in a car on the way to a movie with a guy like Pat Montgomery. It had happened through no fault of her own. Forced to change jobs to meet her rent payment, Candy became the secretary to an undemanding but wealthy owner of a wrought-iron furniture manufacturing plant. The most intriguing routine of a most unintriguing job was to total up the piecework of the many women day laborers who sewed the cushions for padded headboards, barstools, and the like. Over the roar of the foundry, she managed to make friends with two of them, Marie Montgomery and Trudy Temple, who turned out to be, respectively, Pat's mother and aunt. One day Marie called over the din to tell Candy her son was coming home for a vacation and that, since all his friends had moved away from home, she wondered if Candy would mind if he called her. Candy wasn't breathless with anticipation. "But I thought, well, I can always get a free meal out of him."

Her biggest surprise was not Pat himself—he was not handsome but she had dated worse—but the fact that, after their excruciating first date, he asked her immediately for a second. She surprised herself by accepting.

On the day following the abortive first date, they drove out into the desert, looking for an old adobe house Pat had discovered as a child. But Pat made a wrong turn and got lost and they ended up walking up and down across the sand dunes, hand in hand, until the sun touched the horizon and they both remarked how beautiful it was. Candy scampered playfully across the side of the dune and then complained about the sand in her red hot pants.

On the way back into town, they stopped for pizza, then took in a drive-in movie. Candy would later tell Cathy that "Pat likes to work with his hands after all." It was a problem she could deal with, and did. Having put him in his place, she turned back to the movie and acted like nothing had happened. Pat never mentioned it either, but before taking her home, he asked if they could make it three nights in a row.

Candy told Pat to call her the next day. She had no intention of ever going out with him again.

There was no reason to think anything else would happen. On the day after their frolic in the dunes, Candy purposely avoided going home after work, choosing to visit her mother instead. Pat called all night but got no answer. She had washed her hands of him, a fact that Pat failed to realize. He assumed she had simply forgotten about the date, or been called away to some family emergency. It never crossed his mind that she had brushed him off.

Though she was five years his junior, Candy had the worldly wisdom of a much older woman, while Pat in some ways was still as naive as a high school sophomore. Had Pat been more observant and realized that he had been snubbed, he might have disappeared. Instead, when he got back to Dallas he sent her a dozen roses and a humorous card. Inside he had written, "Hope you got the sand out of your pants!" Candy was so touched that she looked up the number for Texas Instruments and called to tell him how sweet he was.

Pat's father was older than the other dads of the Lower Valley. He had married late, so that by the time Pat was a teenager, Jewel Montgomery was nearing the end of his career as comptroller of a small Texaco refinery. In some ways Pat was closer to his uncle Jack, who lived next door and treated Pat like a son, taking him on expeditions into the desert, hunting, camping, and doing all the athletic things that Mr. Montgomery was too frail and asthmatic to attempt. Then one morning in July 1970 Jack suddenly suffered a massive heart attack and died at home before anyone could get to the house. Pat flew home immediately. Jack was only fifty-four.

Pat had been looking for a reason to return to El Paso, but when he got there for the funeral, he was distracted and confused. On the second night home, he called Candy and met her at her apartment. For the next several hours they walked through a nearby park, and for one of the few times in his life, Pat forgot his shyness and talked unstintingly of both his sense of loss—Jack was the first close relative of Pat's to die—and his great hopes for a career in advanced engineering. Somehow, in the way that great tragedies and great victories become compressed and focused in a single moment, the sympathetic, attentive face of Candy Wheeler became that night a symbol for Pat of the fond future in the way that Jack now represented the fond past. And Candy was so taken with his soliloquy that she saw through to a man whom she had not even recognized on the first two dates. He seemed so clever and cute and, above all, generous that she wondered whether this could possibly be the same man who had been so boorish at the drive-in movie.

It wasn't that Pat said anything so very original. The whole of his prior life centered around schools, beginning with Ysleta High, where he was an All-City trumpeter and a straight-A student; Texas Western, the local university where he had to give up hopes of being a professional musician and turn to engineering instead; and finally the University of Colorado on a NASA fellowship. He would have been there still, working on his Ph.D., had it not been for President Nixon's suspension of student draft deferments. Fearing Vietnam even more than he feared a blind date, Pat had taken a job in the Texas Instruments antenna lab, where it was simple to prove to any draft board that the work contributed to the military effort. In fact, Pat was so far ahead of the technical journals by that time, on the very cutting edge of electromagnetic research, that the University of Colorado decided to allow him to supervise his own Ph.D. work for a while, at least until the draft ended and he was able to return for the mandatory campus hours.

Candy listened to Pat's description of theoretical science with only feigned interest, but she managed on two occasions to direct the conversation toward children (Pat liked them) and animals (Pat was allergic to cats and dogs). They agreed to write, and before they parted Pat kissed her at the door.

Two or three days later, Candy ran into Frances.

"I've met the man I'm going to marry," she said.

"What's his name?" asked Frances.

"I don't remember. I think his name is Pete."

Dear Pat,

It's lunch time (I'm at work) so I guess I'll write you, since I said I would. I hope you didn't over sleep too much this morning. It was nice talking to you even though it was past our bed time. Next time, maybe you should call earlier, huh? . . .

How are things in Dallas? It rained out here today—you should have been here with your car since you just waxed it. But it's probably raining in Dallas too, or at least it will soon, just for your car. The next time you're here, if you drive, I'll help you wax the poor thing and then we can do a rain-go-away-for-now dance. Okay? Aren't the responsibilities of ownership terrible? At least the inside of your car is clean.

If you have a few minutes some time, write me and let me know how you are. I like to get letters from people. . . .

As always,
Candy

Dear Candy,

You have got my card by now and know I fell asleep on the couch last night before I could write you. I didn't get up and go into bed until 4 A.M.—I hurt all over! . . .

Did Mother say anything about us being to-gether til 4:30? I don't think she would. Do you know what she told me Sunday about you? She said she liked everything about you except you smoke! I like everything about you except you smoke. I guess we're even—what-not for smoking. . . .

What did your Mom and Dad think of me—you think they think enough of me and you to let you come and visit a weekend? Cause if you can't come here—I'll have to come back to El Paso! If you were here we really could go to Six Flags Over Texas, the Zoo, the Southland Life Building to eat dinner, and we could even stay at my place and go swimming and listen to music or watch TV one evening. . . . Very seriously, have your mom call my mom if you think it would help to get her approval. . . . There's only one way we are going to be able to assure ourselves of our feelings toward one another and that's to see one another as often as possible.

I'll write tomorrow—but I'll think about you all tonight.

Love always,
Pat

Dearest Pat,

Well, how are you? Other than far away I mean.
I miss you.

I just finished rolling my hair and taking my
shower. Now I'm all ready to write you a long letter,
but I don't know where to start. There are so many
things I want to let you know about. I wonder if I
should start with me or Mom. I guess me first.

I like you an awful lot, but I guess you could tell.
Or if you couldn't, I do. (and I miss you.) Tonight I
was telling Mamma about how wonderful you are
and she said, on several occasions, that I was going
crazy. But she also said that it was nice to see me
enthusiastic about someone. She said it had been so
long she thought I had forgotten how. And I think it's
nice that I care about someone again. But most of all
I think it's nice that it's you.

I talked to Mamma about going to Dallas and
she said that if your aunt and uncle invited me to stay
with them it would be okay but that it wouldn't be
nice of me to run down there out of the blue. Also it's
okay to go if some relative wants to take care of me
other than you. Or she stated that if we were
engaged or something like that it wouldn't be so bad.
I told you she'd say "no." Have you come up with any
brilliant plans? Mom also said that if you wanted to
see me bad enough you'd come here, which is true.
Would you come see me? She also said "what would
his mother think?" After all I really haven't known
you very long.

It's Monday now. I just got home from work. I
called Mamma today and she asked me if I was still in
love. Naturally I told her yes.

Please write soon. I miss you lots. (I'm even not
smoking so much.)

Love,
Candy

Dear Candy,

I tried to call tonight about 9:00 your time but
you weren't there so I'll guess I'll go ahead and
write. . . .

*Now for a bout with the intellect—Candy, I've
never been one to say much to others about my
feelings. I guess its because I'm afraid that others
won't feel the same. But I've been thinking and thats
bad—its like trying to make others love you rather
than just caring for others and being glad that you've
felt that way about others. (Does this make sense?)
So I guess one should just be open about one's
emotions. But I guess there's always the other
extreme—saying things you don't really feel . . . if
your not sure I guess you should just let your emotion
guide your actions rather than your speech and only
say what you truly feel when your certain but you
should always let your emotions guide your actions.
(Is this making sense?)—Candy, that's why you need
to come to Dallas, so we can let our relationship
mature and let our emotions become more certain. I
certainly don't want you to think of me as a stranger
as you said. Even though you didn't mean it theres
probably some truth in it. I find that hard to believe
though—cause I miss you so much. I hope I haven't
rambled too much—I'll write tomorrow and think of
you tonight.*

> *Love Always,*
> *Pat*

Dearest Pat,
   *I'm at my Mom's now. I got two letters from you
today. I was completely and totally thrilled. You can
ask my Mom. She keeps telling me I act like an idiot.*
   *You were right about your letter rattling on. (the
one from Tuesday) But everything you said was true.
I mean about emotions guiding, with your mind
controlling (this is what you were saying isn't it) and
not saying what you feel when you feel it for it may
not be what you'll feel later when you've had a
chance to think about. Yes I do know what you mean,
Pat, 'cause I'm the same way. I'm always on the
defensive and as a result no one really knows me.
And it's so frustrating not to be able to say what you
feel, but there's always the possibility that if you get
involved with emotions you could end up getting*

hurt. And it's only human nature to avoid pain (physical or mental). And it is nice to have others love you but sometimes it's hard to love unless you are loved. I mean if you care about people for real it's easy for them to care back. Caring is rather simplified by generalities but loving is more complex. Even though it's easy to love on a low level (like love at first sight or whatever) it's not as substantial as loving on a higher level. And since the higher level is not quite as tangible as the lower level it isn't always recognized or it is confused with an infatuating kind of love. I agree that in order to form a more substantial relationship we must know each other more thoroughly. But I say now that I love you and thats a good start for loving you. Now are you totally confused? But even though I agree that we should be completely sure of ourselves, I'm very impatient. I want to know what is real and what's not right now. But then I always ask for too much. And if life were so simple it wouldn't be a challenge and then it wouldn't be worth living. . . .

Well, I have to go. My Mom is calling me to come visit with them in the den. She asked if I was still writing my true love. Take care of yourself, Pat, and I miss you a whole lot. Please be good.

Love you,
Candy

Darling Candy,

. . . I've got my tape deck playing mood music that I recorded. It would make a great seduction tape—wanta be seduced? It's nice just to sit and listen and think of you and write. (The chess playing seduction scene music from the movie Thomas Crown Affair with Steve McQueen is playing.) Wanta play chess???

When I come to El Paso next let's just be together—oblivious to the world around us and let's just stare into one anothers eyes and smile and giggle and enjoy our love. I miss you so—I'll write tomorrow and think of you every moment till then.

Love always,
Pat

* * *

After Jack's funeral, Pat had taken Candy to meet his grandmother in the hospital. "Mama Mac," as everyone called Grandmother McElyea, had been bedridden for some time and, at eighty-eight, was not expected to live much longer. Ironically, the reason Jack died alone was that the rest of the family was at the hospital with Mama Mac. Candy regarded the hospital trip as confirmation of her suspicions: a proposal of marriage was not far off. She had already decided to accept. Unlike Fred and Dave, Pat had earning power, a good education, and a nice family—and he was so gentle and kind.

Finally Pat called to say he was coming back to El Paso just to visit her, and he ended the conversation with the vague mention of a "gift" he was bringing with him. Candy alerted Frances that the engagement ring was on its way.

But it was nothing of the sort. Instead, Pat ceremoniously presented her with a book called *The Life, History, and Magic of the Dog*, a gift that in future years she would refer to simply as "that damned book." So instead of celebrating their engagement, Candy further cemented their relationship by leading Pat into her bedroom one night. This time she was the aggressor, even though both of them were nervous and awkward. She would later describe it as "a nice, gentle coupling—still no fireworks, but I was more certain then that I wanted to marry him. He seemed so sensitive, considerate, and gentle."

For Pat, it was the weekend that almost broke him, since the rest of the summer was consumed by lengthy long-distance phone calls and two-day weekend trips by plane between Dallas and El Paso.

Mama Mac died at the end of August, and her body was brought back to her hometown of Jacksonville, about 150 miles east of Dallas, for burial. At the funeral Pat's father asked about Candy.

"I've bought her a ring," Pat said.

"Are you sure? What if she says no?"

"This is just the way I want to do it."

Pat's father shouldn't have worried. When Pat flew to El Paso with the diamond, Candy was hysterical with delight. It was only their fourth weekend together, and a scant two months after they had first met, but they quickly agreed that the earliest possible wedding date was the only acceptable one.

They briefly considered immediate elopement, but Candy decided it would be unfair to her parents, so they finally settled on a small ceremony at Trinity Presbyterian Church for parents and close relatives only. By this time Pat's financial resources were severely limited. He had enough for a small U-Haul and a honeymoon night in a motel on the outskirts of El Paso.

> *Darling Candy,*
> *Next Tuesday seems like always and yet tomorrow. I'll be forever happy on that day. We'll be together for as long as we both shall live. And what we make of the rest of our lives will depend on the magnitude of our love for one another and the product of our love. I can think of nothing more worthy of my life than spending it with you. I've often wondered what an all consuming love such as ours would be like. It's a never ending anxiety. An all consuming emotion. An awareness of everything beautiful. And you are beautiful in countless ways. I hope I'll always make you happy. I know that you've already made me overly joyous. I love you.*
> *I'm looking forward to being the father of your babies and teaching them what we both believe to be right. I'd like for us to be the best parents any child would ever desire.*
> *I long for you to be at my side on a cold winter morning so that we might warm one anothers bodies and souls. I want you at my side on warm summer nights so I can love you in a manner so that when I'm gone that you'll always remember. Candace—I love you.*
>
> > *All of my love, forever*
> > *Pat*

One day after the long drive to Dallas, they were settled into an apartment next to an enormous shopping center and Pat was back at work in the Texas Instruments antenna lab. Like most newlyweds, Candy and Pat had unexpected tensions at first. Pat was accustomed to sleeping late in the morning, wandering into the lab about eleven, and sometimes going back to the office late at night when he could have the computers all to himself. Candy, at her best in the morning, found Pat's habits enormously frustrating. The Dallas weather that year was awful, Candy had trouble making friends at the apartment complex, and she couldn't stand being left alone. When she started talking about children right away, Pat suspected that she wasn't as committed to his Ph.D. as he was.

But after that first troubled year, Pat got a leave of absence to finish his degree at the University of Colorado, and they loaded up another U-Haul for the move to Boulder. Unfortunately Pat loaded it the wrong way and, scared that the trailer wouldn't hold up, told Candy they wouldn't be able to stop in El Paso as planned. Even though she had just seen her parents two months before, Candy was so upset that she cried all the way to Colorado. It was an augury of things to come.

Candy decided that the only thing worse than that apartment in Dallas was their new quadplex in Boulder. She hated the cold weather, the altitudes gave her nosebleed, and she was forced to take a part-time job working for a life insurance agent. Pat, despite the poverty, loved it. Besides working on his Ph.D., he worked for the National Bureau of Standards and served as a research assistant. Still, the three salaries combined came to only $300 a month, an amount further reduced by the arrival of a baby daughter in September 1972. Candy joked about it being her "foam-failure baby," but actually the arrival of Jenny made her much happier than she had been during the first two years of the marriage.

Pat's dissertation, considered groundbreaking at the time, was called "Electromagnetic Boundary-Value Problems Based Upon a Modification of Residue Calculus and Function Theoretic Techniques," and about twelve people in the world could understand it. By 1973, they were able to move back to Dallas suburb of Richardson, where Pat started working on Texas Instruments' top-secret military radar projects. A year after that they had saved enough money for their first house, a few miles farther north in the bedroom community of Plano. Their second child, named Ian, was born there in October 1974, and Candy, happy to have one of each sex, promptly decided to have her tubes tied. They also started visiting churches for the first time. Though self-described agnostics, they agreed they should do it for the children.

Like most marriages, theirs had settled into a routine. The excited playful exchanges of 1970 had become joke birthday cards and occasional flowers on anniversaries. But Pat would never again think so fondly of a time as he did that summer he met Candy Wheeler.

Dear Pat,

This is the very last time I'll ever write you. 'Cause pretty soon you'll be with me forever & always.

I just wanted to put this little note in your letter to tell you that I truly love you & I will continue to do so till I die. And even though I don't see how it could be possible, I'm sure I'll love you even more when we're old and grey. I do love you so much, Pat.

Always yours,
Candy

3 · SUPERHUMANS

Ian talked excitedly of *Star Wars,* but Candy Montgomery scarcely listened. She and the kids sat in the expansive parking lot of Texas Instruments, windows of the station wagon rolled down to alleviate the stiffling heat, waiting for Pat's conference to break up. It was a little after 4:30, plenty of time for them to drive into Dallas, get the tickets, find a place to eat, and make it to the 7:30 screening of *The Empire Strikes Back*. Ian would probably be full of Star Wars games all weekend. Pat would want to get down on the floor of the den and do his Darth Vader imitation. Sometimes she thought Pat got a bigger kick out of that game than Ian did. Where was he, though? Pat was late. That was not like Pat.

The name came out of nowhere: "Bethany."

Candy didn't know what the kids were discussing—probably something about brothers and sisters—but she heard Alisa say the name, and suddenly her body tensed all over. The sense of dread rushed back. With it came the strong aroma of something soft and clean and antiseptic; it tickled the nose and infused the sinuses. There was no escaping it.

Allan will be home soon. It will be okay. How long has it been now? Five hours? Six?

This time, though, all the rationalizations fell short. There was an eleven-month-old baby in the house on Dogwood.

She could see Pat walking toward them across the parking lot. He came around to her window and suggested they take the Volkswagen Rabbit instead of the big car. Everything was starting to happen in slow motion again.

Allan will be home soon.

Candy shepherded the kids into the back of the Rabbit, and they continued to talk excitedly all the way to Dallas. As they drove down North Central Expressway, which on Friday nights is the most crowded thoroughfare in all Texas, she searched for diversions. They discussed the dinner plans.

"Remember," she said, keeping her voice down so the kids couldn't hear, "Alisa is a picky eater. We'd better stick with fast food."

Pat nodded and repeated his plans to go get the tickets first in case the movie was sold out. Then Candy fell silent.

That damned smell, why won't it stop?

A little after five the Rabbit pulled into the parking lot of the fashionable NorthPark Shopping Center. Candy and the kids waited in the Rabbit while Pat went to buy the tickets. But just a few minutes later he came back to the car.

"The 5:15 hasn't started yet and there are still a few tickets left," he said. "Why don't we go in now and then eat later?"

That was fine with Candy and more than fine with the kids, so they bought the tickets. Due to the large crowd and the need to get five seats together, they ended up sitting just a few feet from the largest indoor movie screen in Dallas. The kids thought being close to the jumbo screen was great fun, but Candy and Pat had to tilt their heads much higher than they considered comfortable.

Allan will be home soon.

The first time she felt like wretching came about ten minutes into the movie. The scene took place in a blinding snowstorm. A man rode a strange creature, a kind of yak-kangaroo, across a bleak horizonless landscape until the animal fell over dead from exhaustion. To protect himself from freezing to death, the man then slit open the animal's stomach, and its bloody internal organs spilled out onto the snow.

Candy didn't see the man climb into the animal's stomach for warmth, because she had already blacked out. When she came to, three or four seconds later, her eyes were shut tightly and she was holding her breath to get rid of the smell. She clenched the arm rests with both hands.

It was worse now. It was worse now because there was nothing to do, nothing except sit there and pretend to be watching the movie. There were no kids to talk to. No errands to run. She wouldn't even be able to call Sherry that night, because the Clecklers had company for the weekend. Sherry knew something was wrong. When she had come to the house that afternoon to get the card table, she put her hand on Candy's arm and looked into her eyes.

"What's wrong, girl?" she had asked.

"Not a thing."

Sherry looked at her a few more seconds, and Candy started to tremble slightly.

"As soon as I get the folks sent back to Alabama, let's talk, you hear me?"

So Sherry knew. She was the only one who would know. She was the only one who knew Candy as well as Candy knew herself.

Jenny tugged on Candy's arm. "Mommy, Alisa needs to go to the bathroom."

Thank God.

While Candy waited on Alisa in the ladies' room, she tried to collect herself. There was a deep reservoir she was trying to tap. At the center of it was a feeling beyond reason, beyond feeling, beyond thought itself. It was a kind of oblivion. She could cope if she just reached down far enough and found that sanctuary of cold comfort and hardened herself against all unwelcome thoughts. She could build a wall around memory itself if she just concentrated enough.

Black it out . . . you couldn't have done it.

She was all right through most of the rest of the movie. The images passed before her eyes, but she saw nothing. Then at one point, while Luke Skywalker and Darth Vader fought with laser-beam weapons, Luke's hand was suddenly chopped off and it went flying through space.

Candy's body tensed again, and an image of surpassing violence and horror flickered quickly through the back of her mind, an image so terrifying that a year later the memory would still cause her to tremble and choke on her words. Her stomach churned and she thought she was going to wretch. She reached out for that oblivion of unfeeling, but when she did the smell returned, stronger this time, the smell of cleanness and freshness and purity, now corrupted by a second smell, a fouler odor that she didn't want to think about.

She saw nothing else. When the movie ended, she rose as though in a trance and went through the practiced motions of directing children back into the car and answering their persistent questions. Before, they had been a welcome distraction. Now they were simply there. She didn't see them or Pat or anything else for several minutes. Then she heard Pat asking her a question.

"Did you ever return that book?"

Pat was reminded of the overdue library book as they passed near the public library in suburban Richardson on the way back home. Candy answered yes but said nothing more.

Pat pulled back onto the Texas Instruments parking lot.

"What do you think," asked Pat, "should we just get Taco Delight on 2170 or try something like Long John Silver's?"

"Taco Delight sounds like a good idea," said Candy, coming out of her silence, "because I know Alisa likes tacos. Why don't we pick it up on the way and eat at home?"

Ian wanted to go to Allen with Pat to get the food, so Candy and the two girls transferred back into the station wagon. On the way home, Candy occupied herself with thoughts of the evening; the girls would probably play dress-up with Candy's old clothes, and if Ian was agreeable, they would use him as their baby. Five-year-olds generally took any role that was offered.

What about Alisa?

The demons were returning. Both girls sat in the front seat, Jenny against the passenger door, Alisa in the middle. By turning her head slightly, Candy could see the long brunette hair, the olive complexion, the slightly exotic cast to her angular nose and chin, the heavy brows and lashes. Sensitive, finicky, shy among strangers, Alisa Gore was the very image of her mother.

She held her breath to keep the laundry smell from returning.

They arrived home around eight, but this being a June day in Texas, there was still plenty of sunlight left. The girls immediately ran outside to play in the pasture-sized yard while Candy busied herself fixing the drinks. A few minutes later Pat and Ian arrived bearing white bags full of tacos. Pat dumped his load on the kitchen table and announced he was going out jogging while he still had time. He was up to four or five miles on his best days, and he didn't want to lose the conditioning.

The kids ate while Pat was gone. When he got back, sweat pouring off his face and dampening his tee shirt, Candy poured him a big glass of orange juice and he stood in the kitchen, leaning against the counter as he drank.

The phone rang, and Candy picked up the kitchen extension before it had a chance to ring a second time.

"Oh Allan," she said.

Pat perked up at the sound of the name, put down his glass, and moved closer to the phone.

From a thousand miles away came the voice of Allan Gore: "Have you seen Betty? I've been trying to get her for several hours, but she doesn't answer the phone."

Pat couldn't hear what Allan had said, but he could see the lines on Candy's face as they tensed and hardened.

"Oh Allan," she said, "where *are* you?"

The smell returned now, and this time there was nothing she could do to get rid of it.

4 · SIXTH SENSES

Allan Gore had left for St. Paul late that afternoon. It was an awkward time and an awkward trip. For one thing, it was a job that should have been finished two weeks before. When Allan left Rockwell International to join an obscure but promising little electronics company in Richardson, he knew he would have to work long hours, but he tried to avoid weekends whenever he could. This time unforeseen delays meant Allan and two of his colleagues had to return to Minnesota to make certain one of their largest clients, the 3M Corporation, had a fully functional message-switching system by next week. Actually, this was the kind of trouble-shooting job that, given other circumstances, Allan would have loved. He liked the travel, he felt challenged by the work itself, and he especially enjoyed the camaraderie of just a half dozen men trying to hang in there against the colossal electronics firms like Rockwell and Texas Instruments and E-Systems and Northern Telecom and all the other illustrious names that proliferated up and down North Central Expressway in the so-called Silicon Prairie. (The name was a send-up of "Silicon Valley," the cognomen for the area around Palo Alto, California, where the huge silicon-chip industries are based.)

But Allan wouldn't enjoy this particular trip, and for a familiar reason. His wife Betty couldn't stand to be left alone, even for a single night. That's why he had tried to call from the airport before he left: the mere sound of his voice would calm her fears to some extent. At first, just after they were married in 1970, Allan had thought it was a temporary phobia. He assumed it would pass once Betty became accustomed to being away from her family in Kansas. But even now, ten years later, Betty could be reduced to tears by the mere suggestion that

39

Allan was going to be away for any extended period. She had broken down just two weeks before, after he had spent five days in St. Paul programming the new system, and then this week she had grown despondent again when he told her he would have to return. It was not as bad as it had once been—certainly not as bad as the two months in 1977 when business took him to Switzerland and Betty became so upset that she called his boss and complained—but Allan still worried constantly about her emotional state whenever he was out of town.

What made this trip different was the vacation. A week from now he and Betty would be in Europe, vacationing without the kids for the first time in four years, and were it not for Betty's tendency to worry too much about *planning* for vacations, that would be enough to keep her happy. Last night she had been positively radiant on the phone, describing the upcoming trip to JoAnn Garlington as a second honeymoon. Then this morning she had broken down again.

It was not just the business trip that caused it. Betty was almost two weeks late with her menstrual period, and although Allan didn't see any cause for her alarm, she was terrified. The one thing she didn't need this summer was a third pregnancy; the first two had been difficult enough. If she didn't start her period soon, it could spoil the whole vacation, not to mention her teaching the next spring. That morning it was all she could talk about. They had risen a little later than usual, around 6:45, but Betty had been sour from the beginning. She wasn't complaining a great deal; she simply didn't talk much at all. While Allan was dressing for work, she went into the baby's room, took Bethany out of her crib, and changed her diaper. Then Betty poured cereal and juice; they had a quick, silent breakfast. Allan wolfed down the food and went back into the bedroom to start packing.

That's when Betty started complaining. She followed him into the bedroom, half-heartedly helping with the packing but mostly looking for some kind of comfort before he left.

"You know what kind of extra responsibilities you place on me when you leave me alone," she said. And then, her voice breaking for the first time, "Allan, what am I going to do? I just *can't* be pregnant again."

Allan stopped packing for a moment and put his arms around her. It always helped when they talked things through. They moved into the living room and sat together on the couch, and Allan began to speak soothingly and optimistically of the future.

"We've been able to deal with everything else," said Allan, "we can handle this, too. I don't think you're pregnant, but if you are, we can deal with it. Don't let it spoil the vacation."

Betty started to weep quietly, so great was her fear at that moment, but the warmth and assurance of Allan's voice kept her from losing control. On Wednesday she had been to her gynecologist, who had given her a drug to induce the overdue menstrual cycle. But she had only taken the first dose the day before, so it was too early to tell whether the medication would work. Allan said he was sure the drug was probably all she would need.

"I've got to finish packing," said Allan, getting up from the couch and realizing that he was now running late. Betty remained sitting, a troubled expression fixed on her face, while Allan finished getting ready. After a while she got up and went into the laundry room to start her first load of the day. When Allan came back into the living room, she told him about the sewing she intended to do; she was making new clothes for the trip to Europe.

Allan responded reassuringly to everything Betty said. He felt she was definitely coming out of the depression now. He closed his suitcase and briefcase, lugged them into the garage, and put them in the back of the Toyota pickup. Betty followed him out to the back driveway, cradling Bethany in one arm. Allan finished the loading and turned back to Betty.

"Everything is going to be fine," he said. "You know we can deal with anything."

Betty forced a weak smile, and he kissed her gently.

"I'll call from the airport," he said.

Then he climbed into the cab and pulled away, glad they were parting on a happy note.

As soon as Allan arrived at the low-slung brick office building where ECS Telecommunications shared space with copying services, travel agencies, and the like, he headed straight down the hallway to the computer room, where he attacked a programming problem he'd bungled the day before. He stayed there all morning, emerging only at lunchtime to accompany his coworkers to the nearby Long John Silver's. A little after two everything was ready, and he left for the airport, making a mental note to call Betty when he got there. His flight didn't leave until 4:30, but Allan allowed plenty of time so that he could park at a local Surtran station and ride the bus to the airport (ECS was still small enough to care about little expenses like that), and so that he could go by one of the airport banks and buy some traveler's checks denominated in British pounds. Allan liked to take care of things like that before he arrived in a foreign country. He made another mental note—to give Betty the numbers of the traveler's checks when he called her.

Everything went as planned, so that by four o'clock Allan had checked his bags at the Braniff terminal, received his boarding pass, and purchased traveler's checks worth 700 pounds sterling. On the way to his gate, he stopped at a pay phone and dialed home. The phone rang seven or eight times, so he hung up and dialed again. When he got no answer a second time, he assumed that Betty was taking her afternoon walk with Bethany. Just then he saw his colleague, Sid O'Hara, arriving at the gate, so he stuffed the traveler's checks back inside his coat pocket and joined Sid in the boarding area. The two of them could discuss the new software programs on the way to St. Paul.

The flight was uneventful and on time. By 7:45 Allan, Sid, and another colleague named Tom Tansil were all checked into the now-familiar Ramada Inn on Old Hudson Road, their accustomed home when working on the 3M account. They were all starved, but Tom asked if they could wait to eat dinner until after he went out jogging. That was fine with Allan, since he needed to call Betty before he did anything. They agreed to meet again around nine.

Now Allan sat on the bed in his room, going back over everything that had happened that day, wondering if he had forgotten something Betty had said that morning. He dialed the number of his house again, let it ring fifteen times, hung up, then called the operator and had her dial the number. Still no answer. Betty could be moody, but she was never the kind to leave the house in the evening without telling anyone. All Allan could think of was Alisa's swimming lesson. Candy Montgomery would have brought Alisa home around noon, the lesson was at 2, and then they should have been home by 3:30. As far as he knew, there was nothing else that day. Betty didn't like to shop with the baby; she had sewing and laundry to do; there were no other explanations.

Allan picked up the phone again, requested directory

assistance in Wylie, Texas, and got the number for Richard
Parker, his next-door neighbor. When Richard answered,
Allan could hear the voices of small children in the back-
ground.

"Richard, this is Allan Gore. Sorry to bother you, but I'm
out of town and I've been trying to get Betty on the phone. I
think the phone must be out of order. Would you mind
knocking on the door over there just to see if she's home?"

"Yeah, okay, partner," said Richard, a little peeved at the
imposition. "I guess I can run over, but I'm here all alone with
the kids. Cynthia's off playing bridge at a friend's birthday
party, so I've got my hands full. . . . Hold on just a minute,
though, and I'll check."

Richard, wearing only slacks and an undershirt, slipped
out his front door and hurried across the Gore lawn in his bare
feet. Gore always had been a weird guy, kind of quiet and
unsociable. It had been three years since Richard sold them
that house, and he didn't know them much better now than he
did then. Allan was one of those guys who always kept his yard
so neat. Quiet guys usually had neat yards.

Richard rapped hard on the door at 410 Dogwood and
waited for an answer. He rang the doorbell. He waited for a
few more seconds and then sprinted back across the grass. He
couldn't afford to be away from his house; it didn't take an
eighteen-month-old baby very long to get into trouble.

"No answer, Allan. She must be out."

"Okay," Allan said. "Thanks for checking. I'll call her
later."

"Glad to, old buddy."

Now Allan was starting to worry. On an impulse he dialed
the number for Candy Montgomery. She picked it up after one
ring.

"Candy, this is Allan. Have you seen Betty?"

"Oh Allan, where *are* you?"

"I'm in Minnesota on a business trip. I've been trying to
get Betty but no one answers, and I thought you might have
talked to her today."

"I saw her this morning when I went to pick up Alisa's
swimsuit."

"Do you happen to know if she had any plans?"

"No, but I still have Alisa. There *was* a change of plans
this morning. Jenny wanted Alisa to stay over another night, so

they could go to the movies. I just dropped by the house to get the bathing suit and some clothes."

Pat Montgomery, standing next to his wife, noticed the tension in her voice, but Allan was too preoccupied with this new information.

"Did Betty seem all right?"

"She was fine," said Candy. "She did act like she was in a hurry for me to leave."

"Do you know where she might be?"

"Maybe she went to a friend's."

"No, she wouldn't go out this late. It scares her."

Candy's voice was full of concern. "Well, I'm sure there's nothing wrong. When I went over to pick up Alisa's bathing suit she was okay. I remember she was sewing, and we just talked for a while, and she gave me some peppermints for Alisa and told me how she wouldn't put her head under the water unless she got a peppermint afterward. And I took the peppermints and left."

"Is Alisa there now?"

"Yes."

"Could I talk to her for a minute?"

"Sure."

Candy called Alisa to the phone. Allan inquired about the swimming lesson and then asked whether her mother had said anything about going out that evening. Alisa said she didn't remember anything, so Allan told her to have a good time and be polite to the Montgomerys, and then Candy came back on the line.

"Allan, is there anything I can do? I'd be happy to go over to the house and check on them for you."

"No, that's all right, I'll call the neighbors."

"Well, okay, but let me know if I can do anything."

They hung up, and Pat asked Candy what was wrong. She repeated the conversation and then retold her entire day, including the fact that her watch had stopped when she went to Target. As she went on about it, Pat dug into the tacos.

A few minutes later, the phone in Allan's hotel room rang. Allan reached for it quickly, but it was only Tom, asking if Allan was ready for dinner. A few minutes later, Allan, Tom, and Sid all met downstairs in the motel restaurant, but not before Allan had stopped at the desk to leave instructions for his calls to be forwarded to the restaurant.

By this time Allan was so nervous that he had lost his

appetite. He ordered cheesecake but immediately got up from the table to find a pay phone. When he got back to the table, Tom and Sid both tried to help by suggesting that Allan call Betty's friends. But Allan dismissed the suggestion; there weren't any friends close enough to call. Betty never left the house at night. Period. Allan nibbled at the cheesecake and then returned to his room. By now it was close to ten o'clock, well past Betty's normal bedtime, and the phone still rang endlessly.

Allan redialed Richard Parker's number.

"Richard, I still haven't been able to reach Betty. Would you run out back and look in the garage and see if her car is there?"

Cynthia was still at her bridge party, but Richard detected the growing desperation in Allan's voice, so he quickly agreed. He asked Allan to hold and left by the back door this time. On Dogwood, all the garages opened onto the alley, eliminating the need for street-front driveways. Richard went as far as the chain link fence that runs between the two houses and peered into the garage. Then he went back to the phone and said, "Yeah, Allan, there's only one car there, and the garage is open and the lights are on."

"That's strange," said Allan.

He considered the possibilities: it had to be some kind of emergency. Perhaps the baby was sick.

"Give me the numbers for Plano Hospital and the Wylie police," said Allan.

As Richard was looking up the numbers, Allan tried to think of people Betty might tell if she was going to the hospital. He couldn't think of any. He wrote down the numbers as Richard dictated them, thanked him, and hung up.

He called the hospital and the police. They had never heard of Betty Gore. He had run out of names. He felt helpless. He needed to talk to someone, someone who could help him figure this out. Nothing added up. He needed a calm, level head and a sympathetic ear.

He picked up the phone and called Candy Montgomery.

"One car is gone, the garage door is open, and the lights are on," said Allan. "She never leaves that garage door open. Has she called there or anything?"

"Oh, Allan, no, she hasn't. Let me go down there and check the house. Or let me check the hospitals for you."

"Why would a car be gone this late?"

"Allan, let me *do* something."

"No, no, I just wanted to make sure you couldn't remember anything else. I'll get the neighbors to check again."

"Don't worry about Alisa, Allan, we have her and she's fine."

"Okay. I'll call you later."

Allan hung up and felt sick. Why didn't the phone ring? Why didn't anyone know anything? Why couldn't he make the one phone call that would suddenly make everything all right?

For the third time he dialed Richard Parker's house, but this time he didn't waste words.

"Richard, I'm really worried about her. Please go back over there and check *all* the doors and the garage again. If she had to leave in a hurry, maybe she left a note somewhere."

Richard sighed—he didn't like the responsibility and was a little frightened by Allan's panic—but this time he went all the way around the back fence, into the alley, and back up the Gore driveway. He was startled to see that there were two cars in the garage. The smaller one, a Volkswagen Rabbit, was pulled up so far that when he had looked over the fence, he hadn't been able to see it. Richard walked into the garage and tried to open the door that leads directly into the utility room. He could see a light under the door, but it was locked. Something about the house—the burning lights, the open garage, the silence—vaguely disturbed him. He left the way he had come and picked up the phone again.

"Something's wrong, Allan. I don't know what, but something's wrong. Both cars are there and the lights are on, but nobody answers."

"Richard," said Allan, "I want you to go and get in that house any way you can."

Richard didn't say anything for a moment.

"Okay, Allan, I guess so, but Cynthia's not back and I'm still keeping the kids, so I can't spend much time over there."

"I've got to find out what's wrong."

"Okay."

"Call me back when you find out something. Here, write down my number."

"Okay."

Richard took down the number and hung up and took a

deep breath. Then he dialed the phone again and asked for his wife.

"Did you see Betty Gore today?" he asked her.

"No."

He explained what was happening. "Come on home and keep the girls while I go over to check on Betty."

She agreed and hung up. Richard went to find his realtor's keys, hoping he had one that fit the Gore house.

Meanwhile, Allan was growing skeptical of Richard's resolve. He had sounded so tentative when Allan asked him to break into the house, and he had already given a false report on the cars. So Allan called directory assistance again and asked for Jerry McMahan's number. Jerry was a computer analyst at Texas Instruments who lived directly across the alley from the Gores. Allan dialed the number, and Jerry's wife answered.

"Tommie, this is Allan Gore and I need to talk to Jerry; it's important."

"Just a minute." Jerry had gone to bed and was already sleeping. When he came to the phone, his speech was thick.

"Jerry, something is wrong over at my house. I've been trying to get Betty but nobody answers. The lights are on and the doors are locked. Would you get a flashlight and go over there and see what you can find out?"

"Sure, Allan."

"I'll hold the line while you go over there."

"Okay, I'll be back in a minute."

Jerry stepped into a jumpsuit and put on his houseshoes and padded down his back driveway with a flashlight. He walked up into Allan's garage and knocked loudly on the utility room door but got no answer. Then he walked into the back yard and tried to force open a sliding glass door, but it wouldn't budge either. He continued on around to the front of the house, peering in windows as he went, and rang the doorbell, but still there was no sign of life from inside the house. He walked back over to his own house and picked up the phone.

"Allan, the lights are on in there, but I can't see anything wrong."

"Jerry, there is something very *definitely* wrong."

"She's probably just out with friends, Allan."

"No, she's *not* with friends. I've already tried that."

"What do you want me to do?"

"Get in that house and see what's wrong. Take the windows off, force the doors, whatever it takes."

"Okay, but give me your number. I'll have to call you back."

He took the number and hung up. But as soon as he told Tommie what was happening, she grew frightened and insisted that Jerry not go over there alone. So Jerry called Lester Gayler, a barber who lived next door to the Gores on the other side from Richard Parker. Lester's wife answered the phone and roused her husband out of bed. He quickly agreed to meet Jerry in the alley.

Two minutes later, the two friends met behind the Gore house just as Cynthia Parker passed down the alley, returning from her birthday party. From the house, Richard could hear his wife speaking to someone, so he walked out into the yard carrying a big silver ring full of house keys. He was startled to see Jerry and Lester there before him.

"What the hell's going on?" asked Jerry.

"I don't know," said Richard. "Gore just called and said to get in the house. I've got these realtor's keys. Let's try 'em on the doors."

Lester, who hardly even knew Allan Gore, said, "Might as well." Jerry shrugged.

The three neighbors walked together up the Gore driveway. While Richard tried his keys on the utility door, one by one, Jerry and Lester went around to the back patio and tried to force open the sliding glass door again. This was the fifth time the house had been checked that night, but something about doing it as a group invested the procedure with a kind of seriousness that made them all uncomfortable. It wasn't so much the idea of foul play—although that had occurred to them all—as it was the sense of violation. A house is, after all, a very personal possession. If there was something wrong inside, they weren't sure they wanted to see it.

None of Richard's keys worked, so someone suggested they try the front windows. Together they walked around to the street side of the house, and Jerry and Lester started inspecting a large window that opens into the Gore dining room to see if it could be pried open. While they were busy discussing that, Richard went to the front door, thinking he would try all his realtor's keys again. He selected the first key, placed it in the lock, and caught his breath as an icy chill ran down his spine.

The door swung open. He had not even turned the key.

"This door," he said, turning to Jerry and Lester and stepping back away from it, "this door is not locked."

The two men moved away from the dining-room window and joined Richard on the porch, but for a moment no one made a move. Richard stuck his head in the crack the open door had made.

"Betty?" he said. Then louder: "Betty!"

Finally Lester pushed open the door, and the three men entered the foyer, illuminated from both directions by the lights burning in the den to the right and the hall bathroom to the left. Lester started to the left, toward the three bedrooms, and Richard followed. All the hall doors were closed. Lester stopped at the first one, opened it, and flipped on the light inside.

Richard looked over Lester's shoulder: a child's bedroom. Nothing unusual. They continued down the hall to the next room. Meanwhile, Jerry peered into the front bathroom, which opened onto the hallway near the front door, and on the tile he saw a dark, caked substance.

"Oh no," he said, "something bad *is* wrong."

Richard and Lester arrived at the second bedroom. Lester opened the door and flipped on the light. As soon as he did, Richard heard the terrible hacking wail of an abandoned child and the simultaneous exclamation of Lester.

"Oh my God, the baby."

Richard moved into the doorway and saw Bethany in her crib, half sitting, half lying, her legs folded under her, her face blotchy and red, her hair tangled and dirty. Her skin was stained with her own excrement. Her poignantly hoarse crying curdled the blood. She had obviously been here a long time.

"Get her out of here," barked Lester. "Something is very wrong."

Richard quickly reached into the crib and gathered up the baby. Cradling her head against his shoulder, he hurried back down the hall and out the front door just as Jerry was joining Lester at the entrance to the second bedroom. As Richard left, the two neighbors continued together to the master bedroom, but once there, they found nothing.

That left the other half of the house. Jerry and Lester split apart as they entered the living area, Jerry going to the right and into the dining room, Lester left and into the kitchen. They walked slowly, turning on available lights as they went.

Both of them were increasingly aware of a pungent odor that seemed to follow them through the house. They spoke only fitfully.

"Nothing here."

"I'll look in here."

Meanwhile, Richard had left the baby with his wife next door and instructed her to call the police immediately. He searched through a drawer for his handgun and told her to stay inside with the kids until they had figured out what was wrong at the Gore house.

Finally Lester made his way through the kitchen and reached the door to the utility room, between the kitchen and garage. At the same moment that Lester opened that door, Richard appeared back at the front of the house with his gun drawn.

"Oh my God don't go any further!"

Lester shut the door quickly without even entering the utility room, and in the stunned silence of the moment it was difficult to tell whether he was talking to Jerry, to himself, or to someone on the other side of the door.

"She's dead."

Lester had not seen a body. He hadn't seen anything but blood—thick, congealed reddish-brown oceans of blood, glistening on the tile of the utility room floor—and something had told him not to look any farther than that. Some sixth sense took over and told him that the sight on that floor was something too private for him to see. He instinctively moved away from the door.

From the dining room, some fifteen feet away, Jerry saw the look on Lester's face and heard the shock in his voice and moved tentatively toward the utility room. As Lester moved away, Jerry cracked the door open and, without moving any closer, looked in. He got only a glimpse, but it was enough. He shut the door.

"She's blown her head off," said Jerry.

Lester moved toward the telephone on the kitchen counter, thinking he would call the police, but just as he reached for the receiver, the phone rang. Everyone in the room froze.

Lester picked it up.

"Hello."

"This is Allan." He had called because he couldn't wait any longer.

Lester hesitated. "I've got to make a decision," he said.

"What's wrong?" asked Allan.

"I don't know."

Jerry quickly sensed what was happening and strode across the kitchen. "Is that Allan?" he asked. Lester meekly handed him the phone.

"Allan?" said Jerry.

"What did you find?" Allan's voice was tense and shaky.

"I'm afraid it's not good," said Jerry, finding no words to describe what he had just seen. "But don't worry—the little one is okay."

"The baby is okay?"

"Yes."

"What about Betty?"

"I'm sorry, Allan."

"What happened?"

Jerry had to say something. "I don't know for sure."

"What do you think?"

"It looks like she's been shot."

"How? We don't even have a gun."

"I'm sorry, Allan. I wish I had another way to say it."

"Have the police been called?" Now it was Allan who was fighting for the right words.

"Yes, Richard called them."

After a silence, Jerry said, "What about Alisa, Allan? Do you know where she is?"

"Yeah, she's fine, she's fine."

"Allan, I'm sorry. Are you going to be okay?"

"I'm okay."

"Do you have someone there with you?"

"Yeah, I have friends here, I'm okay."

"I wish there was something else I could say, Allan. We'll stay here and explain everything to the police."

"Okay, thanks, Jerry."

Allan hung up the phone. He was stunned and confused and so disoriented that he temporarily forgot where he was. He dialed the room of Tom Tansil; Tom should know. It was as though, after so many hours of dialing and redialing the phone, he couldn't deal with Betty's death any other way. So he called Tom and told him what had happened, and Tom asked whether he wanted company, and Allan said yes, but not for a few minutes. And then, not knowing what else to do, Allan called Candy Montgomery again.

Pat Montgomery was a little peeved when the call came around 11:30, because he and Candy had just gone to bed and were starting to make love.

"What timing," he said as Candy reached immediately for the phone.

"Candy." Allan's voice was distant and flat. "I have some bad news. Betty's dead."

"Oh Allan." Candy's voice broke. "What happened?"

"It looks like she's been shot. The neighbors found her."

"What about Bethany?"

Allan didn't even hear the question. "I know that there have been some things that are bothering her lately," he said, "and I know she's been upset, and she was two weeks late with her period. But I never thought that she would—"

Allan stopped, and Pat noticed tears forming in Candy's eyes.

"But we don't even *own* a gun," said Allan.

"What can I say, Allan?" Candy was almost whimpering.

"Please keep Alisa for a while and don't tell her what happened. I want to tell her."

"Oh Allan, are you going to be all right?"

"Yes, I'm okay. I've got to go."

Candy hung up and began to sob. Pat put his arm around her shoulders.

"Is she dead?" he asked.

"I don't know, I didn't ask. How can you ask something like that? But she must have been, because the neighbors found her."

A gun, she thought. *A suicide. It's all right now because it happened with a gun.*

Allan Gore put down the phone and wondered whom he should call next. He stared at the wall and his mind went blank for a moment. Then he saw Betty, as he had seen her for the last time that morning, as he would see her for months to come. After their argument, she had walked out onto the driveway with Bethany in her arms. Then, as Allan pulled away, she had raised Bethany's little hand and waved it at him, and for the first time that day she had smiled, really smiled, as broadly as she ever had.

5 · BETTY AND ALLAN

Betty was the pretty one. It was not just her mother and father who said so, but a verdict rendered in 1953 by popular ballot at the general store of Norwich, Kansas—Betty was three when she became Most Popular Baby—and then again in later years by the combined young manhood of Kingman and Harper counties. Betty had an innocence about her then, and a wide Hollywood smile that for a while made hers the most coveted female lips in the junior class. Hers was not classic beauty. Her face tended toward thickness and had a dark cast to it; her huge eyes were almost black, her eyebrows narrow and straight, and for most of her childhood she wore harlequin glasses, which remained fashionable in parts of rural Kansas after the rest of the country had moved on to designer frames. But by the eighth grade she had developed the full figure of a woman, long before most of her girlfriends needed grownup bras, and thereafter she would never spend a Saturday night alone.

In public—public being the 414 permanent residents of Norwich—Betty wore her popularity lightly. There were flashier girls, more talented girls, girls who came from more powerful Kansas families. But it was Betty's very conventionality that made her the frequent center of attention. She was the kind of girl who was always being elected vice-president. She played clarinet in the band and guard on the girls basketball team and was competent, if undistinguished, at both. (She quit both, too, after deciding that the Y-Teens and Methodist Youth Fellowship were where her true talents lay.) She tried her best to be feminine, making the most of her infrequent shopping trips to Wichita for dresses, blouses, and shoes. But she could also drive a tractor, and never rebelled against the more

53

tedious family chores—baling hay, dressing roosters, pumping gas at her father's Standard station—that some kids would have resisted. The grey, listless land of Kingman County is not an invigorating kind of environment—the prairie is hard and dry, and there is no such thing as a wealthy farmer—but Betty had the gay, unquestioning optimism of a girl in love with a place for no more reason than that it is *her* place.

Bob Pomeroy, Betty's father, was a Kansan to the marrow, a huge, bearish farmer whose 260 pounds were so well distributed over his six-foot-three-inch frame that he seemed less overweight than simply monumental. He was a man of few words beyond what he needed to transact business, and few allegiances beyond his family and closest friends; but he had that instinctive Kansas sense of community that made him one of the first to show up at the scene of a burning barn or at a grieving widow's hearthside. Bob was noncommittal about formal religion; he was raised a Baptist, switched to Methodism because the kids liked it better, supported the church but left the actual worship to the rest of the family. But he was also the sort of man who never doubted for an instant the existence of the Almighty. He had never held formal office, but he was a pillar nonetheless, not only because of the Pomeroy name (tied to the Kansas land for four generations) but because Bob's granitic perseverance, even in the years when the wind and the freezing rain dashed the crops into fodder, was an assurance that some things never changed. When Bob would walk down the main street of Norwich, his full head of black and silver hair combed back over his large oval face, his shoulders broad as a double-span harness, small children would look up from their play and note his passing with a quiet, tentative "Hello, Mr. Pomeroy," a repeated greeting that would gain in intensity and volume as a smile creased Bob's face.

Bob met his wife in 1948 on one of his rare vacations, a visit to the famous mineral baths in Claremore, Oklahoma, where he hoped to relieve his congenital arthritis. The daughter of a farming family, sixteen-year-old Bertha Hancock was a small, modest girl, with dark hair and delicate facial features, though much more talkative than Bob. The courtship lasted two weeks. A month after that they were installed in a drafty three-room crackerbox on 160 acres outside Norwich, where Betty would spend the first sixteen years of her life, helping Bertha cook on a wood stove and using an outdoor bathroom. She was the first child and the only girl, four years older than brother Ronnie and eight years senior to baby Richard.

On January 1, 1963, a few days shy of her thirteenth birthday, Betty began keeping a diary, using a No. 2 wooden pencil and a large, upright script that would yaw and weave as she tried to control its journey across the thin blue lines of the pages, which were not much bigger than playing cards. The diary had a pale blue binding of simulated leather, with a thong of reinforced cardboard that fit into a gold clasp and allowed her to lock up her secrets each night with the tiniest of keys. When she began, she was (like her handwriting) still awkward and gangly. She struggled against the twin social evils of being too tall and having thick, unruly hair that, regardless of what she did, wouldn't take to that Toni curl. But those anxieties soon subsided as she discovered that flipped hair wasn't a girl's only asset. On February 14 of her seventh-grade year, she was able to write, "I got 19 valentines. One from Leon B. which said he liked me but if I didn't like him to tell him."

For the next six years—until the day in 1968 when Bob loaded her belongings into the back of the family pickup and moved her into a freshman dorm at Southwestern, the cross-state college at Winfield—she wrote something in that diary every day. Sometimes it was just a line about church or athletic events or test scores, but increasingly its contents turned away from mail-order pictures of Troy Donahue and Vince Edwards, or Elvis movies, or books with titles like *Double Date, Three Loves Has Sandy,* or *A Spring to Remember,* to the real thing: boys. Not Leon B., though. Leon made one more appearance in the diary ("Tonight Leon B. called and said he wanted my picture") and then faded into oblivion. Betty had become too popular for shy boys who declare their love in valentines.

In later years her friends would recall Betty as the girl who always had a boyfriend—or two, or three—but who never really seemed to be in love. She was too serious and sensible for that. Not that she didn't like the idea of being attractive; she was quick to notice even the slightest sign of affection, as though she were constantly surprised by her own power over boys. "Tonight a boy stopped to fix his tire," she wrote. "When he left he waved, smiled and said bye to me. He was very cute." And she was always thrilled when Ronnie, her little brother, would report some second-hand compliment from a distant admirer. But on the whole she kept her emotions in check, and thought of the fawning boys as frivolous escorts she could pass the time with while waiting for a real man. No doubt Betty's cool remoteness, not unfriendly but never really uninhibited either, only served to enhance her attractiveness. She was the archetypal nice girl, wholesome, uncomplaining, responsive, intelligent. She was the kind of girl every mother wanted her son to marry.

And, for the most part, Betty could have had her pick of the lot. By the spring of her eighth-grade year, she could write, without a trace of affectation, "I'm about the most popular girl now. The boys are teasing me about Max and James. Harvey winked all day. He's so nice. Jon did too." And the following day: "Harvey wrote me a note. He said he wanted a picture of me and I was beautiful. I was invited to a Hobo Hike." But Harvey was no more lucky than Leon B., for a month later he was out of the picture as well.

Accompanied by her shifting armada of boyfriends, Betty did all the things that teenaged girls in rural Kansas were expected to do. She competed in track meets, joined the scouts, got a part in the school play, went to slumber parties, sent off for an "Art Talent Test," went with the band to the music festival in Pratt, roller-skated, watched the Beatles the first time they were on the "Ed Sullivan Show," went swimming at the lake in Cheney, spent long nights decorating the gym for theme dances like "Apple Blossom Time" and "Hawaiian Luau," discovered hair bonnets and cinnamon toothpicks, went to the Hootenanny in Spivey and the rodeo at Altisa and the Pizza Hut in Wichita, used words like "fab" and phrases like "having a blast," and help plan Twerp Week and Clash Day and Junior Fun Nite. But mostly she went to the movies.

Movies were like a promise to Betty of the world she would enter when she got out of Norwich. It was not that she disliked Norwich, or that she was the slightest bit rebellious; it was just something that she and everybody else always assumed. Betty was the smart one, the one who would leave, the one who would go to college and come back with a degree and a husband who would take her somewhere that was not Norwich. Perhaps he would look like Troy Donahue in *Palm Springs Weekend*, or John Gavin in *Back Street*, or Rock Hudson in *The Spiral Road*, or, as the sixties wore on, the indistinguishable actors who flashed their teeth and physiques in films like *Sex and the Single Girl*, *The Pleasure Seekers*, or

Peyton Place. In Norwich, the weekly movie was one of the summer events around which the adolescent social calendar revolved. The films were shown outdoors, free of charge, as the young daters reclined on grassy hillsides and spread their blankets beneath the trees. (A drive to nearby Kingman, or all the way to Wichita, was required during the rest of the year. Betty made the trip at least once a week.)

Except for movies, the principal occupation of Norwich's teenagers was Riding Around. In the absence of anywhere to go, they made a virtue of necessity by using their cars as ends in themselves, places that were not home and not school but a sanctuary of the young, even if they were just spinning up and down the farm-to-market roads or creeping along the main street of town. An invitation to Ride Around had, in fact, the moral seriousness of any other date, as Betty learned the hard way: "Tonight Mike was gonna come down but before he got here Jon & Wayne came & asked me to ride around. I did & I was sure sorry. Mike's pretty mad." After particularly important Riding Around nights, Betty would come home and write exuberant messages to herself in the diary, punctuated by mysterious letter codes—"C.C.C.C." or "R.R.R.R.R.R."—whose meaning bore an unmistakable relationship to the private rituals honored from time immemorial by young men and women alone at night on dark country lanes.

Norwich was not a cosmopolitan place. Its residents came mostly from the same Anglo-German stock: Protestant, conservative yeomen. For all practical purposes, Betty's perceived world ended thirty miles away at Wichita, and even the family's annual one-week vacation took her to places similar to Kansas—once to a fishing resort in Arkansas, another time to visit relatives in rural Illinois, once to Colorado and Utah. The social upheavals of the age seemed distant indeed. Race riots? There were no Negroes in Norwich and never had been. Crime? People still left their doors unlocked. War protests? Most of Betty's classmates were too young to be drafted during the peak years of the Vietnam involvement anyway. In 1963 she would write in her diary, "Today Pres. Kennedy was shot and killed. Tonight was the carnival. Gary ran the B.B. stand. I shot 2 times and got 2 out of 10. He's such a doll." And in 1968, when Betty was eighteen: "Today was okay. Martin Luther King was assinated (sic) last nite. There are race riots all over. Jimmy came in tonight & we rode around. I Love Him!!"

By the time she made the latter entry, her preoccupation

with Jimmy could have survived World War III. Jimmy Sheetz was what is known in Norwich as "fast," meaning he was a little older (one year ahead of Betty) and a little more sure of himself than the rest, not to mention a lot more handsome. Jimmy won her heart the summer between her junior and senior years when, on one of those lazy nights when three boys were hanging around the Pomeroy house, he surprised her in the kitchen and stole a kiss. The boldness was what got her. Despite her popularity, Betty was never wholly convinced that she wasn't plain, so she tended to cling hard to anything as handsome as Jimmy Sheetz. And he turned out to be her one lasting boyfriend. They were inseparable for her entire senior year, he commuting to a job in Wichita, with Betty's college plans the only thing separating them from marriage. Betty had a single-minded determination to be a schoolteacher and had talked of getting her certificate as long as she had talked about college. At one point she and Jimmy discussed the logistics of her going to college while Jimmy stayed home, and they even set a wedding date, albeit four years away. But then Betty suddenly broke it off. The immediate cause was the school's senior trip, which occurred the week after graduation every year, and which in 1968 took Betty to a resort at the Lake of the Ozarks in Missouri. In three days, duly recorded in her diary, her whole future outlook changed:

Thursday, May 30: Today I met Glenn Welborne from Dallas City, Ill. He's really neat. We danced till we couldn't any longer. We went to an amusement park tonight.

Friday, May 31: Today we went to Ozark Caverns. They weren't very good. We went to a melodrama tonight. Glenn even walked me to the cabin after the dance & gave me a goodnight kiss.

Saturday, June 1: The Dallas City kids left today. Darn! Glenn promised to write. Hope he does. Nothing went on tonight.

A week later, back in Norwich, she told Jimmy she felt "tied down." After ten months of courtship, she gave him his ring back. Glenn Welborne never wrote.

Her trip to the Ozarks, at the age of eighteen, was Betty's first extended stay away from Kansas and apart from her family. And whatever she saw there remained with her. Glenn from Dallas City may not have been the man of her dreams, but he was a foretaste of something beyond Norwich. She wanted to find out what else was out there, and so all of her attention

focused on the fall of 1968, when she would enter Southwestern College at Winfield, Kansas, on an $800 scholarship.
Within a week after breaking up with Jimmy, she was being
courted by five other boys, but the summer still bored her. She
couldn't wait to be gone.

In later years Bob and Bertha Pomeroy would look back
on 1968 as one of the happiest years in Betty's life, a time when
she breathed exuberance and gaiety and when she seemed at
the center of a benevolent, approving universe. Whenever he
could, Bob took snapshots of Betty that year—with Jimmy,
dressed up for a dance; in her cap and gown; in her band
uniform—but one photograph stands out from the others. It
was taken on the night of the homecoming game. Betty had
been elected to the queen's court, of course, and a metal
platform had been erected on the field for the coronation. It
held a large backdrop, decorated with a silver aluminum-foil
half-moon, two or three dozen silver stars, and a curved
banner that fluttered across the half-moon and pronounced in
glittering script, "Some Enchanted Evening." Standing on the
front of the platform are four young women. Betty is the only
one with glasses, and her handsome burnt-orange dress is the
simplest, least distinctive of the four. But the eye is drawn
instantly to her, for reasons that have something to do with her
height but more to do with a certain radiance to her expression. Her smile is wide and natural and fresh, and her eyes are
looking out into the crowd, over the heads of the people who
must have been standing just in front of her, or perhaps they
are looking past the crowd altogether.

The one thing Betty Pomeroy did not excel at was
mathematics. Even high school algebra was such a struggle
that she would usually content herself with a grade of C on an
otherwise stellar report card. And so, of course, she fell in love
with her college math teacher.

Actually it's hard to say who noticed whom first. Allan
Gore, a senior at Southwestern and a teaching assistant in
freshman math, picked her out almost from the first day Betty
entered his class. It was the eyes and the smile that got him,
the innocent sparkle about her, and later it was the way she
always spoke up in class, almost as though she were trying to
please him personally. But Allan was not the sort of guy to
make passes at any girl, much less one of his students, and
perhaps nothing ever would have happened had it not been for

Betty's incipient failure at calculus. Midway through her first college semester, she asked to speak to Allan after class one day and requested special tutoring. All Allan remembered of the conversation is that he wouldn't have refused that smile anything. Allan didn't think it proper actually to date her, so they met at the library a few times to study. The next semester the tutorial sessions simply continued, and, since Allan wasn't her teacher anymore, one thing led to another and pretty soon they were seeing each other every night.

There was nothing very dramatic about the courtship. For Betty it was a continuation of high school; she had always dated one guy at a time, usually older boys, and sometimes for long periods. She adored Allan for all the reasons young girls have always adored their teachers. But for Allan the experience was entirely new. Betty was not only a girl who looked marriageable; she was also the first girl he had ever seriously dated.

Allan had grown up on a farm near Larned, just three counties west of Norwich, but, unlike Betty, he had found no great sense of community there. His father was a reserved, taciturn man who worked wheat and sorghum fields from sunup to sundown and sometimes beyond. By the age of ten Allan was a paid hand himself (ten cents an hour, not bad for child labor in 1957), and he began to develop some of the old man's workaholism. While the town kids were going to movies and dating and driving new cars, Allan remained on the farm, going to Larned only to attend classes at school and then returning to help with the chores or work on his 4-H Club projects. Not that he wanted to be a farmer himself. The late fifties were bad times for family farming in western Kansas (the Gore spread was only 600 acres), and Allan didn't see much future in it. But he worked hard at his 4-H activities anyway, raising pigs, planting soybeans, doing woodworking and electrical projects, even entering competitions for cooking and, one year, "grooming." He raised a calf that was named reserve champion at the county fair (he tried a second time but his entry mysteriously died) and, proudest achievement of all, was named the Kansas State Fair grand champion in wheat competition. To win the big purple ribbon, Allan spent several hours a day for three months picking through wheat stalks with tweezers, rejecting the bad and keeping only the unflawed grain, until he had a gallon jar full of the prettiest amber waves in the West. Congressman Bob Dole gave him a silver tray in front of hundreds of people, and he got a trip to Houston to tour the grain export facilities. More than anything else, that experience made him feel like he had really done something.

Allan was not exactly a loner, but he was not a popular kid either. He played basketball, as every red-blooded boy in Kansas does, but sat on the bench for all of his career. He was a good student but not a great one. The second of five children, he was closest to his older sister, Beth, and when the time came, he followed her to Southwestern College. Allan had saved the money for college himself, mostly by doing farm work, and once he got there, he managed to get two more jobs, washing dishes in the school cafeteria and helping in the mailroom. He dabbled briefly in student politics, taking the conservative side, and eventually became a resident manager in a dormitory. He didn't do it so much for the free room as for the sense of responsibility it gave him. He felt proud to be trusted with such an important job, even though the sophomores did accuse him of being a lackey for the administration. He was excited at the prospect of learning a new field, too, though he had no idea what it would be. He eventually chose a math major after a professor of statistics took an interest in him and helped him get a teaching assistant's job. But in other ways college was no different from Larned. He still worked from sunup to sundown.

Then Allan met Betty. For a man who had had so little experience with women, it was not hard to see why he fell so completely: she worshipped him. To a girl living away from home for the first time, Allan represented all those vistas beyond Norwich that she had always assumed would be hers. Betty had always had an enormous respect for intelligence and found a great security in the assurances of older men. To Allan, Betty was innocence itself: uncomplicated, sympathetic, happy. She wanted kids and so did he. She wanted to be a teacher and she admired her ambition. She had a good solid Kansas family. Both of them had passive personalities, and they shared the naive hope of long, quiet evenings before a fireplace in the country. While dating, they never did anything more ambitious than go to the movies in Wichita; usually they would just spend their evenings at the library. There was nothing torrid about the engagement; they just drifted into it.

A few of Betty's friends in Norwich were secretly surprised when she brought Allan home for the first time. Betty's brothers didn't say much at the time, but they didn't think Allan was much of a physical specimen. One of Betty's girlfriends agreed. Allan was a small, plain man with horn-rim glasses and puffy cheeks and, even at the age of twenty-one, the signs of a receding hairline. He was also shy, which often made him come across as stern or aloof or even snobbish, and he had trouble carrying on a conversation with Betty's parents. To Bob Pomeroy, that was tantamount to being a sissy. At one point Bob remarked to Bertha that, for a guy who grew up in Larned, Allan Gore didn't *seem* like a farm boy. But he was Betty's choice, the same Betty who, Bob rightly assumed, could have had her pick of most of the boys at Southwestern. So they tried to make him feel at home. On one occasion Allan even offered to help out with the work at the Standard station, because he said he felt guilty about accepting the Pomeroys' hospitality and not doing anything in return. So one Saturday Bob put Allan to work stacking a new shipment of tires, a job that had Allan totally exhausted by the end of the day. Bob and the boys would tell that story and chuckle about it when Betty wasn't around. Allan never asked to help out again.

The last entry in Betty's six-year diary was dated May 16, 1969: "Received Allan Gore's ring. Allan graduated May 25th from S.C. with a major in business & math." The only reason they didn't plan a wedding right away is that Allan, like most young men his age, was busy trying to avoid the military draft. Fortunately, he had banged up his knee when he was a freshman, so that summer he flunked his draft physical in Kansas City. He celebrated by asking Betty to join him there, and they spent the next day going from store to store, looking for wedding rings.

In the meantime, Allan had enrolled in graduate school at Kansas State University in Manhattan, and so Betty made plans to transfer there in the spring. Whatever else she did, she was determined not to let anything come between her and her teaching degree. For the next two years, they would have to live on the meager stipend that Allan received for being a graduate teaching assistant, and whatever else they could pick up doing odd jobs. They were young enough not to care.

The wedding was on January 25, 1970, in Norwich Methodist Church among all the friends and acquaintances of Betty's youth. It was a proper wedding in every respect; even though Allan and Betty had been intimate twice, once in a car and once at the Pomeroy house while her parents were away, they didn't consider the marriage consummated until the honeymoon. All they could afford was two days in a motel room in Hutchinson, fifty miles north on the highway, and then they continued on upstate and settled into a one-bedroom basement apartment near the K-State campus. Betty got a job working in a downtown drug store, and for the next two years they managed on about $300 a month. What with Allan's teaching and research, and Betty's classes and job, they saw each other infrequently but made the most of weekends. Meanwhile, Allan exhausted his interest in statistics, after deciding the field was too dry and impersonal, and became increasingly preoccupied with computer analysis. By his second year as a graduate student, he had decided to make a career of it, and soon he was ready to start putting out feelers for jobs.

Betty didn't like contingencies of any kind. She enjoyed the security of knowing where Allan was at all times, of having meals at exactly the same time every day, of knowing not only where she would be tomorrow but where they, as a couple, would be next year. She took great comfort in the regularity of a weekly paycheck and the certitude of a deadline. When she was assigned a paper in her classes, she would characteristically have it completed weeks before it was due. When she and Allan planned a vacation, she would insist that they have all the details decided months in advance. While living in Norwich this had been second nature to her—the Pomeroys' schedule had been the same for years, and the family generally did everything together—but as she and Allan began their dual careers, her punctiliousness began to cause friction.

In February 1971, Allan was invited for an interview at White Sands Missile Range in New Mexico, where job openings would soon be available for analysts who could design programs to test the safety of the nation's ballistic missile system. In March he and Betty visited White Sands together so she could check into transferring to New Mexico State University in the event they moved there. After the interview, Allan was told that the job was his, but that the final offer would have to await the usual security checks and approvals from Washington. Allan and Betty returned to Manhattan to finish the spring semester and wait on further instructions from White Sands, but there were the usual red-tape delays common in the military. By May there was still no final offer, and Betty started to grow very upset. She talked about it all the time, nagged Allan to call While Sands once a week, and was still unsatisfied when he reported back their assurances that he indeed had the job but there was simply a foulup in the paperwork. She began to suspect that Allan didn't really have a job at all and that soon they would have no money. At one point Betty became so worried about the delay that she and Allan had words. Increasingly the lack of an offer became a source of tension that hung over the marriage despite any soothing reassurances Allan could come up with.

In June two things happened: Allan finished his master's degree, and Betty became seriously ill with an ailment known as spastic stomach, which made it impossible for her to digest all her food. When her stomach started becoming distended, Allan took her to a doctor in Larned, who diagnosed appendicitis and wanted to operate. But Betty refused until she got a second opinion from her family doctor in Harper; he said it was the beginning of an ulcer and put her in the hospital. She remained there a week but cried whenever Allan would visit, insisting that he get her out. Shortly thereafter Allan got the final job offer, and Betty's illness cleared up.

There was nothing in the first twenty years of Betty's life to indicate any serious medical problems, at least none of the magnitude that began to afflict her in the spring of 1971. She was prone to colds, menstrual cramps, and minor viruses, but she had no history of ulcers or psychosomatic illnesses beyond one extended period of stomach sickness. It had occurred about the time she broke up with Jimmy Sheetz and when she was starting to make plans to leave home.

Betty and Allan moved to Las Cruces that fall and rented an apartment near the New Mexico State campus. For a while their life reverted to the quiet routine of Manhattan. Allan's assignment was to develop computer software programs that would be used to monitor the private contractor building the Safeguard missile system. Most of the time—when he wasn't simply reading memoranda or passing along routine progress reports—he felt challenged by the work, and Betty enjoyed the life of the new campus. For the first time they had some spending money—Allan got a princely $10,400 per year—which they used to sample the Las Cruces restaurants. They had no close friends, but they occasionally attended campus activities with Betty's classmates.

Then, after a few months, Allan had to leave Las Cruces on a six-week business trip, and Betty's world started to come apart again. When he would call, she would whine and sometimes cry, begging him to come home as soon as possible. She intimated that such long separations weren't proper in a marriage. And then she did something that, in retrospect, was one of the most uncharacteristic acts of her life: while Allan was still out of town, she went home one night with a younger student. Two days after Allan returned, she confessed her transgression, saying she had been confused and scared and hadn't really meant it, and begged for forgiveness. At the time Allan was hurt, but he got over it quickly. In later years he would sometimes wonder whether the incident hadn't been not so much an act of desperation as a calculated attempt to control his behavior. In any event, it never happened again.

Shortly thereafter they moved into their first home, a $9,000 trailer house, and Betty concentrated all her energies on doing her student teaching and completing her degree. When she did, in the spring of 1973, the entire Pomeroy family came down from Kansas for the commencement ceremonies. Betty was the first Pomeroy ever to receive a college diploma, and with high honors at that. To Bob and Bertha, she also seemed happier than they had seen her in some time. She loved the climate and working with the poor Mexican-American kids in her student classroom, and she had even been nominated for a book called *Who's Who in American Colleges and Universities*. Bob was proud enough to buy a copy. The parents were still perplexed by Allan, since he seemed to shrink into the shadows whenever they were around, but they couldn't help but like a boy who was making Betty so happy.

The novelty of military work soon wore off, though, and Allan grew fearful that he would simply continue indefinitely on the same project, without any new intellectual challenges. So one day he found a list of the major American electronics corporations, typed up his resume, and sent it around the country. Most of the companies never responded, but one that did was Collins Radio (later to be merged with Rockwell International), which was headquartered in Richardson, Texas, a bedroom suburb of Dallas. Two months later he stopped there while on a business trip, and Collins offered him a job on the spot. The salary was identical to what he was making, around $14,000, but Allan figured the future opportunities would be a lot greater. As the seventies began, Richardson was just emerging as a major world electronics center, alongside the more established centers of suburban Boston and Palo

Alto. Allan and Betty made a house-hunting trip and found a three-bedroom tract home in the booming suburb of Plano, a town just north of Richardson where some of the streets were so new that front yards were solid mud and the only trees were little leafless saplings held erect with guy-wires.

Once settled, Betty couldn't wait to get a teaching job. She applied immediately to all the nearby school districts (except Dallas, which she considered too large and impersonal), but since the 1973–74 school year was less than two months away, the best she could get was a substitute teaching job at one of Plano's elementary schools. She contented herself with that, and with selling Avon products door-to-door; even though the sales work made her nervous, she wanted to be out of the house during the day. Allan, it turned out, wasn't too thrilled with his new job, either, especially after he found out he wouldn't be doing any computer programming at all. He was assigned to a division that handled telephone message-switching systems, and he was just one step up from a salesman, writing up evaluations of "customer requirements." He was disgusted, and felt a little betrayed, but he bit the bullet and hoped for a reassignment.

Two months after the move to Plano, Betty started seeing a doctor. Her complaints were varied: earache, sore throat, multiple allergies (which seemed to be proliferating as she grew older), occasional upset stomach, fevers. By November 1973, she was receiving regular prescriptions for various decongestants, antibiotics, mild tranquilizers, and other drugs, and she soon had an additional problem: she was pregnant. At first it was cause for celebration—she and Allan had always wanted children, and now that they were settled, the time seemed right. But Betty quickly developed an unusually strong case of morning sickness. The first month of pregnancy brought fainting spells, and soon she was on the verge of a full-blown depression. She switched to a female gynecologist, who made her feel more comfortable than her male physician, and she was given more drugs for the depression.

Outwardly Betty showed the same cheerful countenance and confided her bouts of depression to no one but Allan. She had always been secretive about her problems, even back to her earliest childhood. Allan assumed that her condition would ameliorate as soon as the difficult early months of pregnancy passed and when Betty was able to get her long-desired teaching job. In the meantime they shopped for a church, not so much because of any void in their lives but because they felt they should reestablish some ties for the sake of the children. The one they settled on was Briarwood Methodist, and for a while it helped a great deal.

The main attraction at Briarwood was a minister named Weldon Haynes, an affable, easy-going sort popular with the younger couples for his laissez-faire attitude toward church management. His programs and sermons were contemporary and entertaining, and he pretty much let the members themselves determine the events beyond the sanctuary. Allan and Betty both liked him immediately, and they soon began making friends for the first time since they were married. Among them were Richard Garlington, an engineer at Texas Instruments, and his wife JoAnn. JoAnn was a brassy, self-confident woman, and Richard seemed kind and outgoing. They befriended Allan right away, but at first Betty kept her distance. Then the Gores and the Garlingtons spent a weekend together at a church campout on Lake Texoma, and Betty came out of her shell. By this time, Allan and Betty had almost reversed their roles of five years before: now he was the social animal, while Betty seemed more like the loner.

Nothing improved at home, though. Betty was called as a substitute teacher very infrequently, and even then she considered the job demeaning: she did little more than babysit until the regular teacher returned. For a while she gave special tutoring to the daughter of Catherine Cooper, a teacher at Davis Elementary, but it was no replacement for a classroom of her own. Late that spring Betty returned to her physician complaining of simple depression, much of it caused by her pregnancy and the physical fact she didn't want to face: she was becoming enormous. For Betty, who had always been considered attractive, the disfigurement of bearing a child was just one more turn of bad luck. She decided at one point to use natural childbirth methods, but when the time came that summer, she was so nervous and overwrought that she couldn't relax, and delivery was unbearably painful and troublesome. She finally asked the doctor for an anesthetic.

It was a girl. They named her Alisa, and for a while she restored Betty's spirits entirely. Then Catherine Cooper helped Betty get accepted as a second-grade teacher at Davis Elementary, and she started the 1974–75 school year with new optimism. But it faded fast. Betty was placed in a school that used open classrooms and team-teaching methods, systems she had never learned, and she could never adjust. She had been given a class of second graders, and she found them extremely difficult. When they were noisy, or didn't pay attention, she felt helpless and disgusted. When they didn't finish their lessons by the time for recess, she would hold her class over while all the other students went outdoors. When a student misbehaved in the lunch line, most teachers would simply correct him with a word or two and then look the other way, but Betty would pull him out of line and send a note home to his mother. Some of her fellow teachers considered Betty too stern, but she was simply practicing the same kind of perfectionism that prevailed at home: she couldn't abide her lesson plans being disrupted or her rules being flouted. When it caused friction between her and the children, or her and the parents, she became all the more frustrated and blamed her problems on the open-classroom system, for which she had whole-hearted contempt.

At the same time Allan was unwittingly adding to Betty's burden, first by starting to travel again (his job sometimes called for three- or four-day business trips), and by his increasing involvement in the church. Like most eager newcomers, Allan had been quickly appointed to committees and elected to offices, until eventually he was the chairman of the Council on Ministries, highest lay office in the church. This meant that he was frequently at the church for evening meetings, leaving Betty home with Alisa. What with teaching, trying to care for the baby, and worrying once again about being left alone while Allan traveled to faraway cities or got involved in church politics, Betty became even more bitter. In the fall of 1974 she fell into the deepest depression yet. Her gynecologist diagnosed it as postpartum depression, told Betty to stop taking birth-control pills, and prescribed estrogen and Valium. Her family doctor diagnosed it as "heavy child syndrome," an ailment common to women who have had their first child, and gave her drugs to help relieve her complaints of soreness.

For the next year, Betty would return to the doctor repeatedly, sometimes two or three times a month, with various complaints, including "nervous stomach," sinus troubles, sore throat, swollen glands, tiredness, fear of pregnancy (unfounded), neck soreness, chest soreness, a wart (surgically removed), back spasms (for which she started taking tranquilizers), vaginal itching, laryngitis, breast soreness, fever, earache, sinus problems, and "tingling" in her left arm. Her doctor's usual prescription was drugs and understanding. As time went on, his notes would occasionally include the phrase "anxiety-induced" before the name of the particular ailment she complained of, and he also had the growing sense that sometimes she visited his office as much to *talk* to him about her ailments and get reassurances as to receive any medication. As if that weren't enough, in the summer of 1975 Betty was told that she had been turned down for permanent employment by the Plano school district. Even more insulting was that the woman hired for the job that Betty wanted was fresh out of college, with less teaching experience. Betty's troubled year of team teaching had ended, finally, in the first formal rejection of her life.

Once the sting had worn off, however, Betty redoubled her efforts to get her own classroom, as though something fundamental were at stake. Her desire to be a teacher dated back more than ten years, to her grade-school days, and now she knew she *had* to do it, if for no other reason than to show the Plano administration how wrong they were. For one semester she stayed at home with Alisa, but in the spring of 1976 she got a substitute teaching job at an elementary school in Wylie, a much smaller town than Plano, about ten miles to the east. By that summer she had been accepted for a permanent position, and for a stretch of five months she had no medical problems whatsoever.

But it couldn't last. First there were problems at the church, beginning when Weldon Haynes left for another assignment and was replaced, after a six-month interregnum, by a man named Jack Gorham. Reverend Gorham was a former African missionary, a conservative, and a firm believer in the historical structure of the Methodist church, which tended to be autocratic and rigidly hierarchical. His very presence was a signal that the church management, formerly left to the lay committees, was being taken back by the clergy. JoAnn Garlington was so disturbed with the new order that she quarrelled openly with him and at one point said, "He preaches to us like he's still in Africa and we're a bunch of natives." The Gores agreed, if less openly, and so did a number of other families.

In October 1976 Allan resigned the chairmanship of the Council on Ministries, not only because of the growing disenchantment with Gorham but also because he had finally been freed by Rockwell from the drudgery of telephone-switching systems. This meant both more responsibility and more out-of-town travel. And one of his very first assignments was to install a very complicated software system in Zurich, Switzerland; it would take six weeks. By that time Betty was teaching sixth grade in Wylie as well. Whereas in Plano she considered the students too young for her, now she considered them too old. They were undisciplined and sometimes mean; they were hard to control. Some were even bold enough to call her names. Now Allan was about to leave town for six weeks; they had stopped going to church; she was commuting long distances every day; and suddenly she was back in her doctor's office, with a fresh list of ailments.

That fall Betty was treated for stomach problems, back muscle problems, headache, nausea, "flu syndrome," infected sinuses, a bladder infection, and a genital infection common to women who do not have sexual intercourse often enough. Because of Allan's trip to Zurich, Betty and Alisa went to Kansas for Thanksgiving without him, but the Pomeroys noticed nothing out of the ordinary about their daughter. As soon as Allan returned, however, Betty began to complain: "How long is this going to go on?" For once even Allan was beginning to heed the complaints; he could tell that this was more than just whining. Betty did become physically upset whenever he was absent overnight; and although a part of him resented that because he had always wanted to travel, another part of him knew that something would have to give sooner or later.

So when it became apparent in December that Allan would need to return to Switzerland to finish the job, he tried to make it up to Betty by asking her to come along with him for the week before the spring semester. For the rest of their marriage, they would both remember it as one of the happiest weeks they ever spent together. They rode tram cars in the Alps and stayed at quaint hotels and ate exotic foods and made love every night. On New Year's Eve, they got off the train in Munich and, with no place to go, bought a cheap bottle of wine and went up to a cold hotel room. The wine was awful, there were no sheets on the bed, and they had to make do all through the midwinter's night with a single comforter. But they clung tightly together and felt more in love than ever before.

Betty cried a little when the week was up and she had to

get on the plane back to Dallas, but Allan assured her that he would join her soon, that the job was almost finished. When Betty landed at the Dallas–Fort Worth Airport, though, she found herself in the middle of one of the worst ice storms in Texas history. The streets were glazed for miles around. Even after she managed to convince a taxi driver to take her home, the trip took six hours, and she was terrified all the way. All of a sudden she felt more helpless than ever and almost wanted to cry out: *Why isn't my husband here to take care of me?* For the next two weeks, she kept her recurrent depression bottled up, but finally she couldn't stand it any longer. She called Allan's boss at Rockwell and all but begged him to let him come home. Allan called her from Switzerland. At first amazed that she would be bold enough to call his boss, he finally decided that something *was* seriously wrong and arranged to cut his trip short and turn the work over to someone else.

In February 1977, Allan met with his boss and asked to be transferred to a position that would allow him to work exclusively in Dallas. His request was granted. Two months later, Allan put the Plano house up for sale and signed the contract for a house on Dogwood Street in Wylie. That way Betty wouldn't have to commute any longer. In the fall the Gores transferred their church membership to a little church ten miles up the highway from Wylie, on the advice of Betty's best friend, JoAnn Garlington. Betty managed to get moved from the sixth grade to the fifth that year.

Allan felt like they were starting over, and sometimes he even thought it was all for the best.

6 · GENERAL ALARM

Without exception, each man who saw the lifeless body of Betty Gore the night of June 13 reflexively averted his eyes. Even those who already knew what lay beyond the utility room door were never bold enough to look for more than a moment before closing the door again. Few looked at the head at all—the sight was too horrible—so the early reports as to the manner of death were all conflicting, and usually wrong.

It was a small room, no more than twelve feet long by six feet wide, made smaller by the presence of a washer, a dryer, a freezer, and a small cabinet where Betty had kept toys and knickknacks. In one corner was a brand-new toy wagon and a child's training toilet. Closer to the center of the room, where the freezer stood against one wall, were two dog-food dishes and a bruised book of Mother Goose nursery rhymes. The book had a white cover, which stood out in sharp relief, because in the harsh overhead light that glared off the harvest-gold linoleum, it was one of the few objects in the room not coated in blood.

Much of the blood was not red but black, or perhaps the blood was mixed with some other fluid that had flowed out of one of the gaping wounds in the body. It was difficult to tell because there was so much of it. Betty lay face up, her head next to a front corner of the freezer, her legs stretched out rigidly, pointed toward the far end of the room. The knees were locked, as though she had died at attention and then been laid carefully on the floor. She was dressed in a yellow short-sleeved pullover, so saturated in blood that most of it had turned brown, and red denim pants that rode high on the thigh and were creased horizontally from their extremely tight fit. Her legs were streaked with blood and crisscrossed with slender incisions. The toenails on her bare feet were painted bright red.

Her left arm was the first thing they noticed after opening the door. It lay in a pool of blood and fluid so thick that the arm appeared to be floating above the linoleum. The elbow had a cut so wide and deep that at first glance the arm appeared to be severed. The inside of the cut had turned into something hard and black and shiny. Just below the shoulder, there were three or four equally grisly wounds, as though she had been sliced open with a dull instrument and the blood had long ago run out onto the floor.

To get a look at her face, the men at the scene had to walk around the ocean of red and black and get closer. What they saw was even more unsettling. Her lips were parted, showing her front teeth, the mouth fashioned into a half-grin. Her hair radiated in all directions, a tangled, soaked mass of glistening black. And Betty's left eye was wide open, staring directly down at the gaping black craters in her arm. As to her right eye—she appeared not to have one. The entire right half of her face appeared to be gone.

A few feet from Betty's head, half-concealed under the freezer, was a heavy, wooden-handled, three-foot-long ax.

Officer Johnney Lee Bridgefarmer, a tall, rangy country boy who was patrolling that night in one of Wylie's three official squad cars, was the first man at the scene. He got his orders at 11:18—the dispatcher said two women had called, one of them going on hysterically about a suicide, the other one reporting that the top of a woman's head was blown off at 410 Dogwood. Johnney Lee had been a policeman for less than a year and had never had to investigate anything more serious than a domestic disturbance. So he asked the dispatcher to send his friend and fellow officer, Jim Grindele, to back him up. Less than a minute later he was at the Gore house.

Richard Parker, gun in hand, met Johnney Lee at the door and told him where the body was. Richard had grown even more nervous after the discovery of the corpse and had crawled into the attic, his gun poised to shoot, thinking the murderer might still be somewhere nearby. Johnney Lee strode to the utility room, opened the door, took one look and closed it again. By the time the ambulance arrived, red lights spinning and siren blaring, Johnney Lee was on the phone to his boss, Royce Abbott. Even before the chief could get there, a crowd had started to gather.

Wylie was not a large town—the Chamber of Commerce optimistically listed its population as four thousand—and despite its close proximity to Dallas, it had the look and feel of a country crossroads. By 11:30, just fifteen minutes after the neighbors found Betty's body, a woman who lived on another street a block away was informed of the murder by a neighbor who was spreading the news by car. The wives of Richard Parker, Jerry McMahan, and Lester Gayler all called friends to let them know. Dick Sewell, a dentist who knew Allan Gore only casually, immediately drove to the scene, questioned Richard Parker, and then went inside the Gore home, where he joined three Wylie police officers, the three neighbors who had discovered the body, three ambulance attendants, and Buddy Newton, the local justice of the peace who was called to make out the death certificate. Added to the neighbors who were milling around on the Gores' front lawn, the assemblage looked like a mob scene by the time Royce Abbott arrived.

Royce Abbott, who had been Wylie police chief exactly one month at the time he was called to investigate the biggest homicide of his eighteen-year career, was a crusty, garrulous cop who always had a well-chewed toothpick in the corner of his mouth and who looked, people said, exactly like Warren Oates, the Hollywood cowboy who always played the sinister but slightly comic villain. Chief Abbott parked his car amid the growing traffic jam of official vehicles on Dogwood Street and was met by Johnny Lee Bridgefarmer, who took him straight to the utility room. The chief took a long hard look at the body as the men in the Gore living room craned their necks to see from a distance.

"And look over here, chief," one of the officers said.

Chief Abbott reclosed the utility room door and went into the kitchen, where one of his men pointed at the table. There, spread out next to the remnants of the breakfast dishes, was the *Dallas Morning News*, opened to the entertainment section and folded so as to emphasize a single article, a movie review. The movie was "The Shining." It was the story of a psychopathic ax murderer.

"Looks like one of them cult deals," said Abbott under his breath.

"Call the sheriff," he told Johnny Lee. "We gotta have backup."

The word continued to spread through Wylie, and with it a sense of general alarm. After a few minutes, the original reports of a woman who had blown her head off were changed abruptly to stories of a woman brutally hacked to death in her own home by a psychopathic killer. The residents of Dogwood and surrounding streets double-locked their doors or, in some cases, went searching for children who were still out on Friday-night dates. This was not only a murder; it was the first murder in Wylie in living memory. Even the men inside the Gore home were wary. In the back of their minds was the fear that whoever killed Betty Gore was probably crazy enough to still be in the neighborhood. Abbott dispatched two or three officers to patrol the surrounding streets, looking for suspicious characters. Those men were soon joined by police officers from Sachse, a neighboring town even smaller than Wylie, who had picked up the frenzied radio traffic. As the crowd continued to gather on the front lawn, Abbott questioned Richard Parker and had him repeat the sequence of events leading up to the discovery of the body. Abbott was intrigued by a couple of things Parker said. First, the husband of the dead woman was out of town, but no one had known it until he called. And second, the garage door was wide open all night, when ordinarily it was supposed to be closed—and the garage had a door leading directly into the utility room.

Abbott called the Wylie dispatcher and told her to have the Collin County Sheriff's office bring a camera and finger-printing equipment. Then he went to the bathroom, which leads from the front hallway, and considered the most terrifying evidence yet: there were blood stains on the bathmat, the soap dish, the wall tiles, and the tub. The killer had had enough composure to take a shower before leaving. Now Abbott, like everyone else, was really thinking about psychos.

The phone rang. "I'll get it," said Abbott.

"Hello."

"This is Allan Gore."

"Mr. Gore, I'm Chief Abbott of the Wylie PD. Can you tell me what you know about what happened here tonight?"

"I understand that Betty's been shot?"

"That's correct," said Abbott, observing the unwritten rule of police investigations: never indicate to a suspect what or how much you know until you've heard his entire story.

"I've been trying to call Betty all day," and Allan. "I left for St. Paul on business about 4:30, and I tried to call her before I left but there was no answer. Then I kept trying to get her right up until the time my neighbors told me she was shot."

"I understand," said Abbott. "And when was the last time you saw your wife?"

"About eight this morning, when I left for work."

"And do you know anyone else who might've been around the house today?"

"Well, just Candy Montgomery. She's a friend of ours who was keeping our oldest daughter. She said she came by to pick up a swimming suit this morning."

"All right, Mr. Gore. I'm gonna need to talk to you when you get back. By the way, which airline did you take up to St. Paul today?"

"Braniff."

"All right, Mr. Gore, we're doing everything we can. We'll give you a full report when you get back."

"All right. Thank you."

Royce Abbott pressed down the buttons on the phone and immediately dialed his dispatcher, Kathy Hill.

"Kathy," he said, "I want you to call DFW Airport Security and find out whether an Allan Gore, G-o-r-e, took Braniff to St. Paul, Minnesota, at 4:30 this afternoon. Call me back as soon as you have an answer."

A few minutes later the chief, still waiting on the Sheriff's Office experts, took another phone call. This time the caller was Bob Pomeroy.

"I understand my daughter is dead," said Bob.

"Well, Mr. Pomeroy, tell me first what you've found out so far."

"I heard she's been shot."

"Well, that's correct. Have you talked to her husband?"

"Yes sir, Allan's the one who told us."

"How did he sound when he told you?"

"He sounded shocked, like us."

"All right, Mr. Pomeroy, we're doing all we can, but we don't know any more about it right now."

"Okay, well, thank you for the information."

Chief Abbott was still perplexed as he replaced the receiver. Bob Pomeroy was even more perplexed.

As Bob hung up the phone, a thought flashed quickly through his mind: "No, he didn't. I expected him to, but he really didn't. Allan didn't sound shocked at all."

* * *

Steve Deffibaugh was a corpulent, freckled young man with a stringy red mustache who spent much of his time taking the kind of pictures that, during criminal trials, are always attacked by defense attorneys as "inflammatory and prejudicial." This is because he was very good at his job: he photographed corpses. Deffibaugh was sleeping when the Collin County dispatcher called him, not that such calls were unusual. Deffibaugh had been a cop in McKinney, the county seat, for six years—four with the local police, the last two as a sheriff's deputy—and even in that short time the whole character of the county had begun to change from rural to suburban. Especially along the southern rim of the county, where the small towns were now indistinguishable from the Dallas suburbs, there were far fewer farms and far more office buildings than when he had first joined the force. McKinney itself was still a more or less typical rural outpost—the urban sprawl hadn't reached it yet—but when Deffibaugh got a call to go south, it could be anything. Deffibaugh got those calls more and more often these days, too, since anytime you add people you add crime as well. And Collin County was the second-fastest growing county in Texas.

Deffibaugh assumed it was a routine homicide. He checked his camera gear and discovered he was short on film, but that didn't bother him a great deal since he could usually make do with what he had. So instead of going downtown to the jail to get more, he just packed what he had and started out on the fifteen-mile drive to Wylie. When he pulled onto Dogwood Street, he started to doubt his wisdom for the first time. Outside it was chaos—cars everywhere, neighbors milling up and down the street, the front lawn of the house full of curiosity seekers. Inside it was worse—wall-to-wall police officers, including some who had no official capacity but had simply heard about the homicide and had come to take a look. In all, Deffibaugh figured at least a dozen cops and ambulance attendants had been in the house, in addition to the three neighbors who found the body, and that bothered him. Even in the most carelessly committed crime, the chances of preserving a fingerprint or a piece of physical evidence are less than an oven bet. As soon as he walked in, Deffibaugh could see that this was a messy, complex case that ranged through several rooms of the house, and no telling what had been touched or moved.

Deffibaugh huddled with Chief Abbott and with two other

sheriff's investigators who had been dispatched to the scene. That meant the entire investigative unit of Collin County was present, but from the bare outline of what Abbott told him, Deffibaugh could tell that that wouldn't be enough. He decided to begin shooting pictures in the utility room—the nearer to the time of death they were taken, the more valid they would be as evidence—but in the meantime he asked Chief Abbott to call Dr. Irving Stone. Like a pleader to the Supreme Court, Deffibaugh had asked for the criminal investigator of last resort.

Dr. Stone worked for no police agency and had no particular passions beyond the arcane investigations of the Dallas Institute of Forensic Sciences. The "doctor" before his name referred not to medicine but to his Ph.D. in chemistry, which was the principal reason he was hired in 1972 to be chief of physical evidence at the institute. Stone was short and swarthy, with a perpetual half-grin that gave him a deceptively disarming first impression. At the Dallas County Courthouse he was sometimes called "the Jewish Columbo," a designation rendered half in jest and half in respect for his microscopically inventive analyses of crime scenes. Since the institute was funded as an adjunct to Parkland Hospital, the public hospital of Dallas County, most of Stone's work was for the local district attorney's office or the Dallas Police Department. But one case in four took him to parts unknown, generally to small towns that had neither the funds nor the personnel to handle a particularly messy murder case, and whose officials knew that the difference between a conviction and an unsolved crime could hang on the flicker of an image magnified a thousand times by Stone's microscope.

One thing that could test Stone's habitual good humor was a call at 2:30 in the morning. In this case, he stopped the caller after the word "homicide" and said, "Okay, just give me the address." Then he went to wake up his son Ken. Ken was a first-year law student at Southern Methodist University, but when he wasn't in class he liked to help his father on investigations. Dr. Stone liked having him along, too, since he could often use the extra pair of hands, and police officers weren't always the best people to have handling evidence.

Stone had to look up Wylie on the map, since he had never been there before. It was a long drive, but not long enough for him to feel totally awake even after he got there. That soon changed. Confusion still reigned supreme, inside and outside the Gore home. Stone was distressed by the number of people, but the biggest surprise was yet to come.

After the introductions, Abbott said simply, "The woman is in the utility room. She's dead. Her husband is out of town. The garage door was left open."

"Who's going to process the crime scene?" asked Stone.

"You."

This Stone hadn't expected. He was usually employed as an adviser to policemen, who did the actual lifting of prints and preservations of evidence. But he was prepared anyway. He went to his car and got out the portable crime scene laboratory that he always carried in his trunk. While he was getting ready, Deffibaugh cleared everyone else out of the house.

Dr. Stone was a methodical worker, slow and orderly, who knew that it might be necessary to collect a thousand bits of evidence in order to find the one that solved the crime. He knew he had a long night ahead, since the evidence was scattered all over the house. He was glad that Abbott hadn't told him anything more about the crime, because he preferred to start with a clear head, free of predispositions. He walked slowly through the house, mentally noting which of the rooms seemed to be involved in the actual commission of the crime, trying to formulate a time sequence. He quickly ruled out all the back bedrooms, the living room–den area, and the kitchen, and deduced that the victim and the perpetrator had confined their activities to the utility room, the front bathroom, the front entry hall, the front porch, and perhaps the garage. He decided to start at the point where he thought the crime ended—the bathroom.

With his son helping, Dr. Stone dusted every surface in the bathroom, floors, walls, and fixtures, since porcelain and tile are a fingerprint expert's dream: smooth, even surfaces that hold latent prints like a sponge holds water. He cut blood-stained strands out of the green throw-rug beside the bathtub and scratched dried blood off the tile. From the drain in the tub he retrieved a fairly large clump of hair, which he placed in a bag for later lab analysis. Then he and Ken moved their operation to the utility room itself, where Deffibaugh had already pointed out one of the most promising pieces of evidence. On the door of the freezer, a white surface smeared with blood from top to bottom, there was a clean red thumbprint. It was about midway up the door, the print from a left hand pointing toward the right, as though someone had leaned against the door for support. Unfortunately, it also constituted a very thorny problem for Stone. Television cop shows notwithstanding, fingerprints in blood are the rarest sort of evidence, and, once dried, they are all but impossible to lift without exotic chemicals. Stone had nothing of the sort with him, so he instructed Deffibaugh simply to photograph the print, which is the next best way to preserve it. Deffibaugh did, but since he was low on film, he took only one photo. Then Stone tried to lift it with powder. As he had predicted, he failed, ruining the print in the process.

Next Stone attended to the body itself. He slipped small plastic bags over Betty Gore's hands in the hope that either he or the coroner could find "trace evidence"—skin or hair samples that belonged to the perpetrator. He examined the ax and encased its handle in plastic, but he held out little hope of recovering anything from it, since wood is the worst surface for fingerprints. He placed plastic bags over all the doorknobs in the utility room and bathroom, and ordered them removed. Then he found a pair of sunglasses that had been smashed up and kicked under one of the appliances. While he was doing this, he instructed his son to lift all squares of linoleum that appeared to have full or partial footprints on them. There was so much blood on the floor that it was sometimes hard to say where a footprint left off and a mere smudge began, but Stone told him that, if there was any doubt, he should take it anyway.

While Stone, his son, and Deffibaugh were going about their tedious business, the cops on the outside were still working under the assumption that the killer was nearby. At about 2 A.M., after everyone within blocks of the house had learned of the killing, a man called police reporting that a young girl had just looked out her window and seen a whistling fat man standing under a lamp-post a block from the Gore home. The girl didn't say why the whistling fat man was suspicious, but four officers investigated, including two from Sachse. They searched for half an hour but couldn't find the man. Throughout the night people called the Wylie police, either asking for information or offering it, stirring up confusion that was a foretaste of the investigative chaos that would follow in the next few days.

But the more important investigation was going on inside, where Stone and Deffibaugh moved from the utility room into the living room–den area, still looking for blood, hair, or any other substance that might be traced to the killer. At one point

Jim Grindele, the young officer who had followed Johnney Lee Bridgefarmer to the scene, walked up to Stone and Deffibaugh and said, "Look what I found."

He held in his hand a sunglasses lens, obviously missing from the pair of smashed sunglasses Stone had found in the utility room. Deffibaugh had a flash of anger—the naive cop had obviously moved a piece of evidence before Stone could see it—but he suppressed his rage for the moment.

"Where did you find it?" Stone said.

Grindele led them back into the garage, turned to his right, and pointed to a small closet. For the first time Stone and Deffibaugh entertained the notion that the crime might have occurred in the garage as well, so Stone remained for a while, looking for more evidence. He finally decided that it made no sense, since he could find no blood, no hair, nothing else to indicate that anything went on in the garage. Deffibaugh took a few pictures anyway.

The men worked until dawn, going through the carpet inch by inch, scraping up blood samples wherever they thought the blood might belong to someone other than Betty Gore. One of Abbott's officers, meanwhile, shuffled through some belongings on the top of Betty's bedroom dresser, where a $20 bill had been found. (Deffibaugh duly photographed the dresser, if only to rule out robbery as a motive.) But then the officer found a curious document, a letter of some sort, in a man's oversized handwriting, apparently written to the dead woman quite recently. It was on the final page of a spiral notebook full of similar letters. The officer showed it to Abbott and then, with the chief's permission, ripped it out for later study.

The letter read:

Our marriage has changed a lot since our weekend. Before the weekend I did an awful lot of thinking and worrying about what I was getting out of our marriage and whether or not you were doing things for me. The weekend showed me that what I needed to do was focus on you and us instead of me. I have really tried to do that. I have found that it is even fun to help you (without complaining). We talk more when I do. I have also found that I can place you, us and our family ahead of my job and other activities and still be successful in them. It's the dialogue that does it. Because when we don't, I feel myself slipping back to thinking about me instead of you and us. We have got to get back to a regular (every day) dialogue schedule. I Love You, Allan.

It was almost 6 A.M. when yet another young Wylie officer, Mike Stanley, approached Stone with the evening's second surprise. In his hand Stanley held a bloody fingernail.

"I found this on the rug in the living room," he announced.

"Lemme look," said Stone, taking it from him with some exasperation. "Looks like it could be the victim's. Hold on to it."

Stone had noticed earlier that the body was missing part of one fingernail, and he assumed the nail found by Stanley belonged to Betty Gore. Officer Stanley took the fingernail and laid it on the kitchen cabinet, next to a microwave oven. Then, after a while, Stanley left. He had not been called to the scene. He had just been on duty at the station, heard there was a homicide on Dogwood, and wandered over to see what was going on.

At eight o'clock in the morning, a full five and a half hours since he had begun collecting evidence, Stone took full inventory of what he had: numerous blood samples, a clump of hair from the bathtub, one photograph of a bloody thumb-print, several bloody footprints, a corpse that might yield more evidence later, and a three-foot ax. Until now, he hadn't said much to Deffibaugh or Abbott about what he was thinking, but before leaving, he made two observations.

"It was not premeditated," he told Abbott. "The weapon is too strange, there are signs of a terrible struggle everywhere. It was a crime of circumstance. Second, those foot-prints in the utility room don't belong to a man; they're too small. I think a woman did this. A woman or a kid."

Stone had already given instructions to the ambulance attendants, and now he made one last phone call—to his friend and colleague, Vincent DiMaio. Dr. DiMaio was the senior medical examiner in Dallas County, having performed about 3,500 autopsies in his eight years on the staff, and he was at the morgue bright and early. It was his turn to do Saturday duty, which meant he would be by himself all day.

"Boy," said Stone, when DiMaio came on the line, "have I got something for you. It's an ax murder. A lot of blood. Found some very small footprints in the blood so it might be a woman killer. The ax is in the lab. And Vince—it's a white woman. Good luck."

* * *

Vincent DiMaio told his two lab technicians to put the body on one of the blue plastic carts and wheel it into the examination room. The first thing he looked at himself, though, was the ax. Of all the unusual death weapons he had examined in his career, the ax was one of the rarest. Only once before had he seen it used on a victim, but that case didn't really count, since the person had been strangled first and then dismembered after death. The only thing rarer, DiMaio thought, was that time when a man had been killed with a plain, rounded-end table knife. The killer had tried to stab his victim with the knife repeatedly, but when that failed to penetrate the skin, he'd taken the serrated edge of the blade and literally sawed the fellow's throat open, then jammed the knife down into the chest cavity. DiMaio had had to go fishing for the knife, eventually retrieving it from the man's right lung.

Dr. DiMaio was thirty-nine years old at the time the body of Betty Gore was left at his doorstep, and he could tell stories like the one about the table-knife killer without even a trace of revulsion, often while smiling in a bemused sort of way, as though the homicidal follies of men had long since ceased to surprise him. Perhaps that's because he was a second-generation coroner, the son of the former chief medical examiner of New York City, and he had become a student of grisly untimely deaths in Manhattan even before he reached his twentieth birthday. A small man, prematurely grey, who fancied oversized wire-rim glasses and affected an avuncular familiarity, DiMaio's interest was less with the bodies he examined—after all, nothing could be done for them—than with the people who dispatched them to him so gruesomely. Like all good forensic pathologists, he prided himself on his ability to tell a great deal about the perpetrator just by *looking* at a corpse. But then there was always the one case in a hundred that didn't follow any of the usual patterns. He liked those best of all.

He knew this was such a case as soon as the lab assistants pulled back the sheet. The horrible disfigurement of Betty Gore didn't shock DiMaio, but it intrigued him. For one thing, the victim appeared to be white, middle class, and female, which was a combination he rarely saw. Only one in five murder victims were women, and, of the ones in the Dallas area, most were either black or Mexican-American. Virtually all of them were victims of battering or sexual assault.

Obviously, there was more going on here than assault. But the main thing DiMaio noticed about Betty Gore's body was more foreboding. He could tell almost immediately that, even though the body was covered with perhaps three dozen wounds, there appeared to be little postmortem disfigurement. She had been alive while these blows were being struck.

"Put on some coffee," DiMaio told his assistants. "It's going to be a long day."

For the first hour or so, DiMaio did nothing except look at the body, pacing around the cart, his hands clasped behind his back so he wouldn't be tempted to touch anything. Because of the extreme mutilation it was difficult to take everything in at once, so he began with the hands, hoping to find traces of hair or blood that Betty Gore might have grabbed during a struggle. He did find strands of hair in her hands, as well as some on the soles of her feet; he would have to wait for lab analysis to know whether it was her own hair or someone else's. He inspected all her clothing carefully, had the technicians trim all the fingernails in the hope that she had scratched skin off her assailant, and formed a theory. It must have been a sexual crime. Otherwise, why so much overkill, so much mutilation? So DiMaio had the corpse undressed and ordered the technicians to take anal, oral, and vaginal swabs, looking for semen. All the swabs turned up negative, though. "We *are* dealing with something strange," he said.

After photographing each wound and completing his visual examination, DiMaio began the formal autopsy. Ordinarily he would start from the head and work downward, but he could tell the fatal wounds were in the head area, so he saved them for last. He began instead with the arms, clearing away foreign substances as he went, so that he could see the depth and extent of each wound. On the right arm he found five cuts, none of them very deep, randomly arrayed, as though the woman had been defending herself. On the left arm he found another five wounds, much more serious ones, two of which ran horizontally, as though the ax had been swung side to side. He proceeded on up the body, describing abrasions and chop wounds on the hands, shoulder, and left leg. The only things that puzzled him about this part of the examination were three wounds on the thighs. Those cuts were much lower than all the others, as though struck after the victim was down. But that didn't make sense, when obviously the rage of the assailant was directed at the head and face.

DiMaio moved on to the head. The first thing he noticed was not a cut at all but a small bruise on the left side of the forehead. Why a bruise in the midst of all those chop wounds? He dismissed the question for a moment and took a long look at what used to be the right side of Betty Gore's face.

Half her face was nothing but a mass of tissue and blood. The eye socket and the cheekbone had been pummeled to bits. The bones had been so completely fractured that the eyeball had sunk out of sight, falling back into the sinus. Gingerly, DiMaio cleaned the blood from the wound and began the painstaking work of reconstructing the bones. After getting them all realigned, he could see clearly at last: the damage was caused by six vertical blows, parallel and very deep, and of such similarity that it was obvious to him they had been struck after Betty Gore was down and her head had ceased to move. They could even have been rendered after she was dead. So, despite their apparent force, he temporarily ruled out those blows as the fatal ones.

On the left side of the face he found three horizontal blows of various sizes, suggesting they were struck, unlike the six vertical ones, while the head was still alive and moving. On the right side of the head, near the top, he found a couple of odd-shaped, curved wounds, not especially deep, again indicating they resulted from glancing blows struck during a struggle. He still hadn't found a wound that looked fatal.

With the next wound, all became clear. Near the curious curved wounds was a huge gaping wound that ran almost all the way across the top of the head, from ear to ear. After cleaning away the hair and blood, he could see that it had been produced by at least seven blows. They were so deep, and had been struck with such force, that they had penetrated the skull and gone all the way into the cranial vault, causing a good portion of Betty Gore's brain to seep out onto the floor.

DiMaio now had two groups of blows that could have killed Betty Gore, but he was still not finished. Turning the body over, he found a group of three more deep chop wounds across the back of the head. And for the first time that morning, his skin crawled. Two of the wounds were pointed at the top, but squared off at the bottom. DiMaio could think of only one explanation: the ax had been swung with such force that it stuck inside the head. That meant the killer would have had to wiggle it back and forth, as one does when chopping wood, to remove it from the bone before swinging again. The third blow was so deep, and aimed at such a soft part of the skull, that it had invaded the cerebellum and could have killed by itself.

The rest of the autopsy was anticlimactic. DiMaio found contusions across the front of Betty Gore's neck—as in the case of the forehead bruise, it seemed odd to find wounds from a blunt instrument in the midst of so much hacking—and then he made the usual examinations of internal organs. None of the organs showed anything out of the ordinary, except the endometrium, which was swollen: Betty Gore had been on the verge of having her menstrual period.

Five hours after he began, DiMaio faced a conundrum. The cause of death was obvious—massive head injuries, from any one of three groups of blows—but the pattern of the injuries didn't fit any of the standard motives. If he had to render an opinion, he would still guess it was a sex crime, mainly because the ax is a weapon of passion (it's clumsy and not really as effective as other weapons), because the face was so mutilated for no apparent reason, and because the woman had been chopped so much more than necessary to kill her. But the main thing DiMaio noticed about Betty Gore's body was more foreboding. He could tell that, even though the body was covered with more than forty ax wounds, almost all of them had been inflicted *while the heart was still beating*. It was a thought that gave even the hardened scientist a temporary chill.

7 · MOURNING

Candy Montgomery slept for three hours and then got up, alone, to fix breakfast. Pat and the children and Alisa Gore were all still sleeping. The kids didn't know yet, of course. She and Pat had stayed up talking about Betty for a while, but when Pat was unable to get any information from the police, they gave up and lay staring at the ceiling. Then they tried to sleep. Pat fell asleep first, but Candy kept thinking about the last phone call from Allan. After telling them Betty had been shot, he had called again, the fifth time that night, mainly to give them his flight schedule. But before hanging up, he had said something else.

"I've talked to the police and I mentioned that you were over there, so they'll probably be calling."

It was the first time she had thought about it.

"Yeah, okay," she had said. "Be glad to."

Candy got the breakfast going—Pat would be up early today because he wanted to work in the yard—and then she sat by the kitchen table and looked out the sliding door at the cool grey luminosity, the predawn quiet. The air was still this morning. When the sun rose it would come fiercely and broil the earth again. From her vantage point, Candy could see nothing but the black shapes of shaggy oak trees and the vague outline of the redundant horse corral that ringed the back yard. She felt very much alone.

After a few minutes she reached for the wall phone over the counter and absentmindedly dialed the number for Ron Adams. She had to hear a reaction; the pastor of the church needed to know anyway.

"Hello."

87

He would recognize her voice. "Ron, have you heard about Betty Gore?"

"No."

"She got killed yesterday. They say she was shot."

Ron seemed less shocked by the news than troubled by its implications. Betty and Ron had never liked each other. The Gores had left the church. Ron wondered what he should do.

She explained that Allan was out of town.

"When will he be back? Perhaps I should meet him?"

"This morning." She gave him the flight number, and Ron hung up, perplexed by his dilemma.

Candy turned back to fixing breakfast, and after a while Pat came downstairs. He sat down to have his cereal.

"Kids aren't up?"

"Not yet."

"Darn, I wanted to get out there and mow today."

Candy continued to go through the ritualized movements of a housewife, making the bed, putting away a few toys left out from the night before. She called softly to the kids when it was time for them to get up, and when they limped down the stairs she started a second round of breakfasts.

As soon as the kids were ranged around the breakfast table, alert enough to be arguing about *The Empire Strikes Back*, Pat went outside. After a few moments, they heard the roar of the lawnmower as the engine caught.

"Now when you go outside this morning stay away from where Daddy is until he's finished."

The kids wolfed down their breakfasts and scrambled back upstairs to put on their swimsuits. They wanted to play in the spray from the lawn sprinkler.

The phone rang. It was one of the women from the church.

"Candy, have you heard?"

"About Betty? Just that she was shot."

"I called as soon as I heard, because I thought you said you were keeping Alisa."

"We are."

"Well, don't turn on a radio where she can hear. I haven't heard it, but I understand it's all over the news."

"Oh, is it?" Candy felt a twinge; she stared straight ahead. "Thank you for letting us know."

Candy sat down at the kitchen table. Why was there no one to talk to?

I've talked to the police. They'll probably be calling.

She grabbed the phone and dialed Sherry Cleckler.

"Have you heard? Betty has been shot."

"Betty Gore?"

"Yes."

"How terrible. How did it happen?"

"No one knows. The police won't tell us anything." Candy's voice sounded disembodied, empty.

"Are *you* okay? You sound upset."

"Oh, I'm fine. Just shaken by the news. We're keeping Alisa and Allan's out of town."

"Well, you don't sound fine. After I get all these relations out of my house, I'm coming over and we'll drink a pot of coffee and talk, okay?"

"That's what I need."

"Gimme 'til Monday."

The phone rang again almost as soon as Candy hung it up. Since it was Saturday morning, everyone was home, listening to radios and trading information by phone.

"Candy—JoAnn. Do you know Betty's dead?"

"We heard last night. It's so awful."

"The police just left—they say she was murdered—with an ax. I wanted to call Jackie, but I don't know where she is."

The sense of dread descended again. "An ax?"

"It must have been some very sick person."

"How horrible."

"It's just so terrible, and just when they were getting ready to go to Europe. Betty told me it was going to be their second honeymoon."

"I didn't know they were going to Europe."

"They were planning to leave Wednesday."

"I think Jackie is in New York."

After Candy hung up, she started mechanically cleaning up the breakfast dishes.

An ax . . . it must have been some very sick person.

The phone rang again. Another woman from church.

"Candy, have you heard about Betty?"

"Yes."

"It must have been one of those maniac weirdos."

Candy replaced the receiver and walked out in the yard. As Pat rounded a corner, she waved and shouted to get his attention over the roar of the mower, then motioned for him to shut it off. When the blade stopped whirring, she said, "Pat, they say Betty was killed with an ax."

"Oh God, how horrible."

"They say the police just left."

Pat shook his head and grimaced. He looked into Candy's eyes, as though to say, "I guess we were all thinking it could have been something this bad," and then he restarted the mower. Candy went back into the house, where the phone was ringing again.

"I've been listening on the radio, and they say there were bloody footprints all over the house. How could this happen to someone like Betty?"

"They were planning a vacation, too."

Another call, another exclamation. The phone was ringing constantly.

I mentioned that you were over there.

Candy couldn't stand the phone any longer. She went back out into the yard and looked for something to do. She got the hedge trimmers out of the garage and started clipping the shrubbery around the white fence. It was hard, messy work, but she pitched into it wholeheartedly, rubbing blisters on her hand from pressing the clippers so hard. Pat finished the mowing and told Candy he was going down the street to tell the Greens what had happened. A few minutes later Barbara Green walked over, and Candy put on a pot of coffee. The idea of having a visitor relaxed her a little.

Mainly Barbara just wanted to be certain that Candy would take the news all right. She knew that Candy and Betty had once sung in the choir together, and she assumed they had been good friends. Barbara wanted to offer whatever emotional support she could.

"Wasn't it a fortunate thing that Alisa was here with you?" said Barbara. "Whoever did this might have killed her as well."

"I guess so," said Candy.

The two women talked about Betty in the past tense, and Candy was surprised to find how easy that was. Betty had had her problems at church, but she was basically a good person. She was a hard person to know. *I wonder how Allan is taking it. How will the kids be told?* They talked about all the things people talk about when young friends meet tragic ends.

"What is the world coming to, that something like this can happen in a woman's own home?" said Barbara.

"Isn't it frightening?" said Candy.

After Barbara left, Candy fielded a few more calls, many of them from shocked church members who would naturally call the woman who always seemed to know what was going on.

"We went to see *The Shining* last night and now I wish we hadn't. Who could have such a diseased mind, to use a weapon like that?"

"If they ever catch the person who did this, there's nothing they could do to him that would be punishment enough."

"I just hate it that Betty suffered."

"They say they have a bloody footprint."

After a while Candy left the phone and went into the hall bathroom. Pat came in from his yardwork, passed the open door, and stopped: Candy had her foot up on the sink, and was applying peroxide to it.

"What did you do to your toe?"

"I cut it on that damned door."

Pat had been meaning to fix the metal storm-door facing that was sharp and jagged at the bottom.

"Is it deep?"

"Not too bad," she said. "I wonder if I need a new tetanus shot, though."

A little later the pastor called again to confirm Allan's flight plans; he had decided to go to the airport to meet him. Candy was beginning to see that the whole weekend would be consumed with trying to deal with Betty's death—church members were obviously taking it very hard—and so she called Sue Wright to cancel their plans for the next day. She and Sue were supposed to take two of the church youth groups to Six Flags Over Texas, the amusement park, but this was obviously not the weekend to do it.

"Have you heard about Betty Gore?" asked Candy.

"Yes, I'm just glad you had Alisa with you."

"I know. I was calling to say I don't think we should go tomorrow. I just don't think it's the respectful thing to do. I'm not in any shape to go anyway. I just don't feel like having a big party."

Sue agreed that the outing should be called off and promised to make the necessary phone calls. They talked for a while about the murder, including the fact of the bloody footprint, which was fast becoming the sole detail of the crime known to every person in Collin County.

The police will be calling. A bloody footprint.

Around lunchtime the calls began to dwindle for the first time. JoAnn called once more to report that Allan was home, but that when he was told that Betty was killed with an ax, he almost collapsed.

"Oh no," said Candy. She repeated the news to Pat, who pressed her for more information.

"I don't know anything else. I guess he'll call us when he's recovered enough to handle the kids."

Pat went outside again to finish his work in the yard. Candy sat in a chair by the kitchen table, phone cradled between her chin and shoulder, a pair of garden shears in her hands. As she spoke, she began to work the shears back and forth, pressing with all her might as the metal blades cut through the soles of a pair of rubber sandals. She continued her work for several minutes, long enough for the shears to destroy all semblance of pattern on the sole and to render the shoes into a messy little heap of rubber. Hanging up the phone, she gathered up the scraps she had made and carried them to an outside garbage can.

8 · CONDOLENCES

The first reporters Allan Gore saw were standing on his front lawn. There were four or five of them, clutching notebooks and tape recorders and holding miniature cameras, a contingency he hadn't considered until the moment he returned home. Something was out of kilter. There was something he didn't know. He got out of a friend's car—his colleagues from work had shown up at the airport and insisted on bringing him home—and then looked around, not knowing what to expect. The first familiar face in view was Dick Sewell. Sewell, the curious dentist who had been among the neighbors at the house the night before, had returned that morning to organize a utility-room cleanup operation. Everyone agreed that Allan shouldn't see the condition of that room, nor of the blood-stained bathroom. Now Dick Sewell was the first person to greet Allan at his own door.

"How did it happen?" asked Allan.

"What all do you know?" said Dick warily.

"Just that she was shot."

"Well, that's wrong. The weapon was an ax, and it was very brutal. The crime lab was here until six this morning."

Allan blanched and his knees started to give. He groped for support and found his way inside to a chair. After thirteen hours of turning the news over and over in his mind, of waiting on planes and wondering whether he would ever know Betty's last thoughts, the reality of what had happened was like a final cruel twist that almost broke him. He could feel tears welling up from somewhere deep inside, and for a while he didn't know whether they were tears of grief or of guilt. *He hadn't been there*. Betty had always said he should be there. Then, at the moment she had been more frightened than at any time in her life, *he hadn't been there*.

Allan tried to focus on the things that needed to be done. Stay active, stay occupied, that was what got him through. After he had gotten the news the night before, he had done all the right things, made all the correct calls. He had told his parents, he had talked to the police, and he had made the most difficult call of all—to Betty's parents, in Norwich. Bertha had almost gotten hysterical, until Bob calmed her down and came on the line himself. Suicide had lodged in some part of Allan's mind as a possibility that he didn't want to consider on any conscious level, and when he talked to Bob Pomeroy, he knew Betty's family would never understand that. Later he had felt comforted by the harmless presence in the motel room of Tom Tansil. "You must go home soon," Tom had said, and Allan had nodded and allowed Tom to make the reservations. Allan was so anxious to do the correct thing, to maintain control of himself, that later that night he insisted on going over the 3M project file with Tom, because, after all, they were going to have to carry on without him. When he had reached Dallas, there had been more friends waiting. Even Ron was there, the Methodist pastor from Lucas whom Betty couldn't stand. As Allan thought back on it, Ron had done an odd thing: at the airport, he had given Allan a business card.

Now there was yet another group of friends at the house, including Dick Sewell, who was doing his best to make things easier. Neighbors had started arriving with food; thank goodness Dick was there to take the covered dishes and put them away. Allan felt too tired to face all the decisions. He needed to get his head straight. He needed a sympathetic ear, someone who would understand what he was going through. He went to the phone and called Candy Montgomery.

"Candy, would you and Pat keep Alisa for a few more hours? I just got here, and everything's pretty hectic."

"Sure, Allan, don't worry about her. Just call us whenever you want us to bring her home."

"She doesn't know, does she?"

"No, we've kept her away from the radio."

"I don't want to tell her until everything's quieted down. I need to talk to the police and make some funeral arrangements and get these people out of the house. Why don't you bring her home around 3:30?"

"Okay. Allan, *please* tell us if there's anything else we can do—help with the arrangements or something."

"No, it's fine, the neighbors are all helping."

"Are you all right?"

"I'm fine. A little shaken up, but mostly just tired."

"Allan, I wish I could do something."

"Thanks."

Allan spent the rest of the day making funeral arrangements and attending to the solicitations of relatives and friends. Dick Sewell went with him to a funeral home to pick out the casket, and he was there when Chief Abbott came by to brief Allan on the investigation. It was obvious that the police weren't very far along on the case. They had no suspects anyway. The most intriguing thing Abbott told him was that they didn't believe Betty's attacker was an intruder. Allan wondered why, but not for long. There wasn't time. Neighbors and church members continued to bring food to the house all afternoon, and there were ticklish decisions to be made. Should Betty's funeral be in Kansas, where most of her family friends were, or in Texas, where their personal friends could attend? Finally Allan decided to have a Monday memorial service in Wylie and a Wednesday funeral in Norwich. Both families, Allan's and Betty's, were planning to arrive in Wylie by Sunday afternoon.

By midafternoon Allan was finished with the most pressing duties. Dick and some of the local officials had handled the reporters by giving them a sketchy outline of the previous night's events. Then Dick had left, the police had left, and Allan was alone for the first time since he had tried to sleep in St. Paul. He sat for a few minutes in the living room—den, still trying to get his bearings: everything was happening so fast. Then he called Candy Montgomery again and told her to bring Alisa home.

Candy told Alisa to gather up all her belongings because it was time to go home. Immediately Ian and Jenny got excited at the prospect of a trip, but Candy had to tell them they couldn't go. They whined a little—it seemed like an arbitrary decision—and Alisa seemed perplexed. Candy started getting teary-eyed at the thought of what was about to happen, so Pat insisted on going to Wylie with her. That meant the kids would be dropped at a neighbor's house. As they walked out to the car, Candy kept trying to carry Alisa's bag, but Alisa stubbornly insisted she could do it herself. Candy's behavior was too strange to escape the attention of an intelligent six-year-old. Alisa knew something was up.

Pat suggested they wait an extra fifteen minutes to make sure Allan had enough time to get ready, and then they drove slowly through the countryside toward Wylie. It was almost four when they got there. Allan looked tired when he opened the door.

"Oh Allan," said Candy, grasping him by the arm. "I'm so sorry."

Allan looked at Alisa, reached down and hugged and kissed her. Candy hesitated, then wrapped her arms around Allan's chest and hugged him. Allan gave her a squeeze, and they parted.

Pat didn't say anything. The two men simply moved together and embraced firmly. Neither Candy nor Pat could look Allan in the eye. They held their heads down and stared around the room.

"Is there anything you need?" asked Candy, her eyes starting to water, as Alisa walked on into the living room–den.

"Please," said Allan, "don't leave yet. I'd like you to be here when I tell her. It will help me."

"All right," said Candy, her voice catching. She and Pat moved on into the living room–den and sat on a couch. Candy looked nervously around and noticed, with relief, that the door to the utility room was closed. Allan sat on a chair next to that room, and had Alisa come and sit on his lap. Alisa said nothing. Her eyes were full of curiosity and the childish fear of the unknown.

Allan placed his arm around Alisa's shoulders and looked into her face. His voice was soft and evenly measured.

"Last night," he said, "somebody very bad came in the house and cut up Mommy very bad. And Mommy is never coming back."

Alisa continued to look curiously into her father's face.

"Do you understand?" he asked.

Alisa started to whimper, her eyes watering.

"Who's going to cook dinner for us?" she asked.

A tear rolled down Allan's cheek. "We'll just have to cook for ourselves now."

Alisa was silent for a moment. Then she said, "Who's going to take care of us?"

Allan didn't have an answer for that one. He pressed Alisa's head to his breast as she started to cry.

Candy, who was watching from her seat a few feet away, couldn't say anything because she was crying silently and uncontrollably. She rose from her place, walked across the room, and knelt against Allan's chair, wrapping her arms around both the father and the daughter. The three of them wept together.

"Thank you," said Allan, as Candy and Pat got ready to leave. "Thank you for being here."

On the evening of the same day, four hundred miles to the north, in a small house near the main street of Norwich, Kansas, big Bob Pomeroy sat on a chair in his sparsely furnished living room. He was surrounded by people—almost every family in the county had come by at one time or another that day, bearing food and sympathy—but Bob could just as well have been totally alone. He sat off to one side, reaching deep into himself. For one of the few times in his life, he was unable to act.

For a while Bob had been the only one in the family able to deal with the tragedy. That was his role; it had always been his place to carry the heaviest burdens. After Allan had called with the news, Bob had immediately started bringing the Pomeroys together. He called Richard, the youngest son; then he called his brother Jack, who drove over to Stoney Creek to retrieve the older son, Ronnie, from the country music festival. Then he got in the car and drove a mile east to his elderly parents' farmhouse to break the news to them. Within an hour all the Pomeroys had gathered together in the tiny living room, with Bob trying to soften the impact with suppositions. He guessed that maybe Betty had been killed by a burglar. Or maybe a kid had been playing with a .22 rifle and a stray shot had gone through the window. Or it could have been some kid who was mad at Betty because she had given him a bad grade. But on second thought Bob decided that wasn't very likely.

After a while, though, everybody stopped talking about it, including Bob. The men tried to comfort the crying women. Bertha took it so hard that she had to be given tranquilizers. Then they sat around in the living room and just kind of stared at one another. No one wanted to go to bed, so they sat up all night. Around five in the morning Bob finally lay down for a while, but he didn't sleep. Then, throughout the next morning as the neighbors started arriving, they continued to sit and stare. Whatever happened was beyond comprehension; it was all the more baffling because it happened so far away, in a strange state, where the police didn't seem to know much. Bob comforted himself with the knowledge that, if she was killed by a gunshot, then at least she probably didn't suffer much.

Then, in the early afternoon, Allan had called from Dallas.

"Bob," he had said, "it's worse than we thought."

"What?"

"Betty—she wasn't shot. She was killed with an ax."

Until that moment, Bob had been as stoic as a father can be expected to be, but now he ground his eye into his enormous sleeve. Now he *knew* Betty had suffered. He couldn't even continue the conversation, except to go along passively with Allan's funeral plans. All he could think of was Bertha. There was no way to tell her that. She wouldn't be able to take it.

For the rest of the day Bob had withdrawn into himself, stewing over it, trying to figure out some way to tell her, or better yet, to avoid telling her. Finally, that night, Bob got up from his chair and asked Ronnie to go into the kitchen with him. Ronnie was calm and levelheaded; maybe he would know what was best.

Bob told Ronnie what Allan had said, and then, "I haven't told Bertha or Richard about it."

"We've gotta do it," said Ronnie. "They'll have to know."

Bob waited while Ronnie went to get Bertha and Richard. Then, since there were still neighbors visiting, the family gathered in a small hallway just off the kitchen, the only private place in the house.

It took all of Bob's strength simply to state the bare facts.

"Betty wasn't shot," he said. "She was killed by an ax."

Everyone was speechless for a moment, and then Bertha started to break down. The boys helped her to a chair. But the more remarkable thing was that finally Bob couldn't stand it either; big tears started to roll down his cheeks, and he had difficulty talking. The sight of a 260-pound man crying, the one person who held everything together, was almost too much for the others to take. This family, they began to think, may never be the same.

* * *

Still later that night, in the fashionable, secluded subdivision called Montecito, in the town of Fairview, Texas, Pat and Candy Montgomery were getting ready for bed. Both of them were dog tired. As Candy threw her nightgown over her head, Pat noticed something on her legs. Her thighs were covered with unsightly purple bruises.

"Where did you get *those*?" he asked.

"Oh, just housework. You know how I'm always bumping into the dishwasher."

"You bruise so easily. Come on, we need to get some sleep if we're going to make it to church in the morning."

9 • COUNTRY CHURCH

It was a church service that had first brought Candy Montgomery and Betty Gore together, and it was the church that would lead them to their times of closeness and, eventually, their mutual hatreds. For the Methodist Church of Lucas, Texas, was, more than most places of worship, an institution controlled by and large by women. The epicenter of Candy Montgomery's universe, almost from the day in 1977 when she moved to her dream house in the country, was this drafty white clapboard building known to its congregants simply as "the church." Set back from the roadside, paint peeling, steeple rusted, its floors echoing hollowly under the tread of men's heavy soles, it did not at first resemble a place likely to house the more liberal strains of Methodist theology.

Formed in the time when the land still tolerated cotton and farmers came to the tiny village of Lucas to do their ginning, the church had always been a backwater outpost in a vanishing town. Supported by no more than ten to twenty families, it had managed for long stretches without any full-time minister at all. In recent years, though, it had become a postgraduate receptacle for young seminary students trying out their pulpit skills for the first time, most of them staying a year or less before moving on to less obscure parishes. Most church members were farmers and storekeepers, born into the faith and natural adherents of the easygoing fundamentalism that distinguished them from the other two Lucas churches, Baptist and Church of Christ. Such families sought only a stewardship of quiet devotion and were generally well satisfied with the young divinity students who came to them directly from the Perkins School of Theology, part of Southern Methodist University of Dallas, where the bishop often looked when he needed to fill the empty pulpits of tiny country churches. It was an arrangement that pleased both the parishioners and the parish. All that changed when Lucas Methodist welcomed its first full-time pastor.

Jackie arrived in July 1976, a brassy, convivial sort with a lusty laugh who, at forty-one, was just beginning a career at an age when most had long since settled the patterns of their lives. Normally the arrival of a new pastor would be greeted with unalloyed gratitude, since any ministerial student, no matter how green, was preferable to a vacancy. But Jackie Ponder was not merely a young liberal idealist. The Reverend Ponder was also a woman.

If the Methodists had been searching for inspirational feminists to direct the new ecclesiastical order of the seventies, they could hardly have invented a better role model than Jackie Ponder. She was spiritually self-made. Born an Arkansan, she had grown up in San Antonio, where she attended a strict Lutheran school. At nineteen she married a doctor, raised two children, and wasn't able to enroll in college until the age of thirty. She received an English degree despite having no natural talent for classwork, then, like the female parishioners who would later cling to her, started searching for that "something more" that marriage had failed to give her. For most of her life, she had wrestled with her religious feelings, at one point rebelling against the church entirely and alienating both her mother and her husband. While in her thirties, she declared herself an atheist and went through a dark period of almost total seclusion from everyone except her husband. It was a painful, wrenching time for her and her family. Then, while attending graduate school one summer at North Texas State University and spending all her spare time reading philosophy and psychiatry, she had a mystical experience in which she felt a divine voice giving her instructions to serve as "a channel for His love." Six weeks later, she heard the same inner voice, compelling her to go into the ministry. At first she doubted the evidence—by this time she had scorned the strict Methodism of her youth and advertised her agnosticism—but she finally succumbed. When she did, her sister tried to talk her out of it. Her husband, who had been uneasy but tolerant throughout Jackie's attempts to find herself, became literally sick. At the age of thirty-seven, she enrolled at Perkins. She was one of only twenty women in the school. For the first time, she said, she felt at peace with herself.

Jackie liked to tell people that she lived by only one great commandment: "Love God with all your heart, mind, and soul." It was a simple and infectious idea. Jackie was a big woman, with broad, thick features and an overgrown Afro hairdo, but the most noticeable thing about her was her voice: it was loud and incessant and full of energy. It could fill a room with bravado. Perhaps that's why the Methodist district superintendent accompanied her to Lucas for her visit with the church Pastor-Parish Committee. He wanted to be certain that the congregation would be able to deal with her, not only as a woman, but as a woman who would undoubtedly be more forceful and assertive than any of the ladies of the church. Jackie was as nervous as they were. But if anything won them over, it was her self-confidence. She looked like a person who would *care* about the church and not simply use it as a stepping-stone to another job.

As it turned out, Jackie was not entirely ready for a church pastorate. She was so exuberant about her new life that she was crestfallen when the church didn't instantly fall under the spell of her preaching. At that time the church was divided into two factions, one demonstrative and charismatic, one quiet and traditional. Until Jackie arrived, the two groups had coexisted in more or less mutual tolerance, but things started to fall apart under her leadership. Her confidence in her own spiritual maturity often made her seem harsh and judgmental to those who were less secure. She was a self-described mystic, yet she had no patience with the charismatics. The older farmers in the church could accept her anyway, as a spiritual person who was simply immature, but the young charismatics grew more and more hostile as Jackie pursued a rather aimless, secular method of preaching and church management. When the charismatics asked to have a special prayer meeting to seal off the church from Satan, Jackie flatly refused on theological grounds. It was the first of many no's, and with each passing week, a few more members would stay away. The church had never been very large to begin with. After eight or nine months, attendance had dwindled from about eighty regulars to no more than twenty-five on most Sundays. One of the women who left in a huff decreased the church income by fully one-third. Jackie's husband, meanwhile, was still finding it difficult to accept his wife's new career, and especially disliked the tiny backwater church to which they were now irrevocably connected. Jackie tried to disguise her growing depression, but the fear of failing as a pastor and a wife preyed on her night and day. She continued to pitch into her Sunday sermons with enthusiasm, though, and refused to believe that her commitment to being a "channel for His love" could be frustrated.

If Candy Montgomery had not visited Lucas Church in March 1977, or if Jackie Ponder had not been there to welcome her, the lives of both women might have been very different. Both were the sort of restless spirits who spend their lives expecting next year to be better than this one, and then are consistently and sincerely amazed when it is not. They were, in a word, romantics. Those who didn't know them well might not have thought so. Candy tended toward cynicism, in an offhandedly impish way, while Jackie had a strong streak of vague visionary idealism. ("God is Love," "Love is All" were the constant refrains of her sermons.) But the cynic and the idealist are more closely related than either believes. The two women, almost on their first meeting, became soul sisters.

In a sense both Candy and Jackie had, by early 1977, achieved their earthly ambitions already. Candy's most devout wish since her girlhood had been to marry, live in a big country house, and raise lots of kids and animals. "Lots" had been amended to two children and three pets, but she still felt that a lifelong dream was complete when she and Pat finally had enough money to get their country house. One of Pat's fellow workers at Texas Instruments, Phil Green, had led them out to eastern Collin County one weekend to show them the beautiful shaded countryside among the horse stables and farms along Farm Road 1378, and they had picked out their place on the spot. It was just up the road from the Green house, in a new subdivision called Montecito, on the crown of a hill obscured at the moment by ravines and blackberries and a few oak stands. They got the land for $10,000. The house eventually cost $60,000 more because they insisted that a chic Dallas architectural firm do the blueprints. They accepted the first design submitted: a cathedral look, open and airy, with a lot of exposed beams and skylights, the children's rooms isolated from their own, an oversized double garage, and a workshop and study for Pat. They also looked at the school before making the move: they found they were in a minuscule one-school district, named Lovejoy after a farm family which had donated the land for a tiny red elementary schoolhouse. Far from being disturbed by the lack of urban amenities, the new immigrants of Montecito universally praised Lovejoy School as a return to simplicity and proudly boasted that it had all the advantages of any city district because it had more closely supervised instruction. In February 1977, the Montgomerys made the move from Plano.

So Candy had her house at last, and Jackie had her church. The only reason Candy ventured near Lucas Church the first time was strictly the novelty: she was dying to see a lady preacher. So she dragged Pat to services one Sunday morning and was at first disappointed: the building was cramped and drafty, and it turned out that Jackie Ponder wasn't much of a preacher after all. But after the service she was completely swept away by the warmth and simplicity of the people there, most of them older than the Montgomerys, including a few of the area's farming families. By the next weekend, Pat and Candy had volunteered to help paint the decrepit parsonage, which was vacant at the moment while Jackie and her husband Bill made plans to move to Lucas from Richardson.

For a woman who had never really been interested in any sort of religion, Candy became a dynamo in the church in a remarkably short time. Jackie Ponder's friendship was the sole reason. Candy and Jackie were both loquacious, and the favorite part of their days was the time when they would put on a pot of coffee, take their places around someone's kitchen table, and talk until one of them felt guilty enough to go back to work. It was at such sessions that the two women first began to feel a special kinship, especially since, after a while, they dropped their small talk and started having very intense debates over organized religion. Candy was the doubter, gleefully pointing out biblical inconsistencies and injustices as the two women smoked and drank coffee in the Montgomery kitchen. Both were avid readers as well, although Jackie's tastes ran to philosophers while Candy's didn't extend much beyond the works of Taylor Caldwell and whatever steamy bodice-ripper paperback caught her eye at the supermarket. Nevertheless, it was Candy who became the firebrand intellectual, jousting against Jackie's interpretations of scripture. When Jackie preached a sermon on the Book of Job, Candy told her point-blank that it was the "awfullest book in the Bible" and untrue, because she could never accept a God who played games with man. At times like that, Jackie would tell Candy she was a "seeker," for only someone who cares about biblical truth could be so agitated over apparent inconsistency. This would inflame Candy all the more.

As time went on, they became close confidantes. There was little of the pastor-parishioner relationship in their meetings. In fact, Candy came to have as much influence on the church management as Jackie did, by accepting such unpleasant jobs as writing newsletters, teaching Sunday School classes no one else wanted, church-social planning, and assorted dirty work. By the end of the first year, Candy was church education chairman and would eventually become the highest lay officer in the church. Candy and Jackie were both pleasant, outgoing, self-motivated women, so they had many other friends; but because of their special circumstances, they became more intimate with each other than they could be with anyone else—including, ultimately, their husbands.

The first time they really talked heart-to-heart was a few months after Candy had joined the church, and the subject was Jackie's marriage. Bill Ponder's disillusionment with his marriage had been smoldering for a long time, but especially since Jackie's decision to enroll at Perkins. Then, in the spring of 1977, Jackie decided it would be necessary for them to move into the Lucas parsonage, which at the moment was a rather down-at-the-heels frame house that looked as ugly on the outside as it was pitifully small on the inside. For the first time, Bill balked. Everything up until then had been acceptable because it did not affect his job or lifestyle in any fundamental way. This was different. He argued about it with Jackie, flatly refused at first, then eventually agreed to try it for a while. They moved into the parsonage in June. In August, Bill Ponder suddenly stopped coming to church services. Jackie didn't say anything publicly, but she told Candy the truth: Bill had taken his things and left. He had told her he wanted a divorce, and she was crushed.

One day, visiting Candy as she had many times during the marital crisis, Jackie broke into tears.

"I'm so scared about being single," she said.

"Jackie," said Candy, "you don't know how lucky you are."

If Candy and Jackie had been close before, they now became all but inseparable. At the time it seemed like a natural friendship that was strengthened into something more solid by Jackie's marital crisis. But something else was going on, too. Jackie was about to undergo one of the most significant changes in her life: after twenty-three years of marriage, she would be single again. But the effect on Candy may have been even greater. Candy had been drawn to Jackie because the older woman seemed, from the perspective of a marriage starting to go stale after seven years, like everything Candy aspired to be. Jackie was in charge of her destiny. She was a mother and a wife and a career woman. More important, when something went wrong in her life, she had the ability to change it. When Candy Montgomery said "you don't know how lucky you are," she meant every word.

It was not that anything was terribly wrong with Candy's marriage. On the contrary, Pat had provided everything she had ever expected from him, including a comfortable $70,000 income from his work on sophisticated military radar systems at Texas Instruments. Pat was among a half dozen or so scientists able to do the top-secret government consulting work, and his national prestige in his field meant that the Montgomerys would always be secure. They had their dream house. They had two kids whom they both loved very much. They had a church and a school and, for the first time, a place where they felt they belonged.

"And I," said Candy to Jackie, "am bored crazy."

She didn't know exactly what she wanted, but she knew it was more than she had. Pat was dependable but he wasn't exciting. He worked too much. Sometimes he even worked at home. Their sex life was not what it once was. She felt increasingly used, a paid laborer, a cook and cleaner and nursemaid. (Even though she enjoyed cooking and child care, Pat didn't know that.) She also started to think that perhaps she had missed something by never going to college. It was as though she had jumped straight from childhood to womanhood without anything in between. Jackie talked about books and ideas and writers that Candy had never heard of. Jackie talked about things like "existentialism" and the great German philosophers; admiring Jackie as she did, Candy suddenly wanted to emulate her. She clung to Jackie as the only thing in her life that seemed to transcend the ordinary. And she began to worry, for the first time, about what she might do when both kids were old enough to start school. If she didn't find something else, she would go crazy with tedium.

First she turned to volunteer work. Candy's responsibilities in the church continued to increase, to the point where after a while Jackie asked her to help with outside speaking engagements. Since Jackie was still considered a curiosity at many churches, she was often invited to speak on "Women in the Ministry." In this respect, Lucas Church had a double distinction among feminists, since Candy was one of the top two or three lay leaders. In August 1977, shortly after Bill Ponder moved out of the parsonage, Jackie and Candy traveled to Plano to present one of their Sunday evening programs on "Women in the Church" at Briarwood Methodist. Their duet was a hit, especially with several of the younger couples in the audience who were growing disenchanted with their own church. Those couples included Allan and Betty Gore.

That fall Jackie's church started growing again. It happened for a simple reason: five families moved en masse from Briarwood to Lucas. The exodus had been brewing for some time, mostly because of diagreements with the Briarwood pastor. Once they heard the "Women in the Ministry" presentation, and then visited Lucas, they bolted quickly. The Garlingtons, outspoken JoAnn and her husband Richard, were the first to go, followed by the Gores, the Maples, the Sullivans, and the Williamses. Lucas Church was still small enough to be changed dramatically by the infusion of five families, especially when they were activists. Jackie and Candy were, of course, delighted. These were not only young people, mostly thirtyish couples with children, but they were also liberal enough to pitch into Jackie's "experimental ministry" with a zeal the old-timers didn't have.

It was clear that one of the principal attractions of Lucas was its primitive character, its quaintness. It was the kind of little country church that people wax nostalgic over—even people who never attended a country church or, for that matter, lived in the country. Combined with the newcomers' obvious admiration for the plucky woman pastor, it gave Jackie a blank check to shape the sort of church she had wanted before the charismatics had fled and left the coffers empty. For the first time Jackie started scheduling evening services—she had tried before, but no one had shown up—and she quickly took advantage of anyone who showed the slightest inclination to chair a committee or organize a project. She referred to the new Lucas as an "integrative" pastorate, by which she meant that the parishioners would be expected to minister to themselves as much as she ministered to them. It was not exactly what the more conservative church members had bargained for, but they went along with the changes with their customary equanimity.

In later, sadder times, the year 1977 would be remembered as Lucas Church's golden age, a rich, happy period of fellowship that perhaps reached its most joyous point on a day in late December. On that day the sanctuary of the church was festooned and bedecked with so many cardboard cutouts, construction-paper silhouettes, glittering gold garlands, and pipe-cleaner angels that a visitor, entering unawares, might well assume he had come upon a school pageant instead of a place of worship. The altar itself was all but obscured by the decorative excess. A large Christmas tree stood in one corner, a few feet from the pulpit, just behind an electrically-lit angel with neon yellow hair. A red-suited Santa Claus, rather too thin for the role, sat near the front of the room holding a bag of goodies, while women sliced cakes and parceled out cookies. And the effusion of special effects was dominated by hand-lettered banners, the kind usually seen in high school gymnasia, in this case devoted to such messages as "Alleluia," "And He Shall Be Called Jesus," "Love Your Neighbor," and, on the pulpit itself, "Love is Born." Among the congregation, this special service was known as the Birthday Party for Jesus.

The Birthday Party for Jesus was not the only innovation that Jackie introduced. In a way Jackie was trying to forget her separation from her husband by pouring all her energies into her new profession, but she also truly believed in a wholly democratic, pluralistic approach to church management. She avoided making decisions. She talked constantly of "getting the people involved in the worship service itself." She encouraged her parishioners to redecorate the sanctuary to suit their tastes, even when her policy led to such quirky results as a chapel full of artificial palm trees on Palm Sunday and windows festooned with what were known as "Dolly Parton angels." Jackie allowed laymen to administer sacraments. She made a children's service, complete with puppet shows and funny stories, a part of the weekly worship service. By her own admission, she had no talent for administration; faced with the need for a building fund, she would announce to the church, "Well, it seems we need this money and I guess you all know what to do. Now, let's talk about Love." On Sundays, in fact, she increasingly resembled a reality therapist instead of a preacher. At times she would abruptly depart from a scriptural reading, look into the congregation, and say, "How do those words make you feel? What are you feeling and thinking right now?"

Perhaps the most significant change Jackie made, though, and the one that was universally approved from the pews, was the formation of a choir, something that had always seemed too extravagant and complicated for such a small church. The idea occurred to her when she got to know Elaine Williams, one of the Briarwood defectors, at a women's therapy group both were attending in order to work out their problems with men. (Elaine was married to a photographer, but would divorce him four months later. Jackie's divorce was still pending, but she had already started quietly breaking the news to church members.) A pianist with a strong musical background, Elaine was, as Jackie would later joke, a gift from God. To make it possible for her to become the first Lucas music director, Jackie appealed to the church's principal benefactor, a Dallas attorney named Don Crowder, known chiefly for being the law partner of Dallas Congressman Jim Mattox, and a tireless supporter of the town of Lucas, where he had moved in 1970. Don was not a very religious man himself, but he was impressed by the way Jackie was making the church come alive again, and so he agreed to be the "anonymous donor" funding the part-time music director's job. Elaine was hired.

The importance of the choir quickly came to be more political than musical. The choristers became, by virtue of their constant association with Jackie, the most influential people in the church. They even began to take on all the disagreeable characteristics of a social clique. There was nothing sinister about this, since their only motives were to make Lucas Methodist into a dynamic and exciting place. It was simply that the choir couples—the Montgomerys, the Gores, and three or four others—were all about the same age, with children the same ages, and a stake in maintaining control of the church's future. Jackie was anxious to use that commitment, too, and she did—to organize athletic leagues, recruit leaders (Pat and Candy both held high positions in the church), and get people to come to the church on days other than Sunday.

Even as the church began to flourish again, though, Jackie's personal life remained a source of periodic depression. She was out of town on the Sunday in March 1978 when Don Crowder, as chairman of the Pastor-Parish Committee, announced to the congregation that their minister's divorce was final. Members of the choir had already been told, but some of the older church members were stunned by the news. The fact that Jackie was away at the time made it even odder, in their opinion, since it seemed as though she felt guilty about it. They were right. It would take Jackie a long time to get over her self-doubts—her feeling that perhaps she had sabotaged her own marriage by so single-mindedly pursuing her ministerial career—and her main remedy for her depression was to take refuge among kindred spirits: the other women of the church.

Jackie used to divide her friends into two categories: "front-door" friends and "back-door" friends. Front-door friends were the ones who only came by when they had a reason; usually it was to talk about church business, or to ask Jackie to make a hospital visit, or something similar. Back-door friends were the ones who never knocked, who headed straight for the coffee pot, who felt free to smoke and talk "naughty," and who were, inevitably, women who sang in the choir. These were the ones who knew they were welcome at the parsonage any time and who came often. These were the ones Jackie could bare her soul to. One thing Jackie liked to talk about was sex—never an unpopular subject in this group anyway, but one that was increasingly on Jackie's mind after the divorce. Like most recently divorced people, Jackie wanted to replace her old life with something new and erotic and different. In fact, Jackie was not the only woman in Lucas Church who felt the need to fantasize about sexual adventure. Candy Montgomery and Elaine Williams joked so frequently about leaving their husbands that one Sunday after church, while they were offhandedly talking about "waiting until something better comes along," Diane Maples overheard them and was so upset that she repeated the conversation, very agitatedly, to her friend JoAnn Garlington. Both women thought it scandalous.

Candy Montgomery was a back-door friend. Betty Gore was a front-door friend. When Betty came by the parsonage for one reason or another, the other women would remember to hold their tongues for fear of offending her. It was not that Betty was unsophisticated or unfriendly; it was simply that she had never seemed very outgoing around the other women of the church. She was hard to read, even a little cold at times, and usually she kept to herself. Occasionally one of the children would come home with a story of how Betty had forbidden her daughter, Alisa, to do this or that, and it would always seem a little too strict for the circumstances. Betty had the same reputation at the elementary school where she taught; she was not very popular among her students, and some of the teachers considered her a harsh disciplinarian. Things got so bad during her first semester of teaching at Wylie that a group of fifth graders vandalized her house one night, decorating the front of it with eggs, writing "EGORE" on the front porch in black shoe polish, and ringing the doorbell after everyone had gone to bed. Jackie found Betty blunt but competent. One of Betty's problems, she once remarked to a friend, was that Betty didn't treat Alisa as a child but as a "small adult." The only time Jackie had visited the Gore home was to tell them about her divorce; she thought Betty a bit formal at the time, but given the nature of the call, it was a pleasant enough visit. Since Betty was a teacher, Jackie had asked her to do the children's sermon one week, and it was a big hit. Betty had gathered all the kids around her at the front of the sanctuary and handed each child a toy. Then she began taking the toys away and exchanging them at random—to make a point about how unfeeling and cruel it is to indiscriminately give and take things. The point was well made, but her playacting seemed to emphasize her uncompromising sense of justice and "correct" behavior, even when dealing with children. Betty was a moralist—fond of enforcing rules—which is one thing that made her a bit distant from the other women. That's why it seemed so odd on the day in the spring of 1978 when Betty dropped by the parsonage, bubbling over with excitement, to tell Jackie about her new foster child.

Why Betty Gore ever took such an avid interest in the Texas state foster parents program would remain a mystery, even to her husband, right up until her death. All the evidence of her life indicated that she was awkward around children, even her own, and yet when one of the Gores' ex-neighbors in Plano told them about the program, Betty was fascinated with the notion of temporarily adopting a child. This particular state program involved no permanent commitments; the homeless kids were simply parcelled out to willing households while court judgments of various sorts were being made. So Betty submitted her application to the state, and within a few weeks a six-year-old boy was assigned to the Gores. He stayed only two weeks, without any trouble to speak of, but as soon as he was gone Betty informed the Texas Department of Human

Resources that in the future she would prefer to adopt younger children, and preferably girls. Shortly thereafter she was put in charge of a three-year-old girl, and she hurried over to introduce her to Jackie.

It was not the first time that Jackie would be confused by Betty's behavior. Jackie would go long periods without seeing Betty at all—except at church, of course—and then Betty would burst into the room like they were old friends. Little did Jackie know the real cause of Betty's on-again, off-again friendship. It would have surprised her: Betty admired Jackie above all other women.

Betty was not a great deal different from the other women who admired Jackie. They all loved her, to greater or lesser degrees, in part because they knew what she had gone through in order to put her life in order. That it *was* in order they had no doubt, because Jackie was the strong and wise one, the woman with purpose. Betty had sensed this quality in Jackie on the Gores' first visit to Lucas Church in the fall of 1977. They had visited on the recommendation of the Garlingtons, but the main reason they stayed was the presence of Jackie, with whom Betty instantly felt a kinship. Then, when Jackie came to the Gore home to tell them about her divorce, Betty had been the first to say how she understood completely and would try to help Jackie through the difficult time. Perhaps it was her natural shyness, or the way she expressed her sympathy, but somehow the admiration was lost on Jackie, who found Betty a casual friend but nothing more. Betty was simply never one of the gals.

The year 1978 should have been the grandest, most successful yet for Lucas Methodist Church, and by all outward appearances it was. Membership reached an all-time high, so much so that some of the "old-timers" (who had been there all of eighteen months) grew concerned that the church was in danger of losing its close-knit character. The choir grew and prospered as Elaine Williams, the new organist and director, continued to recruit any member who had the semblance of a singing voice. (Pat Montgomery became an especially prized chorister, not only for his voice but for his ability to read music and conduct in Elaine's absence.) Allan Gore helped organize volleyball and softball teams that summer—the first time Lucas Methodist had ever taken part in the church athletic leagues. The daily coffee klatsches of the church women expanded to include children's birthday parties, baby-sitting co-ops, teas, luncheons, and the like. Jackie's abilities as a public speaker showed marked improvement, as she became more natural and less intellectual in her weekly sermons. There were more and more evening committee meetings as the church took on responsibilities for community social work, foreign missions, and exchanges with other churches. And preliminary plans were drawn up for a new church building.

Still, behind all the gaiety and activity, things were beginning to fray. When the church formed a "couples" volleyball league, Jackie started showing up at games with a man named Chuck, her boyfriend at the time, whom she had no intention of marrying. This was less than pleasing to the older church members, who expected a greater degree of modesty from their pastor. Chuck wasn't the only boyfriend, either. Jackie had several, much to the consternation of those who weren't supposed to know. That same summer the church lost its organist and choir director to divorce: David and Elaine Williams had separated in April after six years of marriage, and by July their divorce was final. Elaine decided that she couldn't support her two children unless she gave up the choir job, and so she resigned and went to work as a technical writer and product developer at Texas Instruments. Richard and JoAnn Garlington, one of the activist couples in the church, spent a weekend at a motel in Dallas going through an intensive therapy program called Marriage Encounter, and as soon as they returned they started proselytizing for the program among other couples. They also started holding hands at all times and remaining entwined in each other's arms throughout church services—a public display of affection that amused some and upset others.

Betty Gore went through a period of despondency that summer, when her initial enthusiasm for the state foster parents program was shattered by a rebellious eight-year-old boy named Danny, who had been abused by his parents, shuffled from place to place by the courts, and arrived at the Gore home with a monumental chip on his shoulder. Betty and Danny were constantly at odds. Danny so frequently disobeyed orders and taunted Alisa that after a while Betty refused to have much to do with him at all; she would go for days without saying anything kind, loving, or even courteous to him. The hatred between Betty and the foster child grew so intense that, on two occasions, Allan sat Betty down and asked her to stop nagging and ordering Danny around because he was "basically a good kid." Betty refused to believe it. Their battle of wills reached an all-time low that fall, when Danny asked Betty if he could have a birthday party. Betty said okay, wrote up six or seven invitations, and told Danny to deliver them at school—but she never followed up by calling the children's parents. On Danny's birthday, only one boy showed up—evidence, Betty said, of how unpopular the boy was. Allan blamed Betty for the fiasco. Soon thereafter, Betty started demanding that the state take Danny back.

Even Candy Montgomery, normally the most carefree and high-spirited of the women in the church, fell into a depression that summer. For months she had been offering her shoulder to Jackie as a prop when things seemed bleakest. Now Jackie was starting to come alive again; she was seeing men now and then, and an old college girl friend named Jeanine had moved into the parsonage to live with her. Just at the moment when Jackie started to put things together, Candy started to fall apart. It was a nameless sort of depression, a sense that something was wrong, that perhaps she had chosen the wrong life. "I've done all the things a wife is supposed to," she would tell Jackie. "The house, the kids, the fancy meals. And then one day I wake up and I say, 'Where's the payback?' And it isn't there." For the first time, Candy started talking to Jackie frankly about extramarital affairs. Candy had it all figured out. She wanted sex without any emotional commitment. She wanted sex on her terms. She wanted sex that wouldn't interfere in any way with her marriage or home life. She wanted sex better than any she had ever had before—the kind women have in Gothic romances, with fireworks and the earth moving and the total loss of control. Jackie didn't take Candy's intentions lightly; she agonized over exactly what to say, and finally said that as a minister she couldn't condone it, but it was a decision that Candy would have to make on her own. Most of her warnings were to the effect that "something bad will come of it." She encouraged Candy to talk to Jeanine, who had once had an affair herself and had a healthy perspective on the matter. Candy did talk to Jeanine. Afterwards Jackie asked Jeanine what had happened.

"There's nothing I can tell her," said Jeanine. "She's already made up her mind."

Shortly thereafter, Candy decided to join the church volleyball team even though Pat didn't intend to play that fall.

10 · CROWDED PEWS

There were no prayers spoken for Betty Gore that Sunday at Lucas Methodist, and yet her death was the one inescapable fact of the day. Perhaps the Reverend Ron Adams thought it indelicate to lead the mourning for a woman who had openly despised him; perhaps he felt embarrassed by the fact that the Gores had abandoned the church several weeks before. At any rate, there was no real need to announce the fearful news. That morning the Dallas newspapers had given the first full accounts of the case, sketchy though details were at the time. The chilling words "ax murder" made certain the news would appear on the front page, complete with lurid approximations of what the body must have looked like. "Think of yourself lying on your back and someone smashing an ax through your head three times," Justice of the Peace Buddy Newton told one reporter. Then, for emphasis, he added, "She was damn near dismembered." It was too sudden and too enormous a crime to be fully real yet. Mostly it was fuel for ghastly speculation. The killer, after all, was "still out there," and it was the kind of thing that could "happen to anybody." One of the newspapers had surmised that the murderer "calmly took a shower" before leaving the Gore home, judging by the blood samples found in the bathroom. The television reports of the crime, which received prominent attention Saturday night on the four Dallas stations, suggested psychotic behavior or worse. The shaded lanes of rural Collin County were not accustomed to such images, and people were suddenly frightened. There had been a run on heavy door locks that weekend, and locksmiths were working overtime to handle the demand for instant installation.

Later no one would be able to remember the sermon of

115

that Sunday morning, not even the man who gave it, for the congregation was stunned to the point of being comatose. They were all like Candy Montgomery, who arrived at church early that morning to teach a Sunday School class, sat solemnly through the services, and then loitered afterwards in the foyer of the sanctuary, chatting concernedly with the other congregants to find out who knew what.

Don Crowder probably wouldn't have noticed Candy if she hadn't sought him out. After the church service, Don stood on the sidewalk outside and rambled on and on about his theories of "the murder" to anyone within listening range. As the church's sole lawyer, he considered it his prerogative, even though Don had never tried a criminal case in his life and had no intention of doing so. Don was one of the church's chief supporters, not because he was a particularly religious man (he would often bolt from the sanctuary early if the Dallas Cowboys were on television that day), but because he loved the little town of Lucas and thought a strong church made for a strong town. He was also the most garrulous member of the church, with a talent for nonstop speaking that served him well on this day.

Oddly enough, Don told his audience, he had been leaving the movie *The Shining* when he first heard about Betty's death. It was Saturday afternoon, and his family had decided to go to see the film on the way home from the boys' track meet. On the way out of the theater, Don's wife had stopped to call the baby sitter at home and reported back the shocking news. All the way home and for the rest of the day, Don had gone on and on about the case. He had known Betty casually, through the church, but that was not what interested him. It was the weapon: such a crude, strange, terrifying weapon. "It had to be a drifter, a transient," he kept telling his family. "How else would you have a weapon like an ax? During the day? In Wylie? Yeah, it had to be a drifter."

Continuing his speculation at church the next morning, he had made a few adjustments—it had to be a big man, he had decided, and it was probably either a sex criminal or a burglar caught in the act—but he was still holding to his original assessment. It was a "drifter." Whoever it was was probably a thousand miles away by now.

Just as Don was explaining how they'd probably never find the killer, Candy Montgomery walked up to him.

"Can I talk to you?" she asked, indicating that she wanted to see him alone.

"Sure." Don noticed that she seemed a little distracted.

Candy led Don out to the gravel parking lot. As they walked, she said, "I guess you know about Betty."

Don started to explain his "drifter" theory all over again, but Candy stopped him. "I guess you know I was there that morning," she said. "I was probably the last one to see her alive."

"Yeah, whoever it was couldn't have been from around here, or he wouldn't have tried a crime like that in the middle . . ."

Candy broke in abruptly with an urgent tone in her voice. "Don, I'm supposed to go talk to the police this afternoon. Is there any reason I should be worried?"

"Shoot, no," said Don. "That's just routine stuff. Whoever did that had to be a very big man."

"You don't think I'm a suspect?"

"No way, Candy, they talk to *everybody* in a case like this. You just tell 'em whatever they want to know. Tell 'em everything. You got nothing to worry about."

It was another scorching hot day, almost a hundred degrees, and Don didn't like standing out in a gravel parking lot wearing a coat and tie. Even though he would have liked to discuss his "drifter" theory some more, he started thinking about how he wanted to strip off his clothes and lie by his pool the rest of the day.

"You got nothing to worry about, Candy," he said. And with that he ended the conversation, called his family over to his brand-new black El Dorado, and drove away. Candy felt comforted by the advice, brief as it was, and began looking around for Pat and the kids. She had to get home to cook dinner.

11 · FATHER'S DAY

Father's Day was duly celebrated each year in the Montgomery household, and despite the aura of gloom surrounding Betty's death, Candy was determined to make June 15 a festive occasion. When Pat woke up that morning, he had been greeted downstairs with the cards everyone had picked out for him on Friday at Wal-Mart. Then after church, Pat's seventy-seven-year-old father, Jewel, came by the house with his lady friend, Ima Jean, and they all had a lavish Sunday dinner together. Normally Jewel was not a very talkative man, but when Pat told him about the death of Betty, he went on for some time about old murder cases he was familiar with from his days back in Cleburne, Texas. After dinner, everybody except Candy went into the living room to play dominoes and "visit." It was a drowsy, leisurely afternoon, until Candy came downstairs to announce she was on her way to the Wylie Police Department.

Pat was a little startled when he looked up from the domino table. Candy was stunning. She had been dressed up for church that morning, but now she had changed from those clothes and was even more elegant. She was wearing a black blouse over a white skirt with thin black stripes in it, a pair of stylish high heels, and dark nylon stockings. Pat thought it unusual for her to be so formal, but all he said was, "Are you sure you don't want me to go with you?"

"No, I can drive myself. They said it shouldn't take long."

Candy was cool and collected by the time she arrived at the squat off-white building that serves as headquarters for the four-man police force of Wylie. That's more than could be said for Royce Abbott, the veteran cop who greeted her. Chief Abbott hadn't gotten much sleep that weekend. Friday night he'd been the second officer on the scene. He'd handled the initial investigation, stayed there with Dr. Stone through the nitty-gritty of the evidence-gathering, and then been up early Saturday morning to organize a door-to-door canvass of the entire southeast end of Wylie, looking for witnesses. Since the evidence was being analyzed at the forensic labs in Dallas and the autopsy was still not complete, all the investigators had were theories. They'd ruled out robbery, since an officer had found a twenty-dollar bill on Betty's dresser, but they hadn't ruled out the possibility of a sex crime or a psycho killing—as Abbott had said when he first saw the body, "one of them cult deals."

By late Saturday, for all their work and questioning, the only thing they had come up with was the testimony of a five-year-old child who said she'd seen a woman come out of the Gore home on Friday morning, get into a station wagon, and drive off. Shortly thereafter, the girl had gone to the home, knocked, and gotten no answer. It had disturbed her, she said, because she could hear the baby crying inside. Abbott thought he already knew who the woman was: Candy Montgomery. He knew she had been there from talking to Allan Gore on the phone at the crime scene. Abbott knew he had to talk to Candy Montgomery anyway, because she was apparently the last person to see Betty alive. And by Sunday afternoon, with most of the obvious leads already exhausted, Abbott had decided that Candy Montgomery was his best shot. Maybe he would be able to trigger something in her memory. Maybe she could remember something suspicious about the house, or about Betty's frame of mind that morning. Abbott was experienced enough to know that criminals who aren't caught soon after the crime frequently aren't caught at all—and two full days had already elapsed since Betty Gore was killed. He was smart enough, too, to know that he needed help. Joining him for the interview of Candy Montgomery were Steve Deffibaugh, the Collin County Sheriff's investigator who had taken all the crime-scene photographs, and Jim Cochran, a distinguished grey-haired gentleman who was a criminal intelligence agent for the Texas Department of Public Safety, the state version of the FBI.

The woman who sat before the three investigators, all wedged into Abbott's tiny office, seemed intelligent, unruffled, and not much affected by the death of her friend. They couldn't have known that she was a little more reserved than usual, nor could they have known the two questions she feared most.

"Mrs. Montgomery, we want to know *anything* you can tell us about your visit to the Gore home on Friday," said Abbott. "Anything or anybody you saw that might be suspicious."

Candy Montgomery's facial muscles never changed one iota from their expression of cool politeness, but inwardly she relaxed. "Okay, I want to do anything I can to help."

"Why did you go to see Mrs. Gore on Friday?"

"I had been keeping Alisa, their daughter, because she and my daughter spent the night at our house the night before. Then that morning the kids decided they wanted Alisa to stay over another night, and I told them I would check with Betty to see if it was okay. But then I had to go to Betty's anyway, because, if Alisa *was* going to stay over, then I had to get her swimsuit so we could take her to her lesson that afternoon."

"How old is the child?"

"Alisa is six."

"And you were keeping her while Mr. Gore was out of town?"

"I didn't know he was out of town, but I found out later that he was when he called me Friday night. He was in Minnesota."

"And how long had you been keeping the Gore child?"

"We picked her up on Thursday afternoon."

"And was Mr. Gore gone at that time?"

"I don't know. I don't think so. He wasn't at home, but it was in the afternoon and he wouldn't have been home from work."

As the questions continued, Candy grew more relaxed. She crossed her legs, confident that her dark nylons covered the bruises on her legs. Her high heels had open toes, but the black part of her stockings obscured the bandage on her middle toe. Inexplicably, the toe began to throb again.

"All right. Now we want to know everything you did and everybody you saw on Friday morning."

Candy patiently repeated the events of June 13, beginning with Vacation Bible School at nine that morning and continuing through the harrowing phone conversations with Allan Gore late that night. The officers frequently interrupted to get precise times, places, descriptions of objects, and the like. But nothing in Candy Montgomery's day seemed out of the ordinary. She had taken the kids to Bible School, then left the church about 9:45, arriving at Betty's around ten. Betty was drinking coffee and sewing something out of yellow material when Candy arrived, but she put everything aside so they could chat and discuss what to do with the children. After a time the two women went outside and played with the Gores' two dogs, and at one point Candy excused herself and went into the bathroom to "pick" her hair. (She had a new permanent which made her hair frizzy, in the then-stylish Anne Murray look.) Candy told Betty about her new business, a wallpapering and painting service she was starting with her girlfriend Sherry Cleckler, and she left one of her business cards on Betty's coffee table. Then, near the end of the visit, she went into the utility room to get Alisa's swimsuit while Betty got a towel. Betty also gave Candy some peppermint candy, with instructions to give it to Alisa if she put her head underwater at the swimming lesson. The entire visit, Candy said, took perhaps fifteen minutes. At one point Abbott stopped her to ask what Candy was wearing.

"I was wearing a burgundy blouse and blue jeans."

"What about shoes? We've picked up some footprints in the hallway," he said, "and we need to screen the prints of people we know were in the house. Can you give me a description of the shoes you were wearing that day?"

"They were blue tennis shoes."

"Rubber soles?"

"Yes."

"Do you have the shoes?"

"Not with me, but I can get them for you. Just let me know when, and I'll bring them to you."

"Yes, we may need those to check against our prints."

They dropped that line of questioning and moved on. Candy couldn't believe the first question had come and gone so easily.

The rest of her day seemed equally uneventful to the attentive policemen. After leaving Betty's, she had driven to the Target discount store in Plano to purchase Father's Day cards. But once there she looked at her watch and discovered it had stopped, since it still registered 10:15. So she asked someone for the time and was told it was 11:10, meaning she was already late for the Vacation Bible School program. She drove straight to the church, arriving at 11:30 for a luncheon. Later she took the kids to Wal-Mart in Allen to buy the cards, drove Alisa to her swimming lesson, attended *The Empire Strikes Back* with Pat and the kids, and didn't suspect anything was wrong until Allan Gore started calling her at about 8:30 that night.

Nothing out of the ordinary, not a single minute unaccounted for, and apparently no help to the police. The interview went on for about an hour and a half, but most of it was taken up with minor details and general background.

As the interview drew to a close, Deffibaugh tentatively suggested another meeting. "Sometimes hypnosis helps a person to remember more in cases like this," he said. "Would you be willing to submit to hypnosis in order to find out whether you remember anything you haven't told us here today?"

"Sure, fine," said Candy. "I want to do anything I can to help you. You call me at any time and I'll meet you anywhere you say."

"Good, thank you for coming down, you've been very helpful."

By the time Candy arrived home she was feeling much better.

"I just called the police station to find out what was going on," said Pat. "I couldn't imagine why it was taking so long."

"They just had a lot of questions," she said. "They don't know anything at all."

"They don't have any suspects?"

"I don't think so."

"What did they want to know?"

"Whether I remembered anything, saw anything suspicious—things like that. But . . . Pat?"

"Yes."

"I lied to them."

"What?"

"I didn't mean to, but they asked me where I was at a certain time, and I forgot and told them the wrong thing."

"Where were you?"

"It was when I went to Target on Friday. I'm not sure I told them the right time."

"I'm sure it doesn't matter."

But Candy Montgomery's temporary anxiety about the time discrepancy in her story paled next to her great relief. The police had never asked her the second question. They had never asked her why the fingernail on the little finger of her left hand was cut to the quick.

She felt so much better that she picked up the phone and called her parents in Augusta, Georgia. She wanted to wish her dad a happy Father's Day.

12 · PRAYERS AND OMENS

The Pomeroys had left for Dallas at dawn, the men of the family hovering nervously around Bertha to make sure she held up under the strain. But at the little Methodist church of Norwich, Kansas, where Betty Gore had spent most of her youth, the Reverend David Smith looked out on a sea of tear-stained faces as he led the prayers of mourning. There wasn't a soul in Norwich who hadn't known Betty; most of them remembered her as a fresh-faced homecoming sweetheart, or an energetic Y-Teen organizer, or simply as the girl who was always around and always welcome, liked by older people and her own generation alike. It was a vision tempered by the passage of time—most of them hadn't seen Betty, except on brief visits, since she was eighteen—and idealized by the suddenness of the tragedy. But the genuineness of the mourning was never in doubt; since the news first became known on Saturday morning, half the town had visited the Pomeroy house, bearing food and offering sympathy. Betty was more than the "quiet, pleasant woman" she was being called in the Dallas newspapers. Here, where she grew up, she was the one so bright and talented that the town couldn't hold her. She was the one who went to college, started a career, married well, and, by all appearances, was thriving in the city. No one could yet comprehend what had happened.

Ronnie, the oldest child now, was making most of the decisions by the time the family departed for Dallas. He and his father conferred briefly about which car to take—they decided on Bertha's Oldsmobile, since it was bigger—and then they set out for the interstate highway some thirty miles to the east. Ronnie's wife Pat came along, too, as well as the youngest Pomeroy child, Richard, and now that the family was alone and together, they were able to speak, if only haltingly, about the crime.

"I guess it was a crazy man," said Ronnie.

"Must've been," said Bob, "but I still just can't understand it."

Bertha remained silent, alone with her thoughts, staring at the white line or the furrows of ripe wheat alongside the roadside. It was harvest time, when she usually busied herself with cooking for the men, but she couldn't focus on the present. Her silence was the most disturbing aspect of the long drive to Texas, for she was the talkative one in the family; the quiet was palpable and painful to everyone else in the car. Bertha thought back to Oklahoma, growing up in Claremore, among wheat fields that didn't look much different from these, and she thought of the year before she met Bob Pomeroy, the year she was thirteen and went to the palm reader with her friends. "You're going to marry a farmer," the old woman had said. "He's going to be from out of state. You'll have three children, and one of them will die."

The memory gave Bertha a jolt; she withdrew even further into herself. Just as Bob was pulling the car onto Interstate 35, he lost power and coasted to a stop. The engine was dead. It would be another hour before Bob was able to flag down a passing motorist, ride to a station, and get the car repaired. The sun was fairly high up in the sky by the time they passed into Oklahoma, but the car remained swallowed in gloom.

They rode into Wylie in early afternoon, with the persistent heat nudging into the upper nineties, and found a dozen or so cars parked on Dogwood in front of the familiar little brick house. Those would be the after-church visitors. Almost as soon as they entered the house, they felt uncomfortable and left out. Unaccustomed to being among strangers, Bob and Bertha waited for people to introduce themselves. Several of the women from the churches in Lucas and Wylie had consoling words for Bertha, but the men seemed more withdrawn. The boys tried to talk to Allan, but he seemed oddly detached, almost as out of place as they were. Alisa was there, and seemed subdued but normal, as though the reality of her mother's death hadn't set in yet. But most disturbing of all, at least to Bob, was the behavior of little Bethany. She had always been an outgoing baby, gregarious even among strangers, but today she was scared and skittish; Allan had to hold her at all times or she would begin to cry. Bob knew the baby had been traumatized by being left alone all day, but he began to suspect there was more to the story he didn't understand.

There was an artificial feeling to the whole afternoon. Everyone felt like an intruder in a group that didn't really exist but was created for the occasion. Certainly Betty had had friends unknown to her family—women from church, from the Marriage Encounter group she so strongly believed in, from school—but most of them didn't seem to know one another. There were also police officers present, shuffling in and out, asking people their names and their relationship to Betty. Two of them identified themselves as Texas Rangers, members of the elite plain-clothes unit that for 150 years has been authorized to enter cases deemed beyond the resources of local police units. Their presence indicated that Betty's murder was growing in importance by the hour; the Rangers invested their time in only a handful of murder cases each year. At one point that afternoon Bob stopped one of the Rangers and asked about the investigation. The officer said, "There's nothing we can tell you at this time." Bob was perplexed; there seemed to be no rhyme nor reason to anything that was happening.

All afternoon Bob stared at the closed door to the utility room, wondering if he would be able to go in. He knew he had to look in there; if anyone in the family had to, it was his job. It took him a couple of hours to summon the courage, but he finally edged over to the door and opened it. It had been cleaned up by the neighbors, of course, but he saw the black squares in the floor where the police had lifted part of the linoleum, the hacking marks on the white freezer door, the doors without doorknobs, and he began to realize the immensity of the suffering. Involuntarily, resisting the image even as it came to him, he could see his daughter, spread out, prone, on the floor of the room. He started to feel sick and closed the door, afraid to break down as he had the day before.

Later that afternoon the phone calls began. Richard answered the first one.

It was a male voice. "I killed her," the man said.

Richard was stunned. Before he could say or do anything, the man hung up. Richard sat in the kitchen, alone, wondering what to do next. He didn't want to place any more burdens on his parents.

A few moments passed, and the phone rang again. He picked it up, more hesitantly this time.

"I killed her," the voice said, "and if you don't keep your daughter off the street I'll kill her and rape her, too."

This time Richard was really shaken up, so he asked his father to come into the room with him. Bob told one of the policemen in the house, and after a brief conference, the family decided that for the rest of the day, older brother Ronnie would answer the phone, since he was a fairly smooth talker and might be able to hold the caller long enough for the police to trace the call.

The man called twice more. His refrain was the same. "I killed her and now I'm going to kill the kid," he kept saying. On the second call, Ronnie was able to engage him in conversation.

"I really didn't do it," he said at one point. "But my girlfriend did and I know where she is."

The caller stayed on just long enough for the police to get a trace, and within minutes a patrol car had been dispatched to the address of the originating telephone. It was not until later that night that the Pomeroys learned the source: it had been a recently released mental patient, calling from a halfway house. They were continuing to question the man, but it seemed highly unlikely that he was the killer. Somehow the news that the man was sick didn't do much to soothe Bob Pomeroy's addled nerves.

The next day brought more of the same chaos. Monday had been set as the day of the memorial service, and every newspaper and television station within a forty-mile radius had heard about it. Many of the reporters had set up a vigil on Dogwood Street, outside the Gore home, anxious to have their cameras poised when the grieving family members emerged to travel across town to the United Methodist Church of Wylie. The morning newspapers had reported the first arrest of a suspect—a bearded, long-haired drifter who had had too much to drink in a Dallas bar and started talking about how he had to get out of town because "they found that woman." A panicky waitress notified the police, who arrested him for public intoxication. After a search of the fellow's orange backpack, though, all they found that might link him to the crime was a pair of "thongs," rubber-soled sandals of the type suspected to have caused the bloody footprints. But the man's thongs were too large to have made the prints. He was dried out and released. Another Dallas newspaper had interviewed a couple in Wylie who went to sleep Saturday night with loaded guns at their bedside, still frightened by the possibility of a maniac on the loose. Tim Jarrell, a reporter for the *Dallas Times Herald*, put his finger on the reason for the continuing hysteria: "There was no apparent reason for the attack. Residents speculate and hope that instead of picking the Gore house at random, the killer had a grudge or some particular reason to choose Mrs. Gore as a victim." It was the first murder in Wylie in twenty-five years. It was committed with a terrifying weapon, against an apparently nonviolent, innocent woman, while she was in her own home, in a nice neighborhood, in the middle of the day. And even though no medical details had yet been released to the public, it was obvious from the few eyewitnesses to the body that Betty Gore had been brutally hacked far beyond what would be necessary to kill her. It was the kind of macabre crime that holds an irresistible fascination for the press and public.

Bob Pomeroy, growing more uneasy by the minute, understood none of this. He didn't understand why the reporters would want photographs of him every time he left the house. He didn't understand why Allan's neighbors would talk to the newspapers, as though they were proud of their grisly knowledge. He didn't understand why many of the people who came by the house didn't seem to know Betty that well. Bob Pomeroy had a lifelong respect for the law and the police, but he didn't understand why the officers wouldn't sit down and talk to him, as though maybe even *he* were guilty of something. Bob began to suspect that he knew much less about his daughter's life than he thought he had known, but for the time being he simply felt left out. In a fit of anger, he called the Wylie police and asked them to clear the reporters off Dogwood Street. When they complied, he felt better for a few minutes.

Allan remained aloof and silent for the most part, though inwardly he felt comforted by the constant buzz of conversation, the steady procession of people through the house, the certainty that he wouldn't have to spend another night alone. Saturday night had been difficult; he had finally called Dick Sewell, the dentist, to get a tranquilizer so he could sleep. Chief Abbott had come by the house sometime during the weekend and told him they were still processing the physical evidence. "We definitely do not think it was a prowler," he had said. Allan had thought that an odd thing to say at the time, but then he didn't think much more about it. He was wondering about other things. He was wondering whether he would forget what Betty's face looked like. He was wondering how she felt at the moment she died. He was wondering whether Alisa would break down later; she was taking everything so well that it almost scared him. Sunday night had been easier; the house was full, with Ronnie and his wife Pat sleeping on the floor in the living room. When he woke up Monday morning, he wasn't feeling quite so empty inside. When the phone rang later in the day he instinctively picked it up.

"Alisa's next," said the caller, and hung up.

The children's names had been in the newspaper. But Allan was too drained to be angry or scared. He calmly reported the call to the police.

According to the immemorial custom of the Southwest, formal sympathy was invariably expressed at mealtime. Within hours of the first reports of Betty's death, all the organizations to which Allan and Betty had ever expressed allegiance had begun to organize cooking assignments. The Wylie neighbors had made sure that Allan had covered dishes waiting when he returned from St. Paul. Then, on Saturday evening, members of Wylie Methodist Church had come by the house bearing a many-course dinner. Now all the other groups, supervised by whatever person seems to materialize at times like that to engineer the fine details of feeding the grieving, were working in shifts. And for the noon meal on Monday, just prior to the afternoon memorial service, Allan knew that members of the church at Lucas would be coming by. The thought didn't make him entirely comfortable, since Betty had quarrelled repeatedly with Ron Adams, the young minister at Lucas, and since Allan hadn't seen many of his old church friends in several months. Betty had loved the Lucas church, but her dissatisfaction with the new pastor ran so deep that the only times she would attend services were when Ron was out of town for some reason. Now, in a final awkward irony, it was the same man who would officiate at her memorial service later that day. It was unavoidable: the Wylie minister had been called out of town.

The only person from Lucas church whom Allan really wanted to see that day was Candy Montgomery. He couldn't think of anyone who knew him better or would be more comforting at such a time. He picked up the phone and called her.

"Candy, I was getting a little nervous wondering about who's going to bring the food today. Do you know who's going to be handling it?"

"As a matter of fact, Allan, I was just about to call you. Barbara Green just called and said the person who was supposed to help her with the food can't do it, so could I?"

"Oh, good, that makes me feel much better."

"And she also wanted me to ask you whether you would like us to stay when we bring the food or just drop off the food and leave the family alone."

"Please stay, just for a little while. I think I'd like having you here."

Candy was relieved and a little anxious at the same time. She was relieved to be able to do *anything* for Allan that might make him feel better, but she was filled with foreboding at the idea of meeting Betty's family. There was another thought gnawing away at her, too, but at such a deep unconscious level that she pretended it wasn't there: she wasn't sure what would happen when she reentered Betty's house.

It was not nearly as bad as she expected, though, perhaps because they were surrounded by people as soon as they went inside. Barbara Green was more nervous than Candy. Barbara was a good friend, and one of her most appealing qualities was a sensitivity to the feelings of others. She couldn't stand to see suffering; in this case, it was almost too much for her. Barbara was also a sheltered person in some ways, unable or unwilling to comprehend how something so awful could happen to someone like Betty. During the drive down to Wylie, she had turned to Candy and said, "I'm just so glad that you weren't in the house, too."

"What?"

"You and Alisa could have been there, too, when Betty was killed. Thank God for that."

Now Barbara seemed a little tense as Allan introduced the two women to all the members of Betty's family. Candy and Barbara didn't stay to chat, but went straight into the kitchen with the food and started putting it away. They worked silently for a while, only stopping to ask Allan questions about what the family might like to eat that night, and then Barbara paused.

"Candy, some of this food has to be put in the freezer," she said, "and I'm afraid I can't go into that utility room."

Candy felt an involuntary chill. She had avoided thinking of it until then. She had averted her eyes from the moment they entered the house. She hadn't even looked at the firmly closed door.

"Would you mind taking the food in?" Barbara said.

Candy knew Barbara was seriously upset.

"Okay," she said weakly.

Candy steeled herself, cradled a couple of Tupperware dishes in her left arm, and opened the utility room door. But as soon as she took her first step, she heard the wild, frenzied sound of mad dogs. She froze; a horrible image momentarily flashed through her mind, and then she turned and looked toward the far end of the room. There she saw the window. She had forgotten, but now it came back to her. There was a window that, due to the uneven slope of the lot, came within a foot and a half of ground level in the backyard. The curtains on the window usually remained open, as they were now, and on the other side of the pane she could see Betty's two cocker spaniels, rearing and jumping and incessantly barking, as though they were engaged in a death battle. At the same time an unpleasant odor swelled into her nostrils, an odor of something sickly sweet and inescapable and wretched. Candy clenched her teeth. She felt naked and alone and wondered whether she should turn and go back to the kitchen.

"Don't worry about those dogs."

The voice came from the adjoining living room. It was Betty's mother, trying to soothe Candy's nerves. "Anytime anyone goes in that room, the dogs bark like that," she said. "They'll quit in a minute."

Candy hurriedly opened the freezer door and made room for the dishes. Her heart was racing.

"Thank you for doing that," said Barbara when she returned.

The church services were to be at two that day, and Allan asked Barbara and Candy to stay with him until then. So the two women sat in the living room and talked about nothing in particular, and even Bertha seemed to perk up a little. She liked both visitors; Barbara and Candy were concerned and comforting and completely gracious. Bertha especially liked Candy's ease among strangers, which was much like her own. Candy didn't say much, but she got up periodically to take care of the dirty dishes and other minor household chores.

"Aren't dishwashers wonderful?" Candy said at one point as she returned to the living room. "I just don't know how I'd get along without one."

"Not me," said Bertha. "I never did ever want one. Some of my fondest times were washing the dishes with Betty after we'd have supper."

It was one of the few times that Bertha was able to talk about Betty at all.

It was odd, but true, that the most nervous person at the memorial service for Betty Gore was the minister who conducted it, Ron Adams. Ron had not particularly liked Betty, not least because she detested him. There was no sense in saying anything about that now, but it had to be in the back of the minds of those who were close to Lucas church. Ron was only there because he was still technically Betty's minister, and because there was no one else to conduct the service. But the service was difficult for him in another way, too. Ron was only twenty-five years old, just starting his ministerial career, and he found nothing in his training to prepare himself for the enormity of these duties. He knew how to conduct a funeral, but he didn't know how to deal with such a horrible death. On Sunday night he had worked a long time on his sermon, afraid that many people would want to treat Betty's death as evidence that God was indifferent or cruel. Ron understood the feeling; he could hardly accept the killing himself. He didn't understand how such a senseless murder could truly be God's will, but he was determined to be comforting to others even though he had no good explanation for them. The hardest part was finding words to describe Betty. "Loving mother," "faithful wife," "committed person of faith"—these were the proper things to say, and he would say them.

Bob Pomeroy had heard his daughter complain about Ron Adams, but as soon as the service began he could tell that this was a different man. Even Ron's own parishioners were surprised. To the 250 people crowded into the little Methodist church off the main street of Wylie, Ron was strong and authoritative and comforting. Normally Ron was a terrible public speaker, slurring his phrases and staring down at his text and occasionally interjecting an "uh" or an "ah" at the most inopportune times. But today he was transformed, as though the tragedy had forced him to grow up overnight. Afterwards none of Betty's friends complained, as expected, that Ron was chosen to lead the service. His voice had been resonant, his prayers deeply affecting.

"How can a thing like this happen?" Ron had said at one

point in his funeral sermon. "How can it happen to a person who is so needed by her family? A mother so needed by her children, a daughter so loved by her parents? . . . Why do things like this happen?

"When death comes by some more normal method, whether organic, by aging, or even accident, it is difficult enough, but an act of violence seems simply incomprehensible. No one has the answers to all the questions of life. . . . Perhaps there will be those who look to God and say that He has some eternal purpose in all this. But surely we can't accept that notion. The notion that God would 'will' something like this upon anyone is intolerable. God does not will evil on His people in this fashion. . . . Occasionally His will becomes *thwarted* by the actions and behavior of humanity which He has elected not to intervene in the processes of. When things like this happen His will and purposes then change to His ultimate will, so that as Paul puts it, 'everything works to the good, to them that love God.'"

One person who heard Ron's words, and would never forget them, was Candy Montgomery. She and Pat sat together near the Pomeroy family, and Pat was so overcome by the sermon that he started to cry, grasping Candy's hands for support. Candy was red-eyed but she never broke down; she was stiff and remote, still thinking about what Ron had said. The act was "unnatural." It was not God's will. It was evil.

Everyone had trouble getting out of the church because of the TV reporters outside, with their minicams and mobile vans. The police were there, too, snapping pictures as people emerged from the sanctuary and recording the numbers on license plates. A group of women joined hands in a circle on the church steps and said a prayer for Betty. Ronnie Pomeroy got so infuriated by one of the TV cameramen that he intentionally backed into the lens of the camera to black it out, causing a brief commotion. Everyone was on edge anyway, especially when they realized that the police were looking for the killer *at the church*. Two sheriff's deputies shielded Allan and the Pomeroys from reporters and then helped them into the car. Shortly before they drove away, Candy Montgomery approached Bertha Pomeroy and offered one last word of consolation.

"I just wish there was something I could do for you," she said.

13 · SECRETS

Friday, June 13, was not a good day to be poor and alone in the vicinity of Dallas. Once the newspapers and radio and television stations had latched onto the story—it was quickly becoming *the* murder case of the year—it was open season on every mental patient, drug addict, or lowlife petty criminal who happened to have been seen by the wrong person or noticed in the wrong place on the day of the crime. Chief Abbott had been devoid of leads on Saturday; by Monday he was swimming in a sea of names, addresses, times, descriptions, and amateur theories, and his phone was still ringing at the rate of once every minute. In Denison, some fifty miles to the north, someone reported a female hitchhiker dressed in blue jeans, halter top, leather vest, and sandals who showed up at Rusty's Paint and Body Shop with dried blood on her vest and feet. A state police officer spent a full day tracing the woman's movements—only to discover that she had been seen by several other people, all of whom noticed no blood. A mental patient in Dallas wanted to confess to the crime, until an officer determined that he had been confined at Parkland Hospital at the time of the killing. A local justice of the peace called to report a strange man following him around and taking his picture; he had to be told that the "strange" man was an undercover officer, acting under orders to take everyone's picture at the memorial service for Betty Gore. Another informant called to report the exact location of the murderer: Room 151 of a Holiday Inn in Dallas. Two officers investigated, and found that the man had aroused suspicion by walking into the dining room on Friday covered with bruises and abrasions. The injuries had nothing to do with the case; he had simply been beaten up.

The collective law enforcement minds of Collin County felt beaten up, too. Now actively involved in the case were the Wylie Police Department, the Collin County Sheriff's Office, the Dallas Police Department, the Texas Department of Public Safety criminal intelligence division, the Texas Rangers, the Dallas County Sheriff's Office, and the Dallas Institute of Forensic Sciences. Chief Abbott was welcoming one and all, so there were no real battles over jurisdiction, as so often happens when small-town police departments try to deal with big-city crimes. But so far the concentrated manpower hadn't done him much good. Policemen continued to comb the neighborhoods surrounding the Gore house, questioning anyone who might have seen something suspicious on the day of the crime. Others patiently checked out every anonymous phone call, no matter how absurd the tip sounded. With the help of Candy Montgomery and Allan Gore, the investigators had been able to find everyone who had contact with Betty in the twenty-four hours before her death, and they were interviewing those people one by one.

When Dr. Stone had finished his first review of the evidence and surmised that the killer was an acquaintance of Betty, Abbott had considered Allan Gore the prime suspect. It seemed too much of a coincidence that he had left town on the very day she was killed. But then Abbott had checked and rechecked Allan's alibi. Allan did indeed have business in St. Paul. There were coworkers with him at all times that day. Everyone attested to his genuine shock and grief upon hearing of Betty's death. So Abbott returned to square one, looking again for someone who had no acquaintance with Betty but somehow could have gained entry to her house and then, for no apparent reason, decided to kill her. Oddly enough, it was the very brazenness of the crime that made it so difficult to solve; it was a brutally brave act, carried out in daylight, by a killer who cared so little about being caught that he took time to clean himself before leaving and didn't even bother to destroy the evidence. The more they studied the facts, the more the investigators came back to the inescapable conclusion that they were looking for a psychopathic personality.

They were also hoping for help from the lab. Dr. Stone had promised them a preliminary analysis of the physical evidence he had collected at the scene, although no one held out any great hope for clean fingerprints. What they did receive on Monday was almost as interesting, though: an analysis of the clump of hair that Stone had found in the drain of the bathtub. According to the meticulous doctor, there were exactly 175 strands found in the tub. All but four of them matched the hair of Betty Gore. Two of them were animal hairs, probably dog hairs. The last two were "foreign"—not Betty's, but human. This meant very little in the absence of a suspect, but it could eventually mean a lot: hair samples were *almost* as distinctive as fingerprints. (The odds of two strands of hair from different people having the same biological makeup are astronomical. It *is* possible, though, unlike fingerprints, which are never identical.) In the course of an investigation the hair could be used to narrow the field of suspects, and at a trial it could be the physical evidence needed to prove that the suspect was in the house on the day of the crime.

In the absence of any new information, the thing to do was return to first sources. That's what Abbott and his colleagues decided, and that's what they did on the evening of June 16, a few hours after the memorial service, when they called Allan Gore in for a formal interview. Officers had talked to Allan several times over the weekend and learned the essential facts of Betty's last day. They had also thoroughly checked out his trip to St. Paul. But sometimes in the formal setting of a police interview, a man will remember more than he thinks he knows. They would have to get it all on the record sooner or later anyway. Joining Abbott for the interview of Allan Gore were two Texas Rangers—G. W. Burks and Fred Cummings, who had joined the case over the weekend—and Joe Murphy, head of intelligence for the North Texas region of the Department of Public Safety. Murphy was a rough-hewn, burly man who lived in Wylie and had offered to help because, among other reasons, he was afraid there was a crazy man on the loose in his hometown. Murphy was forty-three years old, with a face like a cinder block and a reputation as one of the toughest interrogators in the DPS. He enjoyed being thought of as a mean man, especially by the paid informants who occasionally tried to bluff him.

On the night when Murphy and his three colleagues gathered in the Wylie City Hall conference room to interview Allan Gore (Abbott's office was too small), they were strictly gathering information. They had discussed the possibility that Allan Gore might be "involved" somehow, and they intended to look for a murder motive, but mostly they just wanted to listen to his story in hope of discovering something new.

Captain Burks began the interview by asking Allan to review everything he did on the morning of Betty's death. Allan told them about Betty's depression, caused by her fear of pregnancy and the fact that he was leaving for the weekend. He tried to recall everything that had passed between them at breakfast, and said he left for work with Betty still in a "somber" mood. Burks pursued this line awhile, asking whether Betty was normally afraid of being alone, whether she had had any particular "difficulty" with anyone in Wylie. But Allan said she was not really afraid so much as lonesome, and that the only problems she had ever had were with the students from her sixth-grade class, who disliked her so much that one year they had vandalized the house. Most of the other possible murder motives were eliminated by Allan in a similar manner. Did anyone ever make sexual advances toward Betty? Not that Allan knew of. Was Betty secure about her marriage? At one time she wasn't, but the marriage was "improving" due to a church program they had enrolled in called Marriage Encounter.

Allan continued to describe his day in great detail, stopping to explain how he had called from the airport to give Betty the traveler's check numbers, discussed his anxieties with Sid and Tom, continued to call home from his motel room in St. Paul, and finally convinced the neighbors to break into his house. He reviewed all the conversations he had with Candy Montgomery, and all of his movements up until the time he arrived at Dallas–Fort Worth Airport Saturday morning. When he had finished, Burks was still fishing for possible scenarios. Who were your closest family friends who visited in your home? The real answer was none, but Allan named about six families who had been in the house at one time or another. What went on at these Marriage Encounter meetings? Allan tried to describe how married couples would get together to socialize every two weeks. Any problems with teenagers? Not really. Anbody suspicious who's done yard work or home repairs and might know where you kept the ax? A boy fixed the dryer a while back, but I was with him all the time. Have you noticed anything missing from the house? Nothing that I can tell.

The interview went on for a couple of hours, with Burks unable to elicit anything out of the ordinary, at least nothing they didn't know. Murphy took over the questioning near the end, starting with several technical questions about doors and windows: Would the garage door normally be open? Should the door to the baby's room be closed? Then, on the slight possibility that the medical examiner was wrong and there could be a sexual motive to the crime, he asked whether Allan knew of any time when Betty might have had an affair with another man.

"Yes," said Allan, a little hesitantly. "In 1971. We were living in Las Cruces." He briefly related the one-night stand Betty had had with the college student at New Mexico State, then added, "I don't believe that she's ever had an affair with any other man since then."

"Have you ever had an affair yourself?" asked Murphy.

"No," said Allan.

"Do you have anything else that you might say to help us in this investigation?"

"No, I can't think of anything at this time."

When Allan got home from the station, he was physically and emotionally exhausted, but he still couldn't rest. He had been a little edgy ever since he realized that he was considered a possible suspect by the police. Everyone had told him not to worry, since it was their job to consider *everyone* a suspect, but it made him feel uncomfortable nonetheless. Something else bothered him, too. It was a question Burks asked him about Candy. Burks had wondered, when Allan was describing his phone conversations with Candy on the night the body was discovered, whether she had seemed upset. She had, of course—*very* upset—but Allan still wondered what they were driving at. Was Candy a suspect too? Were they that crazy?

The more Allan considered the implications of his interview, the more worried he became. He *was* the only suspect. Who else could it be? Before going to bed, Allan went into Alisa's bedroom and asked her if she would answer a few questions for him about the Friday morning she spent at Bible School with Jenny and Ian. He had never thought to ask his own daughter what she knew about that day, and neither had the police. All Alisa remembered was that Candy had taken them all to Bible School, stayed for a few minutes, and then left to go to get Alisa's swimsuit.

"When did she come back?" asked Allan.

"Around lunch."

"Do you know why it took so long?"

"No."

"Did she go to the store? Were there packages in the car?"

"No."

Allan was getting scared. He didn't know what it all meant, but he did know it didn't look good for him. He tucked Alisa in and went back to his bedroom, but he didn't sleep again that night. After a while he set his alarm for 5:30, because he'd decided he had a lot of business to take care of before noon the next day. That's when he and the Pomeroys were leaving for Kansas, where Betty was to be buried.

At 6 A.M. on Tuesday, Royce Abbott's phone rang.

"Chief Abbott, this is Allan Gore. I'm calling to tell you that there's one thing I wasn't truthful about last night."

"What's that, Allan?"

"I did have an affair."

"Oh?"

"With Candy Montgomery."

14 · ENCOUNTERS

Candy Montgomery would always be able to remember the precise moment when she decided she would go to bed with Allan Gore. It happened on the church volleyball court. Candy and Allan both tried to make a play on the same ball—and collided. It was a harmless bump, really, and went unnoticed by everyone else on the court, but for Candy it brought a revelation: Allan Gore smelled sexy. When she told her friend Sherry Cleckler about it later, Candy said it was odd but true: before the bump, she hadn't been attracted to Allan at all, but the masculine smell changed her mind. Then again, it wasn't entirely that, since she had been talking abstractly about having an affair for several weeks. She had told Sherry she wanted a sexual escapade, and she had even broached the subject with Jackie Ponder. Candy wanted something to shake up her "*very* boring" life with Pat. She was very explicit about the kind of affair she was interested in: transcendent sex. As she put it to Sherry, "I want fireworks."

Then she bumped into Allan Gore and wondered to herself, "Could a man like that make the earth move?" At first glance he didn't look like it. Allan had a receding hairline, the beginnings of a paunchy midsection, and dressed blandly, to say the least. But in other ways he was the kind of man she might be able to have a good time with. She had known Allan for only nine months, but it seemed much longer. Allan was a lot like her: an activist in the church, a lover of kids, the outgoing, personable half of a mismatched couple. Allan sang in the choir, he helped organize the sports teams, he did all the things that Betty never seemed to want to get involved in. He had a sense of humor. It was only natural that the two of them would see a lot of each other, since they both sang in the choir, and even on a good night there were never more than ten or twelve singers willing to give up their weeknights for rehearsal. More to the point, there was a tiny insistent voice in the back of Candy's brain that kept telling her that Allan Gore was as anxious to go to bed with her as she was with him.

It had begun with little things. Allan seemed to joke with her more than he joked with the other women at church. He teased her about her volleyball skills, and every once in a while he'd give her a sly wink, as though they shared some little secret. After choir practice the two of them would sometimes chat a little longer than necessary, or loiter in the parking lot while the others were getting into their cars. The flirting was subtle. Sometimes it was so much like Allan's natural friendliness with everyone that Candy doubted it was a real flirtation at all. Candy was not exactly a wallflower herself, after all, and sometimes she brought out a playful quality in men that was entirely harmless. But then Allan would do something that was unmistakably designed to get her attention, and she would start wondering all over again. One night during choir practice, Allan made funny faces throughout Candy's solo in an attempt to get her to laugh in the middle of a hymn. Pat thought it was funny. Candy was intrigued. She found herself thinking about Allan at the oddest times—while doing housework, for example, or talking to Sherry about how boring Pat was. She also started fantasizing, as she sometimes did, about sex with the man who smelled so nice. Candy was almost twenty-nine years old and, to be totally honest with herself, sexually frustrated. How many more years did she have in order to find out what she was missing? Not many. She decided to do something about it.

She got her chance one night after choir practice had broken up. Allan had already gone out to the parking lot and was just getting into his car when Candy spotted him. She strode up to the passenger side and opened the door.

"Allan," said Candy, leaning into the car, "I want to talk to you sometime, about something that has been bothering me."

"Oh?" he said. "How about right now?"

Candy slid into the seat beside him. She didn't look at him.

"I've been thinking about you a lot and it's really bothering me and I don't know whether I want you to do anything about it or not."

Allan, a little confused, said nothing.

"I'm very attracted to you and I'm tired of thinking about it and so I wanted to tell you."

And with that, she jumped out of the car, slammed the door, and hurried across the lot.

Allan Gore felt shocked and flattered and a little ridiculous. He wasn't shocked by Candy's directness—he had known her long enough to realize that she spoke exactly what was on her mind—but he was totally nonplussed by the idea of another woman being interested in him *sexually*. He was especially surprised, and secretly pleased, that it was Candy. Even though she didn't have what you would call classic beauty, she was one of the most attractive women in the church, in his opinion, and she was certainly the most fun to be with. Then a wave of doubt overtook him: maybe Candy was just flirting, in her own way, because all she really said was that she had been "thinking" about him. But such an odd way to say it.

Allan thought about Candy a lot over the next few days, and he wondered whether she would say anything else the next time they were together. He kept thinking back over what she had said in the car, and wondered whether that was a signal for him to make the next move. He thought about calling her but then felt silly and awkward. He also thought, a littly guiltily, of how different Candy was from his own wife. Betty was as dour as ever, not only because of her problems at school but because Danny, their rebellious nine-year-old foster child, continued to defy Betty's stern attempts at discipline. Then, as if that weren't enough, Betty had decided that they should go ahead and have their next child. They had agreed to have another baby, but this time Betty wanted it planned down to the exact week, so that it would be born in midsummer and she wouldn't have to take any time off from teaching. This was especially ironic, since the Gores' sex life had dwindled to almost nothing and was completely mechanical when they had sex at all. Now Allan was required to have clinical sex with Betty every night during her peak fertility period, in the name of family planning. He felt a little resentful; he had the distinct feeling he was being used. For the first time, sex had become hard work. This, combined with Betty's usual complaints about minor illnesses, made Allan's marital future look bleak indeed when compared to the bright, happy-go-lucky face of Candy Montgomery, full of promise and, he had to admit, allure. That didn't mean he didn't love Betty, or that he would ever do

anything to hurt her. It just pleased Allan that a woman like
Candy would feel those kinds of emotions for a man like
himself.

A week or so after the choir practice, Allan saw Candy
again. It was the night when the Lucas Methodist volleyball
team acted as referees for the other churches in the league.
That meant that they would be staying afterward to clean up
the gymnasium, and it also meant, Allan knew, that there
would probably be an opportunity for the two of them to talk.
Betty was not feeling well, as usual, and Pat never played
volleyball. The only other person left at the end of the evening
was Barbara Green, Candy's good-natured friend from Montecito. They all walked out to the parking lot together, but
when Barbara got into her car, Allan and Candy continued
walking together, more or less naturally, in the general
direction of Candy's car. As they were talking, Barbara drove
up, stopped, and rolled down her window.

"Are you sure I can trust you two alone?" she said.

They all laughed, and Barbara sped away.

As they watched her leave, Allan said, "Now what was it
you had in mind?"

"Get in," said Candy.

Allan slid into the passenger seat of Candy's car.

"Would you be interested in having an affair?" she asked.

Despite all his mental preparation, Allan wasn't prepared
for something *that* direct.

"I don't know what to say," he said.

"It's just something I've been thinking about and I wanted
to say it so I don't have to think about it anymore."

"I don't think I could, Candy. I don't think it would be a
wise thing to do, because I love Betty. Once when we were
living in New Mexico she had an affair and that hurt me a lot,
and I wouldn't want to do that to her."

Candy was surprised to realize how much Allan had
thought about his answer.

"That's fine, Allan. I love Pat, too. I wouldn't want to do
anything to hurt him, either."

"Betty just got pregnant again, too, and it would be unfair
to her, especially since I don't feel the same way about you that
I do about her. So I probably couldn't do something like that."

"Okay, Allan, I was just putting the option out there
because of how I felt and it's up to you to decide. I don't want

to hurt your marriage. All I wanted to do was go to bed. I won't mention it again."

Allan leaned across the seat and softly kissed Candy's lips. Then he quickly got out of the car and went home.

The fall of 1978 was, it turned out, a crucial time for the little country church. It was continuing to grow, for one thing, to the point where a few of the "old-timers"—those families who had been there more than a year—started to worry that too many people would spoil the church's rustic flavor. The *real* old-timers—the less active farming families who had attended the church for two or three decades—were much less sentimental on that subject. They looked at the influx as a good thing: perhaps the newcomers would put enough into the offering plate to get rid of the drafty old frame building and construct a modern sanctuary. Jackie Ponder was not the type of pastor to become embroiled in a matter like that. All she wanted to do was continue to preach about love and accepting others, and try to bind ever closer what she now called her "family of faith." These people were not only her parishioners; they were the closest friends she had in the world. So she never really expressed an opinion on the sanctuary issue at all; she admitted the church needed a new one, but she agreed with the newcomers, too. She had a special fondness for the creaky old place where she had preached her first sermon.

Then, in October, Jackie came face-to-face with the inevitable: she was offered another ministerial position. On the surface it was a much better job than the little one-horse church in Lucas. She would be in charge of the Wesley Foundation, a Methodist educational arm located on the campus of Midwestern University at Wichita Falls, where she could pursue her teaching ambitions while continuing to minister to the congregation of students and faculty who attended the campus church. The job paid $6,000 more than she was getting at Lucas. The only problem was, she didn't want to leave. She could hardly bear the thought of abandoning the close-knit group of parishioners after only two years. The church was just starting to prosper, and Jackie suspected that she needed the church as much or more than it needed her. She quickly, and peremptorily, turned down the job offer. Candy and a few other close friends learned of it only after it was a moot point.

Candy was one of the main reasons Jackie found it tough

to leave Lucas. Even before Candy's recent obsession—her desire to have an extramarital affair come hell or high water— Jackie had always found her to be one of those few women in whom she could confide absolutely. Candy had been a strong arm to lean on during the difficult days just after Jackie's divorce, and in recent months the roles had been reversed, as Candy confided her dissatisfaction with Pat, and her determination to do something more with her life than simply organize PTA meetings, operate carpools, and teach Sunday School classes. Jackie sympathized with the feeling—the emptiness that comes over a woman when she realizes the man she loves is not enough—even though she didn't entirely agree with Candy's solution. Jackie had always tried not to judge others, no matter what, and this situation was no different. She did caution Candy to think about the consequences, especially the effect an affair might have on Pat.

"Pat has already passed up the best I have to offer," said Candy, a little defensively.

Jackie decided to leave her alone.

In November, one of Jackie's fellow ministers called to discuss the Wesley Foundation job again. He was very frank.

"You're making a mistake not to take this job," he said. "This is a big opportunity for you and a step up the ladder, and the bishop doesn't make offers like this every day. This is your next calling. I don't think you can afford to ignore it."

Jackie's rational self had been telling her the same thing, even though emotionally she wanted to remain in the warm environment of Lucas. For one thing, she thought a new minister at Lucas would be able to carry out a major building program, something that the church needed but that she felt helpless to handle herself. She thought about what her friend had said and one day told Candy that she thought she was going to accept the job after all. The two women cried together over her change of heart.

"But it's probably for the best," said Candy. "If you stayed, we'd all just keep playing and not get anything done. The church does need a new sanctuary."

It was December before all the arrangements were made and Jackie left for Wichita Falls. Before she did, Candy impishly mentioned one day that "the affair" had begun. She wouldn't say who the man was, but she seemed ecstatic that it was finally happening. Candy was incredibly detailed about everything; there were secret lunches and little gifts and a few accounts of matters so intimate that even Jackie was a little embarrassed.

"The best thing about it is that both of us have agreed not to get romantically involved," said Candy.

Jackie tried to temper Candy's enthusiasm by reminding her once more of the possible price if Pat were to find out, but Candy seemed to think there was absolutely no possibility of that happening.

On the day Jackie left Lucas, Candy came to the parsonage with a painting of a butterfly. She had done it herself. On the back she had written:

> At last your spirit is free to soar.
> I love you Jackie,
> and you know the best is yet to come.
> Candy

One thing Allan Gore always believed in was that marriages are forever. That's why, when his sexual relations with Betty started to become routine and unimaginative, he cast about for explanations. He enjoyed sex, and he knew that Betty did, too, and there was nothing wrong with them when they were happy and untroubled and together. But lately there was not much enthusiasm in the bedroom. Allan was working hard, even though he didn't travel any longer because of Betty's fear of being alone. Betty frequently came home full of tension from her day at school, and she would sometimes spend most of the evening grading papers for the next day's classes. When you don't spend a lot of time together in the evening, Allan thought, there's usually not much interest in spending a lot of time in bed, either. Allan was afraid they were in danger of falling victim to complete boredom.

One solution Allan considered briefly was a program called Marriage Encounter. Shortly after the five dissatisfied couples transferred their church membership from Briarwood to Lucas, JoAnn and Richard Garlington had gone to a Dallas motel one weekend for a special session in which they talked about their marriage and tried to strengthen their commitment. Allan didn't understand exactly what went on, but he knew that the Garlingtons came back beaming and almost absurdly joyous. They said they were "hooked" on Marriage Encounter and immediately set about trying to get other couples to join. Some of the older church members were put off by the proselytizing. Even though the Garlingtons insisted that Marriage Encounter was only for good marriages, not troubled ones, many people considered it a little presumptuous to be told they needed to go somewhere and be taught how to "communicate" with their spouses. If it had been anyone else but Richard and JoAnn, Allan would have mistrusted it himself, especially since Richard wouldn't tell him exactly what happened during the Marriage Encounter weekend. "You won't understand it unless you go experience it for yourself," Richard said. Allan had to admit that the Garlingtons *seemed* to be happier in the months since they were "encountered," as they put it. Diane and Stu Maples had taken up the invitation of the Garlingtons and gone on the weekend, too, and now they were big promoters of the program as well. One thing the Gores did need was something positive and revitalizing in their marriage. So one evening Allan tentatively suggested to Betty that they give Marriage Encounter a try.

"Why do we need something like that?" she said. "I have so much to do already."

It was true. That was part of the problem. Betty was teaching and taking a graduate course at night and taking care of Alisa and now she was pregnant again. She had time for everything except *talking*, and that bothered Allan. Allan was not nearly so secure and content as Betty seemed to be, now that he had stopped traveling. The very thing that made her so happy made him more than a little resentful. Yet he never brought it up. He didn't have the right words, and he feared doing something else to disturb Betty.

"You don't think there's something wrong with us, do you?" she had said when he brought up Marriage Encounter.

He could tell she would be upset if he told her yes, and so he dropped the subject.

It was Candy Montgomery's twenty-ninth birthday, but the highlight of her day was a phone call that came completely out of the blue.

"Hi, this is Allan."

"Allan!" He had never called on a weekday before.

"I have to go to McKinney tomorrow to get some tires checked on the new truck I bought up there. I wondered if you'd like to have lunch. You know, to talk a little more about what we talked about before."

"Okay, fine. Where do you want to meet?"

It had been two or three weeks since the last time they had talked, on the parking lot outside the gym. They hadn't been easy weeks for her. She felt entirely foolish after virtually throwing herself at him and then being so calmly rejected. Besides being embarrassed, she was afraid it would make Allan think less of her. She would have liked to put the whole incident out of her mind, and the only reason she couldn't was the kiss. If Allan were so dead set against the idea, why had he given her that enigmatic kiss on the lips just before he left? It was not what she would call a passionate kiss, but it was not a brotherly kiss either. It didn't help Candy's peace of mind, either, that she and Pat had been arguing more than usual lately. She had brought home some A+ papers from the English class she was enrolled in, but all Pat would do is glance at them and pretend to understand. His insensitivity infuriated her, and led to harsh words. To Pat they were arguments over "nothing," but to her they represented everything wrong with their marriage. Now, after Allan's call, her old optimism started to return and she allowed herself to fantasize again about what it might be like, even once, with another man.

They met on November 16, at an auto repair shop in McKinney, the venerable county seat a few miles north of Candy's house. Allan broke the ice right away by surprising her with a birthday card. On the front it read "For the Last of the Red Hot Lovers." She opened it to find a small plastic bag of Red Hots inside. It was the kind of hokey gag card that Candy loved, and she was instantly touched. They got into her car and drove to a quaint little teahouse, where they talked about everything *except* themselves for the better part of an hour. Allan talked about Betty. Candy talked about Pat. They compared notes on their children, chatted about church matters. Jackie Ponder's decision to go to Wichita Falls was on both their minds, and they spoke sadly of what might happen to the church once she was gone. Candy got Allan to talk about his work for a while, and he in turn seemed interested when she discussed her creative writing course. Then, after the meal was cleared away and they began to sip their coffee, Allan said, "I've never done anything like an affair before."

"I haven't either," said Candy.

"I would never be able to forgive myself if Betty ever

found out about something like that. I think it would just be devastating to her."

"I feel the same way. I wouldn't want to see anyone hurt by this. Pat *or* Betty. We would have to be so careful that no one would ever know except us."

"I've been thinking a lot about what you said, about not wanting to get emotionally involved. That would be very important for me."

"Me, too, Allan. I just want to enjoy myself without hurting myself or anyone else."

"Well, let's think about it some more and maybe we should think about the hazards some more and whether we want to take that risk."

"Fine. I think we should."

Little else was said that day, but within a week Allan called Candy again while Pat was at work. They chatted more about the risks of having an affair, their fears of doing something that would ruin their marriages. But they also talked about their mutual attraction, and were obviously excited by the prospect of a secret tryst.

"You know, if you don't go to bed with me pretty soon, Allan, then you'll never be able to live up to the expectation I have of you in bed." Candy giggled.

"I know," he said, not laughing. "I've thought of that."

The next month consisted of strategy sessions for what must have been the most meticulously planned love affair in the history of romance. It began with tentative phone calls from Allan, asking about this or that. "When would we do it?" "What if somebody saw us?" Soon after the lunch at the teahouse in McKinney, they arranged to meet for lunch again, this time at the parking lot of Allan's office in Richardson, from which they drove to a nearby restaurant. Allan was accustomed to making his own hours at work, so that was no problem; but they could "save time" if Candy picked him up. From talking about the risks and hazards of an affair, they moved on quickly to a consideration of ways they could possibly *avoid* those hazards. They talked a great deal about "emotional involvement." They both very sensibly agreed that there would be none of that; it was too dangerous. As long as they limited the affair to sex alone, they were safe. They would become closer friends, of course—they already were, just by meeting for lunch—but they were both adults and they would be able to handle the emotional pressures in an adult fashion.

Allan started looking forward to his daily call to Candy from work. Candy, just as starved for affection, looked forward to it as well. Allan was growing much more comfortable with the idea of an affair, mainly because he discovered, to his surprise, that he could go to lunch with Candy, talk with her intimately on the phone, and then go home to Betty and be completely normal. Candy had always felt completely normal around Pat, perhaps because she was confident he would never suspect a thing. Still, Allan and Candy both hesitated to take the plunge.

At the end of November Candy came up with the best stratagem of all: she invited Allan to her house for lunch. She fixed her famous lasagna for the occasion. She also decided, before Allan arrived, that if nothing happened soon, she wouldn't spend any more time on this. She had done what she could to make it happen. It was really Allan's decision to make. He was so damned indecisive that she was starting to think he wasn't aggressive enough to do this anyway.

As soon as Allan walked into the Montgomery house that day, he broke into laughter. For the first thing he saw, hanging above the bookcase in Candy's living room, was a huge piece of butcher paper. On it, in Magic Marker, Candy had made two columns. The column on the left was headed "WHYS." The column on the right said "WHY-NOTS." When she had said she wanted him to come over to discuss the pros and cons, she wasn't kidding. She also knew, from their last few phone conversations, that Allan was leaning toward a decision *not* to have an affair. The cute little sign eased the tension, made him more relaxed.

After eating, they sat in the living room and went over the list an item at a time. They took the "why-nots" first, beginning with the most important one: fear of getting caught.

"But that really shouldn't be a problem," said Candy, "if we're careful."

Allan was much more concerned about one of the "why-nots" farther down the list: the possibility that they would become emotionally involved.

"We need to think about what we're getting into," said Allan.

"Allan, as far as I'm concerned this is just for fun. I'm not serious about it. It's just a companionship thing, and we shouldn't be afraid of it. Whatever happens, we'll do it for a while and then it will be over."

"I'm afraid that I might get emotionally involved."

"We just won't let that happen."

The "whys" on the list were a good deal easier: a sense of adventure, a need for companionship. Candy hadn't gone so far as to put "sex" on the list, but they discussed that one, too.

"We'll always wonder if we don't do it," she said.

"I know," said Allan.

"It's up to you, Allan. I know I can do it. I know I can act in an adult fashion and not take unnecessary risks. I've made up my mind, so just tell me if you want to do it."

They didn't make the final decision that day, but after Allan left, Candy thought to herself, "How much farther can you go?" They had already made too big a deal of something that should have been more natural. It wasn't as though Allan Gore was her fantasy man or anything.

A few days later Allan called again.

"I've decided I want to go ahead with it," he said. They had gone so far with it, Allan had finally decided, that to back out now would be almost a betrayal of Candy. Besides, he thought it would be easier than he had first imagined. After all, they had already had three meetings and it hadn't affected Betty in the least. Why not give it a try, at least once.

Still it didn't happen right away. There were ground rules to be established, logistical problems to be worked out. This affair was to be conducted properly. Candy even made a list of the rules one day so they could discuss them on the phone:

1) If either one of them ever wanted to end the affair, for whatever reason, it would end. No questions asked.

2) If either one became too emotionally involved, the affair would end.

3) If they ever started taking risks that shouldn't be taken, the affair would end.

4) All expenses—food, motel room, gasoline—would be shared equally.

5) They would meet only on weekdays, while their spouses were at work.

6) Candy would be in charge of fixing lunch on the days they met, so that they could have more time. They figured they would need all of Allan's two hours off for lunch.

7) Candy would be in charge of getting a motel room, for the same reason.

8) They would meet on a Tuesday or a Thursday, once every two weeks. This was because Candy was free only on the days when Ian attended the Play Day Preschool at Allen

Methodist Church. She took him each Tuesday and Thursday, from nine to two, but she figured that three out of four of those school days she would need for all the other errands and church and school duties in her hectic schedule.

Finally having checked off every possible precaution like astronauts getting ready for a launch, they set the date for the affair to begin: December 12, 1978.

Candy spent the morning getting ready. First she dropped off Jenny at the little red Lovejoy schoolhouse on Farm-to-Market Road 1378, then she continued on to Allen and deposited Ian at the Play Day Preschool. When she got back to the house, she allowed herself about an hour to fix the special lunch she had planned: marinated chicken, lettuce salad with cherry tomatoes and bacon bits, Thousand Island dressing, white wine, and cheescake for dessert. She packed everything, including a tablecloth, into a picnic basket, and then gathered together a few undergarments and a nightgown and slipped them into her purse. She had everything ready by 10:45. By eleven she was entering Richardson in her station wagon, searching for a motel convenient to Allan's office. She found one right on the freeway, just two or three minutes away for Allan, called the Continental Inn.

It took a few minutes to check in, because the girl behind the counter insisted on seeing her driver's license and getting the money in advance. Candy paid out $29 of the cash she had gotten at the supermarket the day before, and then filled out the registration card with her real name. After all, what difference did it make? Who did she know who had ever heard of the Continental Inn in Richardson? The girl gave her the key to one of the upstairs rooms that were set back from the highway. Candy drove the station wagon around to the back and started unpacking.

The room would do nicely. It was about ten by twelve feet, with one of those old televisions about the size of a Buick. All the shelves and cabinets were built into the walls. The walls themselves were covered with bright yellow fake paneling, which perfectly fit the autumnal decor of the rest of the room: old brown carpet and, on the bed, a spread adorned with leaves and pine cones. By opening the drapes, Candy had a view of a car wash, a "4 Day Tire" store, a Yamaha dealership, and A&A Emergency Plumbing. She went straight to the phone and called Allan at work.

"I'm at the Continental Inn on Central Expressway," she said. "Room 213."

"Be there in a few minutes," he said.

Candy busied herself getting the room ready. First she opened the picnic basket and arranged her marinated chicken feast on the bed. Then she slipped into her favorite peekaboo negligee; it was a soft pink color and almost, but not quite, sheer. It was long, falling all the way to her ankles, and it showed off her body while hiding the slightly too large thighs. She looked at herself in the mirror. For a mother of two, she didn't look bad. Then she sat in a chair by the window and waited.

Suddenly, for the first time since she had propositioned Allan in the church parking lot the month before, Candy started to get nervous. Perhaps it was the coldly impersonal room, perhaps the calculated way they were going about the affair. But she felt herself becoming frightened now that she realized that whatever they did today would be irrevocable. Everything she had done before, no matter how brazen, had been harmless flirtation compared to this. Having sex is not as simple as it seems. It changes people.

On the way to the motel, Allan discovered that he wasn't quite as brave as he had thought, either. He worried that perhaps the only reason he was doing this was to please Candy. He had to admit that Candy was sexually appealing, and yet he didn't want to be full of anxiety all the time. He didn't want to feel like he was feeling now.

But once he opened the door and saw Candy, smiling and seductive in her pink nightgown, Allan felt a surge of bravado. What the heck, thought Allan. I'm here and I'm going to do it.

"I've made lunch," she said, smiling halfheartedly. Allan could tell, much to his surprise, that Candy was even more nervous than he was.

They sat on either side of the bed and made small talk. Allan dug into the chicken and quickly drank a glass of wine. Candy poked at her chicken, tearing off one little sliver at a time.

"I feel like what we're eating," she said.

Allan smiled.

They finished off the dessert and then busied themselves with putting aside the paper plates and containers, as though neither wanted to make the first move. When there was nothing left to do, Candy sat quietly on the chair by the window. There was a moment of strained silence.

"Well," said Allan, "are you just going to sit there?"

Candy smiled. "Yes."

Allan walked around the bed and gently touched her on the shoulder. All of her nervousness dissolved.

The sex was gentle and conventional and satisfying. It was also very brief. Candy was amazed at first by Allan's naivete as a lover. When she stuck her tongue into his mouth, it was apparent that he had never had a French kiss before. The good news was that he was a quick learner. For his part, Allan was positively transported. Candy was so responsive and energetic—she *moved* so much—that Allan found it more exciting than any sexual experience he had ever had. It was good for him because it seemed so good for her. He couldn't keep going very long, but he wouldn't forget the feeling for several days afterward.

Afterwards Candy insisted that they both take showers before leaving. "So you won't smell like me," she said.

Candy felt very well pleased. Despite Allan's apparent inexperience, she hadn't really had to fake her responses very much at all. And he did show great promise as a lover. He wasn't very interesting in bed, and he was certainly quick about it, but he had an advantage most men didn't: the most perfectly shaped penis Candy had ever seen.

Allan would have been surprised to hear his body talked about that way. He was just as satisfied by the lunchtime rendezvous and was looking forward to the next one. When he went back to work, he felt weak all afternoon.

The first time the Montgomerys and Gores ever heard the name Ron Adams was at a very emotional church service in mid-December 1978. Jackie Ponder had nothing but nice things to say about the man who had been appointed to replace her, but her remarks also contained an undertone of regret and sadness. To Betty Gore, JoAnn Garlington, Elaine Williams, and all the other women who had come to regard Jackie as the most positive force in their lives, her decision to go elsewhere could only mean one thing: she was being forced out against her will. It probably had something to do with her divorce and subsequent love affairs. It was all too much for some of the parishioners to accept. Perhaps word had gotten back to the bishop. Regardless of her reason for leaving, though, it was obvious that her replacement was her opposite in every respect. He was a man, for one thing, coming into a church run mostly by women. He was inexperienced, having served only as an assistant at First Methodist in Plano while he was completing his work at Perkins. He was twenty-four years old, even younger than most of the ministers the church had had before Jackie. Everything about him seemed a regression, even before anyone had been introduced to him.

The cards were undoubtedly stacked against him, but Ron didn't help his case any the first time he showed up at Lucas to meet his new parishioners. It was Jackie's last week before leaving for Wichita Falls, and an informal reception was held after choir practice by the Pastor-Parish Committee. While women were crying and hugging Jackie and bidding emotional farewells, Ron stood to one side, very stiffly, and gave solemn, formal answers to everything that was asked him. He spoke of the necessity of a building program. He used works like "task-oriented." He seemed cold and distant and a little haughty. While the reception was going on, several volunteers were busily decorating the sanctuary with tiny angels made out of pipe cleaners and felt. They were particularly proud of the work, since at least four families had been working on the decorations for some time, resulting in literally thousands of toy angels all over the ceiling and walls. When somebody made a light-hearted remark about how well the work was going, Ron took one look at it and said, "This stuff has gotta go." Shortly thereafter, somebody made the mistake of introducing Ron to Betty Gore, who had not only heard the remark but was convinced that Ron was responsible for forcing Jackie out.

"Why don't you go back to your big-city church?" she said.

Ron was beginning to realize what he was up against.

Jackie, for her part, was able to see what was happening and tried to smooth things over. When Elaine Williams came over to say good-bye, they talked briefly about personal matters—Elaine's ex-husband, David, had moved back in with her—and then Jackie said, "Now listen to me. I want you to make this church work. I want you to get along with this man."

Elaine looked across the room at Ron.

"How can I?" she said. "Look at him. He's wearing an orange jacket."

On New Year's Day, 1979, the day Ron and his wife moved

to Lucas, Candy and Pat were the only people who came to the parsonage to help them unload. Candy was not quite as harsh toward Ron as the other women, mainly because she knew that Jackie had made the decision to leave on her own. Candy also felt that, since she and Pat were the most active couple in church, she needed to help temper the ruffled feelings between Ron and people like JoAnn and Betty, who were refusing to give him a chance. Candy tended to laugh at people who were pompous or stiff, so she joked with Ron even though he seldom joked back. She thought he was a funny little guy; she thought it was especially amusing that he "snorted" when he spoke, breathing loudly through his nose. (As a child, Ron had had surgery for sinus cancer.) She dismissed most of his social mistakes as simple immaturity. After all, he was only twenty-four.

But Ron was not the sort to be assuaged with simple good humor. Almost as soon as he moved in, he started making decisions that, to a few of the parishioners, seemed like the intentional destruction of everything Jackie Ponder had built. His first sermon was a disaster. Even Candy had to admit that she had never heard a worse public speaker in her life. Ron frequently stared at the notes on his lectern, made very few gestures, and droned on and on in a monotone punctuated only by short, comical snorts. Candy felt he was speaking at the congregation instead of to it. There was no sense of spontaneity or emotion. Ron was not the type to stop, gaze out over the audience, and say, "Now how do those words make you feel?" the way Jackie used to do. If he had, he wouldn't have liked the answer anyway. Ron was systematic, formal, and a little old-fashioned. He had a program for the worship service—hymn here, sermon here, announcements here—that never altered from week to week. He never encouraged the participation of laymen in the formal service, as Jackie had. He was, in a word, boring.

Though he never said so publicly, Ron had decided early on that some of the younger members, especially the ones in the choir, were "troublemakers" and "carpetbaggers," people from the city who had invaded a small, local church and virtually taken over its management. He thought it especially odd that some of them had to drive thirty miles or more to get to Lucas when there were other, perfectly adequate Methodist churches within a few minutes of their homes. Clearly they had come to Lucas because they wanted a social club instead of a church. It didn't surprise him one bit that they would rather have a "recreational building" than a sanctuary; it indicated their priorities.

Among the choir members, accustomed to being the center of all church business, Candy was the last holdout in Ron's defense. But even she was shocked by his autocratic behavior, how he seemed to be *asking* people to dislike him. One of her duties under Jackie had been to edit the church newsletter. When Ron arrived she changed the name of it to "Adams Apple" and offered to handle all the logistics of getting it out. Far from being pleased, he was desultory about getting information to her, causing delays and wasted time, and on one occasion he trashed an entire issue because Candy had written a sentimental, flowery essay about the meaning of Maundy Thursday. "That's all wrong," Ron snapped. "Jesus didn't *literally* rise from the dead." Candy didn't like some of the things in the Bible herself, but she was still shocked to hear those words from a minister. Then another time Pat was doing one of his popular children's sermons, which were actually puppet shows, and he used Peter Rabbit to represent Jesus. Ron was upset afterward and told Pat not to do it again. One little thing that came to bother Candy was that Ron didn't appear to pray spontaneously; he read all his prayers from a prepared text. But the main thing Candy didn't like about Ron was that he either manipulated people for his own purposes, or discounted them altogether. Ron had had too many chances. Candy finally agreed with everyone else: the man was cold and unfeeling. All he cared about was his damned building fund.

Despite everything, though, Ron might have been able to weather the first difficult year of his ministry were it not for one thing: Marriage Encounter. It started with a dinner invitation. Richard and JoAnn thought perhaps Ron would "come around" if they invited him over and then had a heart-to-heart talk. What they wanted to talk about, unfortunately, was Ron's marriage. They had just returned from another Marriage Encounter weekend, a special "Focus on God" session, and they were brimming over with their brand of emotional honesty. They told Ron they wanted to be totally open with him and discuss their disappointments in his ministry. But then they proceeded to list so many of his personal shortcomings that he became understandably defensive. First, they didn't like his style of preaching. He was rigid, not open to suggestion, and his sermons were boring. Second, he was not coming across as a loving or caring person. He seemed too stern for their tastes. And finally, Richard and JoAnn told him, they were a little concerned about his marriage and his relationship with his young son. In their opinion, Ron treated his wife like property, and he didn't "relate well" to the child. What he and his wife needed was a Marriage Encounter weekend, which would make him a lot more loving and understanding person and strengthen his marriage as well.

Ron listened to the whole speech, and then exploded.

"You're entitled to your opinion," he said, "but you're just plain wrong."

As far as the Garlingtons were concerned, that was it for Ron. They tried to be honest and loving, but Ron had refused to listen.

As far as Ron was concerned, that was it for the "Marriage Encounter bunch," as the Garlingtons and Maples and friends were beginning to be called. Ron had never liked the association of the Marriage Encounter organization with the Methodist church. He disagreed with the whole concept, since all it amounted to was having the husband and wife talk to each other without the advantage of professional counseling or guidance. That was dangerous, he thought, and in the hands of insistent people like the Garlingtons it could get in the way of his ministry. When JoAnn made Marriage Encounter announcements during the worship service, he was furious, especially since it gave the members the false impression that he supported the program. He also had no taste for the public displays of affection that seemed to be required of anyone who had been "encountered." Richard and JoAnn were the worst. They were all over each other at church, wrapping their arms around each other, holding hands at all times, each refusing to leave the other's side even for a moment. They also had the irritating habit of taking communion in "Marriage Encounter style," their elbows entwined like lovers making a champagne toast. For her part, JoAnn Garlington took Ron's dislike of the program as evidence that he didn't know what he was talking about (since he had never been encountered) and that he probably *did* have problems in the loving-and-caring department. She continued to campaign for Marriage Encounter at every opportunity.

Two of the most active lay leaders in Lucas Methodist Church were Candy Montgomery and Allan Gore. So, as 1979 began, they were both wrapped up in the political controversy surrounding Ron Adams, but, unbeknownst to the other choir members, they were more wrapped up in each other. After the first meeting at the Continental Inn, it was obvious that both of them would want more. So a week later, just before the Christmas holidays, they arranged by phone for a repeat performance. This time Candy spent the morning preparing beef teriyaki strips and cheese blintzes. She did change one detail though. When she got to Richardson, she noticed a smaller—and sleazier—motel across the freeway from the Continental. Always the practical shopper, she figured a motel room is a motel room, so why not get something cheaper than $29?

The Como Motel was quite a comedown, even by the less-than-luxurious standards of the Continental. Candy got the impression that the Como didn't have a lot of overnight visitors when she walked into the office and came face to face with a clerk standing behind a plexiglass screen, like a bank teller's window or, perhaps more appropriate, a jailer's. The manager was a greying, avuncular guy in an Alpaca sweater who wanted $23.50 cash in advance, plus a $2 deposit for the key. Candy put her money in the trough under the window, and he passed her a key to one of about thirty rooms grouped in a triangle around the "swim pool" (the sign was short on neon). She drove her car around to the asphalt lot in back.

In months to come Allan and Candy would joke about their room at the Como. Candy always said it smelled like old money. The very sleaziness of the place is what made it so illicit, and so much fun. The room was a little more than a cubicle, ten by ten at the most, done in a sort of tattered harvest gold. The curtains were drooping and frayed. The shag carpet was matted like dirty hair. The bathroom had fake terrazzo flooring, the faucet leaked, and the only furnishings other than the bed were a tiny vanity, a black-and-white TV set, and two hideous captain's chairs with imitation leather cushions. They had a wall phone with no dial on it, two lamps that sometimes worked, and a big fluorescent reading lamp perched awkwardly over the bed.

Here, for the last days of 1978 and the first three months of 1979, Allan and Candy made glorious love every other week, dined on taco salad and homemade lasagna, and sipped cheap red wine out of plastic cups supplied by the management. (They came wrapped in cellophane bags with Walt

Disney cartoon characters on them.) Afterwards they would recline on the harvest-gold velour bedspread—covering the venerable sheets, which often sported suspicious stains—and rest their heads on tiny foam-rubber pillows and talk about their lives and their spouses and their children and their mutual love, the church. They would talk until it was time for Allan to go back to work, or for Candy to pick up her five-year-old at kindergarten, and then go stand in the tub and turn on the faulty shower attachment and wash off the smell of each other. Finally, they would gather up their belongings, kiss each other lightly on the lips, and go back to their normal lives, closing the door behind them. The sign on the door read, "Notice: Contents of Rooms Are Checked Before and After Being Occupied. Anything Missing Is Reported to the Police. Your Car License Is On Record."

Later, when Allan looked back on his whirlwind lunch hours with Candy Montgomery, he would think less of the sex than of the *relaxation* he took there. Those two hours with Candy were often the only time he didn't feel the responsibility for other people's emotions, the awful burden of making Betty happy. In the limited confines of a room at the Como Motel, Allan was a man with no past and no future, able to accept Candy's unconditional affection—she virtually showered him with it—in a way that was simple and guiltless. Candy cooked lavish meals for him, she made the domestic arrangements (checking in), and she was a skilled instructor in lovemaking of a sort Allan hadn't been aware of. Allan had never been with any woman except Betty in his life. This experience was revitalizing, in a way that his life with Betty hadn't been for a long time.

It didn't help that, in the early months of 1979, Betty was starting to grow even more dissatisfied with her own life. She was pregnant again, for one thing, and that brought back the same emotional fears and physical ailments she had suffered through five years earlier, when her first pregnancy brought on a deep depression. Betty's unhappiness and insecurity had always been something Allan could deal with, though. What made it different this time was the situation at church.

No one despised Ron Adams the way Betty did. It had been an almost instinctual hatred, from the day he arrived, and it had very little to do with the pros and cons of his ministry. It was not even anything Betty said to Ron—they had

had very few face-to-face conversations—but the way she would make offhand, sarcastic comments in group meetings. Betty had no particular fondness for the Marriage Encounter movement, for example, but as soon as her friend JoAnn Garlington was asked by Ron not to make announcements at the worship service, Betty leapt to her defense. After Ron's first few weeks as pastor, Betty, JoAnn, and Elaine Williams had formed a sort of alliance against the man and spent much of their time at church whispering snide remarks about his incompetence.

It was true that Ron wasn't a model of diplomacy. Given a personality conflict with one of his parishioners, his solution was either to ignore it or to defy it. One day that spring, Ron's wife, Mary, called Diane Maples to tell her she was expected to help out at the church nursery that week. Diane was a veteran of Marriage Encounter, a friend of Jackie Ponder, a close friend of JoAnn Garlington, and just as dissatisfied as everyone else. "Forget it," Diane told Mary. "I sing in the choir, and I think that's enough church service." Mary didn't like Diane's tone of voice and told her so. Diane got even huffier with Mary. Ron, rather than simply let the matter drop, then made an issue of it by inserting a veiled reference to Diane into the following Sunday's church announcements. "A certain member of this church recently yelled at my wife," he said before the assembled worshipers. "And that's the last time that sort of thing is going to happen."

Late that spring, Ron attended a meeting of the Pastor-Parish Committee to discuss the renovation of the parsonage. This would normally be a fairly routine matter. Since the house stood just a stone's throw from the back door of the sanctuary, everyone could plainly see that it was definitely not in the best of shape. Ron made a formal request for $10,000, to be used for painting and repairs. A brief discussion ensued. Then Betty, unable to control her anger, exploded at Ron.

"Why should we give you $10,000?" she demanded. "Why can't you do the work yourself? We all have to fix *our* houses."

It fell to Allan to try to cover for Betty's feelings when he could—he didn't like Ron, either, but he didn't want it to show—and to reassure her constantly that things would be better after the new baby arrived. Privately, he wished she were more flexible, more secure, more even-tempered, like she had been back in Kansas, before she developed so many minor illnesses and petty complaints.

Candy Montgomery seemed the opposite of Betty in every respect. Candy was always "up," always busy, self-confident, easygoing, warm. She took voice lessons and English courses and helped out at Fire Department fund-raisers and worked as a voter registrar and shepherded two young children from place to place and even helped out her neighbor Peter Haas with his mayoral campaign, and yet nothing she did seemed burdensome or self-conscious. Even her reaction to Ron Adams was different. Betty whispered sarcastically behind his back. Candy frankly told Ron how silly she thought some of his decisions were, and then laughed so he wouldn't take it too hard.

One reason Candy could be so good-natured about "the Ron problem" was that the affair made her feel alive again. At first she was so excited about the sex and the intrigue and the adventure of it all that she had to have a confidante. Normally that would have been Jackie, but after Jackie left she spent more and more time with Sherry, her Fairview neighbor. She even told Sherry about Allan's "perfectly shaped" penis, and then added, "Now if he could only use it in more imaginative ways." Sherry was actually a better confidante than Jackie, because Sherry didn't have any reservations whatsoever. She knew that Candy had felt dissatisfied with Pat, and she could see how much happier Candy was once the long-contemplated affair began. On some days, usually the day after a rendezvous with Allan, Candy and Sherry would meet for morning coffee and go over the juicy details. Sherry always remained light-hearted about the whole business, especially since she had met Allan and told Candy she frankly couldn't understand what she saw in him.

"I can't either," said Candy. "He's not that handsome. He has a receding hairline. He's not what I would call my type at all. I don't *know* what I see in him."

Still, she continued to see him, every two weeks like clockwork, usually on a Tuesday or a Thursday except on those rare occasions when she could get a baby-sitter—usually Sherry—and dare to go to bed with him on a Monday, Wednesday, or Friday. Unfortunately, after the third or fourth time at the Como, she started to have second thoughts. Her doubts weren't spurred by any feelings of guilt. They started, in fact, when she first realized that sex with Allan Gore probably wasn't going to get much better than it already was. The first two or three times it had felt good, but there had been virtually no improvement, and she was beginning to suspect that the man was not capable of fireworks, no matter how much she coached him. The more serious problem was that Candy feared she was beginning to like Allan too much. Sometimes she even thought she loved him. She knew she loved him in the Jackie Ponder sense, but she didn't want to *fall* in love with him. That was too risky.

In retrospect, she would see that it was inevitable. Sex or no sex, she and Allan had both come to look forward to their daily conversations, their shared confidences, their joint dependence. Lately they had started exchanging funny little greeting cards, and whenever Candy had to drive into Richardson on an errand, she would stop at Allan's office and place gifts under his windshield wiper. Sometimes Allan would go out to check his car even when he was staying in for lunch, just to see if he had any brownies or homemade candy waiting for him. Once he found a small ceramic statue of a boy and girl kissing. The inscription on the base read, "Practice Makes Perfect." They had started the affair for reasons of mutual need: they were both starved for affection. But as time went on they seemed less like lovers and more like best friends. During one rendezvous, they had decided to forego sex altogether because they wanted to spend lunchtime talking. She could even talk to Allan about Pat; he was that understanding.

By February she was beginning to feel more than a little anxious about the relationship. Even though it was only two and a half months old, she started worrying that it was turning serious all of a sudden. One day at a lunch she tentatively broached the subject with Allan.

"I think I'm getting in too deep," she said.

"What do you mean?"

"I don't want to fall in love with you. We're getting too serious, and I know this is a temporary thing. I don't want to have to deal with myself later if we go too far."

"How do you know this is getting too serious?" replied Allan.

"I think of you too much."

"But I thought you're the one who said you've got to plow into life and see what happens."

"That's right, I did say that."

"Well?"

"I guess I'm caught in my own trap."

"It won't get too serious if we don't let it get too serious. I think the relationship is temporary, too, but we've got to let it run its course."

"Well, if you're not worried about it, I guess that makes it half all right."

The next week Jackie Ponder returned to Lucas for a few days, her first visit since leaving the church. Ron Adams wasn't too pleased about her visit. It was a direct violation of accepted protocol: once a minister leaves a church, he or she is expected to sever all ties and stay away, so that the new minister can form a bond with the congregation unhampered by feelings for the departed pastor. Everyone else was thrilled, though, especially Candy, who spent much of her time with Jackie pouring out every detail of her affair with Allan. She didn't mention Allan's name—she didn't think Jackie was ready for that—but she did go over all the details of the past two months, including the Como Motel, the token gifts and cards, the sexual excitement. Jackie had a strange premonition about the affair, quite apart from what Candy was telling her.

"Candy, you told me you weren't going to get emotionally involved with this man," said Jackie.

"Yes."

"But you are, aren't you? Something's upsetting you."

"No, everything's fine."

Her denial notwithstanding, Candy decided after Jackie's visit that she really did need to distance herself from Allan emotionally. So the next week, when he made one of his usual phone calls, she expressed even stronger doubts.

"Allan, I don't know if I can handle the way I'm feeling about you."

"What's wrong?"

"I'm still afraid of falling in love, and I know I can't do that. It would be too hard on Pat, and I love him. And I don't want to lose your friendship either. I just don't want anyone to get hurt."

"Why are you talking about hurt when there's no hurt in sight? How can you say how this will turn out?"

"I just have a bad feeling about it."

"This is not like you, Candy. If you back out now, how are you going to know what you've missed? We're only getting started."

"You sound like me."

Eventually Candy allowed herself to be talked into it a second time, mostly because she didn't like the thought of not talking to Allan, and she was afraid they wouldn't be able to continue their friendship without sex. It helped that she and Pat were planning a long vacation to visit her parents in Georgia; that would give her most of April to sort things out and discover how she really felt about Allan.

Allan, on the other hand, doubted that he was capable of falling in love with Candy, at least not in the way she was talking about. He also knew that, for the time being, he needed her. They had something special, something that was renewed each time they caught each other's eye during a church service, or touched hands over a table at lunch, or did something as simple as waste time on the phone. Allan felt better about himself. He didn't want this affair to get out of hand, of course, but so far he was surprised at how little it changed the rest of his life. If anything it made everything else easier. Even going to church was easy, and at first he hadn't expected to be able to do that. He still liked Pat. He didn't think he was doing anything to hurt him. There was no change in his relationship with Betty. Who knew where this affair would end up or how long it would last, but in the meantime he was enjoying it and he couldn't see anything very bad resulting from it. When Candy left for Georgia, Allan missed her and wondered briefly whether her feelings would change while she was away, but he also felt a sense of relief. He hadn't realized, until they took a few weeks off, how much *work* an affair could be.

Allan needn't have worried about Candy changing her mind. When she returned from vacation, it was obvious that she had missed him as much as he missed her. They made a date for the Como, but after the lunch and the sex, they spent most of their time "catching up" on each other's lives. One thing they talked about was Betty's pregnancy. Betty was seven months along, and Allan was starting to feel a little apprehensive. Betty would need lots of attention as the day drew closer, because of her problems with the first baby. And it had crossed Allan's mind that if Betty started having labor pains and he happened to be at the Como that day, he would never be able to forgive himself. So in early June he told Candy he thought they should discontinue the affair for a while, so that he could be available for Betty at all times. Candy agreed completely. Allan loved that about Candy; she *did* understand things like that. She was so different from Betty in that respect. When Allan told Candy something, she would accept it and wouldn't show any negative feelings toward him because of it. Betty would have disagreed and whined, especially when it threatened something she wanted. Sometimes Allan wondered to himself what it would be like to be married to Candy. She was always interesting, a good cook, a good mother. But then he thought, no, that was out of the question. He knew he'd never divorce Betty, no matter what. He believed that marriage was permanent.

Allan couldn't have realized, and Candy didn't tell him, that she was more than willing to suspend the affair for a while, and it represented no great sacrifice on her part. The last visit to the Como had confirmed her earlier fears: the sex was not that great. They spent so much time talking that the physical part was all but obligatory. She would never say no, but Candy was also tired of getting up early on the days they sinned together so she could make beef chow mein, cream puffs, and ham-and-cheese casserole. Allan had come to expect notes and cookies and things left on his car, too. The whole thing was becoming a hassle. Allan was like a toy that seems the most wonderful thing in the world when a kid sees it under the Christmas tree, but after a few weeks becomes a routine part of his life. Not that she didn't like Allan, even love him. Not that she didn't need his companionship. She just missed the magic of those first few weeks.

Sometimes Candy would even admit to herself that she felt guilty about Pat. Poor Pat. He was totally oblivious to everything. She was certain he had no suspicions about her and Allan, even when they cut up at choir practice or exchanged glances during the worship service. Nevertheless, sometimes it was hard to be around Pat, simply because he did trust her so much, and it didn't make it any easier when Pat would tell her how much he liked Allan.

Candy's powers of deception were put to the ultimate test in mid-June when she threw a special sit-down Chinese dinner for the five couples in the choir as well as Jackie Ponder, visiting again with Chuck. The real purpose of the dinner was a surprise baby shower for Betty Gore. It was Candy's idea. She thought it would be fun. It didn't occur to her that it would be awkward, since she had never really felt uncomfortable around Betty even when she was sleeping with Allan every other week. Someone fixed a special cake, everyone brought gifts, and Candy turned out to be right: nobody felt uncomfortable, not even Betty. She virtually beamed with pleasure—one of the few times, in fact, that she seemed completely untroubled and at peace with herself. She was almost "one of the girls."

A week later Barbara Green called Candy to say that the arrangements for the "regular" shower conducted by all the women of the church had fallen through, and she wondered if the Montgomery house could be used again. So Candy hosted a second shower for Betty, just two weeks before the baby was due. Betty was so touched by all the attention that she insisted on going to church the following Sunday, despite her condition, and there were more surprises waiting there. One was the presence of Jackie Ponder, back on a Sunday for the first time. Betty was so carried away that she ran up to Jackie in the crowded sanctuary, threw her arms around her, and started crying.

"We miss you so much," she sobbed.

Jackie was startled, but assumed Betty was high-strung due to the pregnancy. Jackie also considered going by to see the Gores, just to make sure everything was all right, but then thought better of it because Ron was already mad enough that she was visiting at all.

That same Sunday, Judy Swain made a point of seeking out Betty after the services. Judy was a new member of the church, having joined three months before with her husband, and she had been disappointed that she was unable to attend Betty's shower. So that Saturday she had gone out of her way to shop for a present, eventually buying a pink baby jumpsuit. Judy apologized for missing the shower, handed Betty the gift, and waited while she opened it. Betty held the jumpsuit up to the light, as though trying to figure out what it was.

"Oh," she said, in a distracted, vacant voice. She put the suit back in the box without ever looking back at Judy. And then she walked off.

Judy was crushed. The same woman who an hour before had collapsed into Jackie's arms, brimming over with uncontrolled emotion, now suddenly seemed cold and, in Judy Swain's opinion, snobbish. Judy regretted buying the gift at all.

The incident might never have happened had Allan been at Betty's side. Allan understood Betty, and he could cover for her lack of social grace by his own warmth and courtesy. Allan didn't blame Betty as others did, though. He knew that Betty wasn't the most well-liked woman at church, yet he credited a lot of that feeling to her shyness and insecurity. She couldn't act normal around anyone except Allan, because everything the slightest bit unfamiliar threatened her. It seemed a paradox that, on the one hand, Betty would strive to be the perfect woman—raising two kids, teaching school, keeping house, accepting a foster child—and, on the other, be peculiarly antisocial. But Allan understood that both traits were part of the same single-mindedness. Betty was such a proud woman that she had no time for distractions; making the most of her life was her one great devotion.

Bethany Gore was born in early July, and Betty seemed to perk up for a while. As babies often do, Bethany brought Allan and Betty closer together, especially during the week just after she was born, before they told anyone in the church about her.

The feeling didn't last long, though. Now that there was no pressing reason for Allan to be "on call" all the time, there was really no reason for him to put off the affair any longer. But when he and Candy renewed their lovemaking at the Como in late July, it seemed different, lackluster. The sex was still good, Allan thought, but Candy was more reserved than usual; a couple of times she even griped at him, about little things that didn't matter, and that wasn't like her at all. There was something else, too: for the first time, Allan was starting to feel guilty. He thought of Betty, back at the house, taking care of Alisa and Bethany by herself, and he didn't feel very good about himself. That week after the baby had been born was something special. He wondered if there was a way to get it back. He hoped he wasn't making that impossible by continuing to see Candy.

Allan was grateful when Betty finally felt well enough to travel, because that meant they could take off a week to show the baby to her anxious Kansas grandparents. He wanted a reason to be away from Candy for a few days, but he wasn't prepared to tell her that. Before leaving, they agreed to meet at the Como on the following Friday, since she knew she could get a sitter that day.

The Gores didn't arrive home from their Kansas trip until late one Thursday night, and ordinarily Allan would have simply taken off work the next day as well. But he remembered that the special date with Candy was set for that Friday, and he knew she really wanted to see him. If he didn't go to work and she ended up at the Como by herself, the fallout would be disastrous. But when Allan told Betty he intended to go to work on Friday, she objected, arguing that he should stay home and help her with errands. She not only was insistent that he stay home; she was more than a little suspicious about why he just *had* to go to work. So Allan decided the only solution was to somehow get word to Candy that he couldn't make it. First he cooked up an excuse to call her—something to do with church—and then he phoned from the kitchen while Betty was in the master bedroom at the back of the house. Without actually saying the words, he got the message across that he couldn't make it. Candy grew angry when she realized what he was telling her, because now she and Pat were leaving for a week-long vacation and that meant she wouldn't see him for *another* two weeks. Allan didn't want to hang up while she was still mad, so he had to stay on the phone for a few minutes, hoping she would calm down. When he hung up, feeling sheepish and depressed, he walked back to the master bedroom.

"Gee, that sure was a long conversation," said Betty.

Candy and Pat spent the next week in Wichita Falls, fulfilling their long-ago promise to visit Jackie Ponder at her new campus home. Pat had a great time, wandering around the campus and looking the city over. Candy and Jackie had a few private sessions together, but when Jackie asked about the affair, Candy was reluctant to talk about it. One thing was clear, though, at least to Jackie. Candy was really going through some pain. Something was wrong, and it had to be something important because Jackie couldn't even get her to discuss it. Candy and Pat decided to stay on campus through Jackie's Sunday sermon. Pat had brought along his recorder so they could tape the sermon and take it back to Lucas. They both agreed it was a great sermon. It was about Love.

Candy liked the sermon so much that the following Friday she took the tape to the Como Motel so that Allan could hear it. After their usual picnic lunch, she turned on the tape recorder, and they reminisced about Jackie while it was playing. After hearing her talk about love, they made love. It was late when Allan got back to the office.

That night Betty wanted to make love. In one sense that wasn't so odd. The Gores hadn't had sex since the baby was born, at first because Betty didn't feel up to it, later because they were simply out of the habit. Allan had become so desultory about making love to his wife that sometimes they were having sex no more than once a month. But the odd thing about this night was that Betty was so aggressive. It wasn't like her. Allan couldn't remember it ever having happened before, in all the years they were married. But Allan didn't think he *could* do it. He had been with Candy a long time that afternoon, and he was not used to that much exertion in one day. He was out of practice. He was spent. He had no interest in her. He was so surprised by Betty's sexual advance, though, that he didn't even bother to explain. He simply said he didn't feel like it.

Betty began to cry. She felt embarrassed and humiliated and deeply hurt. It would have been different if she were in the habit of making regular advances, but to have the very first one rebuffed was too much for her. She jumped to a lot of conclusions. Allan didn't love her anymore. He hated her because she was fat after having the baby. Allan tried to reassure her, but nothing seemed to work. She had been rejected, and she couldn't stand it. She was afraid she wasn't desirable anymore.

On Monday morning Allan phoned Candy. "I need to talk. When can I meet you and where?"

They arranged to meet for lunch, and Allan poured out the whole story of that Friday night.

"Betty was *very* upset," he said. "She kept saying, 'You don't love me anymore, you don't love me anymore.'"

"You did reassure her, didn't you?"

"Yes."

Candy began to cry. "I think that's a little unfair of Betty, to say things like that after you can't perform one time."

"It upset me, too. It was just that she made the first move."

"What are you going to do?"

"I think, maybe we should end it."

"Now *you're* being grossly unfair."

"I'm afraid of hurting Betty. I think maybe the affair is affecting my marriage now, and if I want to get my life back in order, I have to stop running between two women."

"But what about when I suggested we end it? Remember what you said then? You said, 'No, you have to see this through to the end,' and 'Just because something happens once doesn't mean it will happen again,' and things to that effect. Now that you can't perform with Betty one time, suddenly you want to end it. That's a double standard."

"I'm not saying we should definitely end it. I'm just saying we should think about it. I don't want to hurt Betty."

The issue was left unresolved after the lunch meeting, but they talked several times by phone over the next two or three weeks. Each time Candy grew colder and more antagonistic; she couldn't bear the thought of Allan having so little regard for her feelings. But then she would cry and feel better and tell him that she loved him.

"I do love you, Allan."

"I know, but we've become *too* close. We've become so close that I'm afraid I don't love Betty anymore, and that was never a part of our agreement. We've both been using each other to fill gaps in our marriages, and that's not right."

"It's just so unfair."

After the Friday-night incident Betty Gore fell into a deep despondency that lasted several weeks. At first Allan thought he could talk her out of it by spending more time with her. But soon she was complaining of soreness in her neck and shoulders, and sudden pains of the sort she had when they first moved to Plano. She was sullen and depressed much of the time, especially since she had to start teaching again in early September, and still had the burden of a two-month-old baby. She started seeing her family doctor in Plano again, and he prescribed pain pills to help alleviate some of her complaints. Privately he suspected the ailments were all stress-related.

Later that month Allan satisfied an old ambition of his and quit Rockwell International to join a tiny, virtually new company called ECS Telecommunications. The company had only one product—a telephone voice-message-answering system—but Allan had good friends there, ex-Rockwell employees who dared him to take the chance with a small, ground-floor firm. The only way Allan could have advanced at Rockwell would have been to take jobs that required extensive travel—out of the question, given Betty's fear of being alone. ECS was offering more money and stock besides. It was something exciting and something that Allan really wanted to do, if he could get Betty to go along with it. It took a while, but he convinced her that it wasn't too risky, that he wouldn't have to travel much, and that it wasn't going to require more time than he was spending now. Betty reluctantly agreed—if she hadn't, Allan wouldn't have done it, because he wouldn't have been able to stand the complaining—but she remained fearful and nervous, as she was about any new venture.

The next time Allan talked to Candy, he said that, because of the new job and the additional work, he wouldn't be able to see her as much. Candy was upset; she was beginning to fear the inevitable end of the affair. But she asked Allan if they couldn't meet at least once more. They met at the Como for quick, unsatisfying sex, then spent an hour and a half discussing how they could live without each other. Candy was obviously having second thoughts about breaking off the affair; she had grown too dependent on Allan's kindness. The next time they met, they didn't even bother to go to the Como. Instead Candy fixed a picnic lunch and they drove to a public park in North Dallas and spread their blanket under a tree. The weather was so nice that it gave a bittersweet aura to the conversation.

"I love you so much, Allan. I don't know if I can make it if we break up."

Allan didn't know what to say. He said the usual things about wanting to patch up his marriage.

"Is Betty better?"

"She wants to go to Marriage Encounter now."

"Really?"

"Yeah. I asked her once before, but she always said she didn't think we needed it. I think maybe it will do us both some good."

"You're really going?"

"We're going to the next one—in October."

"I think Marriage Encounter is going to be the end for us."

"Oh no, not necessarily. Let's see what happens first."

On the next volleyball league night, Betty Gore and Judy Swain both had to sit out the game with minor injuries. While they were watching, Judy tried to make small talk.

"Why aren't you playing?"

"I hurt my arm," said Betty. "I don't know what it is, there must be something wrong with a nerve or something. Maybe I hurt it reaching for something, or maybe I was holding the baby in the wrong position. I've been feeling pretty bad lately. I had some soreness in my neck last week, and sometimes my legs ache, but you know, I haven't really felt all that well ever since Bethany was born. It's tough with a baby *and* the teaching and everything."

"You do sound busy," said Judy.

"But I'd never give up teaching, even with the two kids. I just love it. I even miss it during the summers."

"I guess I'm different. I don't mind just keeping the kids and the house."

Betty listened attentively as Judy told her about the pinched nerve in her neck that wouldn't go away. Betty nodded sympathetically. She seemed very lonely. Judy wondered what was bothering her so much that she would pour out all her ailments to a stranger—and the one who had given her the pink jumpsuit, at that. When they parted that night, Betty acted as though she had made a new friend.

Two weeks later Betty returned to her doctor, extremely tense and complaining of aches and pains in her shoulders. When he took her blood pressure, it registered dangerously high, indicating extreme stress or physical exertion. He prescribed more painkillers and muscle relaxants and asked her to come back in a few days. Betty felt a little better after talking to the doctor. What she didn't tell him was that all of her anxieties were centered on the coming weekend: she and Allan were about to be "encountered."

Dunfey's Royal Motor Coach Inn, a fake medieval castle full of tunnels and turrets and gables and the regal purples and scarlets of an adult Disneyland, was the site each month of the weekend called Methodist Marriage Encounter. It was less a counseling session than a total-immersion experience. Though it had the tacit approval of the church, it was run completely by laymen, and it began with a Friday-night dinner at which the rules were explained. Spouses were expected to be at each other's side at all times. Televisions were not be be turned on in the rooms. Newspapers were forbidden. Nothing was to get in the way of the couples *communicating* about their *feelings*.

"Communicating" and "feelings"—those were the watchwords of Marriage Encounter, as Allan and Betty were to find out soon after arriving at Dunfey's and checking into Room 321. They were led into a large meeting hall, with three dozen or so other couples, and introduced to their Encounter leaders, all married couples who had previously gone through the program. It was explained that the couples onstage would talk openly about their marriages, but no one else was expected to speak except in the privacy of their motel rooms. The procedure was that the leaders would propose a question—the first one was "Why did I come here this weekend and what do I hope to gain?"—and then the couples would retire to their rooms to write answers to the question in their individual Marriage Encounter spiral notebooks. (Under the Marriage Encounter insignia on the cover was the Bible verse, "Love one another, as I have loved you.") Once they had written their answers, they were expected to exchange notebooks "with a kiss," read each other's answers, and then discuss how those answers made them feel. When their time was up, they would be summoned back to the main room for more testimonials, followed by additional questions. The group leaders gave them printed sheets explaining "how to write a love letter," "how to dialogue," and "what is a feeling?" and assured them that everything written in the notebooks would be strictly private, known to the couples themselves only.

Allan and Betty, like most couples entering the program, were skeptical at first. It sounded silly, writing things down in a notebook. But they had no choice in the matter. That's what they were told to do. They were sent to their rooms. They started to write. Allan didn't know what to put down. Finally he wrote:

"I wanted to come here because I could see from the examples of Richard and JoAnn, Stu and Diane and especially David and Elaine that it could strengthen or rebuild a marriage. I think too that I haven't felt real close to you for some time and I don't like that. I hope I can learn to talk to you. I hope you can learn to talk to me. I want to be able to understand why you do the things you do, and I want to be able to tell you what I want."

Betty's notebook answer was more specific:

"I came for several reasons. First—for a weekend of relaxation which will probably help my nerves. The relaxation is a period free from the pressures of life at home (not that that is bad) just that it takes lots of energy and time. Second—and most important to get off by ourselves together. It's been a long time since we went to Switzerland. I miss not being able to really be alone and share things, but the time we're home together as a family are too great too. I'm not a person to be left alone at all. I want my husband with me and that's what we'll have this weekend—just us!!

"I hope to gain a little more freedom in expression between us. I don't often hold back my feelings unless I'm mad—then not for long but I feel that sometimes you don't let me know when things are bothering you. We need to work on this!"

As they read over their answers and then discussed what they had written, Allan was pleased to see that Betty really was responding to this concept. After a few minutes, one of the group leaders came by and knocked on their door. It was time for the next session.

The questions became progressively more personal. The next session was called "Focus on Feelings." The couples were asked to retire to their rooms and answer three questions:

What do I like best about you? How do I feel about that?

What do I like best about myself? HDIFAT? [one of many official Marriage Encounter abbreviations]

What do I like best about us? HDIFAT?

Suddenly the Gores were in a realm that brought out emotions Betty had never been able to express before. To the first question, she wrote, "The thing I like best about you is your calmness and your ability to look at everything squarely. You don't know (or maybe you do) how this affects me. . . . You're my tranquilizer. . . ." She liked herself, on the other hand, for her devotion to little things: doing the dishes, seeing that the toys were put away, duties that were important to her even though Allan thought she "overemphasized" them. And her final answer—what she liked about them as a couple—was "that special feeling I get when we're together . . . Warm and happy—It's horrible when we're not—it's like I'm only half me—maybe that means I'm not secure enough. I don't think so—your presence is just important to me."

Allan's answers were much more prosaic. He liked Betty's "dedication to raising the children and [her] job," even though he sometimes resented the attention her teaching got. He liked himself for his calmness and rationality. He liked them for their "promising future." He felt "secure, but not totally fulfilled yet."

The "encounter" session was in full swing on Saturday, and as the day wore on, through meals and pep talks and instructions on how to DILD ("describe in loving detail") or "share our uniqueness" or "open up the gift of dialogue," and as the questions got progressively more personal and incisive, the group started taking on all the outward appearances of a love-in. Encouraged to show affection publicly, couples started emerging from their rooms with arms entwined, holding hands during the meeting-room sessions, and exchanging light kisses at meals. Everyone was issued a name tag. Allan's said "Allan and Betty Gore." Betty's said "Betty and Allan Gore." The couples were encouraged not to carry on any conversations with others without including their spouse entirely. Given the total immersion, the lack of outside influences, the complete concentration on one person for an entire weekend, it wasn't surprising that remarkable things were beginning to happen. Allan was beginning to realize why, when couples emerged from Marriage Encounter, they were likely to become evangelists for the cause.

During their time together in Room 321, Allan and Betty were certainly starting to feel closer. Responding to a question about "masks," Allan wrote, "I wear the mask of the loving husband and father because I want my wife to be happy and fulfilled . . . sometimes I want to have close relationships with persons outside our family and to do so makes me feel that I am taking away from what I should be giving to them . . . I wear the mask of the 'super-worker' . . . I tend to discard the ideas of others in favor of my own." But once he had written it, he decided not to show it to Betty (an allowable Marriage Encounter option). Then when the couples were asked to write a "love letter on feelings of disillusionment," Allan unloosed the dikes: "I have feelings of boredom, emptiness, and sort of loneliness. I don't really know why, but I do. I don't feel like I really know what makes you happy, and that's frustrating. . . . Sometimes I feel like what is most important to you is your classroom—not me. That may not be true, but sometimes I feel jealous of that classroom."

Betty's "love letters" on Saturday began with a confession of her shortcomings ("I wear the mask of the 'Do it all' person") and led up to her most deep-seated fears. "So many times," she began one letter, "I feel that sex is an area that we are a long way apart. I guess part of it is the way I was brought up— that sex is dirty and wrong—and for a long time the fear of becoming pregnant when I didn't want to be. . . . I want to be desirable to you—and I want to make you happy." In response to another question, she touched on an even more general anxiety:

"I guess the thing that I find hardest to talk about is the fear of what is to come. If only all of life would be mapped out so we knew when was the best time to buy a house, when to move, when your parents would die and all the rest of the things we wonder about.

"It's hard for me to talk about sex too (more of the upbringing stuff). Sometimes it's so hard to feel calm and quiet as you need to be to enjoy sex. I guess the relaxation part is the hardest part for me. That's why in Switz. a little (or a lot) of wine helped. It relaxed me so I could really be free to enjoy it all. I've tried several times to have some but what we've gotten tastes bad, or Alisa's up, or it's a school night etc. There's always a drawback. Does this mean I'm not comfortable with sex if I need wine to make love more pleasant? I don't know.

"Also—you know that I've not been very happy at Lucas at church. I guess we'll just wait out the minister because the friends are there that mean so much. But the extent of discontent I feel with the services and the minister ruin and almost diminish any feelings that I gain from church services. How can you feel close to God and one another when the minister doesn't? . . . I need a minister who really says something and is sincere. I'm not sure ours is either. I don't enjoy singing in the choir that much. I feel inadequate as a singer and so why waste my time? Maybe all these feelings are just something that I've invented out of nothing. But I always feel that the choir sounds pretty bad, so why waste time on it."

When the sexual topics started showing up in Betty's letters, Allan felt unable to respond. How could he tell her that one of the reasons he didn't want sex as much anymore is that he was sleeping with Candy? The weekend was supposed to bring about total honesty, but that was one detail he intended not to reveal. When they went to bed Saturday night, exhausted from the long day, they made love before going to sleep—and Allan could tell that the weekend was going to be good for both of them.

Sunday is the final, and the most special day of Marriage Encounter. It begins with religious services, then more group sessions, and then each couple is given a mimeographed sheet. On it is the Big Question of the weekend: "What are my reasons for wanting to go on living?" The couples retire to their rooms for ninety minutes of writing in their notebooks, followed by ninety minutes of dialogue—a total of three hours to do what is called the "matrimonial evaluation." It's a session intended to bring out the intense emotions that have been building throughout the weekend. After the "go on living" session, couples frequently emerge from their rooms with tear-stained faces and tousled hair. In the case of the Gores, it was a totally engrossing—and satisfying—experience. They declared their love over and over, both in letters and the dialogue. They recalled their favorite times together. They remembered their impressions when they first met. Near the end of his letter, Allan wrote: "Before this weekend . . . I was beginning to feel like I didn't know if I really wanted to live with *You*. But just in the short time we've had together this weekend, I have realized that what I was feeling was not 'I don't like you' but more like I don't feel excited about you because I'm too used to the way things are. . . . I want to share a lot more of your feelings and I want to be able to share mine with you."

Betty was equally ecstatic, but near the end of her letter, she turned suddenly solemn:

"Here I sit crying because I am so happy and so proud to be your wife. I've known that all along, but when you really stop to think about it we are so lucky to have each other. Let's don't let anything come between us. We've been through so much, all of it we can look back at as good (except the times you were gone for a long time). Those times I'll never see as good. They were very difficult and when I think of your being gone more I remember those times with dread. The aloneness, the coldness of a house that really wasn't a home without you there, the fear for your safety, because you were where I was not, and I couldn't make sure you were okay. I never really felt fear for my safety at home alone, but the feeling of being alone is the worst possible one to have. It's like you're in a dark tunnel and you've got a long ways to go to the light. The light isn't there till you're home again safe and sound. And sometimes the times you were gone made the tunnel very long."

That night, when Allan and Betty emerged from room 321 for the final time, the entire group gathered to celebrate the sacrament of the Lord's Supper (using an "alternate" modernized text), during which they were instructed to sip the communion wine in the Marriage Encounter fashion, with arms linked. Afterward, in the final emotional climax, they were remarried in a ceremony in which they led each other through the traditional vows. Many of their "encountered" friends surprised them with their presence at the ceremony, and others sent their love through a package of greeting cards, congratulating them on their new commitment. When they got in the car to go home, the radio happened to be on, broadcasting the wrap-up show for the Dallas Cowboys game. Allan switched it off; it was just noise to him, part of a past life.

Then, when they got home that night, they fielded calls until bedtime, all from joyful well-wishers, soon to be part of their "Flame group" (as in "Keep the flame burning"), which would meet regularly to keep the spirit of fellowship alive.

The Gores ran one errand before they returned to Wylie, though. They stopped by the Montgomery house in Fairview to pick up Bethany, whom Candy had kept for the weekend. Allan went to the door while Betty waited in the car.

"How was it?" asked Candy as she handed him the baby.

"It was really good for us."

"What does that mean?"

"I don't know."

The next morning Allan was still riding his emotional high as he dressed for work. On the drive into Richardson, he tried to shut out all sensations except thoughts of Betty. He wanted nothing to do with the outside world. His life had changed. He wanted to concentrate all his thoughts and feelings on his marriage, which was once again the most important thing in his life. Yet when he got to work, he knew that sooner or later he would need to call Candy. She would want to meet him for lunch. He had to face that squarely. He had to be honest.

They met a week later; she brought a picnic lunch and they went back to the park in North Dallas. Allan did most of the talking. He told Candy all about Marriage Encounter and what it had done for them.

"We learned a lot about each other," he said. "I think maybe I was wrong about Betty in some ways. I think a lot of the things she doesn't like about me were based on fears of loneliness instead of bitchiness. We told each other things that we hadn't even thought about."

"That's good," said Candy. "I'm glad."

"I don't necessarily feel different about you," said Allan, "but I do feel strongly that I want to give my full resources to my family. The relationship with you is taking away some of the emotional involvement and energy that I could direct toward Betty and the kids. I'm not sure how long this feeling will last or what will happen, but I know I don't want to interfere with it."

"What does that mean for me?"

"I'm not sure."

Allan suddenly had no desire to go to bed with Candy again.

"I'm not sure I can deal with not seeing you," said Candy.

"I don't want to hurt you. I'm just trying to explain how I feel."

"Does this mean you can't see me?"

"I don't know. They said an awful lot of things at those Marriage Encounter meetings, but they never said you couldn't see someone else."

"You're still using a double standard."

After making the strongest argument ever for breaking off the affair, Allan couldn't bring himself to say the words. They left the issue hanging, but agreed to meet again the next day. When they did, Candy came directly to the point.

"Allan, you seem to be leaving it up to me. So I've decided. I won't call. I won't try to see you. I won't bother you anymore."

"That's fine with me," said Allan. "I can do that."

They both cried a little, because they both knew it was over. Allan was secretly relieved that she had made the decision, not him. That way he didn't have to bear the guilt. He hadn't planned for it to happen that day. That's just the way it worked out.

Candy had mixed emotions as well. She was telling the truth when she said she didn't know how she would deal with the loss of Allan. She had grown comfortable with the idea of loving two people. She loved Allan's casual phone calls and small kindnesses, and she would miss them. The good news was that she didn't have to make any more damned picnic lunches.

Betty Gore continued her regular visits to the doctor even after the Marriage Encounter weekend, mostly to get tranquilizers and painkillers for her various ailments. But one day in mid-October she rushed to his office and was much more agitated than usual: she had discovered a lump on her left breast. The doctor took a look at it and almost immediately diagnosed it as a benign fibrosis of some kind, totally harmless, but just to be sure he sent Betty to another doctor for a second opinion. The other doctor made the same diagnosis and told Betty to stop taking birth control pills and reduce her caffeine intake.

That night Betty told Allan about her fears, especially the panic she felt when she first found the lump. Allan comforted her, and then they sat down to do their daily "ten and ten."

This is a Marriage Encounter routine in which encountered couples choose a topic, write love letters on that topic for ten minutes, then spend ten minutes talking about the letters. Allan and Betty had been doing it faithfully every night since the weekend. They chose the topic of "growing old together."

"There's only one thing that bothers me," wrote Betty. "I'm so afraid that something will happen and I won't get to see the kids grow up and be around to grow old. I guess with a new baby it suddenly occurs to me that something could happen and I won't see her grow up. Now that we're really getting things together too, I'm just very afraid that something will happen and it will all be taken away. Are all my feelings silly? I hope they are just part of my being depressed which I don't really feel too much, but there's definitely something there. I sure have no reason to feel this way."

That weekend the Gores went to church, but it was obvious that Betty was still disturbed by the lump, which hadn't gone away. After church, Alisa Gore had gone home with Jenny Montgomery, a common occurrence, and, as usual, Betty called in the late afternoon to make arrangements for Alisa to come back. Candy set out in the station wagon for the Seis Lagos subdivision—the halfway point between Fairview and Wylie, where they usually met—but was surprised to find Allan there instead of Betty.

"Betty's found a lump in her breast," he said, "and she's very upset."

"I'm sorry to hear that."

"They think it's benign."

"Good."

The next day Candy drove to Wylie to see Betty. As soon as she entered the house on Dogwood, Betty collapsed into her arms, tears streaming down her face. Candy was amazed. Marriage Encounter *had* changed her. It was the first genuine display of emotion she had ever witnessed from Betty Gore. Candy felt closer to her, too, as she stroked her head and told her she was sure it was nothing, she had nothing to worry about.

A few days later Candy received a long letter from Allan. Apparently he was taking the Marriage Encounter experience to heart and expressing himself in writing to everyone. At any rate, he tried to explain why it was better for both of them that they not see each other any longer except at church. "We were both using each other," he said. He also made a reference to the conversation they'd had at Seis Lagos, indicating he thought Candy was "cold" when he'd told her about Betty's lump. He said he would always think the best of her, always love her in his way, but things were better this way.

Candy showed the letter to Sherry Cleckler. Sherry tried to console her, but she was obviously taking things very hard.

"It's so unfair," she kept saying.

Of the dozens of singles bars in Dallas, most of them trendy, stylish, and short-lived, the Currency Club stood out as an exception. Located in the basement of a Marriott Hotel, its warm, dark interior was a haven for lonely people somewhat beyond the point of competing in dress and beauty with the college-age people who inhabited more fashionable places. The Currency Club was a little quieter, its clientele a little older. The dance floor even had a little space for dancing. It adhered to the age-old formula of at least two men to every woman, but most of those men on any given night were between thirty and forty-five. Most of them appeared to be unattached.

Candy sought refuge at the Currency Club in the weeks just after breaking up with Allan. It was difficult to arrange, but Sherry was all for it and wanted to go along herself. With the help of a young girl who worked with Sherry at the beauty salon, Candy and Sherry were able to sneak over to the Currency on nights when their husbands were out of town or involved with other things. Mostly they would just have a few drinks and dance and flirt with the men. On some nights they would meet a special friend named Chuck. Chuck had an eye for Candy, and the two of them would sit together in a booth and sometimes Chuck would put his arm around her. It was not anything too serious, especially since Candy and Sherry usually had to get back in time to relieve the baby sitter, but it amused them for a while and made Candy feel a little better about not having Allan to talk to anymore.

The last week in October the Montgomerys walked next door to the home of their neighbor the mayor, Peter Haas, for his annual Halloween party. Candy was looking forward to the party a little more than Pat, for in the back of her mind she wondered whether Richard, a man she had met at last year's party, would be there. He was around forty, tall and thin, with a mustache, light brown hair with a hint of blond. She had flirted with him, and they had danced a great deal. When they got to the party this year, she was delighted to see that he *was* there again, and she was startled to realize that he remembered her as well. Again they danced together, far more times than they should have, and afterwards they sat together on the piano. Richard was a natural conversationalist, smooth and fluent. He asked about Candy's writing classes (one of her favorite subjects), and she asked about his childhood (one of his), and they talked about animals and children and along the way she discovered that Richard was married and had three kids. At some point Richard leaned over to her and whispered.

"What's your number?"

Candy smiled at him. "Six."

"No. Really. Can I have your number?"

"Oh, you mean my *phone* number. I thought you meant my favorite number." She instantly gave it to him.

Richard called the next day and asked Candy if she would meet him for lunch. Richard didn't know how lucky he was, because Ian had preschool that week and a day was available. When Candy related all the logistical details, Richard suggested that, in that case, why not meet him right after dropping off Ian at school—in other words, at 9:15 in the morning. Richard was a baggage-tag salesman and could pretty much determine his own hours. Candy agreed, and went over to Sherry's later that day to tell her something promising was shaping up.

They met at a shopping center near the freeway in Plano. Candy left her car there and they drove to the Marriott in North Dallas (a now familiar haunt), where they went into the restaurant for a late breakfast. Actually all they had was coffee, several cups of it, as they chatted about their children and their past lives. Suddenly, Richard said, "Would you be offended if I asked you to go to bed?"

"No," said Candy, just as quickly.

Richard was certainly a fast mover. Candy liked that. It excited her. He went to the front desk and got them a room, and they had almost an hour and a half before she had to leave to pick up Ian.

One thing she could tell right away: Richard was going to be a great way to forget Allan. He was *very* accomplished in bed, the experimental type that she had always been looking for, and he was impetuous and forceful and persistent. He called again the very next day, told her how great it had been, and wanted to know when they could do it again. When she explained that she only had Tuesdays and Thursdays free, he said, "Great, we can do it every Tuesday and Thursday." That wasn't exactly what Candy had in mind, but she was lured by the adventure of it all. She confided to Sherry that she had finally found a real lover.

Richard's dates were more romantic than Allan's. Usually Richard would take off the full four hours so they could do other things besides sex. Once they went Christmas shopping at Valley View Mall, where Richard had Candy's picture taken sitting on Santa's knee. Richard took her to some nice restaurants—quite a change from the troublesome picnic lunches for Allan. When they wanted to have sex, they would go to a private apartment in North Dallas; Richard would pay his friend for getting the key for part of the day. The sex was pretty good, especially at first, although as time went on Candy felt the boredom returning as Richard started to run out of tricks.

Everything about the affair was torrid. When for some reason Candy couldn't meet him on a Tuesday or a Thursday, Richard acted really hurt and complained endlessly. Sometimes Candy would give in just to avoid hurting his feelings. In a month and a half, in fact, she probably slept more with Richard than she had slept with Allan in a year. When she *didn't* see Richard, he was always calling. He even came to the house once while Sherry was there. And at that point Candy decided that things were getting out of control. She knew that Richard traveled a lot, and supposed she was far from the first woman he had had an extramarital affair with. He made her feel guilty, in a way Allan never had. He even made her feel threatened, in a way that was both exciting and scary. Sometimes he would try to tempt her into thinking about things she knew she should stay away from.

"Don't you think I would make you happy if we were married?" he would say.

"We would get tired of each other like all couples do."

"You and I? We would *never* get tired of talking."

Conversation like that scared Candy; she didn't want to deal with it.

Finally, after just a few weeks of tempestuous lovemaking, Candy told him she thought they should end the affair.

"I don't think this is good for me anymore," she said.

Richard was not only hurt; he was furious. He yelled at

her, told her she was being insensitive about what they had together.

"I'm cheating Pat, and I don't like that."

Then he refused to talk about it. But this time Candy really had made up her mind. No matter how many times he called, she resisted all his entreaties. He was too big a burden. He was infringing on time she wanted to devote to other people. She was bored with him.

One night shortly after the breakup, Candy and Sherry figured out a way to go back to the Currency Club. There was a great selection of men. Candy danced her heart out and didn't get home until 3 A.M.

The next day she called Sherry to talk.

"Maybe an affair is not what I'm looking for," she said. "I keep looking for somebody to make me happy, and none of them can. Maybe I need to do something for myself."

Richard called one more time, begging Candy to give it another chance.

"I've decided it's not what I want, Richard."

"What do you want?"

Candy didn't know for sure, but she knew where she might start: Marriage Encounter.

Candy had first broached the subject with Allan. She knew she had promised not to call him, but it seemed like this fell under the heading of professional advice. Candy had been amazed by the changes wrought in Betty by the Marriage Encounter weekend. Several of the women at church noticed it, too. The sullenness was gone. Betty didn't seem so cold, or so snobbish. She could talk normally to other people. Candy had another reason for being curious about Marriage Encounter. She had seen it change Allan into a completely devoted family man almost overnight. He was so transformed by the experience that he was truly hurt when he thought Candy didn't show enough sensitivity to Betty's lump. Allan was so willing to please Betty that he had even agreed to her request that they leave Lucas Church. They had started attending Wylie Methodist, but returned to Lucas whenever Ron was not going to be there for some reason or other. (The forgiveness born of the Marriage Encounter experience didn't extend to Ron.)

"Should Pat and I get into Marriage Encounter?" she asked Allan.

"I don't know whether it would be good for you and Pat or not," Allan told her.

Normally Candy would have thought the idea was ludicrous—she disliked the pushiness of the Marriage Encounter people, and she distrusted group therapy—but Allan was one of the most levelheaded people she knew, and it had worked for him.

"I'm having real difficulties getting over us," she said. "I'm miserable. I need to try *something*."

"I'm not sure it would be wise, Candy. They say that Marriage Encounter is definitely not for couples who are having serious problems. And from what you told me about your feelings for Pat, I'm just not so sure."

"You make me so curious about it, though. Does it really work for you?"

"So far it has."

Then Allan confirmed the miraculous changes in Betty since the weekend. Once they had gotten back to Wylie, she had not only wanted to keep up the love-letter writing and the dialogue sessions, but she quickly volunteered them to be leaders for the Flame group in their area. Her enthusiasm ranked with that of JoAnn Garlington.

Despite Allan's mild warnings, Candy added Marriage Encounter to her list. It was a long list she was making, of new and different experiences she intended to try in 1980. As she told Sherry, she wanted to "rediscover me." She wanted to stop looking for fulfillment in men—she had almost decided that was impossible anyway—and try to make something that was truly her own. Maybe she would write a novel. She had tried that once before, and even written about seventy pages based on her mother's family history. Richard had reminded her of it; he thought she was a good writer. She was talking more often to Jackie Ponder now, calling once a week or so to discuss her new resolve. (Jackie was more than a little relieved when she learned the affair was over.)

Another thing Candy decided to do was enroll in special advanced English classes at Plano High School. One of her first papers dealt with Marvell's "To His Coy Mistress," a poem she liked for its depiction of an urgent lover and a reluctant lady. ("The anxious haste of compulsive love and immediate need," she wrote, "produces a frustration that must result in either compromise or incompleteness.") At the same time she pitched herself into the hot political issue of the moment, campaigning door-to-door for a bond issue that would be used for improvements to Lovejoy School. Candy took up painting. And most important of all, over coffee one morning she and Sherry formulated a plan to start their own business: they would paint and wallpaper the interiors of houses. It was all they could think of and it was better than sitting around feeling miserable. Neither of the husbands took them very seriously when they mentioned the business—it was to be called "The Covergirls"—and so they redoubled their efforts to make it work.

Pat had to be talked into Marriage Encounter. He was growing dissatisfied with their marriage, too, but not to the point of thinking anything was *really* wrong. He knew Candy didn't like it when he wouldn't say anything about her writing or her outside activities, but it was because he simply didn't know what to say. He didn't understand writers; he was a scientist. He couldn't say anything intelligent anyway. She thought he didn't have feelings. It was just that he didn't express them very well. Sometimes he didn't express them at all. But he didn't think anything was wrong. And even if something *was* wrong, he didn't think Marriage Encounter was the answer to anything.

Candy dragged Pat to the weekend anyway. She simply had to find out what all the fuss was about. The first couple of sessions, they went to their motel room complaining and making jokes about it, fearing that their worst expectations were confirmed. But after a while, with nothing else to do and the questions becoming more and more interesting, they started truly trying to do the work, write the love letters, have the dialogue; and the process started to have the same magical effect on them it had had on the Gores. Pat, especially, was moved to say things he had never voiced before. And when they got to the final, climactic, three-hour session on why they wanted to go on living, they both collapsed into each other's arms, crying, and then quickly made love before the group leader came and summoned them back to the main hall.

"Oh Pat," Candy told him, "we were so close to divorce at one time. I'm so glad we stuck it out."

She never explained what she meant, and Pat never asked.

Before they returned home, they were asked to write down their Marriage Encounter goals for the year. Candy had only one: "To be happy."

Once the euphoria of the weekend had subsided, the Montgomerys were less enthusiastic Flames than the Gores were. For one thing, they got tired of writing the letters after doing only seven or eight of them; it seemed so much easier simply to speak frankly. For another, they had absolutely no interest in going to the biweekly Flame meetings, to socialize with other "encountered" couples.

"All this is well intentioned," said Pat. "We don't need it." This time Candy agreed.

What she hadn't counted on, however, was the neighborly interest of the Wylie/Plano area Flame leader, Betty Gore. By this time the Gores and Garlingtons had left Lucas Church, but Betty still kept up with Marriage Encounter couples and knew the Montgomerys had been encountered. One day in mid-January, Betty called Candy out of the blue and invited the Montgomerys to spend a Saturday evening with the Gores, discussing their wonderful weekends. Candy, overcome with a vague dread, told Betty she would have to check with Pat first. That night Betty mentioned to Allan that she had invited the Montgomerys over, and Allan panicked.

Allan called Candy from work the next morning.

"I understand Betty invited you over for Saturday night."

"Yeah, what in the world are we going to do?"

"Is it a problem for you?"

"I don't know, Allan. I'm afraid it will be. I'm afraid I won't be able to see you in that context. It might be too painful."

"Would it help if we met for lunch first? Just to see whether we can deal with it?"

"It might."

"Let's have lunch tomorrow and discuss it."

They met at the Italian Inn in Richardson, the first time they had seen each other privately since the affair, and Candy was scared to death.

"Just seeing you like this affects me," she said. "I'm afraid of wanting you again."

"I'm sorry, Candy. I feel guilty about messing up your life."

"I'm beginning to get over it."

"What about your weekend? Did that help?"

"It was good for both of us," she said. "Pat and I talked more on that weekend than anytime I can remember."

Allan asked about Lucas Church. Candy told him the choir suffered by his absence. They caught up on news of the children. As they got up to leave, Allan said, "Well, what do you think? What are you going to tell Betty?"

"I don't think I can come. It hurts too much."

"Well, I know I can handle it if you decide you want to come."

"I don't think so."

A couple of hours later Betty called Allan at work to tell him that Candy had accepted the invitation. Surprised, he called Candy at home.

"What happened?"

"On the way home I decided that maybe this is a good way to *end* the hurt. I shouldn't hate Betty; we should be friends. Maybe it will be over after this."

"Good."

Then Candy called Sherry to tell her about the lunch. "It's good that I went," she said. "I think I've finally gotten Allan out of my system. I found out I really didn't have anything to say to him—and do you know what? His eyes are too close together. By the time it was over I had no desire to go to bed with him ever again."

The evening itself was more boring than awkward. Betty served wine. The men compared jobs and half-heartedly discussed computer programs and the mileage they were getting with their respective cars. They all agreed that Marriage Encounter was a great thing. The kids played with the baby and tried to get her to walk. Everyone was very polite. The Montgomerys left early because they wanted to get the kids to bed.

The next week Candy got an unsigned greeting card in the mail. It read "Good To Have You As A Friend."

She called Allan. "Is this from you?"

"Yes."

"I just wanted to know."

She was over it. Allan could tell by the tone in her voice. He was greatly relieved.

The spring of 1980 was a busy time. Allan was caught up in his work, sometimes spending fifty-five hours a week at the office, and Betty became more active in Marriage Encounter. The Gores even managed a Marriage Encounter weekend themselves. They were starting to feel more comfortable at Wylie Methodist Church, although it was nothing like the excitement of the Jackie Ponder days at Lucas. Allan and Betty both joined the choir there. Occasionally they would go back to Lucas for special occasions like the Easter services. Betty looked healthier than ever and visited her doctor infrequently. They continued to do their "ten and ten" every day, filling two fat spiral notebooks with love letters and then starting on two more, although occasionally they had to use the most trivial topics because they couldn't think of anything they hadn't already written about.

Candy plunged into her "rediscover me" program. Besides her English classes and her painting and her work in the bond election, Candy found a new political cause in the person of Roger Harper, a young candidate for the office of county commissioner who had promised to do something about the outmoded roads around Fairview and Lucas. "The Covergirls" was properly registered as a Texas corporation, the business cards were printed, and Candy and Sherry began to line up clients for the fall, when Ian would start first grade and Candy would have days to herself. In the meantime, she stayed active in the church, serving as the lay delegate to Methodist conferences and meetings. In April she and Barbara Green went together to a spiritual "retreat" at Lake Sharon, where they spent the weekend with other women, participating in lectures and seminars on the Bible viewed from different angles.

While Candy was gone on the retreat, the responsibility for taking care of the kids fell to Pat. It was the kind of job he liked up to a point, but he wasn't the best cook in the world and so the kids weren't always crazy about it. On the Friday night that Candy and Barbara left, Pat played with the kids a while, fed them, put them to bed, and then watched a little television. Starting to feel lonely, he decided to do something he hadn't done in a long time: reread the love letters from the summer he met Candy. He never got tired of them, even though they were kind of goofy and sentimental and immature. So Pat went upstairs to look in the yellow chest where Candy had always kept them wrapped up in a plastic bag. But they weren't there. Perplexed, Pat started a search of the entire house, looking in likely places, getting a little angry that Candy had moved them. Then he remembered that sometimes Candy kept things in her dresser, so he went back upstairs and looked in the dresser drawers. He didn't find the love letters, but underneath some undergarments he found a letter addressed to Candy with no return address on it.

It was obvious what it was as soon as Pat opened the envelope. It was a love letter, but not from him. Pat's hand began to shake. He sat down on the bed and read it all the way through, even to the closing "Love, Allan." He read it again, in a state of shock. It was dated October 1979, and it was a farewell letter. It mentioned "sexual experiences" and how much Allan had enjoyed them. It used the word "affair." Allan told Candy that he felt he had been using her, and that now he wanted to devote himself to Betty because of Marriage Encounter. The letter mentioned the Como Motel; the name seemed vaguely familiar to Pat. Allan told her how great the meals were there. Allan wrote fondly of their lunches together, their conversations, and how they would exchange greeting cards that said "Love Is . . . " on the front. Pat flinched and started to cry when he read that line again. The "Love Is . . . " cards were something he and Candy had exchanged for ten years. That was private. It was *theirs*. The letter mentioned something about Candy being "cold" the last time Allan saw her. Apparently whatever had happened was finished. Still, Pat grew despondent and then furious and then felt very lonely again. Candy wouldn't be back until Sunday. There was nothing to do.

That night Pat only slept about an hour. Half-remembered scenes came rushing back, like the time when Pat had seen Candy sneak up behind Allan and tickle him in church, like how Candy had made such a *big deal* out of Betty's having a baby last summer, with a sit-down Chinese dinner and everything. The Gores had left Lucas Church. Had it been to get away from Candy? At first, Pat kept thinking of the word "divorce." He didn't see any way around it, and yet the word scared him. But then he remembered the Marriage Encounter weekend; he remembered what Candy had said, about their coming so close to divorce. Maybe that had been her way of telling him that she made a mistake. But how could Allan have done this? For a while Pat decided that first thing Saturday he would call Allan and tell him he never wanted to see him or Betty again, and he certainly didn't want their children playing together. Better yet, he would call Betty and tell *her* about the letter; knowing Betty's capacity for holding a grudge, that would be the best revenge of all. But by morning Pat had decided not to make the call after all. Allan *had* ended the affair. He and Betty did have their marriage back together. And Betty was such an unstable personality that she might not be able to handle that at all. It would be unfair to punish Betty; she had nothing to do with it.

But was this something he could forgive? The worst part of it was that she had done it with Allan. Pat *liked* Allan. It was starting to drive him crazy that Candy wasn't home to talk about these things. So late Saturday morning, Pat called Sherry Cleckler at her beauty shop.

"Sherry, I found a love letter from Allan to Candy, and I need to know something. I know she would tell you. Is it over? Is it completely and totally over?"

Sherry was a little panicked by the call. She told Pat to hang up so she could call from another phone.

"Pat, it is over," she said when she called back, "and it won't happen again. It was just a brief thing, more friendship than anything else, and it was just a stage that Candy went through. But she really loves you, Pat. Candy is a good mother and a good wife and a good friend to you, and she made a mistake, but it was only for a brief period and it didn't mean anything."

"Okay. But it *is* over?"

"It's been over a long time."

"I want to talk to Candy about this in my own way, so I don't want you to tell her that I've talked to you. Please promise me that I can talk to her first."

Sherry promised.

That afternoon Pat drove to a floral shop in McKinney and picked out half a dozen long-stemmed roses. Then he returned home and spent the rest of the day in his study, composing a letter to Candy. It was hard work, because Pat wasn't a writer and every word was a laborious effort. The result was a page and a half, mostly faltering attempts to describe his feelings for her, and telling her that, whatever happened between her and Allan, he now realized that it was his fault. He had neglected her. He had caused her to seek affection and understanding elsewhere. He wrapped it up with, "I want our marriage to be good. These roses are how I feel about you."

Candy arrived back home from the retreat on Sunday afternoon, and outwardly everything was normal. Pat was civil but not solicitous. The kids were glad to see her. She started cooking dinner. After a few minutes the phone rang, and she picked it up.

"Don't change your expression," said the voice on the other end.

"What?"

"Pat found Allan's letter," Sherry said.

"What?"

"He found Allan's letter and called me at work to find out if the affair is really over. He told me not to tell you he knows."

Candy hung up but didn't say a word. After dinner she cleared away the dishes and went into the living room and made small talk, dreading what was about to happen, and then a thought lifted her spirits. Maybe Pat wouldn't say *anything*. Maybe Sherry had explained it to him, he knew it was over, and they wouldn't have to discuss it.

But Pat was waiting until bedtime. They went into the bedroom and changed into their night clothes, and then Pat reached under the bed and extracted the half-dozen long-stemmed roses. He handed them to her, and tears began to form in the corners of her eyes.

"I thought I could tell you how I felt better in a letter," said Pat, "and so I wrote it all down. I'm going downstairs while you read this letter. You come on down whenever you feel like it."

Candy sank onto the bed and read the letter through several times. Pat was telling her it was *his* fault. It was obvious that his pain was deep and real. She didn't know what to say or do. She wanted to pull the covers over her head and go to sleep and be a thousand miles away. She simply sat there and continued to cry.

After a few minutes, Pat wondered why she didn't come down to discuss the letter. So he went back upstairs and sat next to her on the bed. But she wouldn't say anything. She wouldn't even look at him. When he tried to touch her, she drew back and said "Don't" and continued to sob. It was a long time before Candy would let him put his arms around her, and then only for a short time, and a long time after that before she could talk at all.

"I'm so ashamed, Pat. I don't ever want to hurt you or the kids."

"I know. Don't worry."

A week later Candy and Pat started making plans for a long-delayed vacation. They would go to South Padre Island, just the two of them, and lie on the beach and treat it like a second honeymoon. Pat was determined to shower her with affection. He brought home a greeting card one night. It had roses on the front, and inside it said, "It's time to get the sand out of our marriage." It was almost ten years exactly since they had run through the desert dunes outside El Paso and first declared their love. Now Pat wanted the South Padre trip to be a new start.

The Gores were planning a vacation, too. They wanted to return to Europe that summer, and try to re-create the magic of the week they had spent together in Switzerland. They would leave in mid-June, shortly after Betty's school term ended.

As the summer of 1980 approached, Candy and Pat and Allan and Betty all agreed that their marriages had never been happier. Life was starting to make sense again.

15 · INTERROGATION

"I did have an affair," Allan Gore told Royce Abbott.

"Oh?"

"With Candy Montgomery."

Chief Abbott was startled, especially since he was hearing such news at 6 A.M., but he kept his voice calm and even.

"Well, I'm glad you told us that, Allan, but to set your mind at ease, Candy's already told us."

Candy had done no such thing, but the last thing Abbott wanted was for Allan to alert her. So Abbott pretended that the affair was of no particular importance to the investigation, but suggested that Allan come down to the station anyway and set the record straight. As soon as he got off the phone, Abbott contacted Joe Murphy, the burly DPS intelligence agent who lived in Wylie. Murphy's specialty was interrogation, and suddenly Abbott felt he was going to need him.

As soon as Abbott called, something had clicked in Murphy's mind. This was the right track. This was a motive, the first one they'd come up with. Love, lust, secret admiration—whatever it was, it was an excellent reason for murder. Husband out of town. His secret lover visiting the wife's house just before she's killed. Small bloody footprints at the scene. Most important of all: *they had both concealed the affair from the police*. That didn't mean he considered them the actual murderers, but perhaps they had made it possible. Perhaps it was a hired killing. But why an ax? Why the overkill? Why do it in the middle of the day? There was a lot Joe Murphy wanted to know.

"I couldn't sleep last night," said Allan Gore when he got to the Wylie police station just after seven that morning. "I got to thinking about some of the questions you asked me last night, and I felt I had to tell you the whole story."

"Start with the first time you met Mrs. Montgomery," said Murphy.

For the next half hour Murphy and Abbott sat listening to Allan's version of the affair. Allan was remarkably composed and unemotional, considering what he was saying.

"Did Candy ever mention getting a divorce?" asked Murphy. "Either you *or* she."

"She mentioned that she had not been in love with Pat, her husband, for some time. She said she was just staying with him until the kids were grown, then she intended to get a divorce. She said she still had her life to live and was looking forward to what life would be like when the kids were grown."

"What about your wife? Did she ever find out that you were having an affair?"

"As far as Betty ever indicating that she suspected Candy and I having an affair, she never let on. I'm not sure if she would have mentioned it even if she had. The past wasn't her concern. Only the present and future was what mattered to her."

"Why are you telling us this now when you failed to tell us last night?"

"Because after I got home last night, I thought about the questions you asked me about my having an affair. And after I got to thinking about it, I asked my daughter Alisa if Candy had taken her to Bible School that morning. Alisa said that she had, but that she had left and came back about lunch time. Alisa gave the time as leaving about 9 A.M. and returning about 12 noon. I felt that that was way too long for her to have been gone from church."

"Do you have witnesses as to where you were that morning, Mr. Gore?"

"Yes, sir. I arrived at my office about 8:30 A.M. and stayed there until I left for the airport. My witnesses there are John Alexander and Kevin Reynolds."

"And are you telling us that you never considered a divorce yourself?"

"I wasn't really in love with Candace. It was just a little fling for fun as far as I was concerned. She wanted it to be the same, but she fell in love anyway."

"Did either you or Mrs. Montgomery have any reason to want to kill your wife?"

"I had no reason to want to kill my wife, nor did I think Candy did. She had a great deal of love and concern for Betty and our children."

"Will you take a polygraph examination in order to verify all you've told me?" asked Murphy.

"Yes, I will take a polygraph."

"Did you kill your wife?"

"No."

"Do you know who did?"

"No."

"Do you have any idea who did or who would want to?"

"No."

"Mr. Gore, at this time we're going to have to read you your legal rights as prescribed by law. You have the right to remain silent. You have . . ."

For a moment Allan froze. As Murphy continued his wooden recitation of the well-known Miranda warning, Allan wondered whether he had done the right thing. He had thought about it before, but now he was certain: *he was a suspect in a murder case*.

As he left the station, Allan told the police that he was on his way to Kansas for Betty's funeral and would be away several days. When he got back to the house, Allan was disoriented. He mumbled a few words to Bob Pomeroy about having to "clear up" some things with the police. He needed to talk to someone. He needed to figure this out. Any other time, he would have called Candy Montgomery.

Doctors Irving Stone and Vincent DiMaio, the two top experts at the Dallas Institute of Forensic Sciences, sat in an office together that same morning, going over photographs of a corpse with a magnifying glass. The corpse was that of Betty Gore, but they were concerned only with her hands. They paused at the second finger of her left hand, having found what they were looking for: half the fingernail was missing, apparently sheared off by the ax.

"Vince, I don't think that's the same finger," said Stone. "I think the nail found at the scene was much smaller."

Stone left the office for a few minutes and went looking for the tiny plastic evidence bag holding a sheared-off fingernail. It was the same fingernail that young Officer Stanley had found on the living room floor of the Gore house, then left lying on the kitchen cabinet next to a microwave oven. One of the neighbors had eventually found it, long after the police were gone, and it had changed hands several times before finding its way to the lab in Dallas.

Now, on Tuesday morning, Stone removed it from the plastic bag and placed it next to the photograph of Betty Gore's lifeless left hand.

"It's not the same," said DiMaio.

Stone picked up the phone and called Stephen Deffibaugh, the sheriff's investigator assigned to the case.

"I think we have the murderer's nail," he said.

What he didn't say was that it might not be valid evidence in a court of law. Too many people had touched it. It had not been properly preserved. Any decent defense attorney could prevent a jury from ever getting a chance to see it.

The case was beginning to "open up," in the words of Joe Murphy. The tiny Wylie Police Department was crowded and abuzz with the movements of city, county, and state policemen, as well as an extra office worker, added to deal with the continuing flood of phone calls from anonymous tipsters, mental patients, and assorted weirdos. But Abbott and Murphy had no time for the press or the phone anymore. After their interview with Allan, they had shifted their investigation entirely. Instead of looking for the killer, they assumed they *had* the killer. Or was it killers? Was it Allan Gore or Candy Montgomery or both? Unfortunately, they had only one witness—the five-year-old girl who had seen a woman in blue jeans come out of the Gore house and drive away in a station wagon. Abbott decided to pay her another visit. She repeated the story for him, and by comparing the girl's memory with that of her grandmother, Abbott was able to come up with an approximate time of 11 A.M. for Candy's leaving the house. He then reviewed the statement Candy had given on Sunday; she had given her time of departure as around 10:20. It was something, but it wasn't hard and fast. Neither the girl nor the grandmother seemed that sure of themselves.

Deffibaugh had a gift for Abbott that day, too: the photographs taken at the crime scene. The most important one was the bloody thumbprint they had found on the freezer. Deffibaugh had taken only one shot of it, since he was running out of film, but fortunately it had come out clear and vivid. Unfortunately, they had no fingerprints of Candy Montgomery. They hadn't taken any on Sunday because she had never been a strong suspect in anyone's imaginings. Now they needed her prints, and they knew they couldn't get those without arousing her suspicions.

Deffibaugh had another lead, too, but it only confused matters more. At the memorial service Monday afternoon, DPS intelligence officers had taken photographs of everyone attending, as well as their cars and license plates. When they ran the license plate numbers through the computer, something curious turned up: David and Elaine Williams had gotten into a blue Chevrolet that was registered to Pat Montgomery. They had already started looking into this organization called Marriage Encounter and wondered what it was. Some kind of wife-swapping club maybe? This would tend to prove it.

At the end of the day Abbott, Deffibaugh, and Murphy all stopped to consider the facts. They had no hard evidence, but they hoped the photograph of the bloody thumbprint would give them some. They believed most of what Allan Gore had told them, but they figured he was still hiding something, too. They could continue to gather physical evidence—the strands of hair found in the bathtub could be matched against Candy's hair, for example—or they could simply form a theory of the case, call Candy in, and hope she confessed.

Late that night, they'd made their decision.

"Call her in," said Murphy. "I think I can break her."

When Candy took the call from Chief Abbott on Wednesday morning, she felt almost normal again. On Tuesday, the local housewives' cooperative had delivered a five-month supply of groceries, so Candy had called Sherry to come over and talk while they stored the cartons and packed things away in the freezer. Sherry was just as anxious to chit-chat, her parents having just left to go back to Alabama after a long weekend. They had taken their grandchildren with them, which meant that Sherry could stay the whole morning. The two friends were able to relax and talk for the first time since Betty's death. By the time Sherry left, Candy was starting to feel better.

Then, while she was having her second cup of coffee Wednesday morning, Chief Abbott called. He sounded relaxed, matter-of-fact. He had just a couple more questions, and he hoped it wouldn't be an imposition for her to come back in that morning. Candy readily agreed.

Within a few minutes Candy had taken Jenny and Ian over to Sherry's house and left for the station, telling Sherry she would only be gone for a short time.

She was ushered into Abbott's office and then left alone. Murphy and Abbott were surprised she got there so quickly and didn't want to talk to her until Fred Cummings arrived. Cummings was a Texas Ranger who specialized in fingerprint work; he would take the prints and match them against the photo Deffibaugh had taken of the freezer door. Also present was Jim Cochran, a DPS investigator who worked under Murphy and who had been present at the first Candy Montgomery interview. He was chosen as much for his manner as his police skill. He was tall, slender, grey-haired and fatherly, a striking contrast to the muscular, intimidating Murphy.

Cummings finally arrived and set up his fingerprint unit.

"We need to take your fingerprints," explained Abbott, "so we can screen out the prints of family and friends who were in the house that day. It's just routine."

After the fingerprints were taken, Cochran, Murphy, and Abbott all crowded into Abbott's office to conduct the actual interview.

"First we need you to go back over your itinerary on the day Betty Gore was killed," said Abbott, "because when we talked to you on Sunday we didn't have all the information that we have now."

Candy repeated the events of June 13, including everything she had told them on Sunday but, in response to their questions, adding more details. She told them about playing with Betty's dogs in the backyard, and going into the bathroom to "pick" her hair, and leaving her business card on Betty's table, and going to the Target store in Plano, but then realizing her watch had stopped and hurrying back to the church. She described each of the four phone calls from Allan Gore. Then, because of some chance remark she made, Cochran got onto the subject of Marriage Encounter.

"Just what is Marriage Encounter?" he asked.

When she gave a brief definition, he pressed her for more information. What was it for? How did the organization work? She tried to explain it as best she could. Murphy abruptly changed the subject.

"Do you know whether Betty Gore was having an affair?" he asked.

"No. Not as far as I know."

"Do you know whether *Allan* Gore was having an affair?"

"No."

Candy assumed they were referring to the time of Betty's death, and she considered her answer truthful.

The interrogators, still very cordial and neighborly, shifted the subject to Candy's marriage. They wanted to know how long she had been married, how she felt about Pat, whether they quarreled often or had any serious problems. She indicated her marriage was fine.

"Have either of you had any outside affairs?" asked Murphy.

"Pat wouldn't do that."

"But you would?"

Candy paused only slightly. "I did."

"With who?"

"I had an affair with Allan Gore."

Candy felt scared, really scared, for the first time. They had known the answer to that question before they asked it.

While they were talking, Cummings came into the room with a fingerprint and laid it on Abbott's desk. Abbott compared it to something else he had on his desk as the interrogation continued.

"Now, Mrs. Montgomery," said Cochran, "I think you can see that there aren't any bright lights here, and this isn't a dark room, and we aren't using any scare tactics like they do in the movies. But we need to ask you to be honest with us about your affair with Allan Gore."

"Okay," she said.

Candy's version of the affair was not much different from Allan's. She mentioned the volleyball game, readily identified herself as the aggressor in the relationship, and told them about the Como and the picnic lunches. They wanted to know how long the affair lasted, and Candy insisted that it had been over for at least eight months.

"Did your husband know about it?"

"Not at first, but he found out." She then described the weekend when Pat had found Allan's letter.

"Was Pat angry?"

"He was mad, and he felt hurt, but he didn't dwell on it for very long."

"What about you? Were you mad at Allan for ending the affair?"

"I didn't want the relationship to end, but I knew that it had to."

"We're going to have to talk to Allan again," said Cochran, "because there seem to be some inconsistencies in his story."

Candy assumed that meant Allan hadn't told them about the affair.

"You *murdered* Betty Gore, didn't you?"

Startled, Candy looked up and saw the burning eyes of Joe Murphy.

"No, I *didn't.*"

Murphy thought the tone of her voice was too calm and collected. This woman was a housewife. Why didn't she go into hysterics?

"Yes, you did," he said brutally. "You're nothing but a murderer. Betty Gore was your friend and you just chopped and chopped and chopped on her. You're nothing but a little cold-blooded murderer, and you sit there and lie to us about it, and you make me so sick that I can't even stay in this room anymore."

Murphy grabbed the doorknob, swung open the door, and bolted from the room. He slammed it behind him. Candy trembled slightly but said nothing.

"All right, Candy," said Cochran, reassuringly, "I can see that something's on your chest. You can talk to me. I understand."

Candy did feel better once Murphy was out of the room.

"I didn't murder her," she said. "I didn't do it."

"Well, I think you did," said Cochran, not too accusingly. "And I think a jury might think you did."

He held up the fingerprint that Cummings had put on Abbott's desk. "If I show them this print, and I tell them this is your print, and I show them the footprints we found in Betty Gore's house . . ."

"They're gonna think I did it, too," interrupted Candy. "But I didn't do it."

"Would you be willing to take a polygraph examination if we set one up for you tomorrow?"

"Yes. If that will prove I didn't murder her."

"Would you care if I looked over your car?"

"No."

"Come on, then, let's walk out there."

As they walked out to where Candy had parked, she felt a lessening of pressure.

"You're trying to pin something on me that's not right," she said. "You're trying to manipulate me to admit something I didn't do."

Cochran peered through the window of her car and noticed a pair of rubber-soled sandals on the floor.

"Would you mind if I kept those shoes for a while?"

"No," she said as she got into the car.

"And I'd appreciate it if we could have the ones you're wearing, too."

Candy felt humiliated as she removed her blue tennis shoes and handed those to Cochran.

"This is not fair, what you're doing," she said.

"If you pass a polygraph examination tomorrow," said Cochran, "then I'll apologize to you for all this."

Candy drove the ten miles to Sherry's house in a trance. As soon as Sherry opened the door, Candy all but collapsed into her arms.

"They think I did it," she sobbed. "*They think I murdered Betty.*"

16 • FRIENDS OF
THE ACCUSED

Don Crowder was peeved when he found out one of the couples from church wanted to talk to him about the Betty Gore murder case. Everybody overreacting to a little routine police investigation. Don was planning to spend the day at the Dallas law office he shared with his friend Jim Mattox, the Congressman. It was a nondescript building on the edge of Little Mexico, just a stone's throw from the behemoth high rises of downtown Dallas where the big corporate law firms made their homes; but it suited Don just fine. Some days he didn't even come into town, because he was finding plenty to do in the little towns out in the country, but when he did drive to Dallas he liked the fact that his office was apart from the rest of the legal community, almost invisible among the furniture stores, Mexican restaurants, and low-slung office buildings of Cedar Springs Avenue. It was a slow day, so Don had the luxury of a long lunch. He had just returned when Rob Udashen, a young lawyer, hurried into his office.

"Do you know a Candy Montgomery?" asked Rob.

"Sure, real well."

"Would she have anything to do with the Betty Gore murder?"

"Sheeit no. Why?"

"Because her husband called and insisted that he see one of us today. The police have interrogated her, and he seems worried that they really are suspicious of her."

"Pat Montgomery is just panicky because they ask everybody questions like that."

"Well, he says the cops have printed her and accused her outright and now they're trying to get her to take a polygraph."

"No shit? Okay, tell 'em to come by the Allen office. I'll

meet 'em out there." Don was still vaguely put out; he had a divorce case and a personal-injury lawsuit he needed to work on, and there was no way this could be *that* serious, no matter what the police said.

Don headed north in his black El Dorado, holding the speedometer steady at sixty-five as he sped up the expressway toward the open country beyond the Dallas suburbs. He parked on the main street of Allen, directly in front of a tiny storefront of rustic wood. "Crowder & Mattox" was inscribed in gold on the window.

Candy looked like she always did—smiling, full of energy, bustling around. She didn't seem too upset by whatever it was that had happened. Pat looked the same, too. Don didn't really notice him. The Montgomerys passed the huge but empty reception desk and went straight back into Don's private office, the one with the autographed picture of President Carter on one wall and various athletic trophies suspended from the fake wood paneling.

"Ya'll have a seat," he said. "What happened?"

"It's probably not as bad as we think," said Candy, "but the police called me back in this morning and they accused me of killing Betty."

"That's ridiculous. Wha'd they say?"

"One of them yelled at me and said I was a cold-blooded little murderer, and then they took my shoes because they said they had some footprints."

"Why they think you did it?"

"I don't know. I guess because I was at Betty's that morning."

"Tell me everything you did that morning."

Candy briefly went over her itinerary, now well rehearsed.

"Sounds like a bunch of hyperactive small-town cops who don't know what they're doing."

"Wait a minute, Candy," Pat broke in, becoming concerned about the light-hearted tone of the conversation. "Tell Don about the affair."

"Hold on," said Don. "Before we say anything else I think you need to retain me right now so that we'll have an attorney-client privilege. Pat, write me out a check, doesn't matter what it's for. Hundred dollars. And put the date and time on it, and then we'll be covered."

Pat took out his checkbook and made out a check for $100.

"And Pat, could I talk to Candy alone for a little bit? It won't be long. Just wait outside or drive around ten or fifteen minutes."

"Okay."

As soon as Pat had gone, Don said, "What affair?"

Don didn't change expressions when Candy revealed how she had had an affair with Allan Gore, but inwardly he was amazed. Allan Gore? Don knew Candy was capable of it—he had always suspected she was a little wild on the inside—but he couldn't imagine Allan doing anything like that. When he tried to visualize Candy and Allan locked in a passionate embrace, he almost wanted to laugh.

"But the affair's over, Don," she said. "It's been over for eight months."

"Candy," he said when she had finished, "is there *anything* you need to tell me?"

Candy hesitated for a second, then went on to repeat everything she had told the police that morning. She added a detailed account of how Murphy had raged at her and stormed out of the room and then Cochran had finished the interrogation.

"They played Mutt and Jeff with you. Bad guy–nice guy. The bad guy makes you scared, and then the nice guy gets you to spill your guts. I didn't know it was this bad, Candy. You're in a mess of trouble, and you need to try to remember everything they asked you for. What about this polygraph thing?"

"They asked me to take a polygraph and made an appointment for me tomorrow. I told them I would so I could show them I didn't murder Betty."

"Well, you're not taking the polygraph. Those things are too unreliable; some people just can't take 'em. You could hurt yourself worse. What we'll do is I'll get my own polygraph man to test you, so we can find out how you test, and then after that maybe we'll let 'em test you."

"Should I call them?"

"No, we'll take care of that. But I'll tell you what I do want you to do. Call all the women at church, everyone who saw you at Bible School last Friday, and ask all of 'em if they remember what you were wearing."

"What?"

"I've been reading a book called *A Death in Canaan* where a young boy was accused of stabbing his mother to death. But the kid was seen in a white tee shirt before the crime and again after it, and it seems to me that that's pretty strong evidence that the kid couldn't have been involved in a bloody crime. Something that brutal, like the kind of corpse we're talking about with Betty, whoever did it would've had blood all over him. So see if you can get Barbara Green and whoever else was there to remember your clothes."

"Don, I think that's dumb."

"Just do it, Candy, and we might get this cleared up right away."

As a boy, Alton Don Crowder had two passions in life—sports and fighting. As a man, he had the same two passions, only he called them sports and lawyering. Of the two, it was the legal work that came second in his heart, a substitute for the professional football career he never had. But like most disappointments in his life, his failure at the Washington Redskins tryout camp of 1966 merely made him a better fighter. The courtroom was not the same kind of arena. In fact, he always felt a little out of place wearing a suit and kowtowing to judges. But it was still a place where you could earn respect. It was a place where there was always one winner and one loser, and the only thing that mattered was which side you were on at the end.

Donnie Crowder was neither a smooth talker nor a particularly friendly person, and those encountering him for the first time were apt to write him off as antisocial. The truth was, he was shy. That's not to say he was a shrinking violet. On the contrary, he was so prone to quick anger and ill-advised confrontations that, as a young man, he carried with him a perpetual air of menace and brutality. He had lost a dozen teeth in brawls and street fights by the time he was nineteen, and he had never overcome his capacity for sudden, uncontrollable rage.

Donnie was always the little guy, both literally and figuratively. Growing up in Dallas in the forties and early fifties, he was the scrawniest, homeliest kid in the class, the one with jug ears, red hair, and buck teeth. "You wanna learn to fight?" he would say in later years. "Grow up with buck teeth." He was the kid who always ended up on the bottom of the schoolyard dogpile, the kid older children made it their business to taunt. His homelife was less than idyllic. Donnie's mother was Irish and feisty and strong willed, a woman who brooked no nonsense and once strapped Donnie into a bathtub and left him in a darkened garage for several hours to teach him a lesson about playing in the street. His father, Alton Dowe Crowder, had spent time in Guam during the war and suffered from clinical battle fatigue the rest of his life. Both parents taught the same lesson: life is hard, and don't expect it to get better.

Donnie fought with his father like he fought with everyone else. They both had hair-trigger tempers. All it took was one reference to his teeth, his intelligence, his family, and Donnie would fling his books to the ground and tear into the kid who popped off. He fought dirty. He kicked and bit and kneed people in the groin and tried to land punches to the throat. He went after kids twice his size. Beginning in elementary school there was rarely a day when he didn't come home bloodied or bruised. Donnie got a reputation as a tough kid, even a bad kid.

Athletics, it seemed, was the one respectable thing Donnie could do. By the age of five he was already playing baseball and basketball. In elementary school he would sleep in his football uniform on the night before Peewee League games. Yet he had no more natural talent for sports than he had for schoolwork. He was gangly and too light; there were always kids who could run faster. All he had going for him was blind competitiveness.

Thomas Jefferson High School, "TJ High," was the site of Donnie's transformation from class bruiser to athletic star. The TJ Rebels were a less-than-stellar football team, losing more games than they won, even though Donnie received constant praise for his passing exhibitions as a roll-out quarterback and bone-crushing flying tackles as a defensive halfback. One of the fringe benefits of stardom, he quickly learned, was that for the first time in his life he could get girls to pay attention to him. He wasn't so brave as to actually ask one for a date, because of his insecurity about his looks, but as soon as he heard a girl was interested in him—usually through the football grapevine—he would go after her with a frenzied passion. He was so sexually aggressive, in fact, that after a time his reputation for that almost equalled his reputation as a brawler. At sixteen, he and his girlfriend were caught making love by her mother. "Yeah," Don would say later, "her mother caught me fuckin' her. It was back in the days when you had to pour me into my jeans, and I couldn't get my prick back in."

In Donnie's senior year, the Rebels won exactly two games, and that almost put an end to his college plans. He was an honorable mention on the Dallas All-City team, but all that was good for were scholarship offers from East Texas State College in Commerce and Hardin-Simmons College in Abilene, schools so small that he was afraid he could play there forever without getting any notice. Then, in the spring of 1961, Donnie was practicing track-and-field one day when he noticed Sleepy Morgan, a legendary recruiter for Southern Methodist University, sitting in the stands. Never shy about showing off, Donnie decided to run past Morgan to see if he could get noticed. As soon as he got close to him, Morgan said, "Hey, can you tell me where Don Crowder is?"

Donnie couldn't believe it. "That's me," he said.

Morgan handed him an envelope, but Donnie was too nervous to open it right away. He stuffed it into his shorts, then sprinted two miles home, went into his room, and very slowly opened it. It was a letter-of-intent for something called a "one-year-make-good" scholarship to SMU. It would put him in the big time, the Southwest Conference. He signed immediately.

The distance between TJ High and SMU was only about ten miles, but for Donnie it was like going to another planet. SMU was an expensive private school, full of the blue-blooded sons and daughters of some of the state's wealthiest families. He started signing his name "A. Don Crowder" instead of "Donnie," and he made one brief run at fraternity life (it ended the day he punched out his SAE pledge leader during a hazing incident), but he still never quite fit in anywhere at SMU except the Cotton Bowl. That's where the Mustangs played their homes games on Saturday afternoons, and where Don not only earned all four years of his scholarship but sometimes defied common sense and his own limitations by playing kamikaze cornerback. His flying tackles against men much larger than he were like those fights on the schoolyard: they made people notice him.

Don arrived at SMU weighing only 140 pounds, distributed over a gangly six-foot frame, and he immediately had to contend with three other high school hotshots who had been recruited at the quarterback position. But he attacked the weight-training program with single-minded zeal and bulked himself up to 160 by the time his freshman season started. By his sophomore year, he weighed 185 and was moved to running back, where he earned a letter mostly because the

other backs were injured. He also played defensive back, and
would have had a chance to play on the starting team if he
hadn't been badly injured during practice. After a particularly
nasty collision, he was carried off the field with blurred vision
and within a few days had surgery for a detached retina. He
remained in the hospital for weeks, his eye patched, lying flat
on his back, and the wisest of the many medical opinions paid
for by the SMU athletic department were for Don to give up
football. That was impossible, Don said; there was nothing else
he wanted to do.

It took Don a year to fully recuperate. It was the year that
weight training became an obsession with him; like the skinny
kid who gets sand kicked in his face, Don wanted more and
more bulk, to the point where he would sometimes spend six
or seven hours a day working out on weight machines. By the
time he reached his senior year, Don weighed an even 200,
more than 60 pounds more than when we he had arrived, and
he was strong enough to win a starting position in the
defensive backfield. The doctors still weren't particularly
optimistic about the eye, but they were sufficiently pleased
with the surgery to leave the decision up to him. Don was the
first man on the practice field that fall. After another terrible
season, head coach Hayden Fry encouraged Don to stay on at
SMU for one final year, making up the year of eligibility he had
lost after the eye surgery. By that time he had already finished
his bachelor's degree. Strictly in order to play football, he
enrolled in law school.

SMU had yet another pitiful season, though, and much to
Don's chagrin, he went completely unnoticed by professional
scouts. Undaunted, he spent most of the spring semester
sending letters and films to pro teams; the result was a single
offer. Otto Graham, head coach of the Washington Redskins,
liked Don's enthusiasm enough to invite him to summer
training camp as a free agent. Unfortunately, Don never made
it past the team medical examination. The Redskins doctor
took one look at the injured eye and refused to approve him.
"You had a good operation on your retina," the doctor said,
"but if you get hit wrong again you could be blind. You've got
one year of law school. Give up the sport."

Crushed, Don tried to talk him out of it. "Ray Nitschke
has a detached retina," he pleaded. But invoking the great
Green Bay linebacker's name made no difference.

"Ray Nitschke is All-Pro," said the doctor. "If you were a

first-round draft choice, I'd let you play. But you're a free agent. Go home."

Twenty-three years old, Don felt frustrated, bitter, and completely disillusioned. It would have been different if he had gone to camp and been beaten out by other players. To be turned away by the team doctor seemed cruel and unfair. He returned to Dallas and spent the summer hanging out in pool halls with his football buddies, where he would drink himself into a stupor, start fist-fights, or pick up women for one-night stands. Coach Fry tried to help him out by offering an assistant coaching job that would pay for his second year of law school. Don was grateful but had no great enthusiasm for the law. He would do it strictly because he couldn't think of anything better.

His attitude began to change, though, as Don entered his second year. It wasn't the classical beauty of the American legal system that first stirred his ambitious heart. Rather it was the realization that great trial lawyers—like Melvin Belli, the man then making Dallas headlines for his defense of Jack Ruby— were almost as famous as great quarterbacks. Don would never be more than an average student, but he didn't intend to spend his legal career writing briefs. He wanted to earn his money in the courtroom.

Despite his mediocre grades, Don managed to get a job the next summer working for a firm run by one of his father's friends. From the lawyer who hired him, Don learned the basics of what he would later regard as his calling. Don called it personal injury law. Some of his wealthier, haughtier colleagues at SMU called it ambulance chasing. The truth was that Don had little choice in the matter. He had made the usual rounds of prestigious corporate law firms in Dallas. None of them wanted him. Either his grades weren't high enough or his combative personality did him in with the interviewers. By the time he received his law degree, Don was more than willing to take the $700 a month his father's friend was offering.

Don's baptism by fire came on a Sunday afternoon in the fall of 1968 when one of the partners handed him his first case. It was set for trial the very next day and was an almost stereotypical personal-injury suit. Don's client claimed he was suffering from whiplash as a result of a car accident that occurred just a stone's throw from TJ High. The defendant had an experienced Dallas attorney on his side. Don studied the case most of the night, showed up at the courthouse Monday in an ill-fitting suit, and called the office later to report, "I kicked the shit out of him."

He had the bug. Personal injury law, he decided, was ideal for him. Each client was an underdog, whether it was the guy who had been hit by a truck or the factory worker whose hand was mangled by a piece of machinery. All the cases were handled on a contingent basis, meaning the lawyer didn't collect anything unless he won the lawsuit. Don was so elated by his first victory that he went on to win nineteen straight cases, losing only when he got so cocky about his prowess that he took an obviously bad case to trial.

Just as Don could never get along with his coaches, he quickly bridled at working for other people and, after only three months, bolted from the firm and hung out his own shingle. It was more difficult now, though, because he was married. Shortly after he started his third year of law school, Don had given up his one-night stands and taken up seriously with Carol Parker, a recently divorced woman he had known vaguely all his life but had never dated. Carol had two children, five-year-old Rhonda and baby Jimmy, and Don fell in love with all three of them. The courtship was brief, and once they were married he redoubled his efforts to make it as a personal-injury lawyer. His success was modest, mostly a series of auto-accident cases that, by 1970, had netted him a comfortable $50,000 a year.

To make things happen faster Don formed a partnership in the fall of 1970 with his father's friend, John Curtis, and an old law school acquaintance named Jim Mattox. Mattox had spent a couple of years as a prosecutor on the Dallas district attorney's staff, but he was ambitious enough to want his own criminal law practice. It was a marriage of convenience. Mattox would be the criminal specialist, Curtis the corporate and securities-law specialist, and Don would handle the personal-injury work. Mattox had also started dabbling in local Democratic politics, and his acquaintance with labor leaders and party officials would no doubt lead to a lot of workmen's compensation cases, which are so similar to personal-injury cases that Don would naturally handle those as well.

That same year Don and Carol had twin girls, Christy and Wendy, and started planning to move to the country. Even though Don had always lived in Dallas, he had a sort of sentimental romantic nostalgia for his father's boyhood on a farm, and he had thought off and on of moving to a rural area where he could have a few acres of his own. He didn't actually make the move, though, until a bizarre tragedy made the Dallas house seem painful to live in. A month before Wendy's first birthday, the baby attempted to crawl up into a built-in shoe drawer, traumatized her trachea and suffocated to death. Carol was distraught for months afterward, and Don decided they had to move to the country. So in 1973 he finally found what he was looking for: a three-acre tract in a brand-new subdivision called Brookhaven Ranch Estates, carved out of an old farm in the little town of Lucas. The new home, which Don designed himself, was a brick-and-redwood fortress with a circular drive in front and a little country creek running through the thickets in the far reaches of the backyard. Don soon added a pool and a tennis court. "You can't miss my house," he would tell first-time visitors. "It's the one with the tennis court out front. It's a pretty good court. The only thing is, my neighbor's horse likes to take a shit on it."

One reason Don was doing so well was that his partner, Jim Mattox, had been elected to the Texas House of Representatives in 1972, one of many liberals who swept in on a reform ticket after a particularly nasty state banking scandal. Ever since then Crowder & Mattox had had a steady flow of unsolicited casework. As time went on Mattox would handle much less, and Don much more of the load, especially after Mattox, making a name for himself as a renegade liberal, ran successfully for a vacant Congressional seat in 1976. But no matter how hard he tried, and how many cases he won, Don's reputation never rose much above the status of a workmanlike, if very successful, lawyer for the injured and abused. As Mattox continued to rise in the political world, bucking an archconservative city, Don wondered whether he shouldn't have chosen politics himself. In 1977, when Congress created several new federal judgeships in Texas, Don was even so bold as to nominate himself for one of them, hoping that Mattox's friendship with Senator Lloyd Bentsen would work to his advantage. Even though he enclosed all his legal articles and summaries of the only two federal lawsuits he'd ever tried, Don's application was politely denied.

Don eventually contented himself with an active life in the local civic affairs of Lucas. He was elected to the Lovejoy Board of Trustees (governing body for the little red schoolhouse on Farm-to-Market 1378), served as City Attorney for the town of Allen, and became active in the Methodist Church of Lucas around the time Jackie Ponder arrived. He coached numerous children's sports teams. He also founded, wrote, edited, and distributed a mimeographed newspaper, first of its kind, called the *Lucas Looking Glass*. It appeared bimonthly, or whenever Don got around to having his secretary type it up, and was mostly a potpourri of Don's own opinions. His column, "Ruminations," ranged from an essay on Eric Hoffer, the longshoreman/philosopher, entitled "A Country of Cowards?" to a grisly description of death in the electric chair (to make a political point) to a long, atrociously-metered Christmas poem, to a lament about how public schools don't offer good organized sports anymore.

Despite his romantic vision of small-town life, Don never made any close friends in the country. He knew everybody, but nobody really knew him. He was not the sort of person to go glad-handing through the PTA meetings, or making social calls for the sake of conversation, and he had an abrupt way of speaking that some people mistook for rudeness. When Don presided over a meeting, he got through the agenda with a minimum of ceremony. Sometimes he would show up in his jogging togs, run hastily through the business at hand, and be off in a flash to get home in time to watch that night's game on television. One thing Don did relish, though, was a good debate, and that made for a lot of long nights spent with the church Pastor-Parish committee after the arrival of Ron Adams. As chairman of the committee, Don felt an obligation to back Ron until someone could prove the man wasn't doing his job. One of the committee members didn't agree, though; her name was Candy Montgomery. He and Candy would have frequent arguments, sometimes verging on shouting matches, over "the Ron problem." Don came to like Candy as an adversary. He liked her energy and her intelligence, but mostly he liked her bluntness; she was almost as direct as he was. After a few months Don came to count Candy among his favorite people in the church, and probably the only real friend he had.

Though Don rarely accepted social invitations, he did agree on one occasion to go with the Montgomerys and a few other couples to a famous country-western dance hall in Plano called the Trail Dust Steakhouse. That's when he discovered the other side of Candy Montgomery. It was after they'd all had dinner and a few drinks. The women wanted to dance, and the men obliged. But Candy didn't dance like the others: she had moves he hadn't seen since college days, when they called it "getting down and dirty." Don was fascinated. "When was the last time you saw someone *shimmy*?" Don asked his wife. The longer the evening went on, the wilder Candy got, until at one point she was dragging people onto the dance floor and draping her arms around them. Don danced with her once and, as he later told a friend, "she practically put her body right through me." Don kept looking over at the table to see what Pat's reaction would be, but Pat had no reaction. He seemed to look at the whole scene with a benign lack of interest. One thing Don was beginning to realize about Candy; there was a lot more to her than what he saw on Sunday morning.

It was very late on the evening of June 18 when Don finally found a few minutes when he could be alone. He had gone to a baseball game after talking to Candy and Pat, but he hadn't been able to concentrate. All he could think of was the strange story Candy had told him. Either she was concealing something or the police were using her to get at someone else. Don was no criminal law expert, but he knew Candy Montgomery, and he knew she was incapable of violence. Normally Don left his legal work at the office, but he had never even been close to a murder case before, and suddenly the hottest one in Texas had been dumped in his lap. Carol went to bed, but Don didn't think he could sleep. He went into his study instead, took out a yellow legal pad, and decided to make a list of reasons Candy could *not* have committed such a crime. First on the list was "size." Don didn't know Betty Gore's exact weight, but he knew she was a big woman. She had never lost the weight from her last pregnancy. Besides, she was big-boned, with bulky arms and a stocky build, while Candy had more regular features. Don estimated Betty was at least thirty pounds heavier than Candy, so how could Candy have used such a large, awkward weapon as an ax? Wouldn't a gun make more sense? Even a knife would have been easier to handle. Don moved on to reason number two: "clothing." Candy had worn the same clothing back to church after going to the Gore home; she couldn't have left such a grisly corpse without getting blood on herself. Finally, Don wrote "demeanor." If Candy had really done this, she would have been a basket case. Instead, she was calm and collected; she was even able to joke about it.

Don wouldn't know until later that Candy was anything but calm and collected that night as she placed the phone calls he had instructed her to make.

"Betty," she said, her voice trembling slightly, "the police have been asking me questions about Betty Gore's death because I was there that morning. And to help them I need to know whether you remember what I was wearing at church that morning."

Betty Huffhines thought for a moment. "No, I can't recall it."

Candy had a sinking feeling at the tone of Betty's voice. What did Betty think of such a strange question? This was going to be awful.

"Oh well," she said, "I just hope *someone* remembers."

"Sorry I couldn't help," said Betty.

Candy tried to collect her thoughts again. Tears were forming at the corners of her eyes. She brushed them away, steeled herself, and called Barbara Green, Suzan Wright, Marie Childs, and Connie Holmes in quick succession. Marie and Barbara remembered that she'd been wearing blue jeans and a maroon blouse. Connie recalled the blue tennis shoes. When she was finished, Candy breathed a sigh of relief. As far as the women of the church were concerned, she could have worn blue tennis shoes that morning. Everything was all right.

Armed with the results of her informal poll, Candy drove to Dallas the next morning so she could give Don a more complete and formal itinerary. Pat came along, too, and immediately went into a meeting with Rob Udashen, Don's young legal associate. Rob told him that, if it turned out that Candy needed full-time legal defense, he would help find a first-rate criminal attorney to take the case. In the meantime, he needed money to cover the hours it was going to take to check out Candy's story and prevent the police from bothering her. Pat wrote out another check, for $2,000, which was all he had in the Texas Instruments Credit Union.

Rob Udashen was twenty-seven years old and the exact opposite of Don Crowder in almost every respect. He was a brilliant student from the University of Texas, where he had graduated Phi Beta Kappa and then been honored as the most outstanding law student in the field of criminal law. He had spent a year after graduation working as a lawyer for prison inmates, then moved to Dallas, made the rounds, and ended up filling the criminal position at Don's firm now that

Congressman Mattox was away in Washington all the time. As much as Don gloried in his own pugnacious, anti-intellectual approach to the law, he had a secret respect for men like Rob. Rob didn't look like a criminal lawyer at all. He was ascetic and bookish in appearance, reserved and scholarly in manner. Don had a hard time imagining Rob coaxing tears from a jury with the eloquence of his summations. But Rob's knowledge of the law was encyclopedic. That's why, on the morning Candy came in to give her statement, Rob was asked to do the interview.

Also sitting in was Rob's clerk, Elaine Carpenter, who had recently graduated from the SMU Law School at the age of thirty-four. For the two young lawyers, it was more excitement than they'd had in all their previous careers. As soon as Candy walked into the office, looking pleasant and respectable and entirely inoffensive, they sensed the uniqueness of the case. Elaine immediately liked her and felt a certain illogical sympathy for her predicament. Perhaps it was because they were both about the same age, from similar middle-class backgrounds. They even looked alike, with the same Anne Murray-style frizzed hair. How could this little woman be accused of an *ax murder*, of all things?

Candy seemed to feel at home right away. The first thing they asked about was her relationship with Allan. They asked her to go over her itinerary on the thirteenth one more time, and then they got her to remember, as best she could, everything the police had asked her. As the interview continued, Rob started to get a strange feeling about Candy's responses. It was becoming clear that this was much more serious than he had thought at first.

"Are you telling me," he said, "that the police said they can match your fingerprints and your shoeprints?"

"Yes, and they took my shoes to check them out."

"And they actually accused you of murder?"

"Yes, they say I'm a suspect. They weren't very nice about it either."

Rob couldn't fathom what was going on. Candy seemed so cool, so detached. If they had just questioned her, that was one thing. But if they had *accused* her, they were not just guessing. Why wasn't she angry, or panicky, or something? How could she sit there and just calmly answer their questions?

When they had finished the interview, Rob gave Candy a pen and paper and asked her to write down everything she had done on the thirteenth, in as much detail as she could remember. While she was working, he and Elaine conferred in another room.

"What do you think?" he asked.

"I don't know," Elaine said. "I get the feeling she might be covering for someone. Maybe she didn't do it, but she knows who did do it. Maybe Allan."

Rob and Elaine had both taken extensive notes during the interview. On one page Elaine had written, "Big void in time at time of murder for client." Throughout the day Candy had been around people who could identify her—at church, at department stores, at gas stations. But at the time that Betty apparently died, Candy could only say that she had driven to the parking lot of a Target store in Plano, where nobody had seen her, and then to the church. No witnesses.

After Candy had finished filling out forms and completing her written itinerary, Rob sent her home with stern instructions not to talk to the police or reporters.

"Reporters?" she said, a trace of desperation in her voice.

"We don't know who the police might be talking to. Just don't talk to anyone without talking to me first."

Don had spent the morning in court, so he didn't arrive at the office until midafternoon.

"A DPS agent named Murphy has been calling me all day," said Rob, "trying to bully us into letting them put Candy on the lie box. So I've arranged for our own polygraph tomorrow afternoon."

"What do you think of her story?"

"We think she's covering up," Rob told him. "There's just something missing. Her alibi makes sense, except for that hour or so when she left the church."

"*Debby!*" Don bellowed, his customary way of getting his secretary's attention. "Get me Candy Montgomery on the phone."

But Candy called first.

"Don, I don't know what to do. I'm over at a friend's house. A reporter came to the house. I'm scared to death."

"Who came to the house?"

"A reporter from the *Times Herald*. Sherry told him I wasn't there, and he went away. But now I'm about to go to pieces."

So the police *had* talked to the media.

"Candy, this thing might get rougher before it gets better.

Why don't you and Pat and the kids leave the house for a few days. Is there somewhere you could go?"

"We could probably stay with the Clecklers."

"See if you can, then, and call me back and let me know where I can reach you."

Pat left work as soon as Candy called to tell him the news. They picked up the kids from school, packed some luggage, and drove over to the Clecklers, about a half-mile away in a mostly undeveloped area still used for farmland. The kids were thrilled, but Pat was growing more worried and perplexed by the minute. He couldn't figure out what was happening, and it was all happening so fast.

That night Don called the Cleckler house.

"I want to prepare you for dealing with the media," he said, "and I think you and I need to meet alone, face to face, about this."

"Okay," she said.

"We might as well do it at my house."

"When?"

"Now."

"I'm on my way."

When Candy arrived in Lucas, Don ushered her into the "family room," a spacious area filled with couches and stuffed chairs and lined with bookshelves.

"Personally, Candy," he began, "I don't think you did this and I think the police are just harassing you for some reason. I talked to all the officials involved, and I think the chances are good that they won't even have enough evidence for an indictment. But listen to me, Candy, I'm your lawyer, and there are three people in the world you should never lie to— your preacher, your doctor, and your lawyer. So don't lie to me, Candy. I don't think you did it, but I think you know who did do it. I think you're covering up something. Who are you covering for?"

"No one."

"Did Allan do it?"

Candy didn't answer. It was the first time she'd thought of Allan as a suspect.

"Did you walk in on something and get scared?"

"Allan didn't do it."

"How do you know?"

"Because I did it."

"What?"

"I did it."

"I don't believe you."

A half hour later, Candy emerged from the family room, red-eyed and ashen-faced.

"What about Pat?" Don asked. "Have you told Pat?"

"No, of course not."

"What would he do if you told him?"

Candy thought for a moment. "He's a very honest person. He might tell the police for my own good."

"Then definitely do *not* tell Pat. Go home and don't talk to nobody, no way."

As soon as Candy left, Don called Rob Udashen. Despite the late hour, Don sounded excited and hyperactive.

"Rob, you aren't going to *believe* this, but what we've got is a self-defense case."

Rob didn't believe it.

A half hour after that, Candy lay next to Pat on the strange guest-room bed at the Clecklers. Pat had gotten paranoid and worried when Candy had stayed away so long, but she had calmed his fears and told him that she would clear up everything the next day with a polygraph examination.

Pat fell asleep first, but after a few minutes he woke up to the sound of Candy's low moaning and inarticulate sounds. In her dream, Candy is driving the station wagon through the countryside. Suddenly she notices that Betty Gore is in the passenger seat. Betty reaches over and grabs the steering wheel, not trying to control the car but to run it directly into the ditch. The two women struggle for the wheel. . . .

Candy woke with a start, one second before the crash. Pat put his arms around her, and she sobbed quietly.

17 · SUSPICIONS

There were no empty pews in the United Methodist Church of Norwich, Kansas, on the morning they buried Betty Gore. The 250 mourners represented better than half the population of the town, and most of them had known Betty all her life. Allan Gore sat with his parents on the front row, feeling vaguely uncomfortable, scarcely aware of his surroundings. The sanctuary was stifling with heat. "Words are so empty," he heard the minister say. Just ahead of him lay the casket. It was closed, of course. The funeral home had said it was impossible to have an open one.

"Betty Gore!" he heard the young minister say. "Such a person! Talk to Bob and Elsie Sheetz. They'll tell you how hard a worker she was when she worked harvest for them . . ."

Allan was confused. He had a gnawing feeling in the pit of his stomach, and yet his face remained dry. He couldn't cry.

"I wish we could gather all the children who have had Betty as a teacher. . . . You know, I think they liked her!"

Sweat started to form on Allan's forehead and at the base of his neck.

". . . faithful, loving wife, a good mother, and a good daughter . . . Thank God for the hope and promise of eternal life . . ."

The funeral meditation had been brief. The pastor led a prayer, and then a woman friend of the family began singing a hymn called "My Friend and I." Allan watched as six men approached the casket and lifted it slowly from its resting place. He didn't recognize any of them. They were "town boys," the kids who had attended Norwich High with Betty, played on the football team, accompanied her to the summer movies and the swimming hole and asked her to ride around in their cars. At the front of the casket was Jimmy Sheetz, the boy who had once seemed the closest to true love Betty would ever come ("He's *so* wonderful," she had written in her diary). Behind him was his brother John Sheetz, and behind the Sheetz boys was Jon Tilson, her other great adolescent love ("I think he likes me best," she had written as early as the eighth grade). On the other side of the casket stood John Thornbro, a three-sport athlete who had dated Betty once or twice ("We played with Wee Jee boards and danced & ate & ate & ate. XX."), and behind him were Danny Liddeke, her class president, and Brent Burford, another star athlete ("Today we practiced for graduation. I get to walk with Brent. It's too good to be true!"). All of them had known Betty well, and yet none of them had seen her for the past twelve years. They had all assumed she was living a wonderful life in Dallas.

Only a few people followed the hearse to nearby Up-church Cemetery, where the graveside ceremony was simple and brief. Allan watched as Bertha Pomeroy started to cry again, leaning on Bob for support. As soon as the casket was lowered into the ground, the Pomeroys started back to the car, where they could break down together in private. There would be dinner waiting at the Pomeroy house, and then Allan wanted to leave immediately for Larned. He was having trouble accepting it all. It wasn't just the shock of her death, or the strangeness of Norwich. It was something only he knew. As he stood there at the graveside, watching the casket and trying to concentrate on the reverend's prayer, he couldn't feel anything. He wanted to grieve, but he knew that whatever he felt wasn't real mourning. When he did finally begin to cry, it was not because he felt a terrible void in his life. It was because he felt ashamed of himself, and guilty. For the first time, he wondered how much he'd ever really loved her.

Texas Murder Victim
Is Former Norwich Girl

announced the *Harper Advocate* on the day after the funeral. Similar reports appeared in several small-town Kansas newspapers. But Kansas was too far away from the scene of the crime to know how rapidly the complexion of the case was changing. That very afternoon, the *Dallas Times Herald* had reported that a "female friend of Allan Gore" was the prime suspect in the murder of Betty, after the discovery of "bloody fingerprints" on the refrigerator door of the Gore home. Betty's death was back on the front page, and a hot item on the six o'clock news. Still, nothing could have prepared Allan for the phone call he received Thursday morning.

"Mr. Gore, this is Texas Ranger Fred Cummings, and I'm calling from Kingman, Kansas."

"Yes."

"Mr. Gore, we're going to be arriving at the Great Bend Airport around one o'clock because we understand that's not too far from your parents' home. We would like you to meet us there if you could, so that we can ask you some further questions."

"All right," said Allan.

But Allan was completely panicked. As soon as he hung up the phone, he knew he would have to tell his family. There was no way to explain police officers flying all the way to Kansas simply to "ask more questions." They would have to know: he was a prime suspect in the murder of his wife. And if he told them that, he would have to tell them the reason. He would have to tell them about the affair.

Fortunately, Allan's older sister Beth was home. It would be easier to say since she was in the room. He gathered everyone into the living room and began haltingly. "I need to tell you something that's very hard for me. I made a mistake. I had an affair with a woman at church."

When the police decided to fly to Kansas for the Gore interview, they weren't simply being melodramatic. They knew that the longer they waited, the more difficult it would be to wring confessions out of the two people they considered prime suspects: Candy Montgomery and Allan Gore. They had gone after Candy first, figuring that she would be the easiest to break. The first indication they had miscalculated came at 5 P.M. that same day. A lawyer named Rob Udashen called the station and asked for Murphy.

"Captain Murphy, I've been retained by Candace Montgomery, who I understand is a suspect in the Betty Gore murder case. And I'm afraid Mrs. Montgomery will have to cancel the polygraph examination you've scheduled for tomorrow. I've already informed a polygrapher at DPS that she won't be there."

"Damn," said Murphy as he hung up the phone.

They had gone too far. They had scared her. They had scared her right into the arms of a lawyer.

Now the investigators felt the press of time, and they

stepped up the pace even more. Later that night—almost midnight, in fact—the chief fingerprint expert for Dallas County turned to Fred Cummings and announced his verdict.

"It's a positive ID," he said. "These prints are the same."

Sergeant Jim Cron, head of the physical evidence section of the Dallas County Sheriff's Department, had spent three hours comparing Steve Deffibaugh's photo of the bloody thumbprint on the freezer door to the fresh prints taken from Candy Montgomery. He had no doubt. That macabre, bloody print found in the utility room belonged to the Montgomery woman. But what about Allan Gore? Cummings and Cochran headed for Kansas.

Unlike Allan's two previous meetings with the police, this one was tense and combative. The two investigators made it clear from the outset that they suspected Allan of a conspiracy to kill his wife.

"We've got evidence that implicates the Montgomery woman," said one, "but we haven't confronted her with it yet. What we want to know is whether you had *anything* to do with it."

"I was in Minnesota the whole time."

"We know you weren't there. What we want to know is what you and Candy talked about before you left."

"Nothing. We hadn't talked at all for several months."

"Mr. Gore, I want you to understand what we're talking about. We feel like we have Mrs. Montgomery cold. It would be much better for you to tell us what you know now than to wait for her to go down first."

"I don't have anything to tell you that I haven't already said."

"I can't very well believe that. Would you be willing to take a polygraph examination to prove that to us?"

"All right."

"When will you be going back to Dallas?"

"I can go right away if it will clear this up."

"Okay, you call us tomorrow, as soon as you get there, and we'll make the arrangements. But if there is *anything* you haven't told us, you should do it before then."

"All right."

Allan was nervous and rattled when he got back to his parents' house. Ray Dahlberg, the local attorney who had accompanied him to the interview, now realized how serious the case was and advised Allan to confer with a Dallas lawyer before taking the lie detector test. By the time Allan flew back to Dallas, he already had legal representation, in the form of Mike Gibson, a partner in the firm that had recently won a measure of notoriety by assisting in the successful defense of multimillionaire oilman T. Cullen Davis of Fort Worth, who was acquitted in the costliest series of trials in the history of Texas jurisprudence. Allan didn't realize that the mere mention of Gibson's name would make reporters and police doubly suspicious of his involvement.

But the ordeal of facing the police and press was nothing compared to what Allan would have to do before he left Kansas. Late that afternoon, he called the Pomeroys in Norwich and told Bob he needed to come down to talk.

Allan asked his older sister Beth to make the two-hour drive with him, and she readily agreed. When they arrived, the Pomeroys were all gathered in the tiny living room—Bob, Bertha, Ronnie, Pat, and Richard. Twilight was approaching, and it had started to rain very hard. Everyone was exhausted from the events of the past week, but at least the funeral was over and they would be able to start over. Or would they? Everyone had a dark intimation even before Allan arrived. If he was driving all the way from Larned just to tell them something, chances were it wasn't something good.

"This is the hardest thing I've ever had to do," began Allan.

The room was silent, except for the sound of the rain pounding against the windows.

"I had an affair with a woman. It wasn't anything. She didn't mean anything to me. It's over now. It's been over more than six months."

Bertha started to cry.

"My God, Allan," she said softly, "how could you?"

She left the room and, as she did, tears started to form in Allan's eyes as well. Beth hugged him gently. Betty's brothers stared at the floor.

"I'm sorry," he said. "The reason I'm telling you this is that I've talked to the police and they tell me this woman is a suspect in the murder. She was the woman who was keeping Alisa that night. I had thought of this possibility myself, but I didn't say anything because I didn't take it seriously until now."

The room remained silent.

"I hope you can forgive me."

Bob started coughing. Ronnie cleared his throat.

"It's so strange," Allan said, "because the past three months of our marriage, Betty and I were closer than ever."

"You say the affair was over?" Bob was the first one to break the silence.

"Yes. It had been over for eight months. Can you forgive me?"

"Did Betty ever know?"

"No, not that I know of."

"Did she know when she got killed?"

"No."

Bob thought for a moment.

"If she didn't know about it when she got killed," said Bob, "maybe nothing ever came of that."

"I just hope you can forgive me," Allan repeated.

"I think I can understand," said Bob.

Allan looked at the boys.

"I understand," said Ronnie.

"I need to go back to Dallas tomorrow to take a polygraph examination," said Allan, "and if it's all right I'd like to leave Alisa here until things are more normal."

"That's fine," said Bob. "I think Bertha would like that."

"Thank you," said Allan.

He and Beth left quickly.

It had been a full ten days since Bob Pomeroy had had a full night's sleep. He was so shaken that he had trouble concentrating on even the smallest task. But it was summer harvest time, and he had a full 160 acres of wheat that needed to be cut. That would be the hardest part, trying to work again. It took enormous effort just to get up that morning, but he did it. On Tuesday the twenty-fourth, he rose before dawn and drove the pickup out to his fields. He pulled his rig out of the shed and started hooking it up to the tractor. Then, as the sun started to rise and he looked up from his work, he saw at least a dozen trucks coming down the highway, trucks he recognized on sight as belonging to neighboring farmers. The men didn't say anything about why they were there. They parked their trucks, shouted a quick greeting, and started unloading their own equipment. By the time Bob had started his tractor, they were already at work, dividing up the Pomeroy Field into areas of responsibility. Bob just sat on the tractor, the June sun beating down on him, staring at the long even rows of grain, wondering what had happened to his daughter.

18 · UNNAMED SUSPECT

Murder is always news. Murder with an ax is the kind of news that gets onto the front page. Murder of a woman with an ax, followed by the mutilation of the body, is the kind of news that television stations can justify putting on their six o'clock reports, since it has the advantages of being bizarre and mysterious, with a hint of sexual deviancy. It helps when the victim is a white, middle-class mother of two who teaches elementary school.

But all of those news "hooks" paled into insignificance on Thursday the nineteenth of June. That was the day the major news media of Dallas learned that the police had a suspect, that the suspect was a woman, and that the woman had had an affair with the husband of the victim. Suddenly reporters' assignments were changed. Police and courthouse "beat" reporters were pulled off the story and quickly replaced with investigative newsmen. Camera crews were dispatched to Collin County, a forty-five-minute drive to the north, to find out where the woman lived and get footage of her if possible, of her house if not. The film couldn't be used yet—until she was arrested, Candy Montgomery couldn't be linked to the death of Betty Gore without the risk of libel—but when and if she went to jail, they wanted to have everything ready to air. On Thursday afternoon, just a few hours after Sergeant Cron's positive identification of the bloody thumbprint, the *Dallas Times Herald* published a page-one story by Gary Shultz, a county courthouse reporter:

Female friend of husband sought
in ax killing of Wylie housewife

The words "female friend" had been chosen carefully. It was the type of phrase that got the point across—she was a friend of

Allan Gore's but not necessarily Betty's—without directly stating the delicate matter of the affair. By that evening, the news was the lead item on all four Dallas and Fort Worth television stations, all of which picked up on the "female friend" usage. Most of the stations simply rehashed Shultz's story, which was being denied by Chief Abbott. The police were as surprised as everyone else by the speed with which the news had spread, and they weren't sure just how to react.

The first one actually to find Candy Montgomery was young Doug Swanson, a 27-year-old *Times Herald* reporter. By checking mailboxes along Arroyo Blanco, the secluded gravel drive where the Montgomerys had built their dream house, he had managed to find the right address. Parking his car on the street, he walked up the steep drive and rang the doorbell. The woman who opened it was Sherry Cleckler, who had come by to comfort Candy after her first interviews at Don's law office that morning. Perhaps not realizing just how spooked Candy was, Swanson immediately identified himself—and all of Sherry's defenses were instantly aroused.

"I'm sorry, she's not here. I'm just the baby sitter."

"Do you know when she might be here?"

"She'll be gone all day."

"All right, thank you."

Sherry closed the door, locked it, and pressed her finger to her lips as she turned and looked at Candy.

"It was a reporter," she said.

"Oh no," said Candy.

Panicked, Candy called Pat at work, and he instantly agreed to come home. Then she called Don, who advised her to get away from the house and, regardless of what happened, not to talk to any reporters. Sherry suggested they go to her house, just five minutes away, and so they gathered up the kids, jumped in the station wagon, and left.

That night Pat, Tom, and Sherry sat in front of the television and flipped from channel to channel in an effort to catch all three major newscasts. Candy wasn't there. She had left for Don Crowder's house. He had called suddenly, wanting to talk, and Candy hadn't known how long she would be gone. When she returned, long after the ten o'clock news, Sherry noticed that she had been crying.

"I can't deal with it anymore," she said. "I'm turning it all over to Don."

"This is the most ridiculous thing I've ever heard of," said Sherry.

Candy didn't even ask what was on the ten o'clock news. She didn't want to know. If there was one thing Candy Montgomery feared more than the police, it was the press. All the police could do was put you in jail. The press could tell the whole world you were there.

By the next morning everyone's paranoia had increased tenfold. First came a front-page report in the *Dallas Morning News*:

Ax case
suspect
hunted

The word "hunted" carried an especially sinister connotation for Pat. He had visions of armies of squad cars spread out across Montecito Estates, searching for Candy and wondering why the entire family had left the house. The truth was far simpler. After the *Times Herald* story Thursday afternoon, the *News* had put one of its young investigators, Bruce Selcraig, on the case, and he had only had a few hours to catch up on all the events of the previous week. He simply assumed, as did many of the investigators on the fringes of the case, that the fingerprint would be all the police needed for an arrest. So he wrote: "A female friend of Allan Gore, whose wife, Betty, was found hacked to death in their Wylie home last week, was being sought Thursday after investigators matched the friend's left thumbprint with a bloody print on the couple's refrigerator, officers said."

Now Pat Montgomery was thoroughly confused by the events of the past two days. The police were not only going to go through with the arrest; they claimed they had a bloody thumbprint that proved Candy did it.

"There must be some explanation for this," said Pat. "Did you open the refrigerator while you were there? Did you lean on it?"

"I may have," said Candy.

"I wonder how they know it's blood."

"I don't want to think about it, Pat."

Pat was not the only person panicked by the news reports. Rob Udashen saw the "bloody thumbprint" story, too. He knew that anytime a case has this much publicity, the police are under a great deal of pressure to make a quick arrest. That meant his time with Candy might be limited. So he went to the office very early, set up a physical examination and a polygraph test for Candy, then called her and told her to come to Dallas immediately. When she got there, he called Elaine into his office, and the three of them started going back over the same ground they had covered the previous day. This time, though, they were all business. They worked fast, taking down every word Candy said, stopping only for elaboration where it was needed. During the interview, Don came into the office.

"Candy, when you get finished with this, I want you to take out a sheet of paper and write down all the reasons you wouldn't have wanted to kill Betty."

"Okay, Don."

"And make me a biography. You know, just the basic details of your life."

"I'm afraid it's not very interesting."

Elaine thought she noticed a slight grin when Candy said that. It upset her. She seemed to be enjoying this too much.

When the interview was over, Rob gave Elaine the names of the doctor and polygrapher he had scheduled for Candy's examinations, and the two women left. Rob was still disturbed by the extensive media coverage. One thing he didn't need was some grandstanding cop to show up at Candy's house with fifteen reporters behind him, so that he could slap the cuffs on her in full view of the world. Besides humiliating Candy, a scene like that would only encourage the cops to charge her with the stiffest crime they could come up with. Capital murder, for example, which in Texas almost always meant the death penalty. He doubted that they could make a capital-murder charge stick, but they might get the indictment anyway, hoping to get her on a lesser charge. He didn't understand why they were talking to the press at all. It was not the way the game was supposed to be played.

Rob decided to call Joe Murphy, the DPS agent he had spoken to the day before.

"Have you decided to let us put her on the lie box?" asked Murphy, hoping Udashen's inexperience would make his job easier.

"No, we still don't want to do that yet. But what I'm calling about is all this information that's been in the press. I don't know how much of it's true, but if it is, then I'd just like to ask you for the courtesy of calling me in the event that you get an arrest warrant. Because, if you're planning to arrest her soon, we'd appreciate being able to bring her up there to you and surrender her, to avoid the press and everything."

"Mr. Udashen," said Murphy, "if we do get a warrant, finding and arresting Mrs. Montgomery will be no trouble for us."

"I'm sorry you feel that way about it."

Rob was still steaming that afternoon when the reporters started calling. Somewhere along the way, word had gotten out that Rob represented Candy Montgomery, so Swanson of the *Times Herald* and Selcraig of the *News* both had calls into him by midafternoon. He returned both calls, confirmed that he represented Candy, and listened as the reporters told him that an arrest was "imminent." They also wanted a comment about the bloody thumbprint reportedly found on the refrigerator in Betty's house.

"I can't believe that's her print," Rob told Swanson. "If it is, then why don't they just come and arrest her? They know where she is. They tell the press that she's being sought, but she's right here. She and her husband and children haven't gone anywhere."

As the questions continued, Rob was a little surprised by how much Swanson already knew. He was aware that Candy had canceled the police polygraph examination, for example.

"I did that to find out what was going on with the case first," Rob explained.

It was to be Rob's final press interview. When he got out of bed the next morning, the first thing he saw was the *Times Herald* headline:

Lawyer dares
police to jail
ax suspect

Since it was Saturday, Rob called Don at home.

"Have you seen this?" he asked.

"Yeah, I saw it. I thought it was a great shot at the cops."

"I don't think so," said Rob. "I don't like arguing the case in the newspapers. But I'm not sure what to tell the media when they call."

"Forget it. I'll handle the media if you don't want to."

"I'm not sure anybody should talk to them."

"No," said Don, "this might be the best thing that ever happened to us. Besides, those hick cops are leaking every damn thing they can, trying to get Candy tried and convicted in Collin County before they even arrest her. The least we can do is talk back."

"I say we ignore it."

"I'll handle it. Tell everybody at the office, from now on, whenever the media calls, I handle it."

Until then, Don had kept the case at arm's length. Rob, after all, was the firm's criminal expert. Don was a civil-court lawyer; he didn't know the rules like Rob did. But he had to admit that once the headlines started getting bigger, he started to enjoy the idea of being Candy's lawyer. He didn't know whether or not she would ever go to trial. Apparently all the cops had was one lousy fingerprint. What were they going to do for a motive?

On Saturday afternoon Don drove over to the parsonage and spent a couple of hours with Ron Adams. Don knew that Ron could keep a secret, but just to be sure, he reminded him of the pastor-parishioner privilege, a legal principle that protects priests from having to reveal information confided during confession or other intimate counseling.

"This church is going nuts over this whole thing," said Don, "and I know you're going to have to deal with it in the days ahead. I don't want the church to suffer. I know that at some point it might come out that Candy and Allan had an affair, and I think it would be better if you talked to people first, to prepare them for that. Candy's going to need their support."

"I understand," said Ron, "and I'll do what I can."

Don had another motive as well. If Ron turned up anything about Betty's personal life that might be helpful to Candy, Don wouldn't refuse that information either. The two men had reached an agreement. They were partners. Ron wanted to hold the church together. Don wanted to keep Candy out of jail. As soon as they had finished talking, Rob drove over to the Clecklers to check on Candy and to ask her if she needed any "counseling."

She was going to need it. The next day's newspapers reported that the police investigation was over.

But still they didn't arrest Candy. Don went to work Monday morning fully expecting a call from Joe Murphy or Royce Abbott asking them to bring her in. But Joe Murphy was biding his time, eliminating all other suspects first.

"Let's let her stew for a while," Murphy told his colleagues. "Let her think about it. Maybe one day the pressure will get to her and she'll just call up and say, 'I did it.'"

For all practical purposes, the formal investigation had ended as soon as Allan Gore returned to Dallas and submitted to a polygraph examination. The examiner was chosen by mutual agreement between the police and Mike Gibson, the attorney now representing Allan. Allan drove to a doctor's office in North Dallas to take the test, but, once there, he had to wait two hours for the equipment to be set up properly. He was scared to death by the time they actually hooked him up, and afraid it would show untruthful simply because of his fear of being charged with something. The pertinent questions were:

"Do you know who caused your wife's death?"

"No."

"On or about June 13, 1980, are you yourself the one who caused your wife's death?"

"No."

"At the time your wife was killed, were you physically present at the home?"

"No."

"Did you plan or set up with anyone to have your wife killed?"

"No."

"Before you arrived in Minnesota on or about June 13, did you know your wife had been hurt or killed?"

"No."

"Do you know anything about your wife's death you're deliberately not telling me?"

"No."

"Are you withholding any information regarding your wife's death that you have not admitted?"

"No."

To each and every relevant question asked during the course of the examination, Allan Gore, in the opinion of the polygraph examiner, was telling the truth.

On Friday the twentieth Pat Montgomery asked for a meeting with his supervisor at Texas Instruments. TI was a conservative, image-conscious company, and he thought it would be best they know that his wife was a suspect in an ax murder. The meeting made Pat nervous at first, but he needn't have worried. Perhaps if he had been a blue-collar assembly-line worker, the revelation would have caused problems. Coming from one of the company's top research scientists, it elicited only the tenderest concern. Like everyone else who knew the Montgomerys, Pat's boss assumed it was merely some terrible mistake; he was more than willing to let Pat have as much time off as necessary to take care of things. And since TI was a company well accustomed to keeping secrets, there wouldn't be any problem on that score either: no one would know about the police investigation except the people Pat wanted to tell. Pat had another company errand to run, too. He dropped by the TI Credit Union and asked for a loan, to help cover Candy's legal expenses. But the loan officer said there was really no way to do that. Pat could get money for a car or a house, but a murder case wasn't really in their line. Pat had assumed as much.

That afternoon Candy called Pat at work and, for the first time, sounded almost hysterical.

"Pat, can you come home *please*. It's everywhere now—in the newspapers and on the radio and TV, and I'm so upset I don't know what to do."

Pat left work right away, and when he got to the Clecker house, Candy collapsed into his arms.

"Oh Pat," she said, "pretty soon everybody will know. Everybody will know I'm a suspect."

"Maybe not," he said soothingly. "I heard something on the radio about a fingerprint they found in the house. Maybe when they finish looking at it, you'll be cleared."

"I hope something happens. I took the polygraph today."

"Maybe they can show that to the police."

Candy didn't say anything.

That morning, after finishing the interviews at Don's office, Elaine Carpenter had taken Candy to St. Paul's Hospital for a physical examination. Stripped to her underwear, Candy was scrutinized by a doctor, who duly recorded the half-dollar-sized bruises on her upper thighs and chest, as well as lesser discolorations on her fingers, ankles and one breast. He described the cut at the hairline of her forehead, which was now scabbing over. He also noted that she seemed full of anxiety, and prescribed Valium and Serax. After that, Elaine and Candy drove to a high-rise office building in suburban Irving, where they had an appointment with a polygraph examiner named Don McElroy. As they sat in his waiting area, Candy seemed even more nervous.

"Now Elaine," she said, "do I tell him the whole story or what?"

"Yes, Candy, that's the point of the test."

"I tell him the truth?"

"Yes, this is *our* examiner. That's why we hired him."

Candy didn't mention the doctor's examination to Pat, nor did she go into any detail about what transpired during her two hours spent with Don McElroy.

"The police might not even believe the polygraph," said Pat.

Pat was getting paranoid about the police. They had suddenly called his wife a murderer. They had been telling the newspapers that they thought Candy killed Betty, a theory that was absurd to anyone who knew both women. They wouldn't cooperate with Rob Udashen. They had even told the reporters where the Montgomerys lived. Pat wondered whether the police *wanted* them out of the house so they could go in with a search warrant and look for evidence. What if they found their Marriage Encounter letters? Worse yet, what if they found Allan's letter to Candy, ending the affair? Pat had to go over to the house anyway, to check on the pets and see that they were fed. He decided he'd be on the lookout for police stakeouts whenever he made the trip, and he made a mental note to find all the letters and bring them back with him.

The pressure lessened a little as the weekend approached. Pat had always liked the Clecklers; this would give him a chance to get to know Tom a little better. That first night Pat and Tom discovered they had both been trumpet players in high school, so Tom got out his old trumpet and they traded it back and forth and blew on it a little bit and reminisced about old band trips. Whenever it was time for the television news, Pat would head for the set and switch from channel to channel in an attempt to catch everything that was said. The bloody thumbprint was still the big item; Pat hoped either that or the footprints they had found earlier would be enough to prove Candy's innocence. On Saturday night, the two couples, Jenny, and Ian all gathered in the living room to look at old slides of Tom's tours of duty in Germany and Vietnam. In the middle of the presentation, Candy left the room to take a call from Rob. When she returned, she was bubbling with joy.

"They've found a woman who says she saw Betty on Friday afternoon," says Candy. "That means I can't be a suspect, because I was only there in the morning."

"Great," said Pat. "I knew something like that would turn up."

Pat was surprised to find how relieved he was. He didn't want to think he had ever believed Candy was involved.

On Monday, the tenth day after Betty's death, Don called from Dallas and suggested that the Montgomerys move again.

"I want to have positive control over the surrender, if and when it comes," he told Pat. "But I don't trust these cops. Do you have any place you can go away from Fairview?"

So, for the second time in four days, the Montgomerys loaded up the station wagon and headed for a new home. They chose Euless, where they would move in with Pat's father, seventy-seven-year-old Jewel Montgomery. This time they were so addled by fears that the police were spying on them that they backed the car into the garage before loading their luggage, then had Sherry drive it to Euless, with Candy lying down on the seat so that no one in the area would see her leaving. Euless was about thirty miles away, a little town on the outskirts of the Dallas–Fort Worth Regional Airport. It was sweltering when they arrived, the first 100-degree day of the year.

They did find a measure of rest in Euless, though. Jewel's house was just a block away from a large park, and that night Pat and Candy walked down there with the kids. Ian and Jenny played on the see-saws for a while, but Ian was so hyperactive that he kept running around and, quite by accident, stepping on his mother's feet. The second time it happened, Candy flinched and grimaced terribly, and Pat suddenly remembered the cut toe he had seen her bandaging a few days before.

"How bad is it?"

"It hurts like hell."

When they got back to the house, Candy took the bandage off and soaked her foot. Pat took a good long look at it and realized for the first time how very deep it was.

"I've got to get rid of that threshold on the back door," he said. "That's dangerous."

The physical pain only aggravated Candy's already frazzled emotions. "I want to be home again," she kept saying. "I want to be in our own house."

"I'll ask Don whether he thinks we could go back over there."

"Pat," she said as they were climbing into bed, "I've got two kids who need me."

"Yes." He held her tight.

"And I could end up going to jail for the rest of my life."

"It's gonna be all right."

The next day, a Thursday, Pat went to work again and called Don to see if it was all right to move back to Montecito. Don gave his assent, since there had been no further evidence of harassment by the police, so Pat called Sherry to ask her to help. Before they could get fully organized, though, Pat got a call from Candy.

"Pat, they're going to arrest me."

"What?"

"Rob just called. They're going to arrest me today."

19 · CENTER STAGE

The one thing Rob Udashen wanted to avoid was flashbulbs. It was the first thing that occurred to him when the call came just after noon from the District Attorney's office of Collin County. He was heartened to hear that the assistant DA, Jack Pepper, was amenable to a quiet, private surrender. The plan was to secure bond before taking Candy to the Collin County courthouse. That way she could be whisked through arraignment and released in a matter of minutes. Pepper even said he'd have it arranged so they could pull into a secluded sally port used for unloading prisoners.

Rob was satisfied enough with the plan—at last, a reasonable person to deal with—but it all depended on having the money for the bond when they arrived. He would figure that out later. First he needed to get Candy under his wing.

"Candy," he said when she came on the line in Euless, "they've issued a warrant for your arrest. Come on into my office and we'll go with you down to the court."

"All right," said Candy dully. The implications hadn't sunk in yet.

Next he called Glen Swanner, the Justice of the Peace who had issued the arrest warrant, and asked about bonding. Swanner agreed to be at the courthouse for the arraignment and said the bond would be no more than $100,000. In most murder cases that amount would not be excessive, but Rob balked. The only purpose of a bond is to ensure a defendant's appearance at trial, and Candy was obviously not a candidate to run off to Mexico. She was a wife and mother, for goodness sake. She'd been under investigation for more than a week; if she'd wanted to run away, she could have done it long before now. As a practical matter, it would be difficult to come up with

238

the $100,000. Bail bondsmen require a 10 percent fee; that meant the Montgomerys would have to pay a nonrefundable $10,000 to keep Candy out of jail. Rather than ask them to do that, Rob called Tom Ryan, a state district court judge in McKinney, to set up a bond reduction hearing.

By the time Rob finished all his calls, Sherry Cleckler had dropped off Candy at the office.

"Here are your options, Candy. The bond is $100,000 because it's a murder charge, and there's nothing I can do to change it today. So you can spend one night in jail and hope we can get it lowered in the morning, or you can come up with $10,000 and spend tonight at home."

"I have to call Pat," she said.

Pat was adamant: he didn't want his wife in jail. They would come up with the money.

Candy walked out of Rob's office and sat down in another room, lighting a cigarette as she did. She had started smoking again. Chain smoking. Elaine Carpenter came in to see how she was doing. Don poked his head in once or twice. Candy was vaguely aware that there were "problems" in the other room. After a while, she got tired of waiting and went back into Don's kitchen. She made coffee and then, noticing all the dirty dishes, started cleaning up the place. She found some baking materials in one of the cabinets and made a batch of chocolate-chips cookies. It all seemed like a lark.

Rob finally tracked down a bondsman willing to handle the case. His name was Jack Swidler. Rob and Candy drove downtown to Swidler's office, a storefront operation in a part of the business district where porno moviehouses and boxing gyms alternated with fleabag mission hotels and beer bars. But there were complications. Swidler suddenly decided he wanted extra surety. He wanted the deed to the Montgomerys' house. Rob left to call the sheriff and explain the extra delay, and Elaine drove downtown to work things out with Swidler.

Elaine was starting to think the whole world was nuts. Witnesses wouldn't talk to her. The police were acting more than a little strange. And now, for some reason, the bail bondsman was afraid that this ordinary little housewife was going to skip town with her husband and two kids and fly to Bora Bora. She was getting angry, especially since she knew this was all a waste of time. The deed to a house was worth nothing to Swidler. Under Texas law, a homestead cannot be garnished or seized under any circumstances—even bankruptcy. She argued with Swidler until he was hoarse, but he wouldn't budge. He wanted the deed, and he wanted a promissory note. Otherwise, he wouldn't make this bond.

Among the media, the word had been out for several hours that an arrest warrant had been issued for one Candace Lynn Wheeler Montgomery of Fairview, Texas. The "female friend of Allan Gore" suddenly had a name, and by midafternoon the name was as close as your nearest radio. Pat had left work as soon as he got Candy's call and arranged to meet Sherry Cleckler at his father's house in Euless. Together they would move the animals and the kids and the luggage back home. They were very conscious of time—they wanted to finish quickly and get home, where they could be reached by phone—so after putting the baggage in the back of Sherry's pickup, Pat packed Ian and Jenny into his Volkswagen Rabbit and headed for Fairview. He had the radio on, as usual, and he had just passed the airport when a news report broke in on the music:

A warrant was issued today for the arrest of a McKinney woman accused in the ax murder of a Wylie housewife. Candace Lynn Montgomery, described by police as a friend of the victim's husband, was being sought this afternoon after being charged with murder in the hacking death of Betty Gore, a schoolteacher found dead in the laundry room of her home on June 13. . . .

As soon as the report began, Pat glanced over at Jenny and knew it was too late. They had both heard everything. They recognized their mother's name, and they knew what murder was. Up until then Pat had managed to avoid telling them exactly what was going on. Ian had asked why they had to live at his grandpa's house, and Pat had told him that the police had made a mistake and thought their mother had done something. He didn't know how he was going to explain this one.

"Daddy, are they going to put Mommy in jail?"

Jenny was always the one who cut right to the heart of the matter.

"Well, we know Mommy," Pat began slowly, "and we love Mommy, and we know she didn't do it. We all love her."

Pat didn't want to say anything more; he didn't want the kids to realize how serious it was. But Jenny was very upset and began to cry. Ian was unaffected, because he didn't understand exactly what was going on. They drove the rest of the way to Fairview in silence.

Around 10:30, Candy called home from Jack Swidler's office. She sounded tired.

"Pat, the bail bondsman says he needs the deed to our house, but everything's taken so long that I have to leave to go to court. You're going to have to drive down here and straighten everything out."

"Okay, what do I need to do?"

Candy spoke away from the phone for a second and then returned. "The deed to the house and a promissory note for $90,000."

"All right, I'll leave now."

"Are the kids all right?"

"They're fine. They want you to know that we all love you."

The job of actually delivering Candy to the courthouse steps had finally fallen to Rob, and at this point it was a thankless task. The delay in getting Swidler to approve the bond had fouled everything up. Around eight o'clock that evening Rob called Don at home. "Judge Ryan just called," he said.

"Ryan's involved in this thing?" said Don. "Wha'd he say?"

"He said 'Where's your client? We're waiting on her.' I told him we're having problems with the bond, but it should be finished any minute now.

"But Ryan said, 'You get that lady up here right now or *else*. Otherwise I'm gonna reconsider that bond reduction hearing you want in the morning.'"

Tom Ryan and Don Crowder had met many times in the courtroom. Neither one of them thought too highly of the other.

"I'll call him," said Don.

But the bond problem didn't go away. Two more hours passed. Rob was calling Jack Swidler's office every fifteen minutes to get reports from Elaine. They always seemed on the verge of some agreement, but then it would fall apart again. When it got to be about ten o'clock, Rob called Ryan again. As he later related the conversation to Don:

"Judge, wouldn't it be easier if we simply brought Mrs. Montgomery in the morning?"

"Mr. Udashen, the answer to that is not only no, it's *hell no!*"

This time Ryan took the offensive by calling Don at home.

"Crowder, you have lied to me. You and your young lawyer have sandbagged me."

Don Crowder's considerable temper started to flare.

"What do you care, Judge? This is not even in your court. It's not in any court. What do you have to do with it? It's the sheriff's matter, and we *will* have her up there."

"You'd better. Right now."

Don hung up, still angry, and immediately dialed Rob.

"*Get her ass up there!* We're pissing off a district judge, and that's something we can't afford."

That's why Pat Montgomery was summoned to Dallas to finish the paperwork, and why Rob was racing up the North Central Expressway as the hour approached eleven o'clock. At least one good thing had come of all this, he thought to himself. It was too late to do the media any good.

When Rob pulled past the brand new Collin County courthouse and turned left toward the Sheriff's Office, he realized how wrong he could be. Bright television lights had been set up at the entrance to the building, there were camera crews and mobile vans everywhere, and at least a hundred people were gathered on the street outside, waiting for the show. As he edged down the street, people peered through the car windows, wondering whether this was the car with the notorious woman inside. He turned left again, into an official driveway, and someone standing nearby shouted something at Candy. Rob couldn't make it out, but it sounded obscene. Candy didn't notice at all.

"What's going to happen?" asked Candy.

Rob was scared, but he tried not to show it. "Don't worry, I have it all arranged. We're going to pull into the sally port, and then they'll pull the door down and close it off to the public."

He continued to edge through the crowd and eased into the garage, nodding at two uniformed deputies at the entrance. They didn't nod back. A headline flashed through his mind. *Lawyer dares police to jail ax suspect.* Damned media.

Neither of the guards made a move to close the door, and once the car was fully inside, it was too late. The throng had surged into the sally port right behind him.

"Don't open your door," said Rob. He needn't have worried. Candy had already locked it.

Rob could see the door to the jail a few feet away. So he reached over and grabbed Candy's hand and said, "Follow me."

Opening his door, he pulled her out behind him. As soon as he did, the crowd moved up close to them, and a reporter for a radio station screamed, "How are you going to plead?"

Candy clutched a book tightly in one hand, looked around her, and smiled faintly.

Just then Steve Deffibaugh emerged from the jail, holding a warrant in one hand and a small card with the Miranda warning written on it in the other. Behind him stood a phalanx of TV cameramen, all pointed in the general direction of Candy. Rob was too stunned to say anything. He couldn't violently object, because everything he did was being taped. He couldn't move forward because the crowd and now Deffibaugh were in his way. So he simply stood there while Deffibaugh approached.

The insistent reporter kept yelling questions. "Are you surprised by the charge?" he said.

Candy looked around again and saw that, oddly enough, about a dozen children were among those watching the scene.

"Candace Lynn Montgomery," said Deffibaugh, his voice quivering slightly as he stared down at the paper in his hands. "You are under arrest." He cleared his throat. "You are under arrest for the offense of murder. You have the right to remain silent. Anything you say can and will be used against you . . ."

As he was speaking, Candy could scarcely hear the words. She was looking at the warrant in his hands. He could hardly hold it still, his hands were shaking so much. She wondered whether he was scared of her or the TV cameras. The thought was funny. She smiled again.

After he had read the Miranda warning, Deffibaugh quickly took Candy by the arm and motioned her toward the jail door. Rob was angry. Why was all this happening for the benefit of the TV cameras? But he was even angrier when they got to the door. Another deputy stopped him from entering.

"No," he said, "you can't go with her."

"Why not?"

"You'll have to go in through the main entrance."

Startled, Rob watched Candy disappearing into a sea of uniforms inside the jail.

"Don't talk to *anybody*," he yelled at her.

He turned around and forced his way back through the spectators, intending to run around to the front of the building. But yet another deputy stopped him before he could get out of the sally port.

"You can't leave your car in here," he said.

"Where can I leave it?" Rob said flatly.

"In the visitors' lot," he said.

Rob got back into his car and moved it to the parking lot, then ran back to the jail and announced himself to the book-in officer.

"Have a seat over there, sir," said the officer.

"I need to talk to my client."

"Have a seat over there, please, and I'll see about it for you."

Glen Swanner, the Justice of the Peace Rob had spoken to earlier in the day, had been as good as his word. The arraignment was swift, and bond was set at $100,000. As soon as Swanner was finished, Candy was fingerprinted and taken into a shower room, where two women deputies named Roberts and Lorance ordered her to take off her clothes. Candy untied her tennis shoes and then unfastened her blue jeans. When she stepped out of them, the women saw the unsightly purple bruises on her legs and the deep cut on her left middle toe. One of them left the room briefly and came back with a camera. All the bruises and cuts were photographed, and then Candy was given a stiff blue prison smock. She had an instinctive dislike for Roberts and Lorance. They were too cold and businesslike. Their attitude seemed accusing.

After Deputy Deffibaugh learned of the injuries to Candy's body, he conferred briefly with Roberts and Lorance and decided she should be examined by a doctor. Deffibaugh had a patrol car called into the sally port, and one of the woman deputies put a pair of handcuffs on Candy.

"Do you really have to do that?" she said.

The deputy didn't bother to answer.

During the short drive to Collin Memorial Hospital, Candy sat in the back seat of the patrol car, handcuffed, with Roberts on one side and Lorance on the other. Far from being awed by the display of police security, Candy found herself growing angry. It seemed as though they were proud of themselves. They *enjoyed* making her feel small. She was the weakest person in the car, and yet they all acted as though she were some dangerous criminal, the way kids acted when they put someone in "jail" under the kitchen table. Under any other circumstances it would be funny. She couldn't wait to get away from these jerks.

At the hospital, there was more showmanship. They made a great scene in the emergency room, hustling her through a crowd of people with exaggerated seriousness. Once in the hospital examining room, Deffibaugh left so Roberts and Lorance could conduct a second strip-search, as though she might have picked up some contraband on the way over in the patrol car. Then he came in and rephotographed the cut on her foot, while a staff doctor examined the bruises and recorded them. He didn't notice the cut at Candy's hairline—the scab on the scar had fallen off that day—and Candy made no effort to help him find it. After the examination, she was handcuffed again and placed in the patrol car for the ride back to jail.

Rob had to wait only about twenty minutes before Elaine showed up with Jack Swidler, the bail bondsman. They had hurried up North Central with all the necessary papers to post the full $100,000. They took them to the bonding desk, but the woman on duty said, "Just a minute, sir," and went into a back room. Ten minutes later she returned.

"This won't be sufficient," she said.

"What?"

"The sheriff says the bond is not in order."

"Well, then, I need to talk to the sheriff right now. There's nothing wrong with this bond."

"Sheriff Burton is busy right now, sir."

"I've got to see him. I'm entitled to some kind of explanation."

"If you'd like to wait, sir."

Unbeknownst to Rob, it was while he was waiting for Sheriff Burton that Candy was being strip-searched, photographed, examined by a doctor, and questioned about the bruises and lacerations on her body. That was something that had never occurred to him, but he knew *something* was wrong.

Eventually Rob got his audience with the sheriff. Burton was adamant. The bond wouldn't fly because it was from Dallas

County. Burton was perfectly within his rights to refuse an out-of-county bond unless it was ensured locally.

Rob went to a pay phone and called Don Crowder at home.

"Don, they sandbagged us. They wouldn't accept our bond. Candy's in jail."

"What the hell?"

"Burton said he couldn't take it. I talked to him. All he'd say was that it was an out-of-county bond."

"The bastards."

"I wasn't ready for them. Candy's spending the night in jail."

"That's all right. You just stick with it. Sounds like something Ryan would pull. I know how to play hardball, too."

"Swidler's on the phone, trying to find a Collin County bondsman that will sign for him."

"Okay, you go on home. The bastards are jacking around with Candy's civil rights, and that's one thing I do know about. Tomorrow morning, if they don't let her go, we'll slap 'em with a federal suit. Bunch of small-town rednecks who think they can write the rules as they go. And Tom Ryan's the leader of the pack."

When Don hung up, he felt a great rush of adrenaline. Things were getting rough. He threw on a bathrobe and went into his study to get out the lawbooks. He remembered that McKinney lay in the federal judicial district of William Wayne Justice, a libertarian renowned and sometimes despised for his left-of-center rulings on civil rights issues. One thing Don would dearly love to see is Tom Ryan being hauled before Judge Justice. It was time to take off the gloves.

On the way back from the hospital, Deffibaugh suddenly turned around and leaned over the seat.

"Well, Candy," he said, "you're being awfully quiet this evening."

Candy hated him. What gave him the right to call her "Candy"? She hated his fat face and his arrogant manner and the way he treated her like a piece of prize property.

"I don't believe I'm required to answer any questions," she said coolly.

"But I know you want to talk about this," said Deffibaugh. "I can tell that you do. Don't you want to say anything to me?"

"No."

She wanted to say "Hell, no," but she resisted the temptation.

"Well, if you want to talk about it, I'll be at the jail all night."

Candy had a quick sinking feeling. What did that mean? Was she going to jail? Why would he assume she's going to be staying all night?

Deffibaugh was quiet for a few moments. When he turned around again, his face was hard.

"There's no *way* you're going to get out of this. You know that, don't you?"

Candy didn't reply.

At the jail, Candy was taken to an isolation cell with padded walls, the kind they use for mental patients. On the way down the hall, she pleaded with the jailer.

"Aren't I allowed to make a phone call?"

"I guess so."

The jailer stood by while Candy dialed her house. Pat picked it up on the first ring.

"They're taking me to a cell, Pat."

"I know. Robert just called."

"What did he say?"

"He said they were having trouble getting the sheriff to accept the bond."

"What does that mean?"

"He doesn't know yet. He says that they'll get a cosigner on the bond and then everything will be okay."

"Pat, I love you. And miss you. Kiss the kids good night for me."

Her voice almost broke.

"We love you, too, and we're thinking of you every minute."

Candy hung up the phone and was escorted to the solitary cell. Up until then she had kept her composure. But when the heavy door was slammed shut, she started to break down. Tears poured out of her eyes. There were no lights in the cell, so she moved as close to the door as she could, to be near the hall light. She was still clutching her paperback book. She opened it and tried to read a few lines. It was called *The Far Pavilions*. After a while she closed it. Pretty soon Rob would be there with a cosigner on the bond and she could go home. Long minutes passed. She opened the book again, but couldn't read. Still nobody came. Against her will, she started to cry again. She flipped through the book, and a bookmark fell out. It was one of those cardboard bookmarks with a Bible verse on it. She read it twice. It was about "strength." Suddenly she realized she was exhausted.

"Okay, God," she said quietly, "there's nothing else I can do. I'm quitting. You do it now."

She lay her head down on the prison cot and was overcome by a real sense of peace. She fell into a deep sleep.

At four in the morning, a deputy banged on the hard metal door and swung it open.

"Here," he said, thrusting a piece of paper at her. "We need you to sign this. You forgot to sign your fingerprints."

Candy didn't get angry, or even say anything. She sat up on the cot, took the paper, and slowly wrote out her name.

I'm tougher than they are, she thought to herself. There's nothing they can do to me that I can't take.

20 · NOTORIOUS

From the moment the first photograph appeared in the *Dallas Morning News* of June 27, Candy Montgomery became the archetypal Scarlet Woman. As long as she was simply a faceless "female friend of Allan Gore," the public imagination had been content with idle speculation about a lurid crime of passion. Photography and videotape changed all that. There were so many photographers and cameramen at the surrender, and again at the bond reduction hearing the next day, that Candy's every expression and attitude was recorded for posterity. It didn't help that she had spent the previous eight hours being shuffled from office to office, and looked tousled and tired by the time she got to jail, but that wasn't what condemned her in the minds of so many. It was her arrogance. It was apparent from all the dozens of photos taken that night that this was no mousy housewife, cowering before the hand of justice. She exuded a haughty independence, beginning with her Little Orphan Annie hairstyle and round, oversized designer eyeglasses. She had worn a striped pullover blouse and faded blue jeans, like an aging hippie, but, worst of all, she looked like she was *enjoying* everything. This time Candy's perpetual look of elfin mischief, accented by her thin, pointed nose and rounded chin, hadn't served her well. For, in almost every photo, Candy Montgomery appeared to be grinning behind her tight lips. The brazen hussy had a smirk on her face.

In oil-company offices and beauty shops and chic North Dallas restaurants, the talk was all of Candy. They called her "Candy" from the beginning, since the name emphasized even more her air of blithe indifference. It filled out the image of a seducing murderess with ice in her veins. And as more and more was revealed about her personal life—including the news that she had been a friend of Betty Gore, a leader in the church, a mother of two, a PTA member—she seemed all the more two-faced. Friends quickly rallied to her defense, unable to believe that she would be capable of such a crime. Invariably, they told reporters that she was "an inspiration," "selfless," "devoted," "articulate," "the type you would never even suspect of shoplifting." One of the most adamant defenders of Candy's character was Ron Adams.

"She's a very pleasant, very loving sort of person," he told the *Times Herald*. "That she would be guilty of what they say she is, is incomprehensible. She's not capable of committing murder. The members of the church are appalled. There's not a person out here who believes for a moment that she's guilty."

Don Crowder called Ron when he read those remarks in the paper. Ron was doing a great job.

Candy had been roused that Friday morning by a jailer who brought her breakfast. Even though she was hungry, the food looked stale and cold, so she drank the black coffee and then pushed the tray back out into the hallway. A few minutes later the jailer returned.

"She didn't eat," he said.

"They never do when they first come," said another one, a little too loudly. "Give her a while and then she'll eat."

Far from scaring her, remarks like that only redoubled her anger. It sounded theatrical, as though they were performing for her. They were saying lines out of B movies, lines that would be laughable if she didn't know that they were intended for her. The one thing she couldn't forgive them for was intentional cruelty.

After breakfast a deputy named Mary came to take her to a holding cell, where Candy would await her first court appearance. When it was time to cross the parking lot to the new courthouse, some two hundred feet away, Mary swung the cell door open and extracted her handcuffs.

"Do you really have to do that?" Candy pleaded.

"No, I guess not."

"Thank you."

"I think you should be prepared, though. There are a lot of cameramen and reporters outside."

"Will we have to go by them?"

"I think so. But just stick close to me."

Mary opened the side door to the jail, and almost

instantly the cameramen started crowding around to get pictures of Candy. Mary tried to push her as fast as she could, but the mob kept the two women from moving very briskly. The farther they went, the closer and closer the cameramen came.

"Mary, I'm afraid I'm gonna fall down."

"Just hold on to me."

"Please tell me where the steps are. I can't see."

"Step," she said as they came to a curb. "Mrs. Montgomery, don't all these people make you nervous?"

"Yes."

"Me, too. So let's just go real fast and we'll get there."

Mary kept up her cadence of "step . . . step . . . step," ever more loudly, as they fell into a rhythm and somehow negotiated the two hundred feet without coming to a dead stop. Once they reached the foyer of the building, they hurried past the elevator and flew up the stairs together, to the relative safety of District Judge Tom Ryan's courtroom.

Rob Udashen was already there; his was the first friendly face she'd seen in hours.

"We've taken care of it," he told her. "We'll have you out this morning."

She was enormously relieved. She scarcely heard the words that Judge Ryan read from his prepared text. But she flinched when he came to the word "murder."

"How do you plead?" he said at last.

Candy looked at the judge, a bearded, white-haired man with glasses, and realized he was speaking to her. She turned and looked at Rob, not sure what to answer.

He whispered, "Not guilty."

"Not guilty," she said meekly.

"For God's sakes, Candy, have you looked at the paper? You sure *look* like a murderer."

Don had decided it was time to take charge of Candy Montgomery's life. He called her at home as soon as he got the afternoon paper.

"Don't you get *emotional* when you're being booked for murder?"

"It's not my manner to get upset, Don. I can't help it. I didn't want to look weak."

"Well, look, Candy, from now on you're out of it.

Understand? We're going to make all the decisions for you, and I don't want you to interfere."

"Okay."

"I want you to defer to me on everything from here on out."

"Okay." She sighed. "I don't feel like trying to figure it all out anyway."

"All right. Now the first thing I want you to do is change your appearance. The least you can do is not *look* like a murderer. I want you to grow your hair out again and get those kinks out of it. Didn't you used to wear your hair different?"

"I had it short and straight before Sherry gave me the permanent. I think what happened is Sherry left the permanent on too long, so it looks hard."

"Okay, get it back to like it was."

"That's all right with me. The curls make me look too identifiable anyway."

"And I want you to lose some weight. Your arms look flabby. If you go to trial, I don't want you looking as big as Betty Gore. And I want you to stop smoking."

Candy didn't say anything.

"Okay?"

"I guess so, Don, but I need the cigarettes. I'm so nervous."

"I don't care. It makes you look too tough. At least don't smoke in public."

"All right, I'll try."

Don had a plan. Like most of Don's plans, it was aggressive and two-fisted and theatrical. It was obvious from the way the arrest was handled that Rob was going to need help on the case. Rob had all the legal knowledge you could ever want, but Don had to face the fact that when it came to one-on-one head-knocking, people could railroad him. Rob was too young and a little too naive. He tended to believe the other guy's bullshit. He was a nice guy in a case that needed a son of a bitch. The morning after the surrender, Rob had finally gotten Candy out of jail by arranging a deal between Swidler and Bob Hendricks, a McKinney state legislator and bail bondsman, who agreed to cosign. But Don was still angry about the way his people had been treated. The slopehead cops and Judge Tom Ryan had won the first round.

Don spread out the newspapers on the desk in front of him. He carefully studied all the accounts of the surrender and was pleased to find a ground-swell of support for Candy among the members of the church. The wisest thing he'd done so far was to get Ron to break the news to the church *before* it hit the papers. Nobody believed Candy was capable of such a horrible crime. Enough publicity would create at least the suspicion that the police were the villains in this story. Don was pleased with the direction the reporting was taking, and he thought perhaps it wouldn't be such a bad idea to keep the story alive. So when Doug Swanson, the *Times Herald* reporter, called Rob that afternoon, Don intercepted the call himself.

"What they're doing to this woman is not right," said Don.

"Are you still maintaining that Mrs. Montgomery is innocent?"

"Absolutely."

"Even in view of the bloody fingerprint found on the refrigerator, and the bloody footprints that match her shoe size?"

"I'll tell you what, Doug," said Don, affecting an intimacy, "anybody who's looked at this crime for more than five minutes knows it had to be performed by a man. Probably a big man. Betty Gore was a big woman, and that was a big ax. I knew Betty Gore. The woman probably weighed one-forty, one-fifty. Candy Montgomery couldn't even lift an ax like that, much less swing it. I've started my own investigation of this case, and I believe in a few days I'll have some new developments to tell you."

"But how do you explain the bloody fingerprint?"

"Oh, that may be her print, I'm not denying that. She was in the house that day. But I don't believe they've got any *bloody* fingerprint."

"What do you think happened then?"

"Well, we've got a number of people we're investigating, but I'm not at liberty to use any names."

It wasn't until the next morning that Rob Udashen picked up a newspaper and realized what Don was doing. Shocked, he called Don at home.

"Don, I don't think these comments in the paper are a good idea," he said. "We've got enough problems with the cops and the courts without making 'em madder."

"I don't know, Rob, I think it puts pressure on 'em, to see that the community is behind us and everything. They've been leaking stuff to the press ever since this thing started—fingerprints, shoeprints, cuts. The bastards."

"I'm just saying I don't think it's a good idea to advertise our intentions. We may be able to beat this thing quietly, with motions and arguments. We may be able to keep it from going to trial at all. Candy hasn't even been *indicted* yet."

"Okay, I see your point. You're the expert. I'll hold off a little bit. But I wish we could do something about these leaks."

"Maybe it wouldn't be a bad idea to get a gag order down the line. But whatever we do, let's play strictly by the rules, so we don't make 'em mad."

"Okay, I got ya."

That wasn't Rob's only surprise that Saturday, though. After the call to Don, he left for his dentist's office, where he intended to take care of something he'd been putting off for months: all four of his wisdom teeth needed to be pulled. But just as the surgeon was about to put him under, he got a call from one of his secretaries.

"You need to call Pat Montgomery right away," she said. "He says the police are at the house."

Stephen Deffibaugh had been officious and polite when he rang the Montgomery doorbell late that morning.

"Mr. Montgomery, I have a search warrant here that gives me the authority to take your car for inspection."

"All right," said Pat warily. "Why don't you come in for a moment?"

"That's all right, I'll just wait here."

"I'm going to have to call my lawyer before I let you have the car, so you're welcome to wait in the living room."

Reluctantly, Deffibaugh stepped into the foyer, looking a little nervous. Pat went to the kitchen phone and called the number Rob had left for them. The secretary promised to have him call right away.

"Who's there?" asked Rob.

"He's one of the sheriff's deputies, and he wants the station wagon."

"Is that the car Candy had on the thirteenth?"

"Yes."

"Read me the warrant."

After Pat read the document, Rob said, "Okay, go ahead and let 'em have it. But watch everything they do."

"All right," Pat told Deffibaugh, "you can take the car. It's in the garage."

"We'd appreciate it if you would back it out of the garage, Mr. Montgomery, so that we can tow it to McKinney. We have a wrecker here."

"All right."

Deffibaugh walked outside to give instructions to the wrecker, then came back in to wait while the arrangements were made.

"Gee, this is really a nice house," said Deffibaugh, looking around at the cathedral ceilings and Alpine architecture.

"Yeah, it's a shame," said Pat, "because we're probably gonna end up losing this house."

After Deffibaugh left, Candy came downstairs to find out what had happened.

"I guess they wanted to check the station wagon for evidence," said Pat.

"Didn't you just wash that car last weekend?"

"Yeah, washed it and cleaned it, while we over at the Clecklers."

"That's what I thought."

Candy had entered a new phase. She was remote and a little nervous, but she remained under control. She hadn't broken down since the arraignment hearing, and there was no further evidence of nightmares. In jail, on Thursday night, she had turned everything over to God, and on Friday afternoon, just to make sure, she had turned everything else over to her lawyer.

"I can't deal with it anymore," she told Pat. "I'm going to let other people deal with it."

But if Candy had reached a new sense of peace, Pat was starting to come apart at the seams. All along he had felt that the next day would bring that one piece of evidence that would clear his wife and end the public ordeal. Now, after a panicky night spent wondering what was happening at the Collin County Jail, he was wracked by fear and frustration. On Friday morning, he had had to wake up the kids and tell them Candy still wasn't home.

Ian didn't seem particularly impressed by the news; he didn't understand it. But Jenny was upset.

"When is Mommy gonna be home?" she asked.

"I think either today or Monday."

"Is Mommy gonna be home for Christmas?"

"Of *course* she is." But as soon as he answered, Pat

doubted himself. Was it possible? Was it possible that Candy, of all people, could go to prison?

Later that morning the lawyers had called to comfort him and to tell him that Candy would be home around noon. Sherry came over to wait with him. When Rob finally brought Candy home that afternoon, they had a tearful reunion, and then Pat plied Rob with all sorts of questions. Rob tried to assuage him by saying they were doing everything humanly possible.

But Pat couldn't shake the feeling that something was wrong with the investigation. That night he tried to get Candy to talk about the case, but she was just as standoffish as Rob had been.

"Don says I'm not supposed to discuss it with anybody," she said.

"Not even your husband?"

"It's not that we're hiding anything, Pat. He just thinks it's better for me not to discuss it."

"I don't understand that, Candy. How can I help if I don't know everything that's going on?"

"I've left all the decisions up to Don. I can't talk about it."

The next day, while Candy was cooking dinner, Pat unobtrusively walked upstairs and quickly started looking through his wife's closet. He was looking for her "thongs," the ones she usually wore in the summer, because he was beginning to wonder whether they made the same type of footprint that was found in Betty Gore's utility room. He looked in the closet, then checked the bathrooms and a few other likely places in the house, but couldn't find them.

"Candy," he said over dinner, "whatever happened to those thongs you used to wear?"

"I gave them to the police."

"No, not those, the *other* pair."

"Oh, I threw 'em away."

"When?"

"I don't remember. A while ago."

Pat dropped the subject.

This was also the weekend that Jackie Ponder came for one of her periodic visits, and Candy was looking forward to it. The visit was all the more welcome, now that Don had forbidden Candy to sing in the choir or go to church that Sunday. He wanted her to stop appearing in public altogether, but she insisted that, once the news media stopped showing up at church services, she would start attending again.

Jackie had been overwhelmed by the news. She was in San Antonio, visiting her parents, when she first heard the name "Betty Gore" on a newscast. She had called everybody at Lucas who had known Betty, to get the details, then grieved for two days. She kept thinking of Betty's terror. She remembered the last time Betty had touched her, the time Betty had run into her arms at the church service. Then a week later, one of Don's private investigators had called Jackie to ask her about Betty, and in the course of the conversation she learned that the prime suspect in the case was Candy. Jackie didn't know what to think. She tried to imagine some circumstances in which those two women would fight, but she couldn't come up with any.

Now she sat in the Montgomerys' living room, trying to comfort them both and, at the same time, figure out what strange chain of events had led to her being a suspect. When Candy would leave the room for even a minute, Jackie would work on Pat, trying to find out what he knew.

"Not much," he said quietly. "She doesn't want to say much about it."

"That doesn't make sense, Pat."

"I know, but I don't want to put pressure on her."

"She's *not* involved in any way, is she?"

Pat paused just a second. "No."

"But you have doubts?"

"Well, what do you think?" asked Pat. "If I know something nobody else knows, I should come forward with it, shouldn't I?"

"Do you know something?"

"Just little things. Little suspicions."

"Like?"

"Like why did she throw away her thongs? And why is she not allowed to talk about the case? And why does she have that cut and those bruises?"

"Have you talked to her about those things?"

"No, I couldn't."

"But what if she were guilty? Just assuming she was?"

"If she were guilty, I guess I wouldn't want her to get away with it. But no matter what happened, I wouldn't give up on her."

Candy reentered the room, and Pat, starting to get

worked up about the case again, said, "I don't understand why you have to be so secretive."

"I told you, Pat, because the lawyers want it that way."

"Candy," said Jackie sternly, "I think you should be more open with Pat."

"About what?"

"Is there anything that happened that day you haven't told us?"

"Jackie, I did *not* murder Betty Gore."

"All right," said Jackie. "I guess that's good enough for me."

Pat still wasn't satisfied, but he resolved not to make matters worse. That evening they decided to take the kids to see a movie called *Herbie Goes Bananas*—it would make things seem more normal—and on the way home they stopped at one of their favorite restaurants, Totino's in Plano. The family outing suddenly turned sour when Candy noticed several people staring at her when they sat down at their table.

"This is awful," she said. "I'm going to have Sherry do my hair all over again tomorrow, so that people won't recognize me."

"I'm not sure they're staring," said Pat.

"This is awful," she repeated.

After Candy's arrest, the police had turned the case over to the Collin County District Attorney, Tom O'Connell. O'Connell was a ruddy-faced thirty-nine-year-old lawyer who had learned to prosecute by the book, first performing court martials in the Army, later under then-District Attorney Tom Ryan. Known by Collin County as the consummate "gentleman lawyer," he was serving his ninth year as DA, but none of the previous eight offered anything like the file that came to rest on his desk that Friday the twenty-seventh. All the police had given him, it appeared, was one fingerprint. He had handled enough murder cases to know that that wasn't nearly enough to send anyone to prison, and certainly not enough to convict a woman with no prior record and a stellar reputation in the community. Since there had obviously been no witnesses to this crime, the case would rely on circumstantial evidence, and, as in all such cases, the more physical evidence he had—fingerprints, hair samples, photographs, and the like—the better his chances of winning. The trouble was, the police hadn't bothered to collect any physical evidence. Candy

Montgomery had been interviewed twice before she even had a lawyer, and yet her body had not been photographed, no blood samples were taken, no hair samples were taken, neither her car nor her house had been searched. It was a minor miracle that, when the woman was booked into jail, a guard had noticed the bruises on her body and the cut on her toe. The examination came two weeks late, but at least they got *some* evidence that there had been a struggle.

O'Connell called in his two top assistants, Jack Pepper and William Schultz, and went over the possible defenses Candy could use. She wouldn't be able to deny the bloody fingerprint, but she could easily say she went into the house after Betty Gore was already dead, saw the blood and the body, and freaked out. It wasn't a strong alibi, but in the absence of eyewitnesses or a confession, it might be enough to raise doubt in the minds of the jury. The other possibilities were a defense of temporary insanity—not likely, because she had no prior history of psychiatric problems—or self-defense. That was even more unlikely, O'Connell decided, because of the number of blows and the fact that she'd lied to the police when they first questioned her. A person who's defending herself doesn't need to lie, and certainly doesn't need to mutilate the body.

So the focus of their preparation, at least at first, would be on accumulating all the physical evidence they could. They would verify her wounds, take hair and blood samples, obtain search warrants for her car. Dr. Stone conducted an inch-by-inch search of the station wagon, poking among the seat cushions, going through the trunk, and finally finding exactly what they were looking for—a small, almost undetectable amount of blood on the parking brake pedal, and an even smaller amount on the floor mat underneath it. Since they now thought that their case might rest on proving that Candy's blood was spilled inside the house along with Betty's, they returned to the Gore residence and retrieved a bath mat, a candy jar, doormats, carpet samples from an area near the front door, and two Band-Aid boxes. Their hope was that, back at the lab, the microscope would pick up more blood matching Candy's.

O'Connell wanted to move quickly for an indictment, not least because the case was getting a great deal of attention in the press, so by the following Monday he started bringing witnesses before the grand jury. One of the first was Barbara

Green, reportedly Candy's best friend, who turned out to be both highly excitable and a stalwart defender of Candy's innocence. When she kept insisting that Candy hadn't done anything out of the ordinary on June 13, the prosecutors tried to get tough with her by reminding her of the perjury laws. As a result, she emerged from the grand jury room in tears and called Candy to relate what had happened.

Don Crowder blew his stack. It so happened that reporters were calling that afternoon for more comments on the case, and Don gave them all they wanted.

"The DA's office out there has gone crazy," he told the *Times Herald*. "They browbeat the hell out of that harmless little woman. It just shows you how desperate those men are. There's no such thing as civil rights in Collin County."

When Doug Swanson called later that day to ask about the cut the police had found on Candy's toe, Don was still fuming.

"That cut was caused by a totally innocuous situation," he said. "In fact, we've got the instrument that caused the cut. I will have three witnesses that will testify to the cut and say how it was committed."

"What witnesses? What instrument?"

"I can't say anything about that right now, because of the way the police are handling this case. That examination they did at the hospital was against Mrs. Montgomery's will. They took her to the hospital under the auspices that she was an injured person. They were really gathering evidence without a warrant. Candy even refused to sign the consent form for the examination, but a sheriff's deputy did it anyway."

"I understand that the police believe there were problems going on between the Montgomery family and the Gore family."

"You're talking about the affair," said Don. "It was something everybody was aware of. All parties knew about the affair, and they also knew that it had ended seven months before. All those differences had been reconciled. That couldn't possibly be a motive for murder."

Again, Rob Udashen didn't know about the interviews until he read the papers the next day.

"Don, you *promised* me you wouldn't do that anymore."

"It's just that I can't take stuff like that lying down."

"Well, at least wait until she's indicted."

"All right, okay. But I think the press is all we got on our side right now. Reporters like underdogs. That's us."

"But every time you talk to reporters, you make the cops mad at us all over again. Don, you called 'em *crazy*."

Rob neglected to mention the most important information Don had given the press. For the first time, he had used the word "affair" publicly, as much as admitting what everyone had been afraid to publish before. From now on there would be no "female friend" euphemisms. The woman's attorney had confirmed it: Candy had been Allan Gore's mistress.

For the next ten days the lawyers on both sides circled like wrestlers about to go to the mat. With grand-jury subpoenas pouring out of the DA's office, and defense motions pouring out of Rob Udashen's typewriter, both sides were playing a defensive game. Rob still held out hope of avoiding an indictment altogether, and to that end he convinced Justice of the Peace Swanner to schedule an examining trial for July 10. If the police didn't produce their evidence by then, the court would be forced to let Candy go free. The DA's office continued to parade witnessess before the grand jury. Often they were working on mere hunches: they subpoenaed Pat Montgomery on the off-chance that he was such an honest man that he would say somethng incriminating about his wife. They planned to subpoena Dee Cathey, a woman who had come forward with stories of how Candy Montgomery and Sherry Cleckler had sneaked out to a singles bar while their husbands were away. Her testimony would tend to indicate that Candy was neither truthful nor faithful. They also strongly suspected that Don Crowder had the clothing that Candy had worn the day of the crime, and they demanded he give it to them for blood testing.

"If you've got her clothing and you don't give it to us," said Pepper, "I'm gonna haul you down here for concealing evidence."

"I'm not concealing any evidence," said Don, "and the clothes are exactly where they should be."

Despite his public defiance, though, Don was secretly afraid.

"They're like a pack of mad dogs," he told Rob. "It's a goddamn runaway prosecution and a runaway grand jury, and they're trying to railroad this thing through before we have a chance to prepare a defense."

In point of fact, Don *did* have Candy's clothing. After Schultz and Pepper started asking for it, Don told Candy to bring in the jeans and blouse. He placed them in a paper sack, sealed it, had the sack signed and dated by a witness, then told Elaine and Rob, "We're gonna play a little musical chairs."

For the next few days, the three attorneys passed the clothing among themselves. Don kept it for a while, then Rob, then Elaine, and periodically each person would transfer it from car to house to office. Whenever Pepper or Schultz would call to ask where the clothes were, Don would simply say, "Right where they should be."

"This way," he told Rob, "there's no way they can get a search warrant, because they can't show probable cause that the clothes are in any particular place."

Finally, they turned the brown paper bag over to Pat and told him to put it on a closet shelf, where it remained until the day of Candy's trial.

Shultz and Pepper were tireless. Next they subpoenaed Don McElroy, the polygraph examiner Don had hired to test Candy the week before, and Don flew off the handle all over again. The attorney-client privilege is supposed to extend to experts and other professionals employed by an attorney, which meant that McElroy wouldn't be allowed to testify about the substance of Candy's story. On the other hand, a grand jury in a small county can do just about anything it wants to, and Don wouldn't be there to see that they played by the rules. Increasingly, Don heard noises in the night and saw shadows on the wall. He began to fear his phone was tapped. On several occasions, he told Rob he thought he had been followed.

On July 2 both Dallas papers reported that the police had found blood in the Montgomery station wagon. To Don, it was yet another infuriating attempt by the police to win the case in the newspaper, and when the reporters called that morning, he unloaded.

"They're looking for Betty Gore's blood on the brake pedal of that car," he told the *News*. "But if that's Betty Gore's blood, there's only one way it got there. It was planted."

"Great," said Rob when he saw the paper. "Now you've accused *them* of a crime."

As it happened, a preliminary hearing was scheduled that day to deal with the prosecution's motions to take hair and blood samples from Candy. But before it even started, Judge Ryan issued a stern admonishment to both sides to stop discussing evidence in the press.

"I would hope in 1980 America that law enforcement and the legal profession have progressed so that pretrial publicity is completely unnecessary," he said. "There is no reason that this case should be tried on the streets of McKinney, Dallas, or anywhere else. Now, I'm speaking my piece in advance even though I've determined that I don't have jurisdiction in this case. Since there's been no indictment, I'm referring these motions back to Justice of the Peace Swanner. That means you guys can still run off at the mouth.

"But let me tell you this. As soon as the case is transferred back to me, there will be no more press conferences and no more discussion of the evidence in this case with anyone."

As it turned out, the press knew everything anyway. Most of what the police knew was distilled for the public on July 8, when the front page of the *Dallas Times Herald* hit the streets with a bold banner headline streaming across its front page:
CANDY MONTGOMERY: IS SHE A KILLER?
'Candy couldn't do that,' friends insist
The article by reporters Doug Swanson and Tim Jarrell broke very little new ground, but for the first time it put all the evidence in one place: the affair with Allan Gore, the fact that Candy was the last to see Betty alive, the hour and a half that morning when nobody saw her, the bloody thumbprint on the freezer door that matched Candy's, the cut found on Candy's toe, the bruises on her legs, and the fact that the bloody footprints in the house were small enough to belong to a woman.

By the time the article appeared, Candy was no longer reading the newspapers or watching the nightly TV newscasts. But Pat was heartened by the fact that, no matter what new evidence was leaked to the press, everyone continued to stand by them. The church had been overwhelmingly supportive. Scarcely a day went by that they didn't receive at least a half-dozen greeting cards or "Have a nice day" cards or "Thinking of you" cards, some of them awkwardly worded, all of them well intentioned. People who hadn't written or seen the Montgomerys in years were visiting Hallmark stores all over America, trying to find messages suitable for a family awaiting a murder indictment. The ones that read "Deepest sympathy," as though intended for a funeral, didn't seem particularly appropriate to Pat, but he filed those away with the others, and Candy wrote replies to them all.

The "one-ringers" had started again, too. Every night before they went to bed, the phone would ring once and then stop. Sometimes it would happen four or five times a night. That was the universal greeting exchanged among Marriage Encounter couples. It meant, "We love you."

On July 9, at 4:18 in the afternoon, the grand jury of Collin County returned the long-awaited murder indictment, thereby formally bringing Candy Montgomery into the jurisdiction of District Judge Tom Ryan. There was a brief flurry of courthouse activity, as reporters at the scene put the word out via radio and wire service. But the more significant result was that now, at last, Bruce Selcraig could reveal what he had known for two days. The *Morning News* held the story out of its early editions, afraid that the rival *Times Herald* would have time to copy it and write their own version, but in the edition that arrived on most doorsteps the next morning, the page-one banner headline said it all:

AX SLAYING CONFESSED, SOURCES SAY

Mrs. Montgomery calls reports of admission 'ridiculous'

The pertinent parts of the article read:

Candace Montgomery secretly confessed to the brutal ax murder of Wylie schoolteacher Betty Gore following a polygraph examination one week after the murder, two independent sources told the *Dallas Morning News.*

The sources said that during a lie detector test given to Mrs. Montgomery on June 20 by Dallas polygraph examiner Don McElroy, the 30-year-old housewife stopped the interview and admitted she killed Mrs. Gore. . . .

McElroy, a former polygraph examiner for the Dallas Police Department, would not comment Wednesday. . . .

In a telephone interview Wednesday night, Mrs. Montgomery denied confessing to the murder, saying: "I think it sounds ridiculous and I think you ought to call Robert (Udashen, one of her attorneys). I can't talk to you anymore." She then hung up the phone.

Udashen, one of two attorneys representing her, would neither confirm nor deny the confession. "I think any communication between myself and Candy and Mr. McElroy is privileged and I'm not at liberty to discuss it," Udashen said.

Sources said McElroy was retained by Udashen in an apparent effort to clear his client.

However, after about an hour-and-a-half on the polygraph

machine, McElroy stopped the questioning and told Mrs. Montgomery he thought she was lying. At that point she admitted hacking Mrs. Gore to death with an ax, the sources said.

Following the conversation, the sources said, McElroy telephoned Udashen and informed him of the confession.

The sources said Mrs. Montgomery told McElroy she murdered Mrs. Gore sometime during the morning of June 13, when she had gone to the Gore home to get a bathing suit for the Gores' 5-year-old daughter, Alisa. She had been babysitting for the daughter that day.

Mrs. Montgomery said she got into an argument with Mrs. Gore about an affair she had with Mrs. Gore's husband, Allan, the sources said. . . .

It's hard to say who was most shocked by the article—Don Crowder, Rob Udashen, Don McElroy, Ron Adams, or Candy Montgomery. All of them were on the phone for most of the morning, cursing and trying to find the source of the article. At one point Don even called the *Morning News* and demanded to speak to Selcraig's editor.

It's easy to say who was *least* shocked by it—Pat Montgomery. He read it three times before leaving for work, and then he read it again. He didn't know exactly what to make of it yet, didn't know whether it was good news or bad news as far as Candy's case was concerned, but somehow it made him feel better. That afternoon he called Rob Udashen's office and requested an appointment. The secretary promised she'd have him call, but by the end of the day Pat still hadn't heard from him. The next day Pat tried again, but Rob was still unavailable.

Actually Rob was busy drawing up legal papers for the motion he had wanted to make for a long time. After the shouting had died down, Rob had gone into Don's office.

"We need to take the press out of this thing," he told him. "We need a gag order."

"I guess you're right," said Don.

21 · SANDBAGGED

Within hours after the *News'* bombshell article, Rob Udashen was on the phone to Jack Pepper, the assistant DA, asking for a gag-order hearing as soon as possible. Rob had an ulterior motive. He wanted to put a stop to the news leaks that were constantly getting Candy's name into the newspaper, but at least as important was the effect it would have on Don's mouth. Pepper seemed more than willing to cooperate. It was scheduled for the next day. Both men agreed it would be best if no one told the press about the special hearing.

The next morning Rob stopped at the house to pick Candy up, and they arrived at the courthouse together. They went straight to Ryan's courtroom, right on time, but found it empty. So Rob had Candy wait while he went back to Ryan's chambers. He found the judge sitting at his desk.

"We're here, Judge," said Rob, poking his head in the door.

Ryan simply nodded.

Rob returned to the courtroom and waited about five minutes before O'Connell and Pepper arrived. But still Judge Ryan didn't emerge from his chambers. After fifteen more minutes, Rob said, "I wonder if he knows we're all out here," but no one else seemed upset by the delay.

Rob let fifteen more minutes pass, then went back to the chambers again.

"We're all here, Judge. We're ready."

"All right."

It took another ten minutes, but finally Ryan emerged in his robes and announced he was ready. The gag order had already been prepared by the DA's office, and it took only two or three minutes to read it and get it approved by both sides.

Rob assumed the hearing was over, but suddenly Ryan shifted gears.

"Now I have one other matter before the court, of grave concern to the court," began Ryan, "and that is the sufficiency of the sureties on this bond. For the record, the surety on the bond, the principal being Candace L. Montgomery—this is you, is it not?"

"Yes, sir," said Candy.

"The surety is Bob Hendricks, who the court will take judicial notice is a local attorney. The affidavit recites that Mr. Hendricks—and I'm just paraphrasing—concerning his financial condition, swears that he's worth at least the sum of two hundred thousand dollars. . . ."

Candy turned and looked at Rob. "What's he saying?" she whispered.

"I don't know," said Rob.

"It's come to this court's attention," continued Ryan, "there's not an affidavit of worth on file with the sheriff's department of Collin County, Texas. And the sheriff is here and I want to find out if that's true. I want to find out the present value of the property, the location and description of the property, and the encumbrances if any, and the net value and also the outstanding indebtedness on the part of the surety for other bonds, if there is any."

Ryan looked up from whatever he was reading. "Are you prepared to offer that type of testimony?" he asked.

"Yes, sir," said O'Connell quickly.

Rob swiveled his head and stared at O'Connell in shock. How could the district attorney be prepared to offer testimony on a matter Rob knew nothing about? They had come to approve a routine gag-order, and now suddenly they were talking about bonds and property and indebtedness.

"All right, call your first witness," said Ryan.

"I call Jerry Burton," said O'Connell just as quickly.

Rob flinched again. Jerry Burton was the *sheriff*. The judge, the DA, and the sheriff all knew what was going on, and he didn't. He was too confused even to object. He didn't even know *how* to object. So he sat and waited to see what they were doing.

Sheriff Burton was sworn, and as he took the stand he handed Candy's bonding papers to the court reporter.

Under questioning from Tom O'Connell, Burton testified that Bob Hendricks, Candy's local bail bondsman, did not have an affidavit of net value on file with the county, and that, even if he did, he was overextended. Rob saw what was coming and leapt to his feet.

"When did you first discover that you did not have the affidavit on file, Sheriff?" asked Rob. His voice dripped with sarcasm.

"Today," said Burton.

"When was that?"

"Today."

"That's all the questions I have for the sheriff."

"All right," said Ryan.

Rob remained standing. "Judge, can I make a statement for the record?"

"Yes, sir."

"I would like to point out that this is the first time I've had notice of the problem. I have not obviously had an opportunity to discuss this with Mr. Hendricks or anyone else prior to today. And I'd like the record to reflect that."

"All right," said Ryan. "You may step down, Sheriff."

Ryan reached for a lawbook resting on the bench and opened it to a page marked with a bookmark.

"Article 17.09 of the Code of Criminal Procedure," he began, "provides among other things that if during the course of an action, the judge in whose court such an action is pending finds that the bond is defective, excessive or insufficient in amount. . . ."

Candy didn't understand all the technical legal language as Ryan read on and on, but she sat up when she heard the phrase "order the accused to be rearrested" and turned to Rob for an explanation.

"Are they trying to rearrest me?" she asked, disbelieving.

"Yeah," said Rob drily.

"Can they do that?"

"Yeah," he said. "Apparently. But don't worry, I'll straighten it out with Hendricks."

Within two minutes of Ryan reading the passage from the lawbook, Sheriff Burton had slapped handcuffs on Candy's wrists. Rob watched her being led away and felt entirely helpless.

"*Exactly* when today did you look up that affidavit?" demanded Rob. He was talking to the sheriff, and his face was flushed.

"I guess just before we came in here."

"While we were waiting for the hearing to start?"
Burton had nothing more to say.

"The bastards," Don said.
"They took me by surprise, Don. I blew it."
"We're filing a federal lawsuit. There *is* such a thing as civil rights, even if those rednecks don't know it."
"Don, you can't go to the press with this," said Rob.
"What?"
"The gag order. They got it approved and signed before they rearrested her. The courtroom was empty. No one knows about it."
"The bastards."

For once in his life, mild-mannered Pat Montgomery was hopping mad. Barbara Green had called him at work to break the news. He didn't even go home first. He drove straight from Texas Instruments to the jail.

Surprised to find the reception area empty, since it was usually full of cameramen and reporters, he marched up to the receptionist.

"I need to see the sheriff," said Pat.
"He's not here," she said.
"Well, you've rearrested my wife and I want to know why."
"I don't know anything about that, Mr. Montgomery."
"Well, I'm not leaving here until I get answers."

Pat went over to the pay phone and called Barbara Green.
"Barbara," he said, "you'll have to keep the kids this afternoon, because I'm not leaving here until I get answers."

Pat took a seat, wondering what to do next. After a few minutes Rob walked in with Bob Hendricks, the bondsman.
"What's going on?" said Pat angrily.

Rob could see Pat was agitated, and attempted to calm him down. He outlined briefly what had happened at the hearing.

"I've got to see Candy."
"I'll try to get you in."

But all Rob's efforts were to no avail. Pat waited at the jail two and a half hours, only to be informed that visiting hours were on Sunday and he would have to wait until then. That evening jail officials agreed to let Rob in to see her for just ten minutes, strictly because he claimed to have legal business.

Since the arrest was made on a Friday afternoon, everyone knew there was very little chance of anything being done before Monday. That meant Candy would spend at least three nights in jail, and the thought made Pat almost physically sick. He drove home and went by the Greens' to pick up the kids. Barbara had saved some Sloppy Joes for him, so he lingered at their house for a while, grateful for the sympathetic ears. Pat dreaded having to tell the children. Jenny already knew something was up.

"Is Mommy ever coming home?" she asked at last.

"Of course, she is," said Pat.

Candy might have broken down again had it not been for Mary. She saw her as soon as the deputy took her to the book-in area, and was glad she was there during the fingerprinting and photographs.

"Aren't you going to strip-search me now?" asked Candy.

"No," said Mary, "we never do that."

This time Candy was placed in the first cell, next to the jailer's office, tinier than the others and generally used as an isolation cell. Since it was still daytime, she managed better this time when the heavy metal door clanged shut. For a few hours she held out some hope of being released, then, aware that it must be well past working hours, realized that she might have to stay the entire weekend.

Rob came to her cell early that first evening, then Elaine the next day. Pat was allowed to see Candy for thirty minutes on Sunday afternoon, but even that time was tense and tearful. He understood what was going on least of anyone.

Neighbors were handling the meals again. On Saturday Sherry Cleckler had come by the house to cook spaghetti and meat sauce for dinner. Barbara Green provded leftovers for lunch. That night, a friend from the church named Larry Sullivan stopped by with a six-pack of Coors and stayed for two hours. Pat had always liked Larry and his wife Terry, but had never known them that well. He already felt himself growing closer to people he had known for years.

Pat and the kids overslept on Sunday morning, but Pat insisted that they go to church anyway. Ron Adams mentioned Candy in his opening prayer, which made the kids feel better, and after services Terry Sullivan brought over an ice chest full of food—barbecued chicken breasts, broccoli, rice, corn, and chocolate cookies. Pat had to save it, though, because Barbara

Green had already prepared a Sunday dinner of roast beef, corn, and potatoes, with peach crunch and ice cream for dessert.

Monday came and went, and Candy remained in jail. Elaine went by to see her that afternoon to tell her there were still difficulties. The legal reasoning was complicated, but it all amounted to two things: Candy's bail bondsman wasn't acceptable, and the only way to get around it was to pay another $15,000.

"Elaine, all I know is I've read *The Rebels* twice and something called *Rocky Candy Mountain* twice, and they refuse to give me any more books, and they refuse to let me take a shower, and I don't even have a pencil and paper to write letters with."

Pat stayed home from work on Monday, expecting Candy to get out of jail, and then fell into a depression again when the lawyers called late in the day to say it would be another day. After the kids were in bed, Pat sat down in his study and slowly started writing a letter.

"These last few days," he wrote, "have been the most trying times of our lives. I want you to know that I believe in you and I love you and I'll always be with you no matter what happens. Don't worry about me—I'll always be with you. And don't worry about the kids. I can take care of them. They, of course, miss you. Jenny has really bugged me about when she can have a pony. Ian wants his own pony. I told her we couldn't afford a pony now or for a while. I want you to know that whenever you think of me, I hope you feel warm all over; because, I'm thinking of you and wanting to be close to you. I can feel your presence, too. I'm praying a lot and I know my prayers will be answered. When you lay down to sleep at night, I want you to know that I'm with you and I'm thinking of you. I love you so much. . . ."

Pat signed his name and addressed the letter, care of Sheriff's Department, McKinney, Texas. It took two days for the postal service to deliver it, and when it arrived Candy was still there to receive it.

As soon as Don got the news of the rearrest, he had personally taken charge of the case. He called Rob and Elaine together over the weekend and mapped out a three-pronged strategy. Rob would work with Swidler, Hendricks, and Burton to see if there was any way to make the original bond acceptable. At the same time, Rob would file a writ of *habeas corpus* alleging that Candy was being held illegally; as a condition of her release, the defense team was willing to settle for a reduction of the bond to $25,000. Don actually held out very little hope of either measure working. But the *habeas corpus* petition would force Judge Ryan to schedule a hearing, and before that hearing was held, Don intended to file a federal lawsuit in the district court at nearby Sherman. It took Don until Wednesday to get the suit properly worded and filed, but once he did, he knew Ryan would be able to feel the pressure.

When the papers were filed, and Ryan was served by the federal marshal, a courthouse friend of Don called to say that the judge was livid.

"Good," said Don. "Exactly what we want."

The lawsuit had named as defendants almost every law enforcement official in Collin County, beginning with Ryan and including District Attorney O'Connell, Sheriff Burton, Wylie Police Chief Abbott, Department of Public Safety officers Burks and Murphy, the city of Wylie, and the county itself. It was also a ten-page laundry list of all Don's grievances, which he knew would be picked up by the press. He accused the Collin County officials of conducting an illegal hearing to put Candy back in jail, of illegally strip-searching her at her original book-in, of leaking unfavorable facts to the news media, and of forcing Pat and Don McElroy to testify before a grand jury in violation of constitutional safeguards. He asked for a total of $1.5 million in punitive and compensatory damages.

Pat was allowed to see Candy on Wednesday afternoon but found it difficult to speak when he saw how much worse she looked. Her hair had gone unwashed three days, and she complained that the guards refused to help her any longer; they wouldn't even bring her a pencil. Pat passed Candy some cards that had been mailed to the house and told her about yet more old friends who had materialized out of thin air after reading about the case or seeing Candy's picture on television.

Elaine Carpenter knew that Pat would be upset by Candy's appearance, so she stopped by to see him that evening. Larry and Terry Sullivan came by a little later, carrying another Coors six-pack, two coloring books, and a Tom and Jerry game. Afterwards Pat put the kids to bed and, hoping he would never have to mail it, started his daily letter.

"I don't think that words can express my love for you," he wrote. "It just seems a shame that when our marriage is the best it has ever been that something like this happens. But we will have to stand up to the test. . . .

"You know, all of a sudden, I feel *so* old. It is hard to remember those early years of our marriage and even before when we were dating. We were both so young. Maybe it's just that experiences such as this age us so fast.

"I hope that everything straightens out soon and all this harassment stops.

"Candy, remember that I love you and that I will *always* be with you. I believe in you now more than I have all our lives and you know that I love you now more than I ever have. It seems so unfair that all this has happened at this point in our lives. But then again, maybe we are more prepared to withstand the assault against you by the authorities and survive in tack now than ever before. I know that this ordeal is hardest on you, but have faith that right and truth will win out.

"I love you so much and will always. . . ."

Candy was not nearly as wasted as Pat assumed. As first-time prisoners go, she was remarkably strong. She tolerated the bad food and the incessant noise from slamming doors, guards yelling at prisoners, inmates' radios, and occasional fights or arguments. Since she was in a maximum-security cell, she couldn't actually see anything, and only once did she speak to another inmate. His name was Phil, and he was having a hard time coping with the solitary cell next to her own.

"I don't think I can do thirty days here," he said. "I'll go crazy."

She didn't say anything. Then, after a moment, he said, "Are you in a padded cell, too?"

"Yes."

"How long have you been there?"

"Almost a week."

"Why do they have you in isolation?"

"They either don't trust me, or they don't trust the rest of the people in here."

The highlight of the week was the day they let Candy clean her cell: she scrubbed the floor and made the sink and toilet look like new. It was just what she needed—activity. If she was going to fall apart, she didn't want it to happen here, where people could see her. She would get through this first;

she could think about breaking down later. It wasn't even that she feared so much. It was the thought that, once it was all over, nothing would be the same. Would she ever be able to fix pimiento cheese sandwiches for the kids and shop with Sherry and play with Sayde, their dog, and forget this had ever happened? Nothing else mattered if she could just have that again.

On Friday, July 18, Judge Ryan's court was again convened to hear motions, and this time Don Crowder was sitting at the defense table. He had stayed out of the forefront of the case until then, because he had clashed with Ryan before and didn't want to hurt Candy's case with his presence. But now he felt he had to be there, if only to come to Rob's defense if needed.

When Candy was brought into the courtroom, Don was standing off to one side, talking to Jack Pepper.

"You know, Jack," he was saying, "you guys ought to feel pretty good. Here you got this big case and all you have to go up against is a guy who's never tried a criminal case and a young kid."

"Yeah," said Pepper, "that's what everyone we've talked to keeps telling us."

He didn't smile when he said it.

Because of the formal execution of the gag order that morning, many people were in the courtroom, including Allan Gore, Barbara Green, Dr. Stone, Don McElroy, Chief Abbott, and the usual flock of reporters. So when Rob began his case, arguing for the release of Candy, he was performing for a sizable audience.

Since one of the matters was a motion to reduce Candy's bond, Pat Montgomery took the stand first to testify about the family's income and financial plight. It was grim: he was down to his last $3,000. As soon as Pat had finished, Ryan snapped at Rob over a minor procedural point, and Don couldn't refrain from getting involved. Since Ryan was refusing to ask Rob's question on the grounds that to do so would constitute an "ex parte" procedure, Don accused the judge of having a double standard.

"Evidently, *you* conducted an ex parte hearing . . . [last week] after the gag rule matter had been settled and decided by you, then in that event you said, 'We have one other matter that needs to be taken up at this point.' Then the sheriff, without notice, without any proper presentation or without due process or without any ability to represent our client and any meaningful hearing whatsoever, you took the testimony from the sheriff and made your decision at that time that this woman should go back to jail after you had accepted the bond."

"Yes, sir," said Ryan, "we have a record on that."

"Well, there'll be another one made, too, Your Honor. But the whole point is, there was no proper notice at that time, no preparation. Evidently, you obviously had talked to the sheriff and the District Attorney's office . . ."

"Now, sir," Ryan interrupted, "don't anticipate things for the benefit of the news media in this courtroom."

"Your Honor, I'm not anticipating anything for the benefit of the news."

"You will testify and argue as to what you know has occurred."

"Well, let me ask you this," said Don, getting angrier. "How could you know that another matter had to be taken up with the sheriff?"

"This Court is not on trial, sir. If that's all you have to say, then sit down."

"You asked me to explain why I believed ex parte conversations, Your Honor—"

"I told you to sit down, didn't I, sir?"

Don sat down. Shortly thereafter, Rob called Sheriff Burton to the stand. The sheriff went over the county bonding procedures, repeated his testimony of the prior week, and said the bondsman, Hendricks, wasn't worth enough to cover Candy's bond. Yet Rob quickly established that the sheriff had arrived at his estimates by examining the tax rolls, which always resulted in a lower valuation than an appraiser would.

"What made you use as a basis the tax rolls, rather than fair market value?" asked Rob.

"If Mr. Hendricks would have been willing to have an appraiser give me a correct appraisal on it," said Burton, "I'd have been glad to take it. That was not afforded to me. The tax rolls was the only means I had."

"Did you ask Mr. Hendricks for that?"

"I don't know whether I did or not. I didn't, no."

"Well, who did?"

"I don't know that it was done."

"Well, it wasn't done, was it?"

"I don't care whether—"

"It wasn't done, was it?"

"I don't know."

Ryan interrupted. "Let's not argue with the witness."

"But the truth of the matter is," continued the sheriff, "I don't care whether Mr. Hendricks writes bonds or not."

The remark made Don furious, and he jumped in impetuously.

"The truth of the matter *is*," he said, rising to his feet, "you simply don't want Candace Montgomery out on bond. That's the truth of the matter, isn't it?"

"That's not the truth of the matter, no, sir."

Don had literally wrenched the cross-examination out of Rob's hands, and he didn't stop. With short, angry questions, he got Burton to admit that the previous Friday marked the first time one of Hendricks's bonds had not been accepted by the county, and that Burton *did* have a sworn affidavit stating the fair market value of Hendricks's property.

"How long have you been determining sufficiency of property values according to the county records?" Don asked.

"I don't understand."

"Since last week?"

"I don't understand the question."

"How long have you used the practice of using to value the property, the county tax rolls? Just this past week?"

"On this case here?" asked Burton.

"No, on all cases."

"Last week," admitted Burton.

"That's all we have, Your Honor."

On re-direct examination, Don continued the barrage, zeroing in on the fact that it had been Ryan, and not the DA's office, that had requested the examination of Hendricks's affidavit in the first place.

"How many times in the past since you've been sheriff has any judge in this county ever requested that before?"

"Requested a security?"

"Requested the same procedures that went on in this instance?"

Burton hesitated before answering.

"It's never happened," said Don.

"It's not at all uncommon," said the sheriff, "for the courts to call my office and ask me to come over, for whatever reason."

"How many times, Sheriff, in the past, since you've been

sheriff, has any judge in this county ever requested such information? The answer is none, isn't it?"

"Well, if you know the answer, why do you ask the question?"

"Because I can't get it out of you, sir. Is the answer none?"

"The answer is none."

"We have nothing else."

The lawyers wrangled among themselves for the better part of three hours, with Don and the judge doing most of the talking. At the end of that time Ryan reviewed the affidavit submitted by Hendricks, asked him a few questions about his property, and then, much to everyone's surprise, declared his net value sufficient.

After exactly a week in jail, Candy was free.

"And y'all better listen to me," said Ryan before leaving the bench. "I don't want to hear or see or read anything in the media that has Don Crowder's name to it, Udashen's name to it, Tom O'Connell's, Jack Pepper, anyone involved in the prosecution of this case, and if I read it one more time, I'm going to put you in jail and then you're going to try your lawsuit from the jail. I'll bring you over here in the morning and take you back for lunch. The show's over, gentlemen, and if you want to test me, I invite it."

Don hadn't realized until that moment just how much he disliked Ryan.

"Candy," he said to her as soon as it was over, "I made a decision today. I'm gonna be your lawyer."

"Good," she said. She had been as impressed as anyone else by the way he chewed up the sheriff.

"I've never tried a criminal case in my life, but I believe in this one too much not to win it."

"That's the way I wanted it anyway, Don. I'd feel like a *real* criminal if we had to go hire Racehorse Haynes or Percy Foreman to pull strings for me."

On the way home Don stopped off to pick up some bean sprouts, berries, and fruits, the kind of food he intended to eat between then and the actual trial. He changed into his running clothes and ran four miles along the farm-to-market road. He felt better than ever. He was in training again.

Allan Gore had watched Candy's imprisonment from afar—he even thought of talking to her at one point, but didn't know how to do it—and followed events through third parties.

Allan felt more isolated than ever in the first few weeks after Betty's death. It seemed that everyone he talked to had some official business: they were policemen or attorneys or reporters or Methodist pastors on missions of mercy. That's why Allan was so relieved when he picked up the phone one evening and heard the voice of someone who had no duties to perform.

"Allan—Elaine Williams."

Elaine hadn't been the Lucas church organist for over two years, but Allan continued to see Elaine and her husband, David, from time to time. She and David had been at the house the Sunday after Betty was killed.

"Allan, I know you have a lot on your mind, but I've been thinking about you and I'd like to talk."

"Sure. What's on your mind?"

"I'm going out of my mind with loneliness. David has moved out again, and this time I think it's for good. We'll be getting another divorce this summer."

"I'm sorry to hear that."

"I don't have many people to talk to about something like this."

"You can always talk to me," said Allan.

They chatted several times over the next week, and then, both feeling the need for a little escapism, they managed some tickets for *A Chorus Line* at the Dallas Summer Musicals. Allan found himself feeling better when he was with Elaine. He could relax; he could even talk about Betty.

A week after that, Elaine called Allan again. She was home alone, because David was keeping their two sons, and she was starting to go crazy.

"Why don't you come over here?" said Allan. "Alisa and Bethany are both back home."

So she drove over and helped Allan fix dinner. Afterwards, they put the kids to bed and then worked on Alisa's wardrobe for the coming school year. That night Elaine didn't leave until almost midnight.

The neighbors noticed.

22 · WARMING UP

The Texas summer of 1980 was the hottest in modern history, three months of unremitting white heat that pressed down on Collin County like a huge woolen blanket. Crops rotted in the field, the earth hardened and cracked, and birds fell out of the trees, dead before they hit the ground. When air conditioning units broke down from overexertion, corporations were forced to send all their employees home, lest they suffocate inside the glass-walled office buildings of Dallas. The Salvation Army started drives to collect window coolers and fans, to be distributed to the poor and the elderly. Still, before the season was out more than a hundred people would die from heat stroke. Parkland Hospital kept two bathtubs loaded with ice at all times, so that emergency patients would have a fighting chance. In mid-June the temperature passed 100 degrees for the first time, and for the next two rainless months it was at least that hot each day, going at one point as high as 117.

There was no escaping the drought, especially for people like Don Crowder who were forced to drive fifty miles a day to or from work. Not willing to risk overheating his El Dorado, Don would remove his suit coat, roll down the windows, and still arrive in Dallas with two damp half moons under his arms. At lunchtime, he would go into the coffee room, strip down to a pair of gym shorts, lace up his sneakers, and start his daily workout. It included fifty quick sit-ups and, if he could stand the midday heat, a mile run through the neighborhood. On the worst days, he would run at dawn, or after the sun had set, but he preferred to do the roadwork at high noon. He wanted to have a beautiful bronze tan by the time of Candy's trial.

After getting Candy out of jail, Don turned all his attention to what he considered a much more important objective—getting Candy out of Judge Tom Ryan's court. Don and Rob prepared motions for a change of venue, hoping that with all the pretrial publicity, Ryan would agree that it was impossible to find an impartial jury in Collin County.

"We need to get this changed to somewhere like Galveston or Port Arthur," Don told Rob. "Some port city where they have killings all the time, and where people understand death. Let's try to get Galveston, because I wouldn't mind spending a few weeks there."

The more important reason for seeking a change of venue, though, was so that Don wouldn't have to face Ryan again. There was little love lost between the two men, perhaps because they were equally pugnacious and strong-willed. Ryan had the irascible manner common to successful men of advanced years—he was sixty-eight—and he apparently regarded Don as a young hothead with less than total respect for courtroom decorum. Yet Ryan was not always known to stand on ceremony himself. His friends called him iron-fisted. His enemies called him arbitrary and vindictive. Because of the civil cases he had tried in Ryan's courtroom, Don considered himself one of his enemies. He also knew that Ryan had a long memory.

Judge Ryan was a conservative Democrat, a member of the same North Texas political organization that had sent Sam Rayburn of nearby Bonham to Congress in 1912, kept him there until his death in 1961, backed Lyndon Johnson through his Senate and presidential years, and consistently elected every judge, state legislator, and district attorney that it chose to put on the general election ballot. Like many other members of the county Democratic organization, Ryan was preeminently a self-made man. Born in Ohio, he had come to Texas with the Army and never left. His first career had been as a bus driver. For twenty-eight years he drove for Greyhound and Continental Trailways. Then, around the age of forty, he enrolled at North Texas State University in Denton and, while he was still driving his bus routes, started studying for his undergraduate degree. In 1958 he completed it, and in 1961, on the day of his forty-eighth birthday, he received his North Texas law degree. He set up shop as a criminal defense attorney in Dallas, handling mostly court-appointed rape and murder cases, then joined the Collin County district attorney's office, where he established a solid record of convictions. He moved to Plano for five years and hung out his shingle again, but then in 1969 he was elected Collin County district attorney. He moved up in 1971, becoming a state judge when a new district was created, and turned over the DA's office to his erstwhile assistant, Tom O'Connell.

Now, after almost twenty years as a lawyer, Ryan neared retirement; as if someone were orchestrating the proceedings from offstage, it appeared that the biggest trial in his entire career would also be his last. Ryan had intended to retire from the bench at the age of sixty-five, but that plan was spoiled when William Clements won the Texas governorship in 1978, becoming the first Republican to win the state's highest office since Reconstruction. Ryan knew that if he stepped down, Clements would appoint a Republican to succeed him, so he decided to stick it out a while longer. The attorneys practicing in Ryan's court weren't pleased by the reversal of his plans, since it meant he was not only his usual testy self, but angry about having to remain in the courtroom instead of going fishing.

Ryan himself was not blind to the criticism. "I could care less," he told reporters when they asked. "I don't care whether attorneys like me. I'm not running a beauty pageant. I'm not running for God. I'm Tom Ryan."

The secret truth was that Don Crowder was not entirely lacking in admiration for Ryan, though he would never admit it publicly. Ryan had an imposing presence, a barrel-chested physique that could have belonged to a very young man, and a bluff manner not unlike Don's own. He was the only judge working who could consistently get Don's goat.

Shortly after Candy's release from jail, the Montgomerys left for a vacation with Candy's parents in Georgia. Don agreed it was a good idea, especially since the lawyers would be arguing over change-of-venue motions in the meantime and there was nothing for Candy to do until that question was settled. Pat was determined to act like nothing was changed. The family was together again, the kids would be happy in Georgia, and perhaps they could escape the stifling heat for a while.

They loaded up the Rabbit and drove all the way to Vicksburg, Mississippi, the first day. The kids had insisted on bringing along Sayde, their dog, and now they insisted on a motel with a swimming pool. Pat managed to find one with both a pool and a lenient policy regarding pets, and they had time to go swimming before dinner. Candy sat in a poolside chair and watched while Pat taught Ian how to dog-paddle. She seemed withdrawn.

That night she lay awake in bed, staring at the ceiling, and Pat wondered how he would penetrate her gloom. He hadn't intended to tell her his secret until the right moment, but now he felt he had to.

"Candy," he said softly, "Don told me everything."

"What?" She started to cry.

"Last night he told me everything. We were just talking and he said I had a right to know."

Pat reached over and tried to touch her, but she quickly drew away from him.

"Don't look at me," she said, her face screwed up in anguish.

"It's okay," said Pat. "It made sense when Don said it. I sure like *that* alternative a lot more than the other one. You're still alive."

"I'm so ashamed, Pat. I can't talk now."

She turned her back to him and pulled the covers over her head.

As soon as they reached her parents' home in Augusta, Candy headed for a phone and called Don's office in Dallas. Rob came on the line.

"He's not here, Candy. What's up?"

"I'm angry, that's what. Don's told Pat everything, and now I've got to explain it to him. He had no right to do that."

"I didn't know that, either, Candy. I agree with you."

"At least Don could've *told* me he was going to do this. If anybody was going to tell Pat, it should have been me."

"I'm sorry, Candy."

The change of venue hearing wasn't held until late August. It should have been wholly routine. Rob conducted the questioning of seven witnesses—four attorneys, the managing editor of the McKinney newspaper, an architect in Lucas, and a McKinney social worker—and then submitted nine sworn affidavits. Without exception, they all testified that every living, breathing person with access to a radio, TV, or newspaper, thought Candy Montgomery was guilty of murder. On cross-examination, they all said that they as individuals were capable of being fair and impartial jurors, because they didn't believe everything they read and heard in the media.

Like most venue hearings, this one was predictable. The defense elicited the fact that people already had preconceived opinions. The prosecution responded by getting them to say that they would be able to ignore those preconceived opinions. (Tom O'Connell also called four witnesses of his own, all of them past or present county employees, including one constable named Jerry Kunkle who vouchsafed the opinion that most people thought Candy was innocent.) That left the decision up to the judge.

The difference in this case was Ryan. He sat through most of the hearing puffing on a cigarette, but after each witness had been examined, he exercised his privilege to question them himself. Most of his questions were intended to show friendships or professional relationships between the witness and Candy's attorneys, but in a few cases he was simply catty. To Howard Shapiro, a former Collin County prosecutor who had gone into private practice, Ryan asked, "When you were a prosecutor, did you ever prosecute a murder case?"

"No, sir."

"I don't think you ever got out of misdemeanor court, did you?"

Of Jim Bray, a Plano attorney, Ryan asked, "What is your relationship to defense attorneys?"

Bray didn't answer right away, so Ryan continued. "Is there one? Did you all go to law school together?"

"No, sir."

"You don't know how they happened to pick you out?"

"No. I have no idea."

When another attorney, George Parker, took the stand, Ryan started in again.

"For the record," he said, "you are an employee of Mr. Bob Hendricks who was the bondsman in this case?"

"That's correct."

"In fact, you were his runner from the office to get her out of jail the first time she got out of jail?"

"That's correct."

"Mr. Hendricks is a member of the Legislature, is he not?"

"Yes, sir."

"Running for office in November?"

"Correct."

And when Gary Patton, an ex-prosecutor in neighboring Denton County, took the stand, Ryan was even more explicit.

"Did you participate in that murder trial when the Texas Ranger was killed over there [in Denton County] on a narcotics bust?"

"No, Your Honor," said Patton. "Not directly."

"Were you in the office at that time?"

"Yes, I was."

"And that received as much if not more publicity than this case has received, has it not?"

"Yes, I would believe so."

"And he got a fair trial in Denton County."

Patton mumbled something inaudible.

"Well," said Ryan testily, "he was tried in Denton County."

"Yes, sir."

"And he got a jury in Denton County?"

"Our office did, yes."

"Well, you were in the office. Didn't you take a little pride in selecting a jury in a murder case of that significance?"

"No, Your Honor, in fact, I did not take a direct part in that case, directly out of my own decision. It was not a capital murder case."

"That's probably why you're not over there prosecuting."

"No, that's not true."

Don Crowder, silent until then, stood up and spoke rapidly. "Your Honor, we're going to object at this time to the adversary role the court is now attempting to play in this process. Also, the sidebar remarks you're making to the witnesses put on by the defense."

"Sidebar remarks, sir, I will sustain," said Ryan. "The law gives me province to interrogate witnesses."

"We understand, Your Honor, but we think you're going out of that province at this point. We want it on the record that we object."

"All right. Let's proceed."

Ryan turned and looked at the witness. "You may stand down and go back to Denton County."

The sarcasm was not lost on the newspaper and television reporters in the audience. At the end of the hearing, Ryan announced he would make a ruling on the requested change of venue within a week.

"I'll give you one guess what that'll be," said Don under his breath.

* * *

On Friday night, the first of August, a neighbor of Allan Gore's noticed a strange car parked on the street in front of the Gore home. It had been there since about 6:30 in the evening, and when the neighbor went to bed, it was still there. The following Thursday, the same neighbor noticed the same car— a 1971 black-over-blue Chevrolet Monte Carlo. Again it arrived after 6:30 and remained after the neighborhood's customary bedtimes.

Acting on information from a confidential source, investigator James Cochran of the Texas Department of Public Safety went to the office of Elaine Williams on August 19 and asked her if she owned a 1971 black-over-blue Chevrolet Monte Carlo, license plate number PFN 16. She said she did. Cochran asked her if she had parked it in front of Allan Gore's residence on the nights of August 1 and August 7. She said she had. She added that she had left Allan's house around 1 A.M. on both evenings.

Only the week before Elaine had gone to lunch with her friend, JoAnn Garlington. She had gotten to know JoAnn at Lucas church, and later through Marriage Encounter, when she was about to marry David for the second time.

"I do wish you would use more discretion," JoAnn said.

"What?"

"You and Allan. Everybody in the world knows about it."

Betty Gore had been dead exactly two months.

Dr. Fred Fason was a good-humored, fatherly charmer with a huge nose, bushy eyebrows, and a sweet, intelligent mouth that didn't seem to fit the rest of him. He invariably described himself as "a River Oaks shrink." River Oaks was the Beverly Hills of Houston, a place full of shaded drives and iron gates and mansions built by people with too damn much money. A lot of it eventually made its way to Dr. Fason, who dealt with a lot of Valium-addled socialites and impotent millionaires in the course of his career. Dr. Fason didn't mind if people knew that, either; it was the only advertising he had.

That's why, when a lawyer from Dallas named Crowder called Fason sometime in early August, he was quick to tell him that he didn't care much for courtroom work. It was bad PR. But when the attorney outlined the case, Fason was sufficiently intrigued to say that *perhaps* he would agree to serve as a consultant, and he would see the client once for diagnosis.

Candy and Don flew to Houston, where Fason administered a battery of tests. Afterward, he pronounced himself hooked on the case.

"If she'd turned out to be a sociopath," he told Don, "I would've dropped this case like a hot potato. But I think she's being completely honest. I guess I'm your man."

The real test didn't come until two weeks later, though, when Candy returned to Houston, accompanied by Elaine Carpenter. Elaine noticed that Candy seemed more detached than usual, almost numb, on the plane ride down, and when they were forced to wait on Fason in his dark, antiseptic reception area, Candy grew even more vacant.

When Fason arrived, he offered a cheery greeting and then ushered Candy into his spacious office. Elaine started to follow.

"No, no," said Candy. "I'll be all right."

Candy felt very comfortable around Dr. Fason; she found him businesslike and yet playful at the same time.

After Candy disappeared, Elaine settled back in a chair and perused a few old issues of *Texas Monthly*. An hour passed, with no one coming or going, so she moved on to *Reader's Digest*. Another hour passed. Elaine got up from her chair and started pacing about, bored to tears and wondering what could be going on inside.

Suddenly she heard a shriek. It was loud and eerie, and it came from Fason's office. Then she heard several more in quick succession; they were low-pitched, like moans, or like the noises people make when they're having nightmares. They sounded asexual; she couldn't tell whether they came from Candy or someone else. And they wouldn't stop.

Frazzled and panicky, Elaine didn't know what to do. So she ran over to the desk of Fason's secretary, picked up the phone, and hurriedly dialed the Dallas office. She managed to get Rob on the line.

"Rob, she's been in there for two hours and I've been hearing some screams. Should I go in and interrupt?"

"No," said Rob. "I guess we should have told you more about this. Just stick with it. Fason might be getting exactly what we need."

It was Fason's voice that got to Candy—soft, deep, resonant, the source of his power and his art. He was a psychiatrist, but he was also a first-rate clinical hypnotist. On this day he began with a speech about the need to "be completely open and level," because if Candy wasn't, or if she didn't think she could be, the interview was over.

"No, there's no question about that," she assured him.

"All right," he said. "I want you to start and tell me about what happened that day."

"That's what I don't want to talk about."

"I know that's what you don't want to talk about."

"I try very hard not to think about it anymore."

"I know."

But Candy reluctantly agreed to relive the morning of Friday, June 13, for Fason's benefit. She began with Vacation Bible School, and ended up telling Fason everything—more than she had told Don, more than Pat knew. Then they talked a long time about "control" and "anger" and Candy's deep-seated unconscious fears.

After a couple of hours, when Fason was certain that he had established a trust with his patient, he decided to try hypnosis. Candy was remarkably susceptible; she went under quickly, and her hypnotic trance was deep. Fason's smooth, soft voice carried her as far under as it was possible to go, until her body was totally relaxed; then he took her back in time to June 13 and Betty Gore's utility room.

"When I snap my fingers," he said at length, "you will begin reexperiencing and relating that time to me as you go through it. One. Two. Three. . . ."

He snapped his fingers loudly.

"Begin. What's happening, Candy?"

She said nothing; her face wore a worried expression.

"What's happening, Candy? You can tell me."

He waited for a response that didn't come.

"What thoughts are going through your mind? . . . I'm going to count to three. When I reach the count of three, your thoughts and feelings will get stronger and stronger . . . stronger and stronger and stronger . . . so strong that you will have to express them and verbalize them. . . . One. Two. . . . Stronger and stronger . . . so strong you will have to get them out. *Three.* Let them out. What's that you're feeling, Candy?"

"*Hate.*"

"Okay. You hate her. Express your feelings . . . stronger and stronger."

Candy started to whimper.

"You hate her," repeated Fason.

"I hate her," she whispered.

"You hate her. You hate her. Say it out loud."

"I hate her."

"Louder."

"I hate her. She's messed up my whole life. Look at this. I hate her. I hate her."

"When I count to three I want you to back up in time again, Candy. I want you to go back in time to where she's shoving you. You're in the utility room and she shoves you. Just relax. One. Two. Three."

Candy whimpered and moaned softly.

"What is happening? Go through it. The feeling is very strong. One. Two. Three. She's pushing you."

Candy moaned again.

"What's she going to do? What's happening? Tell me. What is it?"

Candy tried to say something.

"What? Louder."

"I won't let her hit me again. I don't want him. She can't do this to me."

"The feelings are getting stronger," said Fason. "Stronger."

Candy squirmed on the couch but didn't respond.

Fason time-regressed her yet again, this time asking her to go back to "the first time you ever got that mad."

"Do you recall ever being that mad before?" he asked. "Do you recall it?"

No response.

"When you were little. Let's go back, back in time. Let's get in the time machine and go way, way back in time. Back when you were little. One. Back, back in time. Two. Three. The time machine stops. How old are you, Candy?"

"Four."

"Four. Tell me about it. What made you so mad?"

"I lost it."

"What did you lose?"

"Race."

"You lost the race."

"To Johnny."

"Do you like Johnny?"

"He beat me."

"What did he say when he beat you?"

No answer.

"How did you feel?"

"Mad. Furious."

"What are you going to do?"

"I'll break it."

"Break what?"

"The jar."

"So what did you do?"

"I broke it."

"How did you break it? What happened?"

"I threw it against the pump."

"Are you scared?"

Candy nodded. "My mother took me to the hospital."

"What did your mother say?"

"Shhhhhh."

"Did what?"

"Shhhhhh."

"What did she say?"

"Shhhhhh."

"When I count to three, your feelings will be stronger and stronger. One. Two. Three. What are you seeing?"

"I'm afraid."

"What are you afraid of?"

"Hurts. I'm afraid."

"What are you afraid of? Are you afraid of being punished for your anger? Is that what you're afraid of?"

"It hurts." She rubbed her hand across her head.

"Your head hurts? Where does it hurt?"

"I'm scared. I want to scream."

"When I count to three, you can scream all you want to. One. Two. Three."

Candy shivered but made no sound.

"Just kick and scream all you want to," said Fason. "It's okay. It's okay to do it."

Candy shrieked, an eerie, wailing sound that could be heard through two walls of Fason's office.

"It's all right," he said. "Just kick and scream all you want to."

Candy was breathing hard.

"How did you feel when she said, shh?"

"I'm afraid I'm going to kick and scream."

"When I count to three, you're going to kick and scream all you want to. One."

"I can't."

"Yes you can. Two. Three. Kick and scream all you want to."

She screamed even louder. "It hurts," she yelled and then screamed again.

As soon as she stopped, Fason thought it wise to start bringing her out of the trance. It would take more interviews to sort out the details, but in his mind he had done what Don Crowder asked him to do. He had found the source of Candy Montgomery's rage.

It was four hours before Candy and Fason emerged from the office. Candy looked thoroughly drained, and yet somehow serene. She was exhausted, but Elaine thought she looked better than she had in weeks. On the way back to the airport, and then on the plane to Dallas, Candy began to talk about the experience. Under hypnosis, she said, she had been very animated and yet remained quite calm. Whatever else had happened in that room, Candy had found peace there.

Candy and Elaine made two more trips to Fason's office in Houston, and each time Candy returned feeling better than when she had left. All of her sessions were tape-recorded and sent to Don in Dallas. Don was ecstatic about what he found on them. But one, in particular, he played twice to make sure he was hearing right. It seemed that Fason had put his arms around Candy in the middle of the session, to comfort her.

Don called Candy immediately. "What the fuck is this stuff?" he demanded.

"I don't know," said Candy. "The sessions are pretty rough, and I cry a lot. But I don't know. I didn't have any idea."

Don had grown so curious about hypnosis, and intrigued with the idea of using it at the trial, that after Fason had finished with Candy, he asked him to come to Dallas so that the defense team could observe Candy under hypnosis. Fason agreed, and flew to Dallas for a full day of work with her. The attorneys watched Fason put her under, then apply the usual tests that proved she was truly hypnotized and not faking it. He said, "You will feel no pain," and then pricked her finger with a pin. She didn't move or change expression. He said, "It's getting very cold in here—below zero," and goose bumps appeared on her arms. Then he asked her many of the same questions he had asked during the Houston sessions, allowing her to go on at length as Don and Rob, amazed, stood by listening.

"Doc, I have an idea," said Don after the demonstration. "One of the problems we have is that Candy doesn't show enough *emotion* when she's in public. She looks cold as ice. I'm afraid it's gonna hurt her when she takes the stand. For a while I was gonna have her take acting lessons, but I decided not to, because the press might find out. So what I'm wondering is—is there a way to program her into showing emotion when she testifies?"

"You want emotion?" said Fason. "I can get you emotion. The emotion is in there. We just need to release it."

So Fason put Candy under again and planted a so-called "trigger phrase" in her subconscious. He told her that, when she heard that phrase, she would break into tears. She nodded.

Fason counted to three and brought her out of the hypnosis.

"All right, Candy," said Don, "I want to go over your testimony just one more time."

"Are you kidding?" she said. "I *hate* to do that."

"It's important. Now start by telling me everywhere you went the morning of the thirteenth."

Don led her through the events of that morning, and then, when he got to the most crucial moment of all, uttered the trigger phrase.

Candy looked confused for a moment. She twisted her face for a moment, and almost started to whimper. Then she suddenly hardened and gave Don a blistering glare.

"You bastard," she said. "You set me up. Listen, you do anything you want, but you don't mess with my mind."

Don dropped his programming idea.

As far as Don Crowder was concerned, the technical part of the case was complete. Everything from now on would be psychology, strategy, outguessing the opposition. Don felt that he already knew what every single witness would say, including the ones that were subpoenaed by the state, and he had even gone so far as to try to make friends with some of them. The only important one who would not talk to him was, of course, Allan Gore, so Don successfully filed a motion to take a deposition from Allan. Mostly Don just wanted to make sure there were no surprises. He wanted Allan's itinerary for Friday the thirteenth. He wanted a description of the Gores' involvement with Marriage Encounter (to show that all was not well with Betty's marriage). And he wanted to get Allan to say that Candy had no reason to kill Betty.

Don got most of what he wanted, but something about Allan's responses to the questions disturbed him. For one thing, Allan flatly denied that he and Betty were having any marital problems. He also denied that he had ever told Betty about the affair with Candy. Don found that hard to believe in view of the fact that the Marriage Encounter program was all about "communicating feelings" and "honesty"—and that the Gores attended the Marriage Encounter weekend during the same month the affair ended. Near the end of the session, in the midst of a series of questions dealing with the affair, Don suddenly asked, "Have you seen Elaine Williams in the past, in the same regard that you saw Mrs. Montgomery?"

"No," replied Allan.

"Have you ever had any affair with anyone other than Candy Montgomery?"

"No."

Don had one more touchy bit of business to take care of before the trial. About a week before the scheduled trial date, he called Candy and told her that it was time to let a few more people in on the secret. She could tell Sherry Cleckler and Jackie Ponder. Then, a few days before the trial, Don set up a meeting at Lucas Church for Betty Huffhines, Barbara Green, Marie Childs, Sue Wright, Judy Swain, and Ann Cline.

"Ladies, what I'm about to tell you," Don began, "is the hardest thing I've ever had to do. Don't interrupt me before I'm finished. This is a bizarre story, but compared to the alternatives, it makes sense."

When he narrated the story, some of the ladies gasped audibly. Barbara Green began to weep. Betty Huffhines's jaw hardened. All of them were too stunned to say anything.

"I realize some of you have been used," Don admitted bluntly. "But it was necessary."

Betty Huffhines was incredulous. "You expect us to believe that story *now*?" she said.

"I'm afraid it's the only story that adds up."

Four days before the trial, Jackie Ponder came from Wichita Falls to visit, and Candy knew she would have to tell her. Once she did, Jackie exploded.

"I *refuse* to believe that, Candy," she said. "Why did you keep that from me?"

"I had to. But I never lied to you."

"You did lie to me. I asked you point-blank and you lied."

"I didn't murder Betty Gore."

The next day Don called Candy in to go over her testimony. He was mean and harsh as he ran through the questions. Candy was almost in tears by the time it was over.

"I hope you can cry on the stand."

"I can't do it, Don. I can't let people see me like that."

"Do you *want* to go to prison?"

Afterwards, Elaine Carpenter tried to soothe Candy's nerves, by suggesting that Don sometimes overdid it a little.

"No," said Candy, "Don's just doing his job. I understand. I appreciate how nurturing he's been through all this."

After that final rehearsal, Don told Candy he didn't want to see her anymore before the trial. He wanted to distance himself from her emotionally. He didn't want to feel sorry for her. He didn't want to feel anything except the rush of adrenaline a man gets when he's ready to enter righteous battle.

That same day, Don took a call from Bruce Selcraig, the investigative reporter at the *News* who had broken the polygraph story.

"Bruce," he said, his voice full of bravado, "this will be a trial like none other in Texas. We're going to do things that have never been done in an American courtroom. And I'll guarantee you right now, they're scared to death. I've got them right where I want them. If they put on some of the witnesses I've heard they will they're gonna bomb. After the first day, I'll have center stage and I'll never lose it, because I've never been as prepared for a trial in my life as I am for this one."

"What about Judge Ryan?" Selcraig asked.

"Ryan's not a bad judge," said Don. "He's just very concerned about his image. He thinks he may be lionized after all this is over. He'll be groomed like a stud horse for this. You remember when they made a film of the Tex Watson story and they had the scene for the extradition hearing in Collin County? Well, they had an actor for Ryan, and he was disappointed. That's what we're talking about."

To get a little rebuttal, Selcraig then called Ryan at home and, much to his surprise, got him to talk. Apparently he was looking forward to Monday's proceedings just as much.

"I run a tight courtroom, I'll tell you that," Ryan said, "and I call 'em the way I see 'em. I could care less about what the lawyers are calling me. I go to bed each night after the news and I think about my day for about fifteen seconds, that's how much it bothers me. But I'll tell you this, I love every minute of it. I'm really the nicest little old man in Collin County. I'm just no Casper Milquetoast."

One person who wasn't giving any interviews was Candy Montgomery. On the day before the trial, the family went to church, but Candy decided not to sing in the choir after noticing TV newsmen outside the sanctuary. That night, after the kids were in bed, Candy and Pat huddled together on the living room couch, his arms closed tightly around her.

"I'm so afraid," she said.

Pat held her closer.

Five miles to the south, Don Crowder lay motionless under his sunlamp. The long hot Texas summer had given way to chilly fall nights and overcast days, but Don was undeterred. By 9 A.M. the next morning, his bronze tan would be perfect.

23 · THE BIG TOP

In the exact center of McKinney, Texas, ponderous, bulging at the seams, a solid stone fortress the color of coffee stains, the Collin County courthouse stood empty and abandoned. It was 106 years old, built when the frontier was young and a scaffold was kept in the basement for public hangings on the courthouse square. It was the same building where, in 1921, the whole state of Texas converged to find out whether a farmer named Ezell Stepp would get the noose for cracking the skull of a field hand and then stuffing his body down an abandoned well. (Stepp was found guilty and hanged promptly.) It was the same courthouse where Charles "Tex" Watson, the football-hero-turned-Manson-cultist, was held for extradition in 1970, before eventually being send back to California for trial. More recently, it was the courthouse where Robert Excel White was sentenced to death in the electric chair with national television cameras rolling. White was one of the first men convicted under a new law that came into effect after a landmark Supreme Court ruling that the death penalty was constitutional. The presiding judge that day was Tom Ryan. When he asked White if he had anything to say, the prisoner said simply, "Yes I do. I killed those people and my conscience bothers me." Ryan, for the only time in his judicial career, couldn't speak. He had to leave the bench for a half hour before he could regain his composure and pronounce the death sentence.

Yet since July 1979, the drafty old building had been vacant. Collin County had modernized and moved two blocks east, where the jail had electronic doors, the offices were centrally air-conditioned, and the tidy, compact courtrooms seated exactly sixty spectators each. Judge Ryan had decided that wasn't enough. The new courthouse simply wouldn't do as an arena for the battle of titans that was coming. This, Ryan had told everyone, would be his final trial before retiring. In terms of public interest, it would be perhaps the biggest trial of his career. He wanted it in the old courtroom, where he could squeeze in at least 250 people, with room in the balcony for all the reporters who cared to attend. The padlocks would come off the doors, and a four-man cleaning crew would spend a week getting everything ready. By the time they finished, it would be restored to all its former grandeur. The courtroom itself was three stories high, floor to ceiling, and it extended the full length of the courthouse's second story. Ryan's bench, standing on a raised platform at one end like a colossal altar, so dominated the room that even people sitting on the back row seemed to look up at him. From the three-sided balcony, once reserved for black people and now for the press, the view would resemble a crowd scene out of *Ben Hur*.

Ryan also ordered extra bailiffs, to keep spectators from mauling one another in the scramble for seating.

Candy rose at seven, left Pat sleeping in bed, and went downstairs to start fixing breakfast. No one had said things should be any different on this day. They had tried to keep it that way, make their lives as normal as possible. But now, in the cold light of the early morning, the only person moving through the still sleeping house, Candy grew frightened. The normalcy was no longer comforting. Things weren't normal. She lit her first cigarette of the day and started breakfast. It helped when Sherry came over; Sherry had sensed what Candy might be feeling, so she showed up unexpectedly at the front door. Still, they didn't talk about the trial. Candy only alluded to it once.

"I don't think I've ever been so dependent on other people as I am today."

Don had been very explicit about what Candy was to wear. She was to look sober and matronly. Her hair was once again short and wavy. The colors she chose were dark and subdued. She wore earrings and a blue, loose-fitting dress with a hemline well below her knees. Over her shoulders she draped a white woolen sweater. The women asked Pat for an opinion when he came downstairs. He said he thought she looked fine. Soon Rob Udashen was at the door; Candy gave Pat a quick kiss and then was gone. Pat would follow in his own car.

Candy and Rob made small talk on the way to the courthouse. At one point, in her usual direct manner, she asked a brutally simple question.

"What are the Texas prisons like?"

"There are two women's prisons," he said. "There's one that you definitely do not want to go to. The other one is not that bad."

"How do they decide which one you go to?"

"You'd go to the good one."

Rob entered McKinney on Highway 5, drove past the new courthouse complex, and turned left onto Louisiana Street. From two blocks away, he could already see his worst imaginings coming true. The crowds were thronged up and down the courthouse steps and ranged around the square, apparently trying to push up close enough to the doors so that they could rush in and claim seats. Cars were parked in every available space for several blocks around.

Rob was grateful when a deputy sheriff recognized his passenger and waved him into a special roped-off parking area near a side entrance.

At about the same moment, Don Crowder was turning his El Dorado onto Louisiana Street. Far from fearing the crowds he saw ahead, he got a great rush of adrenaline. He could almost feel the concrete runway of the Cotton Bowl beneath his feet.

For the people who waited so patiently on the courthouse steps on the trial's opening day—most of them housewives from surrounding towns—the first few hours must have seemed tiresome. First Judge Ryan cleared the courtroom of all spectators so he could have room for the panel of two hundred people who had been subpoenaed for jury duty. Then the entire morning was taken up with motions, the formal reading of the indictment, and an explanation of the qualifications necessary to be selected as a juror. In an attempt to save time, Ryan asked a number of questions himself—and quickly eliminated thirty-two of the first eighty-four people called because they admitted they weren't able to be objective. It was not until after lunch that the real winnowing process began, in which each side has the opportunity to question prospective jurors for evidence of bias or prejudice. O'Connell went first, straining to make his mild voice heard in the cavernous courtroom, slowly and carefully explaining legal concepts to the jurors: circumstantial evidence, "reasonable doubt," the presumption of innocence, the range of punishment. He also pretty much summed up his case by saying, "The ultimate fact issue to be proved to a jury is that a defendant killed the deceased."

After his speech, O'Connell asked fairly routine questions of the panel members, and only three had responses out of the ordinary. One woman admitted that she would find it "difficult" to convict a person if the case were based on circumstantial evidence. Another woman testified that Don Crowder had done legal work for her in the past, and was her neighbor in Lucas. And a man told O'Connell that Crowder was the track coach of his daughter.

O'Connell asked each of the three if anything about their admissions would have a bearing on their ability to "follow the law" and "render a fair and impartial judgment." They said they could be fair. Even though O'Connell could have struck them from the panel, all three were subsequently selected. Don Crowder was more surprised than anyone.

But Don took a different tack when it came his turn to question the panel. He began by making a joke about "this late hour." After all his physical training for the trial, he said, he felt like he was about to collapse on his feet. He briefly touched on the legal concept of "reasonable doubt"—requiring the state to "prove beyond a reasonable doubt" that a person is guilty—and then asked routine questions about jurors who might be related to police officers or members of Marriage Encounter. Finally, in the midst of a rather tiresome recital of areas that had already been covered earlier in the day, Don paused for a moment.

"It's not proper for me at this time to discuss the facts with you," he said, "and of course Mr. O'Connell didn't discuss the facts with you either. But there is something I've got to tell you now for me to be able to discuss the law with you."

He waited for just one beat.

"On Friday, June the thirteenth, 1980, Candace Montgomery killed Betty Gore. She did so with an ax. She did so in self-defense."

The sixty-two jury panelists were stunned. Two women started to cry. Candy, seated at the defense table, started to tremble. She fought back tears and held a clenched fist to her mouth. Don cast a quick glance over at the prosecution table, and thought he saw O'Connell's face flush more deeply. He turned back to the panel.

"The homicide was justified," said Don. "We haven't chosen to try our case in the papers. That is the reason you've never heard that before from anybody until now. This is the place where the trial takes place. Right now. Right here. This is where it all starts. That's where all of the evidence will come from. If you're going to convict, then make sure it comes from there."

Don pointed at the witness stand in front of the judge's bench.

"We have quite a story to tell," said Don, aware now that all eyes were riveted on himself. "Quite a story. And it hasn't appeared in the papers. And you haven't got a hint of it most likely. And you won't until it comes from the witness stand. I hope it will make you feel better that Mrs. Montgomery will take the stand. She intends to testify. Testify completely and fully as to the event that occurred."

He briefly ran through Texas law as it relates to self-defense, and asked the panel as a whole if there were any disagreements with that law. The room remained silent.

"Now if you've read the newspapers," he began again, "you know that there is an affair involved here. Mrs. Montgomery sinned. She acknowledges it. But she is not on trial here for that sin. Some of you—I'm sure many of you—are Christians on this panel. I'm sure many of you have very strong feelings about the Seventh Commandment. About adultery. There's nothing wrong with having those strong feelings, and I'm not asking you to forgive her. Not at this stage, or ever. Nor is she. But we're asking can you decide this case on the evidence, without letting the affair muddle your mind? If you cannot, please speak up now."

The room remained silent.

At the conclusion of the emotional speech, one of the panelists, a Mrs. Fiorini, raised her hand and asked to be dismissed.

"Why is that?" asked Don.

"Well, I'm already shaking like a leaf from what I've heard already and it really does make me nervous and I'm not sure I want to be in judgment of another person."

Ryan immediately excused her. Another woman asked to be excused on the same grounds. Finally the attorneys made their strikes, and Ryan announced the jurors. Nine of the twelve were women. Conventional wisdom held that a majority-female jury is bad news for a female defendant, because women are presumed to be harder on other women than men would be. But other aspects of the panel seemed more favorable to Candy. Two jurors, for example, had spouses who worked for Texas Instruments, Pat's employer. Five others were connected to the electronics industry, including two with ties to Rockwell International, where Allan Gore had once worked. The men included a "sales engineer," a quality control supervisor, and the head of corporate security for EDS, the huge electronics firm owned by H. Ross Perot. The women included a teacher, three secretaries, and five housewives. This was preeminently a jury of Candy Montgomery's peers, for they inhabited the same affluent, white collar, suburban world in which she had spent all of her adult life.

Before recessing for the day, Ryan told the jury not to discuss the case with anyone, especially reporters; not to watch television; and not to read the newspapers. Then he held everyone else in the courtroom while the jurors were escorted by bailiffs to their cars. Only then did he release the rest of the spectators.

When it was over, Pat walked to the front of the courtroom and wrapped his arms around Candy, and she felt like collapsing. She brushed tears out of her eyes and politely turned away the reporters who had come down from the balcony in hopes of getting a word or two. Don told Pat to get her on home, and then he quickly left the building, not wanting to talk to Candy.

Outside, on the steps of the courthouse, a television reporter saw Don leaving and stopped him on the way to his car. Don tossed his jacket over one shoulder and agreed to a quick interview. Little did he know that, even as he spoke, a mobile transmitter was piping his remarks directly to the 6 o'clock news.

"All I know," he was saying, "is that two of those women in there were crying their eyes out."

That night Allan Gore called Bob Pomeroy in Kansas.

"They selected the jury today," he said, "and they want me to go down there tomorrow."

"I'm gonna come down, too, Allan. Bertha just couldn't stand it, but Ronnie says he'll go with me."

"Okay, fine. And you should know that they kind of threw everybody a curve today. They're going to plead it was self-defense."

"What?"

"That's what they told me."

"They're saying Betty tried to kill that woman?"

"I guess so."

Bob was incredulous. He couldn't sleep again that night. He and Ronnie got up early Tuesday morning and started the long drive to Texas. On the way they talked about the latest shock in the year's long series. They also talked about Allan—and wondered why he kept acting so strange. He didn't seem to *care* about this trial. He'd called several times during the summer to give them news of the case, and he would constantly make references to how hard the whole thing was on the Montgomerys, how much money Candy was losing. Once Bob had grown tired of it and gotten angry.

"Allan, I could care less," he said. "If she killed Betty, I don't care if it costs her every cent she has."

"Well, yeah," Allan said, "I can see that."

Allan had never given the slightest indication of whether he thought Candy was guilty or not. Bob figured that maybe the Montgomery woman was still in love with Allan, and when she found out he was planning his second honeymoon, she'd flown into a rage and killed Betty. But that was only theory.

The police hadn't been any more helpful. Bob had called Chief Abbott a couple of times, but Abbott never would say anything about the evidence. Then he kept trying to contact Tom O'Connell that summer, but the district attorney wouldn't return his phone calls. It was driving Bertha crazy, the *not knowing*. He had tried to make it easier on her by taking her on a vacation up through Colorado and Utah, but on the very first night she broke down in the motel room. "I just don't know if I can ever get over this," she said. Bob didn't know if he could, either.

"Ronnie," said Bob, now that they were on the highway, headed for the trial they hoped would explain everything, "how does a person commit some crime like that and then say it was self-defense four months later? You don't say, 'I had to do it,' four months later. That's something you say right after you kill somebody."

"Seems that way to me, too," said Ronnie.

Ronnie could only stay one day. He had to be back at work. Bob thought he'd get himself a motel room in McKinney and stay as long as it took.

Like everyone else, Bob Pomeroy was taken aback by the

crowd scene outside the courthouse. It was even worse on
Tuesday. Some women from the First Assembly of God of
Princeton, Texas, had set up tables on the courthouse square,
where they were conducting a bake sale. There were three
mobile television vans at curbside. And everywhere you
looked, there were lines of women, waiting patiently in the
hope that a seat would be vacated and they would be allowed
into the inner sanctum. At first Bob despaired of getting into
the courthouse himself, but he went around to a side door and
told a deputy sheriff who he was.

"Hey, Mr. Pomeroy," the deputy said, "you don't ever
have to wait out here. Every morning when you're ready to
come in, you just knock and you can go in and get a seat before
everyone else."

"Thank you," said Bob. He would later remember it as
the first and last act of kindness he received from the
government officials of Collin County. Bob went inside and
chose his seat—on the front row, slightly to the right. He
wanted to have a clear, unobstructed view of every witness.

On Tuesday, the expected feud began. Before the first
witness was called—even before Candy had been formally
arraigned—Judge Ryan announced, "I have one other matter
before the court."

"Counsel will recall," he began in his deep, growling
voice, "that on the eleventh day of July, 1980, this court issued
an order restricting news releases. . . . Among the parties
enjoined was the law office of Mr. Crowder. . . . Yesterday
afternoon, this court, after the jury was selected, was leaving
the courthouse at 5:35 and observed within the immediate
proximity of the court, a news conference with a television
media being conducted by one of the defense lawyers, Mr.
Don Crowder. In the court's opinion, it was a direct violation of
this court's order.

"Is there any reason or do you have anything to say, sir,
why this court should not find you in contempt of this court for
violation of the order this court entered on the eleventh day of
July, 1980?"

Don rose quickly to his feet. "Your Honor," he began, "I
thought the order was lifted, especially since we met last
Friday and invited the news media into your chambers and
invited photographic sessions to be taken between the attorneys and the court and there was no reason to believe at that

time based on the comments you made over the weekend to the news media, that the gag order was anything but lifted at that time. Furthermore, let me ask you this—"

"Sir," Ryan interrupted, "you're not asking this court a question. I asked you if you would like to make a statement."

"I'm responding. Furthermore, yesterday you instructed the jury they were to have no contact whatsoever with any medium, news or otherwise. . . . There was no reason at that time to believe . . . that there was any further need for the gag order. If I am in error, it is an innocent error. Certainly not intended. And I believed at that time that the order had been lifted and there was no further purpose for it."

"All right, sir," said Ryan. "This court will find you in contempt for violation of its order that was entered on the eleventh day of July, 1980. Your punishment is assessed at one hundred dollars fine, plus costs, plus twenty-four hours in the Collin County jail. But out of an abundance of precaution, so your confinement will not interfere with your proper representation of your client, I will suspend the issue of that commitment until the day next preceding the conclusion of this trial."

Don sat down. The trial hadn't even started, and already Ryan had made him fighting mad. The jury was brought in. Don tried to swallow the bile gathering in the back of his throat.

O'Connell rose and made a brief opening argument, which sounded more like a schoolteacher's lecture on "What is a trial?" than an impassioned plea for justice. He asked the jurors not to take notes. He asked them to "bear with us" through the tedious parts. He told them how exhibits are numbered. He told them the names of the prosecution witnesses who would testify. And that was about it.

He called his first witness: Allan Gore.

Allan seemed wholly unemotional. His face was blank, indifferent. He answered all questions in the same monotonous, evenly modulated tone. At first his voice was so flat that the jury had to strain to hear him, but he finally raised it to a barely audible level. Allan's cool recitation of facts was fine with O'Connell, who favored a logical, workmanlike approach anyway, but it struck Bob Pomeroy—and the jury—as exceedingly odd. Wouldn't a man show a little emotion at the trial of his wife's accused murderer?

After reviewing the pertinent facts of Allan's life, O'Connell led him very methodically through everything he did on the day of June 13. He mentioned that Betty had been upset that morning, out of fear that she was pregnant, but he noticed nothing else out of the ordinary. Allan described his frantic calls that evening, trying to locate Betty, including the four he made to Candy.

"When you told the defendant that your wife had been killed," asked O'Connell, "what response if any did she make?"

"Shock and surprised," said Allan. "Seemed like a normal shock reaction to something like that."

"There was nothing that seemed to be out of the ordinary or unusual about her reaction to it?"

"No."

O'Connell pressed on, skimming lightly over the visit the Montgomerys made on Saturday when they brought Alisa home, and had Allan point out on a diagram where he kept his ax (on a nail in the garage).

"All right," said O'Connell, removing a three-foot, wood-handled ax from under the clerk's desk. Candy, her face graven in stone, suddenly realized what he was doing, and turned her head away. "Let me ask you . . . whether that looks familiar to you."

Allan looked at the ax indifferently. It was still splattered with dried blood.

"That does look like my ax."

Don Crowder relaxed. He had been worried about Candy's lack of emotion. This guy was a machine.

Next O'Connell set out to establish what he hoped would be sufficient motive for murder. He asked Allan to describe the affair. But when he got to the end—the difficult breakup—Allan acted as though everything had been quite cordial.

"What was the defendant's reaction to your discussions with her with respect to not seeing each other again, as you recall?"

"The final decision to terminate the relationship was a mutual one."

O'Connell dropped the line of questioning and, shortly thereafter, passed the witness.

As Don Crowder began his cross-examination, Bob Pomeroy received his first major shock. Asked Betty's height and weight, Allan said he didn't know.

Bob leaned over to whisper to Ronnie. "He's been married to her ten years and he don't know her height and weight?" Bob considered that one fact more damning than anything else Allan had said.

Don moved on to Marriage Encounter and had Allan give a brief description of how it worked. To emphasize just how immersed in Marriage Encounter Betty was, he also had Allan identify a number of photographs—one showing a Marriage Encounter bumper sticker on the family car, another showing a latch-hook rug hanging over the Gores' fireplace, emblazoned with the Marriage Encounter emblem, yet another showing Marriage Encounter stickers she used on correspondence.

Next Allan was asked to testify about the friendship between Betty and Candy, detailing several occasions when they visited each other and mixed socially, including the baby shower for Bethany in 1979. At the end of this sequence, Don asked, "Do you know of any motive that Candace Montgomery would have had to have killed your wife?"

"No, I do not."

The second shock for Bob Pomeroy came when Allan admitted that, on the night he discovered Betty was dead, the thought of suicide entered his mind. It was a thought that had certainly never entered Bob Pomeroy's mind. He wondered why Allan would even consider it.

Continuing, Don also got Allan to admit that Betty was "extremely depressed" that day, then had him detail other times in her life when she was equally depressed, notably just after pregnancies. Finally, in an effort to further emphasize his point about Betty's depression, Don introduced a copy of the newspaper found by police on the Gores' dining room table— the movie review of *The Shining*, about an ax murderer, which originally led Chief Abbott to think the crime was the act of a cult.

Don's questions about the affair were much more explicit than the DA's had been. He got Allan to go into great detail about the Como Motel. Allan was also happy to admit that the affair had been less than passionate most of the time.

"Fact of the matter is, Mr. Gore, neither one of you were very good at this, were you?"

"No."

"So what started out as a lukewarm affair and evolved into something that was nearly intellectual, finally ended up in nothingness, didn't it?"

"Yes."

Don then firmly established that Allan and Candy had never been intimate after October 1979, when the affair broke up, and he got Allan to say that, to his knowledge, Candy had never been in his garage or seen his ax. The final question of the day was whether Allan Gore could attest to the reputation of Candy Montgomery for being a peaceable and law-abiding citizen. Allan Gore said he could. Her reputation was good.

By Wednesday morning, when the prosecution case continued, Candy had decided she liked Tom O'Connell. From her seat at the defense table, she could look directly across the room and study him as he sat hunched over his papers or conferred with his assistants. She wondered why his face was always so red. She tried to think about anything except what was happening directly in front of her. Don had told her to stop taking Serax before coming to the courtroom, because it was starting to make her look like a zombie in the papers again, but she didn't want to be emotional. She hated journalism. Every time she took a step or made a move there were twenty people there to record it, and she knew it would thrill everyone if she would totally break down. That's the one thing she refused to do. She could wait until she got home to do that.

Still, it was almost impossible to keep her composure when Allan's neighbors took the stand Wednesday morning. Richard Parker went first, followed by Jerry McMahan and Lester Gayler, and each time they came to the part where they opened the utility room door and closed it so quickly, Candy shuddered and felt a physical sensation of disgust. But that was not as bad as the testimony about Bethany, the baby left alone in her room for thirteen hours and covered in excrement when she was finally found. I don't care, Candy told herself. I will not be interested in this trial, she kept repeating. They can't make me look at the pictures of Betty. I'll refuse to look at them.

Late that morning O'Connell called the first "church" witness, Betty Huffhines, who had been one of the first people to see Candy after the killing. A natural redhead, Betty's hair seemed even redder than usual as she took the stand. O'Connell led her through her conversations with Candy at Vacation Bible School that day, which she said were wholly unremarkable. Then, on cross-examination, Don asked her a series of questions about the community and church projects she had worked on with Candy.

The same pattern applied to the testimony of Suzan

Wright and Barbara Green. O'Connell established that they had seen Candy both before and after the killing, and that she had seemed normal each time. No one could testify with any certainty exactly what she was wearing. They did remember her "explanation" of where she had been that morning—first at Betty's, then at Target, where she realized her watch had stopped. On cross-examination, Don simply bolstered what O'Connell had already established and got the women to add further information about Candy's reputation for being a charitable, civic-minded housewife. He even managed to get into testimony, over O'Connell's objections, that Barbara Green considered it "inconceivable" that Candy Montgomery could have committed murder.

After the women testified, Ryan broke for lunch. During the recess, he sidled up to Don.

"What the hell is O'Connell doing?" he said. "His witnesses have all turned into defense witnesses."

Don smiled. "I know."

The crowds were starting to get rowdy. By the third day people were literally shoving and pushing for seats. As the trial resumed, a woman holding a baby yelled at the deputies guarding the outer door.

"You mean I've been standing here holding this child for two hours," she said, "and you're not going to let me sit down?"

Those who did have seats had learned to bring their lunches in paper bags, so they wouldn't have to give them up during the midday break. But in an effort to restore order and give others a chance, Ryan banned food from the courtroom. The weather was unseasonably cold, and there were strong drafts in the old building, further adding to the discontent of the crowd.

O'Connell started his parade of police witnesses on Wednesday afternoon. Officer Johnney Lee Bridgefarmer, first at the scene, described the blood-soaked utility room and the body. A second officer, Michael Stanley, testified about how he found the fingernail and showed it to Dr. Stone. Peggy Sewell was called strictly to describe how she found the same fingernail the following morning, on the kitchen cabinet, and then gave it to Cynthia (Mrs. Richard) Parker, who testified she delivered it to Royce Abbott. Lest the point be lost on the jury, Don Crowder's cross-examination stressed that this is not commonly the most expeditious way to preserve evidence. He also got Abbot to say that—given the amount of blood left in the house, the fingerprints, the hair, the fingernail, and the time of the offense—it was a "careless" crime.

Stephen Deffibaugh took the stand for one reason—to introduce the photographs he had taken that night. After the usual objection that they were "inflammatory," Ryan admitted them. Candy averted her eyes as the grisly photo of Betty's body was passed to the witness box. Don had tried to get her to look at it two or three times, but she refused. Now she tried to block out an unpleasant mental image. She felt some comfort in that. She didn't have to look at anything.

"That's not a pretty sight, is it?" Don said, gesturing toward the picture.

"No, sir, it's not," said Deffibaugh.

Candy began to tremble. She buried her face in her hands. It was the same position she would maintain almost all day Thursday.

Seats for the trial's fourth day were hotter than season passes to the Dallas Cowboys football games. O'Connell expected it to be the prosecution's final day, and the rumor on the streets was that Crowder would open the defense portion of the trial by putting Candy herself on the stand. The women had started lining up on the courthouse steps at six in the morning, long before sunrise. Some of them claimed vantage points where they could watch Candy as she got out of her car; maybe, if they were lucky, she would even *say* something as she walked by. Tom O'Connell was as curious as everybody else to find out what she was going to say. He frankly considered self-defense a weak story. Unfortunately, it was the one defense that was impossible to prepare for until you had heard the defendant's explanation. All he could do was prove that Candy did the crime, and then go after her on cross-examination when she told her cockeyed story.

Fred Cummings, the Texas Ranger, and Jim Cron, the Dallas fingerprint expert, took the stand to testify that Candy's bloody thumbprint was found on the freezer. An analyst from the Southwest Institute of Forensic Sciences testified that Candy's blood was found on the doormat at the Gore home. But it was not until Dr. Irving Stone took the stand that the jury was first exposed in any direct way to the frightful mess found in the utility room the night of the thirteenth. Stone, who handled the collection of evidence that night, was the first man to examine Betty's body, which he noticed right away was surrounded by dried, congealed, caked blood. He described the blood-covered ax, the blood-smeared doors and door-knobs, the bloody footprints made by a pair of "thongs." He described how the bloody thumbprint on the freezer door was photographed and preserved. He described the bathmat, apparently stained by blood after the perpetrator showered. And he said that two hairs found in the bathtub were probably Candy Montgomery's. Finally, completing the chain of evidence for the bloody fingernail found on the carpet, Stone testified that the nail found by Stanley, shown to Stone, left on the counter, picked up by Peggy Sewell, passed to Cynthia Parker, turned over to Royce Abbott, given to Fred Cummings, and finally examined by Stone again—that that fingernail was, indeed, the fingernail of Candy Montgomery.

After O'Connell had finished the direct examination, Ryan declared a fifteen-minute recess, and Candy asked Elaine to go with her to the witness room. She had to take a Valium. There would be no other way to get through the medical testimony.

Unbeknownst to O'Connell, Don Crowder had met with Dr. Stone, and his colleague, Dr. Vincent DiMaio, three weeks earlier. They had been the first two outsiders to learn the complete self-defense theory that he intended to put forth at trial. They had been remarkably cooperative and, being scientists, very intrigued by the whole business. Don now felt he knew their every answer long before he asked the questions.

Stone now testified that, in his opinion, "quite a struggle" had taken place in the utility room, and that many of the wounds to Betty Gore's body could have been inflicted after she was already dead. He also confirmed Royce Abbott's opinion that the crime had been carried out carelessly.

"If someone had planned to murder Betty Gore," said Don, "could you imagine it could have been carried out anymore ineptly than this one was?"

"Probably not."

Then, a few questions later, "Is there anything in your investigation that would rule out the fact that Candace Montgomery may have attacked in self-defense?"

"No, sir."

"When we were talking in my office one time, you told me that this appeared to be a case of 'overkill.'"

"Yes."

"What did you mean by that?"

"It's cases of homicide where there is inflicted to the body far more damage or injury than is necessary to take the life of that person."

Vincent DiMaio, the Dallas County medical examiner, testified immediately after lunch, and the more cynical members of the defense team suspected that O'Connell scheduled him that way for maximum effect. In excruciating detail, he described the corpse of Betty Gore, from the dried blood on her skin to the rigor mortis in her joints, and then one by one he listed every single wound on the body. Frequently, he said, he found "gaping wounds." He also found "chop-like wounds." He found parts of the body "severed." He described skin that was "sheared off."

When DiMaio came to the right side of Betty's face—the ghastly mess where her eye used to be—Bob Pomeroy winced and felt sick. From his seat on the front row, he could hear every word DiMaio said. He didn't want to know any more about the suffering. Bob thought about leaving, but decided he could take it. He couldn't stand not to know everything.

The last wounds DiMaio described were the massive gashes to the back of the head, which had literally ripped open Betty's cranial vault and allowed her brain to seep out.

There were, in all, forty-one chop wounds. Forty of them occurred while Betty Gore's heart was still beating.

On cross-examination, DiMaio said that a beating heart doesn't necessarily indicate a person is alive, and that Betty was probably unconscious during most of the destruction. He went on to testify about the effect of adrenaline on the body—specifically, that the secretion of adrenaline can make a scared person stronger and quicker than he would otherwise be. Don led him back through the description of the wounds, emphasizing the apparent randomness of the blows, and at the end of three full hours of bloody testimony, asked, "Is there anything in your investigation that would rule out that Candace Montgomery acted in self-defense in killing Betty Gore?"

"No, sir."

A few minutes later Tom O'Connell stood up at the defense table.

"If it please the court, ladies and gentlemen of the jury, the state will rest its case in chief at this point."

Ryan asked the bailiff to take the jury out of the

courtroom. The prosecution's case was finished, and what was proven so far was that Candy Montgomery had killed Betty Gore. The body had been mutilated. Candy had seemed unremorseful and, in fact, had concealed the crime. The defense knew all this. They were greatly relieved that none of the surprise witnesses had materialized. They had feared that O'Connell would bring in women to testify about Candy's "loose" character—her trips to the Currency Club, for example—or that one of the jail witnesses would claim she had confessed the crime.

Still, Don was taken aback when Ryan said, "Are you prepared to go forward, Mr. Crowder?"

Don approached the bench and told Ryan that he certainly wasn't. It had been a long, grueling day of tedious police and medical testimony. It was already the middle of the afternoon, and Candy had been so upset by the autopsy testimony that she had taken a tranquilizer.

"Judge, I intend to call the defendant as my first witness, and I thought our prior agreement was that we could begin our case at the beginning of a trial day. I really need the evening to prepare my opening remarks."

Ryan was unfazed. He thought there was plenty of time left in the trial day, and it was foolish to waste the court's time and the state's money by sending everyone home.

"I don't think she's capable of testifying at this time."

"When do you anticipate she will be?" asked Ryan.

"Could we have about a ten-minute recess?"

"All right. Ten minutes."

Don took Candy into an empty witness room and said, "You're going to have to testify today. Are you ready?"

Candy looked at him with glazed eyes. She started to shake. "I'm tired."

"Candy, we don't have any choice. You know what we've been through. You know what to say. I know you're tired, but I also know you're tough. Now pull yourself together."

Late in the afternoon of October 23, 1980, the curiosity-seekers and reporters, policemen, and attorneys who had waited all week finally got what they had come for. Candy Montgomery took the oath and slid into the witness chair, situated directly in front of O'Connell, so that she had to look straight into the eyes of the twelve jury members and, beyond them, the mostly female members of a hushed audience. Now everyone would hear for themselves whatever it was that Candy Montgomery could possibly say for herself.

She was less than a model witness. Her voice was clipped and nasal, her manner cool. Somehow she had regained that air of haughty reserve that served as her defense against the world. As Don began the questioning—about her children, her upbringing, her community and church activities, her friendship with the Gores—Candy gave short, functional answers. She sounded like a stuffy schoolmarm, over-enunciating her sentences and wringing all the emotion out of her voice.

Don moved on to the morning of June 13 and led Candy through the events of that day, beginning with her breakfast with Jenny, Ian, and Alisa, and continuing through her storytelling session at Vacation Bible School. During a pause in the questioning, Don walked over to the defense table, leaned over, and asked Rob, "Is this going as bad as I think it is?"

"Worse," Rob said evenly.

So Don decided to gamble. He decided to be brutal. He decided to take Candy directly to Betty Gore's house and make her describe every single detail and movement that she could remember. If necessary, he would make her describe every blow of the ax. Someway, somehow he intended to make her reveal something of herself besides the tight, thin lines around her mouth.

The story Candy Montgomery was about to tell did not spring suddenly out of her conscious memory. As late as two months prior to the trial, most of the facts of the case—what actually happened inside the utility room—remained unknown. Dr. Fason had changed all that by putting her under hypnosis and literally forcing her to relive every moment. She had been through long, wrenching hypnosis sessions on three separate occasions. After those sessions she had been forced to repeat the events of the thirteenth in private sessions with Don and Rob. When her conscious story conflicted with her unconscious story, she had been confronted with the lie and forced to admit the facts she would rather have forgotten. After six intensive sessions—three under hypnosis, with a psychiatrist, and three conscious—the best possible reconstruction of the killing of Betty Gore emerged.

24 · PASSION PLAY

Candy wasn't expected until noon, so when Betty responded to the polite knock that morning, her face bore an expression of surprise and pained suffering. No doubt she had just sat down to rest for the first time that day after putting Bethany into her crib for her midmorning nap. She probably hurried to the door so the noise wouldn't wake the baby. In her hand Betty held a half-finished cup of coffee, and from behind her came the muffled sounds of *The Phil Donahue Show*. Since she didn't intend to go out that day, she was dressed for housework: tight-fitting red denim shorts, a yellow short-sleeved pullover, and sandals. She pulled the front door halfway open and peered out.

"*Betty*, I have a *special* favor to ask you." Candy was not long on greetings and salutations, but no one minded her abruptness; the friendliness in her eyes and her smile was greeting enough. "The girls wanted Alisa to go see the movie with us tonight, and I told them that if it's okay with you, it's okay with me, and I'll be happy to take Alisa to her swimming lessons to save you the extra trip."

"Yes, that's okay," said Betty, appearing a little distracted. "Come on in."

"I thought it would be," said Candy, "and so I just ran down from Bible School to get Alisa's swimsuit."

The two women walked into the living room—den, which that morning was dominated by a large playpen in the middle of the floor, with toys and children's books strewn around it.

"The only easy way to do it," said Candy, "would be for Alisa to stay another night with us."

"Okay," said Betty. She switched off the television and walked into the kitchen. "Want some coffee?"

"No thanks."

Candy took a seat in a chair next to the sewing machine, where she noticed that Betty was making something out of yellow cloth. Betty came back and sat on the other side of a small table. She still seemed tense, as though she were anxious for Candy to leave.

"So where's Bethany?" asked Candy.

"Bethany got up very early today, and she just went back to bed."

"Oh no!" said Candy, frowning. "I wanted to play with her."

"Candy, if you're going to take Alisa to her swimming lesson, remember that she doesn't like to put her face under water," said Betty. "So when she *does* put her face under, be sure to give her peppermints afterwards. That's the reward we use."

"Okay," said Candy, "and while I'm thinking about it, I need to get directions to the lessons because I'm not sure I remember."

"Oh, it's easy. It's right off Parker Road, coming the way you came into town. I forget the name of the street but it's the only one there, right after 2514 makes that left-hand turn. It's the second or third house on the left."

"Okay, I think I remember."

Betty was loosening up a little, as though the small task was a welcome interruption to all the morning chores.

"I've been so busy getting ready for our trip," said Betty, "but there's still so much to do. We're leaving Wednesday and taking the kids in the Rabbit to Kansas."

"Oh, that sounds great," said Candy. "Rabbits are great for vacations. We took our Rabbit down to Padre Island last month and had a great time, even with the kids."

"Well, the only problem is that Alisa wants to take the puppy to Kansas, and I've told her that's just impossible in a Rabbit, but she wants to do it anyway."

"You mean you have a puppy and I haven't even *seen* him?"

"Oh yes, he's about six months old now."

Candy jumped up from her chair and walked over to the sliding glass door that opens into the backyard. "I *have* to go play with him then."

Betty followed Candy out onto the Gores' concrete slab that passed for a patio, while Candy knelt down and let the frisky little cocker spaniel nuzzle up to her legs. An older dog followed him.

"What's his name?" she asked.

"Chito."

"Princess and Chito—I just love cocker spaniels. He's cute."

"Alisa just can't bear to leave him here alone."

The women went back into the living room–den and sat again in the two chairs.

"I almost forgot to tell you—I have a new business," said Candy. "Sherry and I are going into business together once the kids go back to school. Pat thought we would never do it, but we're incorporated and everything, and now he's starting to change his tune. We're lining up jobs for papering and painting. Do you need anything papered?"

"I don't think so."

"Let me show you these business cards Sherry and I had made up. They're so cute."

Candy fished in her purse until she found one of the cards. She placed it face up on the table between them. The card featured two cartoon women holding brushes and, next to the illustration, the legend "The Covergirls," with their names and home phone numbers at the bottom.

"That's cute," said Betty.

Candy glanced at her watch. "Well, it's getting late and I have some errands to run." She put her purse in her lap. "I need to be going. You want to get me Alisa's suit?"

Betty didn't stir from her chair. Her face was blank, her eyes unfocused.

"Candy," she said calmly, "are you having an affair with Allan?"

Candy was stunned. "No, of course not," she answered, a little too quickly.

Betty squinted and a steeliness crept into her tone. "But you *did*, didn't you?"

"Yes," said Candy, quietly now, "but it was a long time ago." Candy was still and her eyes avoided Betty's. Betty said nothing at all, staring past Candy's head, transfixed, sullen.

"Did Allan tell you?" Candy looked into Betty's face for some sign.

"Wait a minute," said Betty. She rose abruptly from her chair, walked through the open door of the utility room and out of sight. While she was gone, Candy wondered how recently

Betty had found out. Pat had said that, if Betty ever found out, she might not be able to take it. Candy also realized, with a quiet panic, that she had nothing to say to her.

After a few seconds, Betty reappeared in the doorway, her face tensed. In her hands she clutched the wooden handle of a curved three-foot ax, the kind used for chopping heavy firewood. There was, oddly enough, nothing very threatening about her stance, since her hold on the implement was rather clumsy and she held it away from her body, the blade pointed at the floor. Candy was more worried about what Betty would say than what she would do.

Candy stood up but didn't move from the chair.

"Betty?"

"I don't want you to ever see him again." Her tone was deliberate and had a hard edge to it. "You can't have him."

"Betty, it's been over for a long time. I'm not seeing him. I don't want him."

Betty continued to stand in the doorway, though her grip on the ax was loosening. She seemed uncertain, as though realizing that people have little to say to each other at times like this.

"Betty, don't be ridiculous," said Candy, hoping to diffuse her anger with a wave of the hand. "It was over a *long* time ago."

"Well, don't see him again," said Betty. It was an order.

Candy reached down to the chair seat and picked up her purse.

"Under the circumstances," she said, "I think I'll just bring Alisa home and drop her off right after Bible School."

"No," said Betty harshly. "I don't want to see you anymore. Just keep Alisa and take her to the movie, because I don't want to look at you again. Bring her home tomorrow."

Betty laid the ax against the wall, just inside the living room—den, and walked past Candy into the middle of the room. "I'll get a towel from the bathroom," she said, speaking over her shoulder. "You get Alisa's suit off the washer."

All Candy wanted to do was get out of the house, because she suddenly had a sick feeling in the pit of her stomach. So she moved toward the utility room, dropping her purse in a chair as she walked by. She found the swimsuit on top of the washer. As she was picking it up, Betty reappeared behind her.

"Don't forget Alisa's peppermints." The tone was softer now, more reassuring, as though Betty's anger had subsided.

The two women met at the utility room door, and Betty handed the towel to Candy.

"That's okay, I have some peppermint at home I can give her."

Betty moved over to the fireplace and reached into a candy bowl. "I'll give you a few of these anyway."

Betty walked back to the utility room door, where Candy was fidgeting with her purse. Candy wrapped the swimsuit in the towel and stuffed it into the handbag. Betty gave her the handful of candies, and she dropped those in as well. Then Candy rummaged around for her sunglasses. When she found them, she folded her regular lenses and put them in the purse, still holding the sunglasses in her hand.

Candy looked up at last. Betty was looking at her intently, but the expression was no longer one of rage. It was a face full of pain. For a brief moment Candy thought of how Betty would cry after she left, and she felt a stab of conscience. They both hesitated, as though something important would be settled by the tone of the parting. Reflexively, clumsily, Candy reached out and placed her hand on Betty's arm. When she spoke, her voice dripped with pity.

"Oh, Betty, I'm so sorry."

All at once Betty's rage erupted. She flung the hand from her arm and shoved Candy's chest with both hands, with such force that Candy stumbled backwards into the utility room. Betty grabbed the ax resting by the doorway and rushed in after her, holding it like a weapon, diagonally across her chest. The blade still pointed at the floor.

"You can't have him," Betty screamed, crowding Candy, moving closer. "You can't have him. I'm going to have a baby and you can't have him this time."

"Betty, don't," said Candy, reaching out to put her hands on the ax as Betty moved in. "This is stupid. I don't *want* Allan."

For a moment neither woman moved. Both of them gripped the ax firmly by the handle; it hung between them like a curtain. Then they both tightened their grips, their eyes locked, and Betty began to jerk the ax, trying to control it.

"Betty, don't do this," pleaded Candy. "Please stop."

"I've got to kill you." Betty spoke the words slowly, with a distracted, impersonal finality.

As they grappled for control, Betty gave the ax a violent

wrench with her wrists and jerked upward. The flat side of the
metal slapped against the side of Candy's bobbing head.

"Betty, what are you doing?" Candy stepped backward,
further into the utility room, and grabbed her head with one
hand. "Betty, *stop*."

Candy looked at her hand; it was streaked with red. Then
she looked back at Betty, and saw her raising the ax blade over
her head, almost to the eight-foot ceiling, as though to smash
her with a single powerful blow. Candy screamed at the top of
her lungs, a high-pitched, pleading sound, and jumped
sideways into a cabinet, spilling books and knickknacks onto
the floor.

Even though Candy had no place to hide—Betty was
between Candy and both exits—the ensuing swing of the ax
missed her entirely and landed harmlessly on the linoleum.
The blade made a dull thud, bounced once, and sliced a gash
in Candy's toe, exposed by her rubber sandals. Just as it did,
Candy reached over and grabbed the weapon by the blade,
wrapping her fingers around the thick heavy metal. Her
pleading turned now to anger. She said no more.

With the exaggerated blow and the drawing of blood,
some primal instinct unloosed the surging rage of both
women. As soon as Candy grabbed the blade, Betty started
shoving and jerking the handle in an effort to get the ax back.
But Candy held on tightly, and the struggle degenerated into a
wrestling match to gain control of the weapon. Betty thrust
and jabbed the ax at Candy's body, kicked at her legs, kneed
her in the thighs. Candy responded with wrenching motions
intended to jerk the handle out of Betty's hands. From a
distance, nonsensically, came the frenzied, high-pitched sound
of barking dogs. Betty moved her hands farther up the handle,
trying to get leverage, and at one point bit Candy on the
knuckle in an effort to make her let go. As soon as she did, her
head bent, her body temporarily off balance, Candy shoved
the ax against Betty's body with all her might. Betty reeled
backward and fell sideways against the door of the freezer, her
feet slipping a little on the linoleum.

Candy didn't hesitate. As Betty struggled to regain her
balance, her body temporarily facing away, Candy raised the ax
with both hands and brought the blade down on the back of
Betty's head.

The blow resounded with a hollow pop, like the cork
coming out of a wine bottle, and then blood gushed across the

back of Betty's neck. Candy dropped the ax, jumped away from Betty, and felt time shift into slow motion. Betty began to slump toward the floor, blood pouring out of her skull, but she continued to struggle to regain her feet. Terrified by the blood and the certainty that she had just killed her, Candy bolted for the living-room door but, as though dreaming, felt an eternity pass as she tried to reach it. She finally put her hand on the knob, started to pull—and *Betty slammed her body against the door.*

Candy looked up and saw blood spreading across the side of Betty's face. Betty had picked up the ax again, like some nightmarish vision of a dead person who still stalks his killer. Tears spurted out of Candy's eyes. The barking of dogs, wolfish and primitive, grew louder still.

"Let me go, Betty, please Betty, let me go."

Betty's voice came from a thousand miles away: "I can't."

Candy grabbed the ax again, and for the next few eternal moments, the women did a macabre dance around the utility room, once again jabbing and pushing with the ax that hung between them, Betty's head now dripping blood onto the floor until the linoleum was slick with crimson. They circled endlessly, one temporarily losing her grip, then gaining it again before she could be shoved away. At one point Betty bumped up against the freezer again, and as she did, Candy removed one hand from the ax and grabbed the knob of the door leading to the garage. She pulled it open a few inches, but then Betty managed to shove her away from the doorway, slam it shut, and push in the lock on the knob. Both women began to kick as they jockeyed for position. Their shoes made squeaking noises on the sticky red floor, and above the steady electrical hum of the washing machine, they both grunted and breathed heavily. Betty removed a hand from the ax and grabbed Candy's hair. Then Candy slipped on the blood and went down hard directly in front of the freezer. As she did, Betty tried to raise the ax again, but, growing weaker from the loss of blood, couldn't get it up in time. Candy tackled her by one leg, and she sprawled forward, almost on top of Candy. By the time they were both upright again, the ax was between them, and they continued to fight over it from sitting positions.

Candy shoved Betty hard, jumped to her feet, and lunged at the garage door again, but this time the knob wouldn't turn. She pivoted as Betty moved back toward her.

"Betty, don't," she said. "Please let me go. *I don't want him. I don't want him.*"

Betty's eyes flared in one final paroxysm of rage, but her reply was eerily restrained. Placing one finger to her lips, the other hand still gripping the ax, she breathed out from somewhere deep in the back of her throat.

"Shhhhhhhhhhh."

The eerie susurration echoed through the subconscious of Candy Montgomery like a psychic alarm. She grabbed the ax once more and used it aggressively, pushing the wooden end against Betty's thighs and legs. From beyond an open window came the hysterical canine sounds, desperate now, the barking and howling of a frightened creature. Candy jerked violently and then leaned backward with all her might, wrapping both hands around the blade. The handle was becoming covered with blood, and when Betty tried to pull just as hard, as though the combatants were having a tug of war, her grip couldn't hold the surface. Her hands slipped off and she plunged backwards into the room. She wouldn't stay down, though. She got up and lunged back toward Candy, but not before Candy had time to raise the ax and bring it down with all the adrenaline-fueled strength she could gather.

Disoriented by the loss of blood, rushing forward toward her opponent, Betty ran directly into the blade, redoubling its force, as it came down directly across the top of her forehead, piercing the skull and making a sound like a coconut being cracked open with a machete. Betty threw her arms straight up in the air. Candy raised the ax again and brought it down on the forehead, again cracking the skull. Betty groaned and clutched her head. Great fistfuls of hair came loose in her clenched hands. Candy struck a third blow, missing the head and slicing into her elbow. The bone snapped, and the arm swung limp at Betty's side. Candy swung for a fourth time, and a fifth, turning the top of Betty's head to a ghastly red paste, carving gashes in her arms as Betty vainly tried to block the metal with her own flesh. Betty's eyes rolled, and her head bobbed and weaved instinctively, trying to avoid the next swing, but the blows continued. Her legs began to buckle, but *she still wouldn't go down.*

Some inner fire continued to fuel Candy's hatred. She chopped and hacked and raised the ax again. Betty's legs flexed and became tangled; one of her shoes went sliding across the floor. She swiveled in a half circle, weaved, knelt, and finally sat, her head slumped forward, her back to Candy. But she still wouldn't fall, as though her entire purpose in her last moments now was to frustrate Candy's will to destroy. Candy continued to swing, even after Betty's back was turned, landing repeated blows to the shoulders and the base of the skull. Then she cracked another time across the top of the head. Betty's brains began seeping out of the cranial cap. She twitched and lurched backward, her bloody head thudding against the linoleum and landing between Candy's legs.

Candy screamed and swung at the woman who wouldn't die. And through some remarkable motor reaction, Betty moved one last time, drawing her legs up into a fetal position until Candy's flailing ax hacked them back down onto the floor. Then, with Betty's head still between her legs and a dead body lying prone across the red floor of the utility room, Candy swung the ax at least a dozen more times, this time aiming at the face, trying to obliterate that look that had once made Candy want to reach out and say, "I'm so sorry, Betty." There was no pity or remorse or conscience now. Candy destroyed Betty's face out of pure unadulterated hate—anger over what this woman had done to her, rage that now her life might be changed because of this stupid woman. Candy swung the ax at the immobile head until she had no strength to swing any longer. She stopped, literally, at the point of exhaustion.

Candy dropped the ax and kicked it aside. Her hands fell to her knees, her head drooped between her shoulders, and her chest heaved as she gulped air rapidly, trying to feed oxygen back to her overtaxed heart. She stepped back a few feet, away from the body, suddenly afraid to look at it. She walked to the other end of the utility room, where she was enveloped by the electrical churning of the washing machine, and then back the other way. She closed her eyes tightly and then opened them again. When she did, she saw splatters of blood all over her blouse and blue jeans, and she became vaguely aware of a sickening antiseptic smell: the odor of fabric softener, the odor of the room, now mixed with some other smell, of violence and fear and dread. She suddenly had the sense of being covered with grime, contaminated. She wretched and gagged on the phlegm in the back of her throat. Her stomach contracted, and she could feel the bile rising into her mouth. Afraid of being sick, she turned abruptly, walked rapidly through the living room, and entered the bathroom.

She threw back the curtain and stepped directly into the bathtub, keeping her clothes on. When the spray began spewing out of the shower head, she held up her arms and watched the water cleanse away the telling red blotches. Much of the water splashed onto her blue jeans and blouse, until, afraid of getting all her clothes wet, she turned off the water and stepped onto the bathmat. She removed a towel from the rack and dried off her arms. She stopped to look in the mirror. She straightened her hair. She was beginning to feel normal again.

Candy left the bathroom and walked into the living room, hesitating before she got to the utility room door. She paused for a moment; something stopped her. A sound. The dogs—the dogs in the backyard were barking at something. She turned and went back into the bathroom and rummaged around in the cabinets until she found some towels. She carried them into the utility room and, being careful not to see anything, fell to her knees and started scrubbing the floor with one of the bath towels. But the blood wouldn't go away. The more she scrubbed, the more it seemed to spread across the floor, soaking her towel but making an even greater mess. She stood up and went to work with a clean towel on the freezer, rubbing hard with circular motions, but the blood simply smeared across the smooth white surface. She tossed the towel aside, stood up, and supported herself with one hand against the freezer.

Suddenly she heard the sound again—louder this time, and more real—and she looked up and caught her breath. At the end of the room, through a low window framed by frilly curtains pulled back to let the sun in, she saw Chito and Princess, staring directly at her, barking at the top of their lungs and jumping back and forth against the pane. *The dogs had seen everything.* She was shaken by the thought. She looked down at the floor, seeing where the body was but not looking directly at it, and then extended her leg as far as she could, stepping over the prone corpse of Betty Gore to get to the other end of the tiny room. She unfastened the curtains and pulled them across the window, but the dogs continued to bark. She spoke to herself. "You have to be normal," she thought. She stepped back over the body and picked up her towels. "This is silly," she thought. "There's too much blood."

For the first time she thought of something beyond the house: Ian and Jenny, Bible School, the show at eleven o'clock,

Father's Day cards, swimming lessons, movies. All the normal things she was supposed to do that day. "One thing at a time," she thought. "Do one thing at a time." She looked for her purse and caught sight of it on the chair. She searched the floor until she found her glasses. She thought of her car. For a moment she couldn't remember where it was. She stood in front of the fireplace and peered out the front window of the house, wondering whether it would be there. She saw it and sighed with relief. She walked very deliberately, like a person who's had too much to drink and tries to disguise it by doing everything too precisely.

She left by the front door, closing it behind her. As she crossed the threshold, she saw a streak of red on her foot and looked closer. The toe was bleeding profusely from a deep gash. Until then she hadn't even noticed it, but now the toe began to throb with excruciating pain.

She looked at her watch; it read 10:20. Plenty of time to go to Target and get the Father's Day cards and then go back to the church. Then she looked at the watch again. It had stopped. It was broken. It had stopped the moment she had soaked it with the spray from the shower head. She got into her car and headed into the uncharted farm roads of rural Collin County, driving aimlessly, trying to decide what to do next. The one thing she didn't think about was what she had left behind in the utility room. No one must know about that. No one, ever, must know. And maybe if she didn't think about it long enough, even she would believe that it never really happened.

25 · JUDGMENT

The huge courtroom remained silent. Candy Montgomery's voice barely rose above the traffic noise from the square. Bob Pomeroy studied her face. She was a halfway attractive woman, he had to admit. She sounded unreal. He could summon no anger toward her.

"What did you do when you got back to the church?" asked Don.

"I explained to Barbara why I was late."

"Did you lie to her?"

"Yes."

"Did you consider telling anybody what had really happened?"

"I was afraid to and I was so ashamed. I didn't want anyone to ever know."

"Did you think you'd be believed?"

"No."

"You were having trouble believing it all happened at the time, weren't you?"

"Yes."

"People at the church, of course, knew you and Betty had been friends, didn't they?"

"Yes."

"Then what did you do at the church?"

"There was supposed to be a luncheon for the Bible School teachers. And I can remember getting the meals ready for the kids and seeing to it they were taken care of. And I can remember somebody handed me a plate. And I can remember sitting there, trying to eat. And thinking all the while that I had to be normal. And I would feel the blood running down along the side of my face. And I would have to get up and I'd go check on the kids or something so that I could blot it so that no one would see it."

Candy was lapsing into her monotone again. While describing the struggle, her cheeks had trembled and she had sobbed silently. But now she regained her composure. Don feared that her testimony seemed too rehearsed.

"Mrs. Montgomery, I want you to be honest with this jury," he said. "You're not happy this situation took place."

"No."

"But you feel genuine anger to this day, don't you?"

"I am angry that it has happened, yes."

"Why is that?"

"Because it seems so pointless."

"Pointless?"

"Yes. I didn't want him. I kept trying to tell her that."

"You didn't plan it, did you?"

"No. And she put me into that position. It's caused me to lose everything that is important to me. And it hurts."

"But you'd had an affair with her husband."

"But it was over."

"But you had an affair with her husband, didn't you?"

"Yes."

Don paced across the front of the courtroom and passed in front of her. He turned when he reached the clerk's table.

"The two of you put her in that position, didn't you?"

"Yes, we did."

Don reached for something beside the table, blocking Candy's view with his body.

"When you went over there," he said, "did you mean to kill her with that ax?"

"No."

Don picked up the object and placed it on his right hip. Time for a bootleg play, he thought to himself.

"But you did kill her with the ax, didn't you?" he said as he walked back toward the witness box.

"Yes."

"This ax right here—"

"*Don't make me look at it.*"

Don grabbed the ax with both hands, brought it into full view, and thrust it toward Candy's face.

"*Don't!*"

"You killed her with this ax right here, didn't you?"

Pat Montgomery could hear the scream in the witness

room, thirty yards and two walls away. Tears burst out of Candy's eyes and she seemed to rise out of her chair.

"You killed her with this ax right here, didn't you?"

"Yes," she said, so he would take it away.

One of the woman jurors dabbed at her reddened eyes with a tissue. Another squirmed in her seat, offended by the cheap trick. She, too, had wondered why Candy seemed so cold and impersonal, but she also felt an odd sympathy toward her. Her story hung together; it didn't seem whitewashed. But how can you be sure? She wanted Tom O'Connell to be tough, to pry open every part of the story, to find the one lie in it that would make it all come apart.

Don led Candy through the rest of her day—the swimming lesson for Alisa, the family trip to *The Empire Strikes Back*, the four phone calls from Allan Gore, each one more desperate than the last. Then Candy admitted all her coverups and evasions of the following week, as she tried to avoid detection.

After a ten-minute recess, Tom O'Connell drew a deep breath and plunged in. This is what he had been afraid of. Candy had been intelligent, attractive, and direct. She handled herself well. And she used the best possible explanation—the "I freaked out" excuse. He would probe at her story, trying to pick out the discrepancies.

O'Connell asked Candy to repeat much of her account of what happened in the utility room, but with much less detail. She didn't hesitate in answering, and there were no contradictions. She even added small details at certain points, like the fact that the peppermint candies were located in a glass bowl on a shelf just to the left of the fireplace. It was the kind of detail a bald-faced liar wouldn't know. O'Connell dwelt for some time on the fact that a bloody sunglass lens had been found in the garage—an apparent contradiction in her testimony that the entire fight had taken place in the utility room. But when O'Connell really pressed her, Candy abruptly switched her cool pattern of response and snapped back. Finally, O'Connell scored most of his points by emphasizing her lies and coverups after the killing.

"Would it not be a fair statement," he asked, "to say that had the fingerprints not been found, that perhaps we might not have ever known the true story?"

"I doubt that."

"Doubt what? That we would or wouldn't?"

"I doubt that you would have never found out."

"Why is that? You weren't going to tell anybody."

"I don't think I could have lived with it for very long."

"You lived with it long enough to find out whether there was going to be any direct connection between you and the offense—"

"I did not hold off because of the prints."

"I didn't ask you that. The question was that you held out telling anybody at least until the comparison was made, didn't you?"

"No."

"Who did you tell before that if anybody?"

"I told no one before then."

O'Connell got to her one other time as well. Going back over the affair, he took a chance and suddenly asked, "Was the affair with Allan Gore the first and only one that you've had since your marriage to—"

Don Crowder was on his feet in an instant. "Your Honor, we object to this. Whether there is or not, it wouldn't be material to these proceedings."

"Objection," said Ryan, "is overruled."

O'Connell looked back at Candy.

"Would you repeat the question?" she said.

"Was the affair that—"

Don tried again. "Your Honor, that's *not* proper. It's not proper at all and we renew our objection."

"Objection is overruled," growled Ryan.

"Was the affair that you had with Allan Gore," said O'Connell, "the first and only affair that you've had since your marriage to Mr. Montgomery?"

"It was the first one, yes."

"Well, was it the last one?"

Candy flushed deeply. "No, sir."

"The affair with Mr. Gore terminated as I understand from the testimony, in October of '79. Is that correct?"

"Yes."

"Since that time, who else have you been involved with?"

This time Rob Udashen objected, thinking perhaps Don was simply posing his objection in the wrong form. He was overruled.

"There was one other man," said Candy, "that I saw very briefly. From about the beginning of November until mid-December."

"And that also is of '79?" said O'Connell.

"Yes."

"What is his name, please?"

"I will not give you his name."

"I'm sorry," said O'Connell, disbelieving. "I didn't hear the answer."

"I said I will not give you his name."

"Why not?"

"Because it's irrelevant. And I would not want to damage his family."

"Well, I appreciate your concern at this point in time. But I'm going to have to insist that you answer the question."

Don rose again and asked to have the jury dismissed. Ryan complied, and briefly the lawyers argued over the relevance of the man's name. The judge then pointed out that Don had gone on endlessly about Candy's reputation as a pillar of society, active in church, and the like, and the prosecution had the right to show otherwise. All objections were overruled, and the jury brought back.

"Who was that individual?" asked O'Connell.

Candy said Richard's name quietly.

"Richard who?"

She repeated the last name.

"Spell the last name."

Candy hated O'Connell for this. She spelled it.

But shortly thereafter, O'Connell dropped the line of questioning. There are prosecutors who froth at the mouth like mad dogs and wave their arms and work themselves into a frenzy of moral outrage, but O'Connell wasn't one of them. He saw no reason to go into the nitty-gritty details of a man's love life. It was not his style. He would stick to his original plan, and try to expose the cracks in her story. He wandered from place to place, from the utility room to Jackie Ponder's divorce and back to her furtive coverups of the weekend. (He missed the most damning one, the fact that Candy had scissored her "thongs" to pieces and dumped them in the garbage. Don had conveniently left that out of the direct examination.) He emphasized the fact that a year-old baby had been left in the house alone by this woman who prided herself on her motherhood. He pointed out Candy's repeated lies to her friends. And then, abruptly, he stopped.

"You may stand down," said Ryan.

It was over.

* * *

As the jury filed out of the courtroom, Candy could think of only one thing at first. She had to get to Pat before anyone else did.

"Pat doesn't know," she told Elaine. "He doesn't know about Richard."

As soon as Ryan adjourned for the day, Candy got Rob to escort her across the hall, and when everyone had left they closed the door. At first Pat put his arms around her. Then haltingly, trying to get it over with quickly, Candy told him that she had been forced to reveal another affair that day.

"What?"

"I didn't want to tell you. I was afraid it would hurt you."

"Who?" Pat started to cry.

Candy gave him the name.

"I don't believe it," said Pat, and he started to bawl like a baby. Candy started to cry, too, and tried to touch him. Pat turned away and walked across the room. He stared out at the throngs on the courthouse square, studied the television reporters, dabbed at his eyes. Then he wept some more, still shaking, unable to get himself under control. On top of all the other pressures, it was too much.

"Pat, it's not *that* bad." Suddenly Candy turned huffy. Pat wept more loudly.

Don opened the door to the room and stuck his head in. Pat and Candy weren't speaking. Candy sat pouting in one corner, Pat stood in another. The room was full of iciness and depression.

"All right," Don announced, entering the room, "we're about seventy-five percent of the way home, folks."

They said nothing.

"Let's don't blow it now."

Don walked over to Pat's corner and placed an arm on his back.

"Look, Pat, I know this is hard to take."

Embarrassed by his tears, Pat tried to look at Don.

"She shouldn't have done it, Pat, but it's over." Don looked Pat in the eye. "It doesn't matter if she fucked a hundred men as long as she doesn't do it again. Now come on, we've got to pull this thing back together."

On the way out of the courthouse, fighting his way through the thicket of reporters, Pat ran into a parking meter and bruised his wrist badly. That night at home there was little to say. Pat watched the Channel 8 news and tried to sort out his feelings. A little later, Ron Adams came by for what he called "counseling." He told them he knew they still loved each other. Pat felt comforted by his words. He tried to put it all out of his mind. Don seemed elated by the events of the day. Pat wanted to feel the same way. He wanted to be prepared for whatever might remain.

When Tom O'Connell left the courtroom that day, the first person he saw in the hall was Allan Gore.

"I think we may have trouble with this whole thing," said O'Connell.

"Well," said Allan, "whatever happens, I guess it's for the best."

In his hand, Allan carried a paperback copy of *Shōgun*. He had read most of it in the witness room that week.

For all practical purposes, the trial was over. Barring any unforeseen bombshells, the twelve jurors either believed Candy Montgomery or they didn't. Still, Don went on to bolster her testimony in every way he could imagine. First he called Dr. Robert Bright, a handsome, articulate pathologist who had been hired to analyze the autopsy. Bright said most of Betty Gore's gruesome face injuries were probably sustained after she was dead, and that the other wounds indicated that a struggle had taken place. For the spectators, it would have been fairly boring testimony, except that Ryan kept reacting to the testimony. He swiveled nervously back and forth in his chair, played absentmindedly with a rubber band, rolled his eyes, sighed deeply, looked at his watch, and increasingly unnerved Don and made him lose his concentration. When Don asked a question about adrenaline, Dr. Bright started a long, rambling answer.

"Mr. Crowder," interjected Ryan, a little testily, "I'm going to insist we conduct this examination in question and answer form. I will not permit narrative testimony."

"Your Honor, I'm doing the best I can," said Don. "I'm asking him the questions."

"Yes, sir, I understand that."

Don detected a note of sarcasm and snapped angrily back. "I don't recall, Your Honor, this interruption with Dr. DiMaio's testimony yesterday or Dr. Stone's when the exact same questions, many of the same were asked, and many of the same type of responses were given—very very long responses at times." He grew angrier as he spoke. "We'd like the record to show how the judge is interfering with the questioning of the witness and has continued to do so since this witness took the stand."

"Ladies and gentlemen," said Ryan, "will you go with my bailiff, please."

As soon as the jury had left, Ryan opened up. "I've been very patient all morning," he said. "There's no necessity to dictate into the record anything that the court says because it's already in the record. The record speaks for itself."

"We have to preserve the record, Judge," said Don. "You have interjected your bias in this trial from the very moment it started. We want the record to show that. We want the record to reflect that for appellate purposes."

"Let me tell you something," Ryan retorted. "I am going to run this court in an orderly, professional manner. And I anticipate the same from the attorneys. We discussed this in great detail one day last week. How this trial would be conducted. And there are not going to be any personal attacks on the presiding judge of this court."

"That's fine with me," said Don. "As long as you stay out of it."

"Will you let me finish what I'm saying?" said Ryan.

"Your Honor," said Don, ignoring him, "I won't be lectured or bullied in this courtroom. I'm representing a woman who may go to jail for her life. I'm going to perfect the record and have the record show it, and the record of this trial shows from the very time it started to now, you have interjected your bias and continued to do so, and no, I will not lay down for you."

"All right, sir," said Ryan. "For that remark this court is going to hold you in contempt. I am going to assess your punishment at a hundred dollars in costs, seventy-two hours in the Collin County jail, effective immediately when this court stands in recess this afternoon.

"Bring the jury in. Let's proceed."

Now fully expecting to spend the entire weekend in jail, Don continued his questioning. Ryan posed no more objections from the bench.

Dr. Ronald Washington, the first doctor to examine Candy after her confession, detailed the bruises on her chest and legs and the cuts on her head and toe. Dr. Maurice Green, the Dallas psychiatrist who started seeing Candy after her visits to

Houston for hypnosis, testified that since the killing she had been numb and detached. He described her condition as "dissociative reaction," in which a person induces amnesia in himself in order to suppress intense anger or rage.

"When I initially saw her," said the doctor, "she continued to tell me that she had feelings of anger towards Betty Gore. I explored this with her. And she felt that Betty Gore had triggered something within her that had caused her to commit acts of violence, and as a result of this, Betty Gore had in essence, like ruined her life. Ruined her family's life. And her friends' lives, in many ways."

Dr. Green went on to say that Candy's suppressed anger was triggered during her struggle with Betty, and that the overkill was a "depersonalized" act. "Almost as if she were a spectator. As if she was watching it. Wasn't really involved. In other words, she felt it wasn't really me that did that."

On cross-examination, Dr. Green admitted that "dissociative reaction" implied no mental illness, and that Candy always knew what she was doing—*except* when she was swinging the ax at Betty. "She just kind of went berserk—momentarily." His ambiguous explanation of her behavior—she was sane enough to know what she was doing, but not sane enough to stop hitting the dead body—led Tom O'Connell to question the whole concept of "dissociative reaction." What about her subsequent lies to her friends and to the police? Was that "dissociative reaction"?

"To some extent," said Dr. Green.

Dr. Green was nervous and sweaty throughout his testimony, an indication to several jurors that he had a personal stake in trying to help Candy. Most of them disregarded his remarks.

After a failed attempt to get religious testimony introduced—Don had found an SMU theologian willing to say that Candy did not violate the second commandment, but Ryan ruled that theology had no bearing on the case—the regional executive of Marriage Encounter took the stand, primarily to refute a rumor. Lest the jury be in doubt, Don wanted it on the record that Marriage Encounter was neither a cult nor a wife-swapping club, but a church-sanctioned program.

Pat Montgomery ended the first week's testimony. Don called Pat strictly to indicate that after everything that had happened, he still stood by Candy. For the first and only time

in his life, Don called him "Dr. Montgomery," referring to his
Ph.D. in electrical engineering. Pat answered a few routine
questions dealing with Candy's feelings about violence—she
didn't allow toy guns or let the kids watch shows in which
animals are killed—and about the Montgomerys' friendship
with the Gores. Then, in his proudest moment, Pat told a
favorite story about Candy once rescuing a stray kitten. Don
had him repeat the story about the weekend when he found
Allan's farewell love letter. He had him run quickly through
the events of the thirteenth, to show the jury how it fit with
Candy's version.

When Pat was finished, Ryan surprised everyone by
announcing that the trial would be suspended until he could
hold a full psychiatric hearing to determine Candy's sanity. In
view of Dr. Green's "dissociative reaction" remarks, Ryan said,
he was obligated to make sure she was legally competent to
stand trial. He asked the lawyers to suggest psychiatrists and
scheduled the hearing for the following Monday morning.

Everyone went home except Don Crowder. As soon as
Ryan rapped his gavel, Don was arrested by the sheriff and,
with reporters and cameramen following along every step of
the way, escorted two blocks to the county jail.

"Chickenshit," Don muttered, apparently not caring who
heard him. "Son of a *bitch*."

The defense team had offered a motion for Don to be
released on his personal recognizance, the normal procedure
in the case of an officer of the court, but Ryan refused the
motion without comment. Don was fingerprinted, booked,
and mug shots were taken, but they never actually got him
into a cell. Rob Udashen had called an attorney in Austin, who
ran over to the Texas Court of Criminal Appeals, found the
chief justice, and got him to approve a writ of *habeas corpus* on
the spot.

Don was a little disappointed. He had been looking
forward to the headline-making drama of spending Saturday,
his thirty-eighth birthday, in jail.

The weekend should have been tense and nervous, a time
for second-guessing the events of the past five days, but
instead it was merely passing time. Candy, like everyone else,
became mentally exhausted when she thought of the trial, so
she put it out of her mind. On Friday night, she and Pat went
to the Lucas parsonage for a dinner of barbecued chicken,
potato salad, and ranch-style beans served by Ron Adams. The

Greens were there, and the Sullivans, and they found it was remarkably easy not to mention the trial. They went to church on Sunday—against Don's wishes—and on Saturday afternoon Candy drove to McKinney to be examined by Dr. Thomas Thornton, the court-appointed psychiatrist who would testify at her competency hearing.

"Most people never get the chance to prove they're sane," she joked as she left.

The newspapers found out Candy was competent to stand trial even before she did. The psychiatric results were in the Sunday *Dallas Morning News,* angering Judge Ryan so much that the next day he tried without success to find out who leaked the information. The newspapers and TV stations still couldn't get enough of the case. Pat watched and read as much as he could but kept all the accounts away from Candy. Especially disturbing was an article by Bruce Selcraig in the Sunday *News* in which many of the trial spectators were interviewed.

"I just wish they'd stop all this and put her away," said one woman, speaking for the clear majority of the curiosity-seekers. "I know they have to hear all this evidence stuff—now don't you dare use my name—but everybody knows what she did."

The depressing thing about the comments in the newspaper, Pat thought, was not that they were so vindictive. It was that, apparently, the women hadn't bought Candy's testimony about what happened in the utility room. If that were true of them, it might be true of the jury as well.

Candy was subdued over the weekend but never morose. She cooked and cleaned and chatted with Sherry. She called Don to find out how much longer the trial might last. Not long, he said. On Sunday night she slept only fitfully. Sometime during the night she started unloading a dishwasher and noticed that her mother was looking over her shoulder, trying to help. Her mother spoke in a sweet, saccharine tone as she pulled a pocket knife out of her skirt and laid it on the kitchen counter. "You'll need this to defend yourself," she said. "Here, take it." And then she disappeared. When Candy reached for the knife, she saw blood on her hand and stopped. She woke up sobbing.

It took less than fifteen minutes to pronounce Candy competent, and then the trial moved quickly toward its conclusion. Don's most important remaining witness was Dr. Fred Fason—and a magnificent witness he was. He was one of those people whose physical appearance is instantly likeable, a big bearish Santa Claus of a man, wise yet jovial. His deep rumbling voice was hypnotic, his manner smooth and confident without seeming arrogant. He seemed to be having great fun on the stand.

Fason outlined the twenty or so hours he had spent with Candy, describing her as being in a "detached, mildly depressed emotional state." He also backed up Dr. Green's diagnosis of a dissociative reaction. What he meant by that term was entirely different, however. He said Candy's dissociative reaction had begun before she was six years old and continued to the present—in other words, that it was a constant condition of her personality and not something that had been caused by the events of the thirteenth. She was a person excessively concerned about what other people thought of her—a common trait in people suffering from dissociative reaction—so she tried to keep up a public front at all times. She wanted others to consider her warm and loving and concerned for animals and children, a person who didn't have a violent or vindictive bone in her body. No one is *that* pure, so she had suppressed a great deal of anger over the years in order to satisfy her ideal self-image.

That's why Fason turned to hypnosis. It was the one way to get past her conscious image of herself and find out what dark realms lurked behind her cool, reserved exterior. His explanation of how hypnosis works—short-circuiting the normal, conscious defense mechanisms, making a person childlike and ingenuous, subject to suggestion—was intelligent without being too academic.

Fason described how he had led Candy, under hypnosis, through the events of June thirteenth, in an attempt to find the precise moment when she erupted in rage, went off the deep end, and killed Betty Gore. He found that moment: the point during the struggle when Betty Gore, bloodied but still battling, had pressed her body up against the utility room door, stared into Candy's eyes, and said, "Shhhhhh." Reaching that point in the chronology, Fason "age-regressed" Candy to try to find any other incident in her life when she had been that angry. He discovered such an incident at the age of four.

As Candy recalled—still under hypnosis—she and an older boy were racing to see who could get to an outdoor water

pump first. The winner got to pump water into a jar. Candy
lost the race and was so mad that she took the jar away from
the boy, threw it against the pump, and shattered it. A piece of
glass popped up and struck her in the forehead, and blood
streamed down her face. She was taken to the hospital for
stitches, but in the emergency room she was so frightened that
two attendants had to hold her down, kicking and screaming.
Her mother came into the room.

"Shhhh," she said. "What will they think of you in the
waiting room?"

When Fason asked her to express her true feelings about
the incident—it was not a conscious memory—Candy had
screamed and moaned uncontrollably. She had never been
able to express her fright before then, *because of what the
people in the waiting room might think*. This was a woman who
suppressed rage all of her life because of what others might
think of her.

Fason was quick to add that he was not saying Candy went
berserk in the utility room. He was saying that there was a
connection between the shushing by her mother at age four,
and the shushing by Betty in the heat of the struggle. The
blind rage was the result of a lot of things—the association in
her mind between Betty and her mother, the association of
pain with the sound "Shhhhhh," the need finally to get rid of
hostilities that had been building up inside her for twenty-six
years.

The "Shhhhhh" theory made Don nervous—it sounded
too bizarre to be understood by a jury—and so he pressed on
to more mundane explanations of Candy's behavior. In Fason's
opinion, Candy had lied to the authorities because of her
shame over being capable of such violence. It was a shame so
intense, he said, that she still didn't totally admit to herself
that she had done it. And Fason stated his emphatic opinion
that Candy never consciously intended to take Betty Gore's
life.

Tom O'Connell suddenly felt trapped again. Fason was
testifying that Candy's urge to destroy Betty Gore was the
result of a "disorder" but not a mental illness. She was sane
enough to argue self-defense, but not sane enough to be
responsible for the forty-one blows. It was like having a self-
defense and a temporary insanity plea at the same time, and
reaping the benefits of both. And despite his attempts to point
out the inconsistencies in Fasion's reasoning, the doctor held
firm on cross-examination. Candy's *initial* impulse, he said,

was one of self-defense. At some point during the struggle, she changed, lost control, was transformed into an unconscious killing machine. After that, she couldn't even see Betty Gore. Hers was, quite literally, a blind rage.

Don's defense was complete, but he had one more duty, he felt. He wanted the jury to know that Betty Gore wasn't a mild-mannered, sugar-and-spice schoolteacher, blameless and pure. According to the ancient custom of criminal defense attorneys everywhere, Don wanted to throw a little dirt on the victim.

The parade began with Catherine Cooper, the Plano schoolteacher who had shared a team-teaching class with Betty right after the Gores had moved to Texas. Catherine testified that Betty had "more than the ordinary amount of conflicts that a teacher has with parents," that she didn't communicate well, and that she could be extremely tactless. She was known as a harsh disciplinarian—perhaps too harsh—and her problems had led to her not being hired permanently by the school district.

Ann Cline, a Marriage Encounter member, testified that Betty had once received threatening phone calls from a parent, that Betty was very moody, and that she would go through periods of deep despondency. She had little patience. She made derogatory comments about Ron Adams during church services. Ann was followed by Judy Swaine, who said many of the same things and testified about Betty's spurning of her expensive shower gift. Don also used her presence on the stand to point out that Betty was a much larger woman than Candy.

"By the way," said Don, "are you about the same size as Mrs. Gore?"

"I'm approximately the same height. I'm about a size larger."

"All right. And could you stand for the jury one more time?"

She slid out of the witness box and stood beside it, furious at Don for using her as an example of how overweight Betty had been.

Finally, to get the story from the horse's mouth, Don called the object of Betty's scorn, the Reverend Ron Adams himself. Ron quite willingly related instances of Betty's open defiance of him, often manifest in childish ways. On cross-examination, O'Connell questioned Ron about his discussions with Candy since the killing, and at first he tried to avoid answering.

"You asked her," said O'Connell, "whether or not she was involved in the killing, didn't you?"

"I refuse to answer that, Your Honor," said Ron, "on the parishioner-priest privilege."

"You'll answer his question," said Ryan.

Don gave Ron a nod of the head, as though to say, "It's all right."

Ron started his answer. "We talked about—"

"Wait a minute," interrupted O'Connell. "Are you answering the question because Mr. Crowder says you can or the judge told you to answer?"

"The judge indicated it was my responsibility to answer the question," said Ron.

Ron answered the question.

Don was ready for his last gambit. He asked for, and received, a hearing to determine whether the jury would be allowed to hear the testimony of Don McElroy, the polygraph examiner who had questioned Candy about a week after the killing. Polygraph examinations are not accepted by the courts as factual evidence, and they are usually kept out of trials by the objections of defense attorneys. In this case, a defense attorney wanted the polygraph results admitted, because it bolstered his client's testimony. After both sides questioned McElroy as to the relevant answers Candy had given during the examination, O'Connell—to the surprise of everyone— said he had no objection to the polygraph examination being introduced. Ryan said he needed the night to study the law.

"Don't get your hopes up," he told the lawyers. "I'm not in the mood to change the law of the state of Texas over one case. Or attempt to. I know what's going to happen."

But the next shock came Tuesday morning, when Ryan *did* admit the polygraph testimony after all. It was some indication of how desperate the prosecution had become. O'Connell was hoping to prove there were inconsistencies between what Candy had told the jury and what she had told McElroy. But Don was secretly exultant. On the important questions—like "Did you go to the house of Betty Gore with the intention of harming her?"—he knew Candy's answers had been irrefutably truthful.

The defense rested.

* * *

For his rebuttal testimony, O'Connell tried to fight the self-defense story with everything at his disposal. Deffibaugh and Stone were recalled to testify about the sunglass lens found in the garage. How could Betty's bloody lens be there if the fight had been confined to the utility room? Deffibaugh even said that, over the weekend, he had revisited the Gore home and tried to figure out a way for the lens to get from the utility room to the garage. Short of going into the garage and placing it, there was no way.

Next O'Connell tried to repair some of the damage created by Don's anti-Betty witnesses. He called JoAnn Garlington, the first witness who seemed actively hostile to the defense. JoAnn was now convinced that Candy was lying about the killing and, out of loyalty to Betty, took the stand to say the most extraordinary things.

"I have never seen Betty being unkind to anyone in the six years that I've known her. . . . I've never even seen her raise her hand to her child."

Don felt sure he could dispel JoAnn's vision of saintliness by reminding her of a conversation he had had with her only a few weeks before.

"We both agreed [Betty] was an extremely moody person, did we not?"

"No, we did not."

"We didn't?"

"No."

"Was she a moody person?"

"Not to my knowledge. Not any more moody than anyone else would be. Than any normal human being is."

"You didn't tell me she was a moody person?"

"No."

"You didn't tell me she had highs and lows? Almost constantly?"

"No."

For the first time, Candy felt loathing for a witness.

O'Connell called two of Betty's fellow schoolteachers. Both of them said she was a nice woman. So did a friend of the family. In an attempt to show how cold and hostile Candy was, O'Connell also tried to introduce a television videotape taken one morning when Candy was arriving for the trial. The cameraman had stumbled on a tree root in his attempt to follow Candy into the courtroom, and when he did, she had angrily said, "I hope you fall." Ryan ruled the tape inadmissible as evidence.

Finally, in an effort to counteract the testimony of Dr. Green and Dr. Fason, O'Connell called a Dallas psychiatrist named Dr. Clay Griffith, who testified that in his opinion Candy did not suffer from a dissociative reaction, and in fact had acted with calculation and self-control before, during, and after the crime. Since he had never examined or met Candy, Dr. Griffith's testimony was based entirely on a reading of the court record. And his knowledge of the case was so sketchy that his opinions were almost entirely discredited on cross-examination.

Shortly after that downbeat session, the prosecution rested. The jury was sent home and final arguments set for the following morning, a Wednesday.

Don Crowder was looking forward to his summation as the crowning moment of his legal career, an hour he had looked forward to for so long that he had dozens of pages of scribbled notes, phrases dashed off here and there, quotations that came to him in the middle of the night, numbered points he reminded himself to make. He had rehearsed the speech in broad outline the night before he addressed the jury. Once he began, he was a possessed man, feeling every bit of the outrage that he had so carefully nurtured. It wasn't that he felt the authorities had been unjust to Candy—he had put her out of his mind entirely—but that he felt he had the only logical explanation of the killing, and there was no way O'Connell could shake it.

He opened his speech to the jury with some reminders about the presumption of innocence and the concept of "reasonable doubt." Then, using large posterboards placed on an easel, he reviewed the testimony of each witness, emphasizing the references to Betty's size, her moodiness, her obsession with Marriage Encounter. He stressed that the affair had been over for eight months. He reminded the jury of the carelessness of the crime. He said the medical testimony indicated that most of the ax blows were rendered after Betty was already dead. He pointed out that an ax was an extremely clumsy murder weapon, and that more practical ones—like knives and scissors—were readily available. He tried to explain "dissociative reaction" one more time.

"She was aware of doing the act," said Don, "but didn't comprehend what she was doing. Much like a defensive back in the National Football League when a receiver enters his defensive area of the playing field, tends to hit that man as hard as he can. Maybe even harm that man. But it's not a conscious thing. He's reacting to the ball and the man. He may think about it afterwards. He might have thought about it beforehand. But he's conditioned to inflict punishment."

In reviewing the testimony of Dr. Fason, Don avoided mentioning the "Shhhhhh" anecdote, because the newspapers had had a field day with it, and Don didn't entirely believe it himself.

Don moved on to Betty—her depression, her tactlessness at school, her problems in communicating with others.

"Judy Swaine," he added, "testified she was approximately the same height and one size larger than Mrs. Gore, and if you recall, Mrs. Swaine was a very good-sized woman."

And finally Don tried to deal with the most troublesome aspect of his whole case: the overkill, the forty-one blows.

"I know that there are things in this case that still bother you," he said. "I'd be a fool not to recognize that. How in God's name could one human being inflict the kind of punishment Candy Montgomery inflicted on another? Well, I've got an answer. When Betty Gore came at Mrs. Montgomery she was no longer a human being. She was an animal. She had turned into something less than a human being. She was an animal in search of prey. She was ready to attack. . . .

"John Steinbeck once wrote that there are those among us who live in rooms of experience you and I cannot enter. But if you're worried about whether or not Mrs. Montgomery is ever going to be punished in this case or has not been punished in this case, don't worry about it any longer, because she lives in that room of experience and we can't enter it. She lives in it and she's locked in it and it now constitutes a cell—a jail cell. And her family has moved in it and Betty Gore threw away the key on June 13th.

"They've lost their home. They're heavily in debt. . . . They're moving away from this area to start anew. They've been punished and they'll be forever punished. There won't be a day in the life of Mrs. Montgomery that she'll ever put out of her mind that she committed this act on June 13th, 1980.

"But you have an opportunity here to allow a family to stay together. Don't rob two children of their mother—"

There was a loud and collective gasp from the audience. Ryan looked sternly into the crowd but didn't say anything.

"Don't rob a husband of his wife," Don continued. He was getting ready for his finale.

"There's been an American tragedy played out in this courtroom," he intoned gravely. "But conviction—a conviction is not a proper solution to that particular tragedy. Perhaps there's forces working in this case that you and I can't understand. To a woman named Gore, an event of massive tragedy took place on June 13th, a Friday the 13th, and this case will end very nearly on Halloween. Maybe there's something involved here we can't understand. Something greater than all of us. But you can understand *this*—that the state has not proved its case. That reasonable doubt exists. Good luck to you."

Don, at long last, was finished.

Taking center stage for the state, O'Connell summed up his approach to the case in the third sentence he spoke.

"I don't know if final summations are all that important to juries," he said. "You've sat there as we have and listened to the testimony, and I'm sure can draw whatever reasonable inferences and reasonable deductions that the law in fact permits you to do."

After a long introduction—full of generalizations about the duties of jurors—O'Connell made the one strong point he had to make: Betty Gore was not present to give her side of the story. Yet he didn't mention her by name. She was "the other party." He reviewed all the physical evidence, which didn't make any difference at this point, since Candy had admitted to the killing. Then he tried to attack the "reasonableness" of Candy's self-defense plea by musing on the evidence of the mysterious sunglass lens. There's something wrong when the defendant's testimony and the physical evidence are at odds, he seemed to be suggesting. He pointed out that Candy was a good liar, since none of her friends had detected her deceptions after the killing. He reviewed the discrepancies in the polygraph examination. And he was most effective when dealing with the psychiatrists.

"To say that that relates back to something that happened when she was four years old and it was her mother she was after is just incredulous," said O'Connell. "I really think it is, and I think it's insulting to the intelligence of the jury. I think it's insulting to put that on. . . .

"You're not going to swing an ax twenty-eight times or forty-one, or however many times it was in this case, and not know what you're doing."

The jury, suddenly, was out.

* * *

"Ya'll go on home and get something to eat," said Don. "This is gonna take a long time."

As he watched Candy and Pat leave the courtroom, Don turned to Rob Udashen. "We did everything we could do, Rob, and now if they send her to prison, we can't let it get to us. If the worst happens, we're just gonna walk away from it."

Pat and Candy lunched on Salisbury steak, macaroni, and iced tea, but the anxiety was too much for them, so they drove back to the new courthouse, where the lawyers were waiting, and sat around sipping soft drinks with Don.

"You know, Pat," said Don, "what I said in there is true. No matter what happens ya'll are gonna have to get out of town. There's no life here for you anymore."

A deputy sheriff came into the room and motioned that he needed to speak to Don. Don got up and conferred for a moment.

"Good God, where's Candy?" Don said.

She was in the restroom. But when she emerged, she was told to go into the attorney's conference room with Don, where an armed guard would be posted at the door. The Sheriff's Office had received a death threat against both Candy and Don.

They all sat nervously in the small room, wondering whether the Montgomerys should be escorted home again. Then, in the middle of the afternoon and long before anyone had expected it, a bailiff came to the door and told the attorneys a verdict had been reached.

Don couldn't wait for the car to be brought around. He told the Montgomerys to wait for their escort and then sprinted out the door and ran the whole two blocks to the old courthouse. He flew up the stairs and burst into the courtroom, only to find that a twenty-man cordon of deputy sheriffs had formed a human wall between the spectators and the attorneys, just in case there were problems when the verdict was read. Don went into the judge's chambers. O'Connell was already there.

"One of the TV stations wants to tape the verdict," said Ryan. "Do either of you object?"

Don didn't say anything. O'Connell hemmed and hawed for a few moments, then said, "I really don't see any point in it, Judge."

"All right," said Ryan.

When Don told Candy what the judge had suggested, she felt enormous relief. After the trial she would thank O'Connell for that.

"All rise," said the bailiff.

Ryan strode out, mounted the bench. "You may be seated, ladies and gentlemen," he said.

"I have some instructions for the attorneys, the parties, and the spectators. When I read the jury's verdict into the record I want no reaction from anyone in this courtroom, whatever that verdict might be. No vocal reaction, no physical reaction. And don't think I'm picking on y'all. That's a standard instruction I give every time I get a jury verdict. Because I want to thank you for being as nice as you have been up to this point and I deeply appreciate it.

"All right, bring the jury in."

The jurors filed in. Don and Candy studied their faces, for any sign of emotion, but could find none.

"Mr. Foreman," said Ryan, "has the jury reached a verdict, sir?"

Bob Snyder, the head of corporate security for EDS, stood up. "Your Honor, we have."

The bailiff carried the verdict to the judge.

"We, the jury," Ryan read, pausing just a beat, "find the defendant not guilty. Signed, Robert F. Snyder, Foreman."

As though frozen in time, the room was silent and motionless.

"Each member of the jury that concurs in this verdict, will you indicate it to me please by raising your right hand?"

They all raised their hands.

"The court will accept the verdict and order it filed."

Candy started to cry. Don put his hand on her shoulder.

"Congratulations, Candy," he said.

Pat rushed past the bar and let Candy collapse into his arms.

"Dadgummit, Don," Pat said, "I love ya."

There was no general celebration. Five minutes later, when the Montgomerys started down the courthouse steps, there were scattered cries of "Murderer!" from the assembled crowd. For the first time since the trial began, Candy felt genuinely afraid.

26 · OUTRAGE

For the jury, it had not been an agonizing or even a particularly difficult decision. When the door of the jury room swung shut, everyone had assumed at first that they were in for a long haul. One woman, fearing they would have to stay overnight, complained that she didn't have a change of clothes. They asked the bailiff to bring food and drinks, wanting to get as much done that day as possible.

Bob Snyder, an ex-military man who handled all security operations for H. Ross Perot, had gained the respect of everyone for his apparent levelheadedness and knowledge of trial procedure. He was quickly elected foreman. He stood up to speak.

"I'm as offended as anyone by the affair Mrs. Montgomery had," he said, "and I don't approve of it morally. But I think, as far as this decision is concerned, we should put that aside. It can't affect our thinking in the case."

To the surprise of most of the jurors, no one offered any objections, although two of the female jurors did say that they, too, wanted it known that they didn't approve. Then Snyder moved on to the brutality of the crime—the forty-one blows. He wasn't sure that *that* should be a paramount issue in the deliberations either.

There was only mild disagreement on the overkill question, with the jurors eventually deciding that, regardless of whether it was a single gunshot or a hundred whacks with an ax, it was just one killing. The only question was whether it was murder, voluntary manslaughter (a lesser charge that Ryan had placed in their instructions), or not guilty. After a mere half hour of discussion, they were ready to take their first vote—on the question of murder only. Snyder suggested a secret ballot.

He collected the papers and read them aloud. Three voted guilty. Nine voted not guilty.

Since no one knew who the three hard-liners were, a general conversation ensued. It turned out that the principal concerns were why Candy hadn't run away instead of killing Betty, and why she had left the baby in the house. The women jurors were especially concerned about the baby issue, but as the discussion continued, a consensus emerged that Candy had been under sufficient stress to cause her to completely forget the baby was in the house. Next they discussed flight.

"Why didn't she just get out of there?" one woman asked.

"Sometimes you just don't have control over your body," said another.

Bob chimed in that, as a combat veteran, he could easily understand the kind of irrational impulses Candy must have felt.

He then called for a second vote. All twelve voted not guilty of murder.

Next they considered voluntary manslaughter. This time the issues were more cloudy. On the first ballot, the jurors split, six guilty and six not guilty, and everyone groaned at the implications.

They discussed some of the evidence, including the issue of the mysterious sunglass lens. But after hashing and rehashing that aspect of the trial, they finally decided that they didn't know exactly what point Tom O'Connell had been trying to make.

"Besides," said a juror, "those sunglasses could have gotten there any number of ways."

The baby issue came up again. The general feeling was that it was unfair for Candy to go scot-free after such a terrible death. But Snyder, perhaps sensing that the discussion was aimless, kept calling for additional ballots.

The next tally was four guilty, eight not guilty.

He called for another: two guilty, ten not guilty.

Finally, there was only one holdout for a conviction.

"How are we going to get at the problem?" one of the women asked. "If somebody asks a question, we'll know who the holdout is."

So Snyder ordered everyone to write something down on a piece of paper. Those who'd already made up their minds would just scrawl something. The one with the question would write it down. When Snyder looked through all the scraps of paper, there was only one with writing on it.

"I've resolved my question," it read. "I'll vote acquittal."

"Well," Snyder announced cheerfully, "we're ready to go, then."

When the bailiff opened the door, though, the jurors suddenly weren't so sure. They could hear the incessant din of reporters and cameramen crowding around to get pictures of them as they came out. It occurred to them that the verdict was going to be unpopular, and some of the women wanted to ask the bailiff for extra protection. They got it, but no one really relaxed until they had all been safely bundled into their cars by sheriff's deputies and driven out of sight.

For the first few days after the verdict, it seemed as though the twelve jurors were the only people in the world that believed in Candy Montgomery's innocence. After leaving the courthouse, the Montgomerys went home and invited people over for champagne and bologna and cheese sandwiches. Candy was beaming.

"Oh Pat," she said, "you know what the best thing is? I can go to the grocery store again. I can write a check again. I can just be *normal*."

"Candy," said Don, overhearing her, "you can't be normal."

"Everybody knows I'm innocent now."

"Candy, all they said is you're innocent of murder."

"So?"

"You're still guilty of adultery. That's what these people can't accept."

The newspapers and television news shows were full of followup stories, many of them featuring interviews with "the other jury," the people who had lined up each morning on the Collin County courthouse steps for seats at the most sensational trial in Texas. Most of them were women. Most of them were more than willing to be quoted. They were uniformly "disgusted," "appalled," "disillusioned." The headline in the *Dallas Times Herald* read:

Woman hacked 41 times
in self-defense, jury rules

The apparent inconsistency implied by the headline pretty much summed up public opinion.

Two days after the trial, the hate mail started arriving. It came from all over the country, most of it unsigned, some it containing such grisly attempts at humor as drawings of Betty Gore, blood gushing from forty-one places in her body, or, in one case, a newspaper photograph of Candy's face that had been scissored into twenty pieces. Many of the most hateful letters were signed by avowed Christians, quoting scripture and warning Candy that she had escaped mortal justice, but that God had a terrible surprise waiting for her. One letter was composed of the word "SHHHHHHHH" scrawled dozens of times up one side of the page and down the next. At first she opened the mail herself, but after the sicker ones started arriving, she turned them over to Pat. Some of them were so offensive that he destroyed them forthwith.

Halloween fell three days after the verdict, and at an adult party in North Dallas, three of the invited guests came dressed as Candy Montgomery, complete with cardboard axes and signs on their backs—"Whisper to me at your own risk" and the like. An unsigned poem was sent to the offices of Crowder & Mattox. The first page had a cartoon likeness of Candy, holding a bloody ax and grinning diabolically. The title of the poem was "Candy Is Bad For Your Health":

> Candy Montgomery was a whore
> She screwed around with Allan Gore—
> When Betty Gore brought it up,
> Candy used an ax to cut her up. . . .

> In Collin County, murder's O.K.—
> If you go to church and pray,
> And don't worry, adultery's cool
> If you teach Sunday School!

The doggerel went on for twelve similar stanzas. It had obviously been copied and widely circulated.

Four days after the verdict, on a Saturday, Candy went shopping for the first time at her usual McKinney supermarket. She was so unnerved by the stares that she returned home without buying anything.

Six days after the verdict, a Dallas television station aired a documentary on the trial. A reporter held the bloody ax in his hands and repeated again the facts as the public knew them: a woman had taken this very ax and mutilated another woman with forty-one blows, and the jury called it self-defense. Pat was so angered by the sensationalism of the report that he briefly considered filing a complaint with the Federal Communications Commission.

By November 5, eight days after the verdict, the Montgomerys had decided to leave Dallas forever.

Bob Pomeroy, lonely and tired, had gone and checked out of his motel in McKinney as soon as the verdict was rendered. He had tried to find Tom O'Connell afterward, but, as usual, the district attorney didn't have time for him. The police had never explained anything to him. The prosecutors had never had time to explain what they were doing. Bob felt he knew less about his daughter's death after the trial than he had known before.

Still, Bob had very little interest in the question of whether Candy Montgomery had been technically innocent or guilty. He had no anger that she was going free. A thought had suddenly occurred to him as he was watching the closing arguments in the trial, and now as he drove back to Kansas, he couldn't shake it. When Don Crowder had started to make his summation, he had spent twenty minutes on *Allan's* testimony. Almost everything Allan had said had benefited the defense. Bob had known that Allan was a strange bird, and he'd been acting weird since the killing, but he'd never wanted to face the possibility that Allan simply didn't care whether Betty lived or died. Suddenly Bob felt tired, and much, much older.

27 • EVIDENCE OF LOVE

The ancient Spartans worshipped a goddess called Hera Aphrodite. She represented the full range of womanly virtues: marriage, fertility, love, beauty, the nurturing of children, and sexual fulfillment. Over time, though, her worshippers separated into two cults—one devoted to Hera, one to Aphrodite. Hera became the goddess of marriage and the hearth; she was a strong goddess, tied to the earth, patroness of warriors. Aphrodite became the goddess of love, beauty, and the sexual life of women; she reportedly came from the sea, and prostitutes claimed her as their guardian. Mythology records that Hera, the wife of Zeus, became uncommonly jealous of Aphrodite, Zeus's mistress. Marriage and love, once united in a supreme white goddess, had become warring forces within the soul of every woman.

Betty Gore and Candy Montgomery were women more similar than either would have liked to admit. They were small-town girls, Betty almost stereotypically so, and they were post–World War II babies. Neither woman would be called beautiful; both were "pretty." They married into the upper middle class, choosing men devoted to the glamour field of the seventies: electronics. They thought themselves—and they were—resolutely typical.

Betty and Candy also came to share the great malady of the day: their marriages were going sour. Yet so grand were their hopes and adamant their intentions that, for a time, they didn't admit this even to themselves. For Candy, her settled life brought on feelings of inexplicable dread and self-doubt, feelings so vague at first that she didn't know herself why she

had sudden bouts of ennui and mental fatigue. For Betty, her
fantasy of married life—a strong, wise husband who made all
the decisions and stood behind her at all times—deteriorated
into the bitter realization that in many ways she would always
be alone. Each woman, to a greater or lesser degree, blamed
her husband for the malaise. They thought of their husbands as
weak men, men too passive and indecisive to fulfill the strong,
fatherly image they once held of them. They constantly
wanted their men to be more than the men themselves wanted
to be.

When it came time for each woman to make a choice in
her life, they diverged at last. Candy followed her own
instincts, tried to "rediscover me," sought refuge in the lives of
her children, in civic affairs, in going back to college, and
ultimately in the self-absorption of sexual adventure. Betty
sought a more private refuge. It depended on no one but her.
Through Marriage Encounter, through her devotion to per-
fecting the daily routine of life, she hoped to win her husband's
love. Had Candy chosen any other man to have her harmless
fling with, the Greek tragedy would never have happened.

What really happened in the utility room?

As late as three years after the killing, this was still a very
pertinent question to the general public of Collin County and
environs. Perhaps never before had there been such wide-
spread disagreement with a jury verdict, and such a universal
feeling that something important about right and justice had
been sacrificed when Candy Montgomery was allowed to walk
free. The trial had asked all the right legal questions, but
somehow it seemed that a lot of larger moral questions had
gone begging. Even after Candy's story had been picked apart
by lawyers, analyzed by psychiatrists, held up to the cold light
of logic, there was something missing. Perhaps it was something that only Betty Gore could have explained.

Still, it was possible to know a great deal about Betty's
mental state on the morning of her death. She was depressed
over her late menstrual period. Allan had just left to go out of
town—always a traumatic event for her. She felt like the entire
responsibility for the upcoming vacation had been dumped on
her. She had taken at least one drug—the one her gynecologist
had prescribed to induce a period—and she was in the habit of
taking tranquilizers and muscle relaxants for any number of

psychosomatic ailments. Betty was also subject to various imbalances associated with the menstrual period and would often go into a deep blue funk during the premenstrual phase. She may even have suffered from a clinical ailment known as premenstrual syndrome, in which case her hormonal imbalances could have induced manic-depressive behavior just before her period. Into her life, unexpectedly, walked Candy Montgomery, and her mind started making random connections. Betty was probably pregnant again . . . the last time she was pregnant Allan became distant and disinterested . . . he spoke of Candy a lot . . . Allan and Candy . . . and *presto!*—the thought she'd been unwilling to face for months bobbed to the surface.

"Are you having an affair with Allan?"

"No, of course not."

"But you *did*, didn't you?"

Candy, far from trying to lie her way out of everything, abruptly *admitted* the truth. She even made it worse by blithely excusing herself.

"But that was a long time ago. . . . Did Allan tell you?"

On one of the lowest days in her life—the day all her fears and insecurities had come together at once—Betty's first instinct was a mild form of vengeance: she wanted to teach Candy a lesson. Much of Betty's life involved teaching lessons to people, whether they be misbehaving ten-year-olds or rebellious foster children or insensitive Methodist ministers or . . . brazen hussies like Candy Montgomery.

But in this case, as in many previous cases, Betty's solution was awkward. Perhaps because she had just been reading about *The Shining*, perhaps for some other reason, she thought of the ax. It wasn't much good if you wanted to kill someone, but it was great if you wanted to terrify them. Betty was not a violent woman, but even if she had been, there were much better weapons available. She wanted something intimidating, not something functional.

Once Betty returned to the living room–den area with the ax, though, even she realized how ludicrous the whole scene was. She didn't raise it up over her head or rush at Candy. She said, "You can't have him this time." (The words "this time" indicated she connected Candy to the other time she was pregnant.) And then she quietly put the ax down. No doubt she felt foolish about the whole thing. She may have even been afraid that Candy was secretly laughing at her. The worst part of it was that Candy obviously hadn't been scared at all. Betty tried to make small talk, forced herself to be more normal for a moment, and even helped Candy by arranging for Alisa's swimsuit and towel. She wanted the whole thing to be over.

The crucial moment—far more important than Betty's cryptic "Shhhhhh"—came when Candy made her feeble, patronizing apology. If Candy had simply bundled up her belongings and left as quickly as she could, the whole confrontation might never have happened. Instead, after refusing to accept any guilt because "it was over a long time ago," she suddenly said, "Betty, I'm so sorry." Even that wouldn't have been so provocative, but Candy *touched* Betty. Betty didn't like to be touched anyway; at a moment like this, it must have set off an alarm.

Yet Betty was still not homicidal. She shoved Candy into the utility room, gaining the obvious advantage. The normal thing to do, if she intended to hurt Candy, would have been to lunge after her with her fists, or perhaps kick her while she was falling backwards. Instead, Betty turned her face away from Candy so she could pick up the ax. Again, the act made no sense unless she was thinking, "So she wasn't scared by the ax, huh? Try *this* on for size."

Once the struggle began, Betty abstractedly said, "I have to kill you." As any rookie police psychologist knows, real killers don't announce their intentions. Again, the threat was a form of intimidation. Candy, in the meantime, screamed, "I don't *want* him, I don't *want* him," a peculiarly selfish way of describing why an affair is over. Not "I made a mistake." Not "I'm sorry." Not "I'll never do it again." But a constantly repeated phrase that indicated Betty's husband was not even desirable to Candy; she had used him up and tossed him aside.

The sight of blood changed everything. Blood induces mild shock in even the most levelheaded people, especially when it is *their own* blood. Candy had no way of knowing the extent of her injury. She reached up and touched her forehead, and when she looked at her hand it was streaked with blood. She became panicky. Betty gained control of the ax and raised it over her head, as though to slice Candy in half. Candy became convinced that the fight was real.

Even at that point, it's unlikely that Betty was trying to kill Candy. For one thing, she already had Candy cornered in one end of the utility room. She had sole control of the ax. Candy had nowhere to hide. Betty could pick her moment. And yet, in that very tiny, confined space, she missed Candy entirely. The ax blade hit the linoleum, bounced once, and gashed one of Candy's toes. It's possible that even in her final, desperate moments, Betty never intended to murder Candy. Yet the combination of the blood, the ax, the strange behavior, the exaggerated swing—all of these things could very well have convinced Candy that her life was in danger. And after that, all bets were off.

Finally, there is no doubt that something passed between the women in those frenzied moments that defies all the best efforts of psychiatrists, lawyers, and policemen to explain. For by the time Candy stood victorious over Betty Gore's lifeless body, there was still within her a desire to make the other woman disappear, to eviscerate her face and make her suffer even after death for what she had done in life. At some point the issue between them ceased to be Allan Gore and became something else, something that only the chemistry between those two very different women could define. Candy the free spirit and Betty the moralist. Candy the gadabout and Betty the duty-bound housewife. Candy for whom a husband was the means to an end, and Betty for whom a husband represented everything stable and meaningful and secure about this life. Candy the woman who didn't like the Bible because God sometimes played games with man. Betty the Marriage Encounter organizer, making a religion out of family. Regardless of what may have happened to Candy when she heard Betty's eerie "Shhhhhh," it can't be denied that Betty was like the judgmental mother-figure Candy had been trying to escape all her life. Candy was independent; she answered to no one. She despised those who sat in judgment of her. Betty and Candy, Candy and Betty—two versions of womanhood, caught in a tragic collision of insecurities, doubts about themselves, and the awareness, perhaps, that neither one of them had really learned how to love.

28 • AFTERMATH

Two months after the trial, Candy and Pat Montgomery pulled up stakes and left Texas for good. Reporters gathered on their driveway even as they were loading the car. Pat found a job doing military research in the engineering department of a major southern university. They bought a smaller house in a well-to-do suburb, joined the local Methodist church, and tried to forget. Candy changed her name back to "Candace," because, she told Pat, "I don't feel like a Candy anymore." For the first year she rarely left the house and tried to avoid close friendships. Then she volunteered to work at a rape crisis center, helping young girls deal with the police, until, bowing to Pat's wishes, she gave that up and went back to college. She started another novel and began submitting fiction to women's magazines. Most of her stories had happy endings. Gradually she got involved in the church again, but it wasn't the same. She missed Jackie and Sherry. She tried to return to Lucas to visit, but Sherry talked her out of it twice. What Sherry didn't want to tell her was that many of her ex-friends thought it best that she was gone.

At Lucas Methodist, Ron Adams stayed long enough to patch things up—the congregation was traumatized and would remain so for many months—and then moved on himself, to another tiny parish, in Caddo Mill, Texas, feeling his work in Lucas was finished. Three years after the trial, he was divorced and had moved again, to an associate position in a church in Duncanville, Texas.

Two weeks after the Montgomerys moved away, Allan Gore and Elaine Williams were married in a quiet ceremony. Allan sold the house on Dogwood to accommodate all the children—Elaine's two boys and his two girls. There were

355

immediate problems with Alisa. She refused to accept her stepmother. With each passing day, she showed new signs of neurosis, until she began "acting out," a psychiatric term for uncharacteristic behavior that, in this case, was an impersonation of her mother. She locked herself in the bathroom until she got her way—something she had seen her mother do once. She exerted a strong influence on her baby sister, Bethany, until the younger girl, perhaps wanting to emulate her sister, developed the same sort of neurosis, only milder. Elaine's boys never got along smoothly with the girls, even after the entire family started going to psychiatric counseling sessions. The only time the girls seemed to behave normally was when they visited their grandparents, the Pomeroys, in Kansas.

Bob Pomeroy was shocked when Allan revealed his marriage plans just three weeks before the wedding. Words were exchanged. Bertha became upset all over again. Later that year Bob learned from a neighbor that Allan and Elaine had begun seeing each other within weeks of Betty's death, and he was so perturbed by the news that he confronted Allan with it, threatened to hire a private detective, and demanded to know whether Allan had anything to do with Betty's death. Allan confessed to the dates with Elaine, but he couldn't begin to explain his complex feelings for Betty. Then, after the girls returned from a visit to Kansas, Allan and Elaine decided to make a new rule. The Pomeroys were interfering with Alisa's and Bethany's ability to accept their new mother. From now on, the Pomeroys would only be allowed to see the girls one day a month. Ronnie Pomeroy went to Texas to talk Allan out of the new rule, but it held fast—and for a few months the whole Pomeroy family made a monthly weekend trip to Texas, where they would stay at a motel room in McKinney and take the girls to amusement parks and lakes. But Alisa didn't respond at all to the family therapy, and within a year began exhibiting physical symptoms of her trauma. She became anorexic, losing weight rapidly, unable to hold down food even when forced to eat it. Only when she was allowed to spend two weeks in Norwich, Kansas, did she begin to recover; Bertha stuffed her with as many potatoes as she could eat. After more than a year of therapy, even the child psychologist admitted that Alisa would never accept Elaine as her mother. The Gores, grateful that Alisa's health was improving in Kansas, simply let her stay there for the following school year. Bethany, dependent on her big sister, soon joined her. Alisa attended the same schools and churches Betty once loved, and seemed as happy as it was possible for her to be. A year later, the Gores brought the girls back to Dallas to try once again to forge a new family.

Bob Pomeroy cut back his farming operations to running a few head of cattle on a small portion of family land he'd kept. He also sold three-dimensional fluorescent religious pictures at the weekly flea market in Wichita and in the summer of 1983, took over the Doughnut Delight in downtown Norwich. Bertha returned to work at the local farm-machinery factory.

Don Crowder went into a mild depression in the two months after the trial, when he realized that most of his Collin County neighbors blamed him for what they regarded as a miscarriage of justice. People avoided his glance at church. The parents of children on his soccer and track teams turned a cold shoulder. Only his fellow lawyers encouraged him, as letters poured in from defense attorneys all over Texas, impressed by his defiance of the odds in the first criminal case he'd ever tried. A year later, Don accepted his second criminal client, a troubled young black girl who had wandered away from a Job Corps Center in McKinney and murdered an elderly woman who had offered her a drink of water. Don argued an insanity defense—the girl, born in Bedford Stuyvesant and raised in Watts, had been abandoned by two sets of parents, later abused, and was feared even by her own relatives—but she was convicted of murder and sentenced to ninety-nine years.

Judge Tom Ryan retired and then, in that grand tradition of the Texas judiciary, promptly began hearing cases again in Dallas County annex courts.

District Attorney Tom O'Connell ran for reelection in November 1982 but was roundly defeated by a relatively unknown Republican named H. B. Ownby. Ownby's campaign consisted of huge newspaper ads featuring newspaper clippings from the Candy Montgomery trial. "REMEMBER OCTOBER 1980?" they read. Sheriff Jerry Burton left Collin County to drive a truck in Oklahoma.

Jackie Ponder eventually moved to Texas Women's University in Denton, where she founded a Women's Resource Center and worked in the campus ministry. She continued to correspond with Candy and kept up by phone for a while, but as time passed their friendship began to wither away. She thought about Betty a lot. She especially thought about the moment when Candy looked into Betty's eyes, saw how full of pain her face was, and suddenly said, "I'm so sorry." It was the moment that triggered the paroxysm of rage that altered so many lives. But it was also, Jackie thought, the moment when Candy really looked at Betty for the first time. She hoped Candy remembered it, too.

A NOTE ON TECHNIQUE

This book is a factual account that is necessarily dependent on the recollections of others. It was assembled over a period of two years, from interviews, court documents, letters, and other material supplied by more than one hundred people. But since it reaches into personal matters beyond the scope of the public trial, it could never have been completed without the full cooperation of two people: Candace Montgomery and Allan Gore. Both submitted to dozens of hours of interviews, often touching on matters very painful to them and to the interviewers alike, and willingly trusted us with letters and diaries that made it possible to get closer to the truth about the women this book describes. Those interviews were supplemented by separate sessions with the people closest to Betty Gore and Candy Montgomery, notably Pat Montgomery, Bob and Bertha Pomeroy, and Elaine Gore. Only one restriction was ever placed on the authors: it was agreed from the outset that the children of both families would not be subjected to interviews.

There were remarkably few cases of conflicting accounts of the same episode. When this did occur, always in minor instances, we chose the version that seemed most likely. One name was changed. "Tina," the five-year-old girl who saw Candy Montgomery leave Betty Gore's house on the day of the killing, is a pseudonym. Of all the principals, only two chose not to be interviewed. They were Barbara Green, who felt traumatized by the emotional strains of the case, and Judge Thomas Ryan, who declined requests for interviews on the grounds that it would be unethical for him to comment on the case privately.

Many of the principals had become distrustful of reporters

by the time we began our research, and so we're doubly grateful for their decisions to share their recollections and insights. Especially generous with their time were the Reverend Jackie Ponder, Dr. Fred Fason, Tom O'Connell, Don Crowder, Captain Joe Murphy, Deputy Stephen Deffibaugh, Dr. Vincent DiMaio, Dr. Irving Stone, and Reverend Ron Adams.

In addition, we would like to thank the following people who assisted with various troublesome aspects of the story: Dr. Alvin Snider, Rob Udashen, Elaine Carpenter, Alice Rowley, Betty Huffhines, Bruce Selcraig, Doug Swanson, Connie Holmes, Marie Childs, Ronnie Pomeroy, Richard Pomeroy, Sherry Cleckler, Elizabeth Ann Cline, Dr. Guy Abraham, Judy Swaine, Kathy Cooper, Chief Royce Abbott, Richard Garlington, JoAnn Garlington, Sue Smith, and Richard Parker. June Leftwich, of the Dallas Public Library, provided invaluable assistance.

All editorial decisions were our own.

ABOUT THE AUTHORS

JOHN BLOOM and JIM ATKINSON are prizewinning reporters who live in Dallas. John Bloom is currently a film critic for the *Dallas Times Herald* and a contributing editor of *Texas Monthly* magazine.

Jim Atkinson is a founding editor of *D* magazine and a contributing editor of *Texas Monthly* magazine.

FROM THE BESTSELLING AUTHOR OF
THE PROUD BREED

W I L D
S W A N
by Celeste De Blasis

Sweeping from England's West Country in the years of the
Napoleonic Wars when smuggling flourished and life was led
dangerously, to the beauty of Maryland horse country—a
golden land already shadowed by slavery and soon to be
ravaged by war—here is a novel richly spun of authentically
detailed history and sumptuous romance, the story of a
woman's life and the generations of two families interwoven by
fortune and fate, told as it could only be by the bestselling
author of THE PROUD BREED.

Don't miss WILD SWAN, available in paperback July 1,
1985, from Bantam Books.